WITHDRAWN

D1351452

TEACHING ABOUT RACE RELATIONS

Routledge Education Books

Advisory editor: John Eggleston
                 Professor of Education
                 University of Keele

TEACHING ABOUT RACE RELATIONS
Problems and effects

Lawrence Stenhouse, Gajendra K. Verma, Robert D. Wild and Jon Nixon

with contributions by
JEAN RUDDUCK, PATRICIA SIKES,
ALISON BERRY and DAVID SHEARD

Report of a project supported by the Social Science Research Council and the Calouste Gulbenkian Foundation

Routledge & Kegan Paul
London, Boston, Melbourne and Henley-on-Thames

First published in 1982
by Routledge & Kegan Paul Ltd
39 Store Street, London WC1E 7DD,
9 Park Street, Boston, Mass. 02108, USA
296 Beaconsfield Parade, Middle Park,
Melbourne, 3206, Australia and
Broadway House, Newtown Road,
Henley-on-Thames, Oxon RG9 1EN
Printed in Great Britain by
St. Edmundsbury Press, Suffolk
© University of East Anglia 1982
No part of this book may be reproduced in
any form without permission from the
publisher, except for the quotation of brief
passages in criticism

Library of Congress Cataloging in Publication Data

Main entry under title:
Teaching about race relations.
(Routledge education books)
'Report of a project supported by the Social Science
Research Council and the Calouste Gulbenkian Foundation.'
Bibliography: p.
1. Race relations - Study and teaching (Secondary) -
England - Case studies. I. Stenhouse, Lawrence.
II. Series.

HT1506.T4   305.8' 007' 1241   82-5405
ISBN 0-7100-9036-6   AACR2

NEWMAN COLLEGE
BARTLEY GREEN
BIRMINGHAM, 32.

CLASS 370.19342
BARCODE 00452017
AUTHOR STE

This report is dedicated to the teachers and the pupils who took part in the project and placed their experiences – including their difficulties – on record to help their colleagues and peers.

CONTENTS

ACKNOWLEDGMENTS

We should like to record our sense of debt to:

- our steering committee, who gave up their time without reward. Their advice and criticism was of great value, but they are not responsible for our errors and omissions. They were: Miss Elaine Brittan, Professor Jerome S. Bruner, Mr Geoffrey Caston (chairman), Miss June Derrick, Mr Mike Feeley, Dr F.S. Hashmi, Professor Richard Housden, Professor Denis Lawton, Professor Alan Little, Mr Barry MacDonald, Professor James McFarlane, Dr J.A. Maraj, Mrs Jane Orton, Professor Edwin Peel, Mr James F. Porter, Mr David Sheard and Ms Vivien Stern;

- Marion Pick and Gwen Strange, who typed versions of this book in manuscript, and Wendy Lawrence, who typed some parts and some corrections.

1 INTRODUCTION

Lawrence Stenhouse

This is a report of the work of two linked research projects mounted at the Centre for Applied Research in Education (CARE) of the University of East Anglia during the period October 1972 to September 1975. Their intention was to explore some of the problems and effects of teaching about race relations. One project was supported by a grant from the Social Science Research Council and the other, by the Calouste Gulbenkian Foundation. The programme was directed by Lawrence Stenhouse and involved a team of three researchers in the study of forty schools throughout the country. It combined a measurement programme on a pre-test post-test basis, designed and executed by Gajendra Verma, with a programme of case study, executed primarily by Robert D. Wild. The experimental teaching took place in the spring term of 1974.

Publication of the report has been delayed by several factors, including problems encountered by project staff and, more recently, problems facing publishing houses.

As will later become clear, the project aimed to study the problems and effects of teaching about race relations by working with three groups of teachers, each of which adopted a different approach. One group comprised teachers who used drama as a means of dealing with race as a classroom topic. The field-worker responsible for studying these cases was unable, in the event, to deliver a report.

A further setback to the project schedule was the sudden illness of the project director at the climax of the dissemination phase in January 1976: he was prevented from returning to work until September of that year.

Despite the gap in the data and the problems of illness, the report was substantially complete by 1977. Jon Nixon, who teaches drama in a London comprehensive school and is a part-time doctoral student at the Centre for Applied Research in Education, contributed two drama case studies using materials held by the project supplemented by interviews with the teachers concerned. He also added three further studies based upon his own work and upon his own study of another teacher. By the same date a collection of teaching materials was also complete, based on those used by the teachers of the project but re-edited by a sub-committee of teachers working with consultants.

The original intention was to publish report and materials together, but it was not easy to find a publisher. When we did,

1

he asked that the materials be re-edited from loose-leaf form
to book form and be up-dated. This considerable task was
accomplished and three books were prepared, edited respect-
ively by Dave Dunn, Dave Sheard and John Waddleton with
assistance from other members of the teacher team. The publisher began lay-out work on these books, but, in the face of
revised estimates and declining textbook sales, finally found it
necessary to withdraw from the contract.

The project report is now published by a publisher who does
not have a schools list and to whom, therefore, the teaching
materials have not been offered.

We have already been made aware, through our contacts
with researchers and teachers, that the aims and conception
of this project run counter to what the majority expect of it.
Its purpose is expressed in its title. It seeks to throw light on
the problems and effects of teaching about race relations to
adolescents in order to strengthen the basis of teacher judgment. It does not hope to solve those problems and recommend
a particular curriculum or method of teaching, since any
school's response will be influenced by its situation, and by
the strengths and weaknesses of its staff. It would seem absurd
to expect that the pattern of teaching in a school in Brixton
or Moseley should be similar to that in a school in Lincolnshire
or Cumbria. The most important decisions will be made by
schools themselves: the function of the project is to inform
those decisions.

Since there is a good deal of confusion about the issues at
stake in teaching about race relations, it seems best to set
these down as we see them.

Ours is, and will remain, a multi-racial society, and of
course a multi-cultural one. Pluralism adds immensely to the
social resources of any community; but it is also a source of
conflict, and ethnic and cultural boundaries often coincide
with boundaries of power and class and access to the good
things society has to offer.

Not so far behind us is a society that was a confederation of
much more culturally homogeneous local communities (still
recollected in dialects), where the stranger in the inn was
'outlandish', at best the object of social caution, at worst of
persecution. Still fresh in history is a colonial past with all
its pressures towards a conception of hierarchical relationships among races and cultures. Its interethnic assumptions
are embodied in English literature, from Macaulay's 'Essay on
Clive' to Biggles.

Schools have traditionally been concerned with transmitting
moral standards as well as knowledge, and both moral standards
and knowledge seem problematic in the area of race.

The problems that we find ourselves facing as teachers are
potentially quite frightening and are not to be solved by mere
goodwill. Personal and professional understanding and art in
teaching are necessary, as is a modesty of aspiration as an

armour against disappointment. Progress in educational practice
is measured in decades - even generations - rather than in
weeks or terms. Education will not solve the problems of community relations: adult society cannot delegate the reconstruc-
tion of culture to schools.

There is, of course, a case for attempting in schools to
increase pupils' respect for and interest in people who are
culturally or ethnically different from themselves. This is true
whatever the identity of the pupils may be, though the need
in Britain is probably greatest for the white majority. One can
see that in primary schools much can be done through careful
choice of materials for reading and of themes in art and the
social subjects. And throughout the school system, this is to
an extent still true. When a school is itself multi-cultural or
multi-racial the quality of its life as a community is of first
importance in terms of influence on race relations.

This theme is not, however, the one pursued in this research,
which by its brief is restricted to the problems and effects of
teaching about race relations to adolescents. Such teaching
will normally take place within a subject department or an integrated faculty, and will be an aspect of its general teaching.
In the last resort we do teach about our multi-cultural society
and race relations within it not because of a sense of social
mission (though some may), but rather in the light of an educational aim. We encounter race as teachers of social studies or
humanities, of sociology or history or art or music or literature
or drama. To avoid the topic of race in such areas is to falsify
the relationship of our subject to real life outside the school.
And in one way or another, race and inter-racial attitudes arise
in all these subjects, and enter into many O-level and CSE
syllabuses.

The aim of this research is to help teachers who will teach
about race relations in the fourth and subsequent years of the
secondary school by documenting the problems and effects of
such teaching. Its assumption is that the teacher concerned
would wish, so far as possible, to contribute to interracial
respect and to combat racism. But how much can be achieved
in changing attitudes and values is, it must be conceded,
questionable.

We imagine, therefore, that the majority of teachers will wish
to teach about race in their subject areas because it is there -
like war or social class or the family. Although they will hope
to influence attitudes for the better, and will try to do so, in
the last analysis they will teach race in their subject so long as
they are not shown to be doing harm.

In our project teachers have gone a little further than this.
They have been prepared, in the hope of obtaining positive
results, to emphasize the theme of race in their teaching of
humanities, social studies or drama for a specified school term.
They have done so to make it possible to study the problems
and effects of teaching about race relations. The aim of this

study has been to help all teachers who face race as a theme, whether it arises in the normal course of their subject teaching or is introduced as a separate topic.

Perhaps a good starting point is to clarify criteria of decision-making. As a teacher, would you teach subjects or topics (the Black Hole of Calcutta or 'The Merchant of Venice', for instance):

(a) even if this led to a deterioration in inter-racial respect?
(b) only if this did not lead to deterioration in inter-racial respect?
(c) only if this led to improvement in inter-racial respect?

We assume that some of our readers will take position (b), though some will take (c), and some who take (a) would teach reluctantly in the face of evidence that the results of part of their teaching were unhelpful to racial harmony.

A further point. This project is about teaching not in multi-racial schools, but in all schools. And the issues dealt with are socially important for all schools. The condition of race relations in Birmingham, Bradford or Brixton could be in the hands of voters in Brampton, Bournemouth and Boston.

The report we offer falls into two sections: the measurement results, and the case studies of classroom teaching. Our aim is to write for teachers and for those interested in education rather than for researchers and those interested in research, though we hope we have given the latter sufficient information to support critical responses.

2 THE TEACHING STRATEGIES WITHIN THIS PROJECT

Lawrence Stenhouse

One group of teachers in our project, those employing teaching Strategy A, as we called it, worked within the tradition of the Humanities Curriculum Project (HCP). There is a story behind this and it would be misleading not to tell it.

The Humanities Project - of which I was director - was, like most patterns of action research in education, complex and multi-faceted. Its occasion was the raising of the school-leaving age, and its justification in political terms (for policy and pedagogy must both be satisfied in education) was seen in the possibility of its offering an ethical basis for the accountability of teachers to pupils, parents and society for their handling of contentious controversial issues in the classroom. Its definition of content was 'controversial human issues of universal concern', and on the difficulties of handling such content was built its pedagogy: a discussion of evidence in which the teacher acted as a chairman aspiring to procedural neutrality.

This is not the place for an extended discussion of the project, but it is probably worth making two asides which relate the work of that project to the work of this one.

First, the context of the Humanities Project was the raising of the school-leaving age (ROSLA). In that context, it might be seen as a bid for an area of mixed ability working across the whole school in the fourth and fifth years. There are schools that have used the project materials and teaching style in this setting; when discussion groups contain the full range of ability, the challenge of difficult reading materials can be met, and met to the advantage of pupils at all ability levels. Schools that have responded to ROSLA by streaming or banding in humanities seem to have created problems for themselves; and they are the majority.

Second, the procedural neutrality of the teacher as chairman rests on the premise that he is not personally neutral. He adopts a procedural neutrality to avoid asserting his views with the authority of his position behind him. He is likely to adopt the stance of neutral chairman because he believes that it furthers discussion as a search for truth and avoids the shaping of view by mere conformity or rebellion. Simply, he will be seen by the pupils as listening more than teachers generally do and not taking sides in pupil discussion. It is appropriate to claim, not that the HCP style of teaching is the right or the only way to teach, but that it is an intelligent, professional response to the problem of pupil discussion which is designed

5

to promote autonomy and responsibility, and to the problem of the school's responsibility to parents in the circumstances of a pluralist society.

For an account of the Humanities Curriculum Project the reader must go elsewhere (Humanities Project, 1970). Here there is space only to clear up two areas of potential misunderstanding.

Within the Humanities Project there was a good deal of discussion as to whether or not Race Relations should be tackled. True, it was a human issue of universal concern: but was it in a political sense controversial? Did the existence of race relations legislation justify politically the schools' taking a line on race relations irrespective of the feeling of parents? The project staff were divided as to whether the project's logic held in this topic area.

However, the staffs of the Schools Council and Nuffield Foundation urged the project to include race relations among its themes. They had apparently been under some pressure to see that an appropriate Schools Council project did explore problems and possibilities of teaching in this topic area, and they believed that the non-authoritarian stance of the Humanities Project was likely to be effective to some degree in improving inter-racial respect.

Presumably, the argument would be that part of the problem in race relations is prejudice, in a literal sense: a disposition to make ill-founded judgments or experience uncritical reactions before examining the evidence. If so, the examination of evidence under neutral chairmanship might be conducive to the undermining of prejudice and to reconsideration.

Although there is a reasonable expectation that reflective discussion of evidence might be expected to undermine inter-racial prejudice, it is important to notice that this changes the logical basis of the Humanities Project. The initial justification for the HCP strategy was based on the school's accountability to parents and pupils, and was thus essentially political. The educational advantages of the strategy could thus be explored in the experiment rather than assumed to justify the experiment. Essentially, the educational (as opposed to the political) justification of HCP came from the results of the experimental work.

In the event, the Humanities Curriculum Project did experiment in teaching about race relations - but cautiously. This was unique among its themes in being evaluated separately, and the experiment was mounted in three schools inexperienced in HCP as well as in three of the experienced experimental schools. Some of the results of the evaluation have been published (Bagley and Verma, 1972; Parkinson and MacDonald, 1972; Verma and Bagley, 1973; Verma and MacDonald, 1971); others are available for consultation at the Centre for Applied Research in Education, University of East Anglia, Norwich.

The findings were summed up by Verma and MacDonald (1971)

in the following passages:

> We have thought it important to stress the limitations of
> the programme, to ensure that the data obtained are
> treated with caution, but it may still be useful to sum-
> marize the trend of the results. Given the prudential
> nature of the concern which motivated the setting up of
> this pilot study, the major finding is that no marked
> deterioration in the attitudinal or personality character-
> istics of the pupils was manifested in their test responses
> after exposure to the teaching programme. The effects of
> the experiment, although not generally significant, tended
> to suggest a shift in the direction of inter-ethnic tolerance.
>
> The combined picture of the results seems to indicate that
> there was no general tendency towards intolerance after a
> seven- to eight-week teaching programme. There is no
> evidence to suggest that the students generally became
> less sensitive to or tolerant of members of other racial
> groups. These results cannot be considered as constitut-
> ing proof. Analysis of the pilot study along other lines is
> incomplete, but a decision has already been made to pro-
> ceed with the editing of a full collection of materials on
> race, on the grounds that none of the problems encoun-
> tered in the course of the study would justify the abandon-
> ment of further research. No teacher involved in the pro-
> gramme abandoned the course, or found it necessary to
> reject any of the premises described earlier. In February
> 1971, each of the schools which participated sent team
> members to an evaluation conference at which they expres-
> sed willingness to undertake the teaching of race with
> other students in the future.

What conclusion can one reasonably draw from these findings? It seems clear that, in a human issues programme based
on the HCP teaching strategy, there is little case for leaving
out race relations as a topic because of a fear that inter-racial
attitudes will, overall, deteriorate rather than improve. On
the contrary, attitudes appear on the whole to improve a little
as a result of such teaching.
It is important to get two points clear.
First, since the aim of teaching in HCP is to develop an
understanding of human issues, one would presumably teach
about race relations even though this did not improve inter-
racial attitudes. Our assumption was, however, that one might
not teach about race relations if it led to a deterioration of
attitudes. Of course, this makes race relations a special case.
Few people would exclude twentieth-century European history
from British schools on the evidence that it led to less sympathetic attitudes towards Germans (though perhaps they
should show more concern about this than they do). However,

in a multi-racial society one might well be prepared to argue that race is a special case because of the presence of institutional racism alongside the recognition in our race relations legislation that we should be committed to the impartial treatment of all citizens.

Second, there was no basis in the work done in the context of the Humanities Project for suggesting that the topic of race relations ought to be taught neutrally, and we never at any time made this suggestion. What we claimed was that those who were teaching neutrally could appropriately teach about race relations. There was never any suggestion that teachers who normally advanced their own views in social studies or humanities should change their stance and teach neutrally in the area of race relations, and we had no data to support such a conclusion. No more was claimed than that the Humanities Project offered an intelligent and cogently argued curriculum for experimental development in schools and was therefore a worthwhile extension of the range of choice open to schools and teachers. It is difficult to implement, and some schools find a rigorous curriculum based on an innovative teaching strategy too demanding, given the level of priority they are prepared to give it.

On the basis of research results and of the two positions just outlined, it was decided to publish a collection of materials on race relations. Normally the Schools Council does not (or did not) subject the teaching materials of its projects (as opposed to their research reports) to scrutiny. However, in this case the project wished them to organize a conference at which the materials and their content could be introduced to workers in the area of race relations and to members of those communities that have a basis in racial identity. A copy of the collection of materials on race relations was therefore sent to the Schools Council to support the request for a conference.

The present account of what happened is necessarily based a good deal on hearsay.

Some of the members of the committee of the Council that received the materials were alarmed by them, either in their own persons or because of anticipated reactions or both. Their alarm was apparently not without some foundation, for when they consulted some leading figures in the area of race relations, they had an unfavourable reaction. Whether it would have been possible to allay fears by presenting the materials in the context of the research is difficult to know at this time. As a matter of fact, they were examined out of this context.

The result was that the Schools Council, as copyright holder, vetoed publication of the materials. They cited as reasons for their veto the inclusion in the collection of expressions of extreme views (National Front and Black Power); the use of community newspapers, which by virtue of their departure from norms of spelling and syntax might bring the Black and Asian communities into disrepute; and the problem of misunderstanding or half understanding likely to arise because of the high reading level of the materials.

The project's response to their criticism was to suggest that the collection be re-edited by a group of teachers, part nominated by the project and part by the Schools Council programme committee. At this point the Council said that the most fundamental objection was to the neutral role of the teacher. The director of the present project asked them to provide further support in order to develop and document other, non-neutral strategies for teaching about race relations. Not surprisingly - given that they probably saw him, erroneously though understandably, as advocating rather than investigating a neutral stance in teaching about race relations - they declined to do so.

The Humanities Project's other sponsors, the Nuffield Foundation, and the consultative committee supported the project in this rather difficult situation and the committee passed the following resolution:

The Consultative Committee recommends that the team carry out further research into the methods of teaching race, under independent sponsorship, drawing on the work and experience already gained by the Humanities Curriculum Project.

We in fact approached the Social Science Research Council (SSRC), who provided a grant of over £43,000 for further research in problems and effects of teaching about race relations. The Gulbenkian Foundation also provided a grant of over £18,000 to include in our work a study of the problems and effects of teaching about race relations through drama. The resulting research, which is reported in this book, took place in the period 1 September 1972 to 30 September 1975.

Since the proposal was put to the SSRC and the Gulbenkian Foundation in terms of a project to explore and report on 'the problems and effects of teaching about race relations', it was necessary to study such teaching.

There is a serious problem here. Any teaching within an experimental framework must satisfy educational as well as research criteria. Let us imagine, for the sake of argument, one hundred possible ways of teaching about race relations. Of these, twenty-five may seem unpromising from the point of view of the research worker. Of the remaining seventy-five, twenty-five may seem unpromising or even educationally inadmissible to teachers. There remain fifty possibilities advocated by teachers and worth studying from the standpoint of public research. These are open to us, but were we to use any of the fifty methods that seemed inadmissible or unpromising we could rightly be accused of using the pupils involved as 'guinea pigs' without due regard to their own rights and their own advantage.

This means that the researchers must work with teaching that is endorsed by the teachers - and, less importantly perhaps, by themselves - as offering promise of advantage to the pupils.

At this point it might seem that in the experiment we were conducting it was necessary only to find a group of teachers interested in or already engaged in teaching about race relations and then to study what they were doing. But it would be difficult to operationalize and utilize such an experiment. There are many reasons for this, but we shall content ourselves with two here: the need for support, and the need for definition.

Taking a thorny problem such as teaching about race relations and at the same time studying one's own work and making records of it available to researchers is an extremely tough assignment. It is difficult enough to undertake the study, but to make one's problems public in the context of a research is even more taxing, because of a traditional secrecy in the teaching profession about the existence of problems. This tradition is breaking down, but we have a long way to go. Accordingly, we believe that any action research of the kind we are discussing must try to bring groups of teachers in individual schools into more openly co-operative working relationships and into relation with teachers in other schools. Support can be drawn from the mutuality of conferences and meetings at school, district and national level (though it doesn't always work out that way: competition too often creeps in). Setting up a supporting structure of conferences among teachers within a project creates a sort of discussion club about the problems in hand, and a tradition emerges. We don't think it possible or desirable to have a research and development project in which such traditions are avoided. But it does distinguish teachers working within the 'project club' from those outside it.

In the sector of our programme supported by the SSRC we recruited two groups of teachers: one group who would teach by Strategy A, the HCP strategy, and another who would teach by Strategy B, in which the teacher expressed his social commitment in the classroom. In the Gulbenkian wing of the programme we recruited a group of teachers interested in teaching about race relations through drama (Strategy C). We recruited Strategy B first because there was more work to be done with these teachers and in their support. Strategy A came before Strategy C, partly because there was a delay in receiving our funding decision from the Gulbenkian Foundation, and partly because the progress of our research was delayed a little by our principal research worker on this wing of the project suffering a motor accident.

The samples of local education authorities, schools, pupils and teachers are fully discussed later in this book (Chapter 4), where the issue of their representativeness is examined. What we want to do here is take you through the experiences of the teachers involved.

The Strategy B teachers ultimately involved came from six-teen schools. Their local authorities had agreed to meet their expenses in attending project conferences. Although a minority of the teachers had made an initial decision to take part on the project, most were nominated by their schools, which in turn were nominated by their local authorities. Some local authorities declined invitations to take part, as did some schools.

Those Strategy B teachers who were able to do so attended a conference in Norwich on 24-29 May 1973. For this conference I wrote a paper on behalf of the project team; and it seems worthwhile to print this in full since we still feel it might be a reasonable point of departure for a school in thinking about its teaching in this area.

SSRC PROJECT: THE PROBLEMS AND EFFECTS OF TEACH-ING ABOUT RACE RELATIONS

Draft Working paper for the conference of Strategy B

Experimental Teachers, Norwich, 24-29 May 1973

THE NEED FOR CONSENSUS

If teachers from some forty-five schools are to co-operate in a research and development project, there must be con-sensus about aims and procedures. Without such consensus it will be difficult to communicate with one another and to report the work we have done to teachers who have not taken part in the experiment. The consensus we achieve should discipline our experiment without constraining it. There must be room within the consensus for experimental initiatives and for individual style.

GENERAL EXPERIMENTAL DESIGN

In the nature of the case the general experimental design has originated with the research team. This design had to be set out in order to attract the support of sponsors and local authorities which makes the experiment possible. The research team must now make sure that the general design is acceptable to all those taking part.

It is proposed that three groups of schools - about fif-teen in each group - should be involved in the project. Each group should be involved in teaching about race rela-tions to pupils in the fourth year. Each group should follow a different method or procedure and so far we have called these Strategy A, Strategy B and Strategy C.

Strategy A schools are expected to use the approach of the Humanities Curriculum Project, in which the teacher plays the role of a neutral chairman.

Strategy B schools are expected to use an approach in

which the teacher feels free to express his own or the
school's commitment in the classroom.

Strategy C schools are expected to use an approach
based on drama.

It is desirable for experimental reasons that the weight
of the teaching should fall in the second term of the
fourth year. This will allow us to administer tests in the
first and third terms. It will also allow us to test the same
pupils a year later in the fifth year.

Our basic assumption is that all three approaches will
in some sense work, but that each will throw up different
problems and provide different insights. At the end of the
experiment we hope to have information and materials
which will make it possible for schools to make an eclectic
approach to the problem of teaching about race relations,
drawing on three strategies. We do not think there will be
one 'right' way of teaching about race relations.

Our experience suggests that the work in the experimental schools will be demanding on teachers in terms of
skill, amount of work and psychological pressure.

It is important to note that the experiment rests on
the assumption that there is something to be gained from
an attempt to handle race relations as a topic with adolescents. There are those who believe that race relations
should not be handled as an explicit topic and others who
believe that it should not be handled with adolescents
unless it is part of the school's programme from the first
year.

STRATEGY B: THE TASK OF THE CONFERENCE

This paper is being produced for the Strategy B conference in May 1973. In suitably modified form it will go
to the Strategy A conference in July 1973 and the Strategy C conference in September 1973.

As a result of the May conference, teachers in Strategy
B schools will have to achieve consensus in a general
description of the work they propose to undertake. It is
part of the task of the research team to help in this.

On the basis of our present experience we can make
some suggestions as to how adequate consensus can be
achieved; but they are only suggestions.

It seems profitable to try to be clear about our premises
- how we see the situation - and our aims - what we intend
to do about it. We may well need to go on to examine the
implications of our aims for practice and to define the kind
of teaching materials required. Some consensus in the
definition of terms is also desirable.

STRATEGY B: PREMISES

Premises define how we see the situation at the beginning of our experiment. We hope to learn from the experiment so that our premises should be treated as provisional; as hypotheses.

One assumption has already been stated: that it is worthwhile to teach adolescents about race relations.

Other premises will have to be agreed at the Conference. But some questions can be raised here:

(1) Is racial prejudice characteristic of our society and shaped by social experience?

(2) Is racial prejudice related to the psychological needs of individuals or of groups?

(3) Can schools influence attitudes?

(4) Are schools involved in transmitting racial prejudice - e.g. through textbooks, etc? If they are, is this avoidable?

(5) Are we to regard ourselves as teachers as free from prejudice or as implicated in prejudice?

(6) What is the nature of the teacher's commitment in this area?

(7) Is the school entitled to work against prejudice if parents are prejudiced?

(8) How do we view the relationship between information, understanding, empathy and attitudes?

(9) What should be the school's attitude towards well-informed hostility to people who are distinguished as a group on racial grounds?

(10) Is it more important to assert that all people are similar or that all people are different?

(11) Do we have to take a line on heredity v. environment?

(12) What importance do we give to cultural differences?

(13) Ought all groups to be assimilated or integrated into society, and if so, in what sense?

Many of these are extremely difficult questions. Probably we cannot hope to find even provisional answers to them all. But they ought to be on our agenda.

STRATEGY B: AIMS

Premises are our expression of the situation as we see it. Aims are general statements of our intentions as teachers. When we have more than one aim we probably need to state our aims in order of importance. If two aims come into conflict, which ought to win?

The following are examples of teaching aims which might be discussed (among others) at the conference:

(a) to attack/undermine (racial) prejudice in students;
(b) to attack/study critically (racial) prejudice and
    discrimination in society;
(c) to develop tolerance/respect for people of other
    races/people different from ourselves;
(d) to encourage pupils to react to difference with
    interest rather than hostility or fear;
(e) to provide much fuller and more accurate information
    about other cultures, racial difference, our multi-
    racial society;
(f) to develop an awareness of other cultures, and of
    differences of value among cultures;
(g) to help students to develop an awareness of their
    own cultural identity;
(h) to help students to respond at an interpersonal level
    to people from other cultures;
(i) to help students to question critically racial and cul-
    tural generalizations and stereotypes;
(j) to develop students' capacity to criticize attitudes
    towards other cultures and other races when these
    carry the authority of the adult world or the school.

IMPLICATIONS

There are two alternative or possibly complementary
approaches to spelling out the implications of an agreed
aim. One is to analyse it into behavioural objectives, that
is, close specifications of how students should perform as
a result of the course; the other is to spell out the implications for the teaching strategy and materials. Either
approach is acceptable from the point of view of the experiment. More information will be available at the conference.
    Out of our discussion we should perhaps hope that some
agreement about the use of terms emerges: e.g., race,
ethnic, culture, tolerance, respect, prejudice, discrimination.

This paper is very largely concerned with focusing the issues
and providing an agenda for the conference. It arises from the
problems of educational experiment.
    The conference itself involved intensive work and consider-
able pressures as a group of teachers sought a common identity
and basis for working, while a group of researchers working
as staff of the conference kept pressing the deadline within
the conference for a common statement of intent. Part of my
role was to draft and re-draft a statement which attempted to
build on the various statements and papers produced by
teachers within the conference, and it would be disingenuous
to pretend that this was not a position of considerable influence,
which must give me a good deal of responsibility for what
emerged.

The working paper that was adopted by the conference was as follows:-

CENTRE FOR APPLIED RESEARCH IN EDUCATION,
UNIVERSITY OF EAST ANGLIA
SOCIAL SCIENCE RESEARCH COUNCIL PROJECT:
PROBLEMS AND EFFECTS OF TEACHING ABOUT RACE
RELATIONS

STRATEGY B: *Working Paper from the Norwich Conference May 1973*

This Working Paper is an attempt to catch the consensus which emerged from the conference. Please comment if you feel that any correction is necessary.

We have set out the paper under the general headings used at the conference:

PREMISES   These are statements made in the conference about the situation as the participants see it and they provide a basis on which Strategy B is built.

AIM   This is intended to be a brief statement of the intentions and purposes of the teaching.

ROLE OF THE TEACHER   This is intended to catch the practical implications of Strategy B for the teacher's approach.

PRINCIPLES OF PROCEDURE   These provide an amplification and clarification of the implications of the aim.

TEACHING STRATEGIES TO BE EXPLORED   These point towards problems of content and method in the classroom. It will be important for teachers and schools to try some of them in practice and report results.

The practical side of the experiment is in exploring and testing the teacher role and the strategies.

- What problems do these raise?
- How do they work out in your school?
- How do they need to be changed?
- What do they really look like in practice?
- What do you think are the effects on pupils?

PREMISES

(1) 'Prejudice' is taken to mean prejudgement which involves undervaluing or penalizing people.

(2) Racial prejudice is a characteristic of our society, related to and influenced by social factors, experience and the acquisition of cultural attitudes.

(3) Social, economic and institutional factors are influential in the maintenance of prejudice and discrimina-

tion in our society.
(4) Racial prejudice is also related to the psychological
    needs of individuals and groups.
(5) Elements in our society often play upon ignorance
    and fear in order to maintain prejudice and discrimin-
    ation.
(6) Schools often transmit accepted social values which
    may themselves be factors in racial prejudice.
(7) Schools may transmit prejudice through structure,
    curriculum content and textbooks.
(8) Schools ought to attempt to teach about race relations
    and to diminish prejudice, discrimination and tension.
(9) This is a task for all schools, not just multi-racial
    schools.
(10) Schools are entitled to work for better race relations,
    even if the parents are prejudiced and discriminatory.
(11) It is important that teachers examine their own pre-
    judice.

AIM

To educate for the elimination of racial tensions and ill-feeling
within our society - which is and will be multi-racial - by
understanding prejudice, by developing respect for varied
traditions, and by encouraging mutual understanding, reasonableness and justice.

PRINCIPLES OF PROCEDURE

(1) We should help pupils become aware of their own atti-
    tudes.
(2) We should assist pupils to detect bias and the motives
    behind this.
(3) We should help pupils become aware of the emotional
    content in racial tension or conflict.
(4) We should make clear the historical and social factors
    which help explain the presence of racial/ethnic
    groups in society.
(5) We should help pupils to see that many problems
    which appear to stem from racial causes may be pre-
    dominantly social.
(6) We need to help pupils to see the possibility of organ-
    izing for change.

ROLE OF THE TEACHER

The teacher should be an example of a person critical of
prejudiced attitudes and opinions held by himself and
society at large and trying to achieve some degree of
mutual understanding and respect between identifiably different human groups.

TEACHING STRATEGIES TO BE EXPLORED

(1) We need to introduce into the classroom a structure and an atmosphere conducive to effective teaching about race relations.

(2) It is important, particularly at the beginning of the work, to set up situations which help teachers to know more about their pupils and their attitudes.

(3) We need to help pupils to look at their own views and criticize what they see.

(4) We should in general focus the work on the experiential and the emotional, factual materials being built round that. Most of the factual data need to be in teachers' books rather than in pupils' materials.

(5) It will be necessary to examine critically the bias and prejudice expressed in textbooks and other resource materials as well as generally in the arts and literature and mass media. (It may be difficult to deal with all aspects in the classroom.)

(6) We should help pupils to question critically racial and cultural generalizations and stereotypes; and to criticize their attitudes towards other races even when these carry the authority of the adult world or the school.

(7) Race relations can be regarded as an aspect of social tension, and there is a need for a study of tension both in society at large and in face-to-face groups such as the teaching group. (This presents problems for the teacher: there are possibilities in simulation, and observations and group self-analysis and drama; but release of tension in the classroom can be frightening and difficult to handle.)

(8) We should not treat prejudice and discrimination only in the context of colour, but should explore the nature of prejudice in general and of prejudice and discrimination in religious and nationalist contexts (e.g. Ireland).

(9) It is particularly important to make clear the social, historical and institutional factors shaping prejudice and not to stress individual guilt about the past; but it is important to stress individual responsibility now.

(10) We should try to develop an awareness of other cultures and of differences of values of other cultures.

(11) We need to generate interest in and respect for both differences and similarities.

(12) We need to help people to respond at an interpersonal level to people of other races.

(13) We should value the choices a plural society can give rather than conformity in the name of integration.

On the basis of this position, the project central team was commissioned to prepare or to seek out and recommend teaching materials to support the teachers who were working within the experiment.

We cannot pass on from this conference without noting that there was a strong note of dissent from the majority view. One school withdrew. The conference ran from 24 to 29 May. On Sunday, 27 May, the following statement was issued by the members attending from Archbishop Temple's School, London:

Sunday 27th May 1973

Statement to SSRC Conference on the Teaching of Race Relations
From the representatives of Archbishop Temple's School, London

We came to this conference with some experience of teaching in multi-racial schools, some experience of living and working in multi-racial areas of London, and with some hope.

We appreciate the initiative of the University's project team in calling on teachers to participate in putting out teaching materials. We think it would be generally agreed by participants that we gave ample voice to our convictions, basing them on our experience and study in and outside the teaching situation.

The mode of procedure at the conference seemed to allow for the incorporation of these views, with modifications, into the aims, strategies and premises of the project.

We list below some of the contributions we made to the conference which are missing from the formulated document.*
We believe these contributions are fundamental to the problem we are discussing:

(1) That the problem of race relations is basically a problem of racism and not of prejudice.
(2) By racism we mean the systematic oppression of a group of people for socio-economic purposes. Attendant on this definition is the conviction that racism must be eliminated. No amount of knowledge of 'cultures' will do this. An obvious example is contained in the history of the Raj in India. Two hundred years of rule may have bred a complete understanding of Indian civilization, culture and habits, but this understanding did not alter the structure of the Empire. A contemporary example is South Africa. In that context, understanding black culture facilitates control.
(3) We believe that education and the school curriculum have a role to play in the elimination of institutional racism.

*An earlier draft of the document printed above.

(4) We do not believe that the contradictory approach
which places the onus of racism on the child and
his or her family, can work in conjunction with the
realization stated above.

Because of this, we feel we are obliged to withdraw from
the second part of the conference which deals with teaching materials.

(Signed:) Farrukh Dhondy Hilary Boudillon Barry Simner

Farrukh Dhondy shortly afterwards published an extended
statement of his position in the 'Times Educational Supplement'
(2 November 1973). It is too long to reprint here, but it is well
worth studying and discussing in any school or teachers' centre
group.

It is obviously impossible for us to represent Dhondy's view,
but we need to make one or two points.

The team from Archbishop Temple was working in a multi-
racial context. The withdrawal of the group was an immense blow
to the other teachers at the conference, and the remainder of
the proceedings were conducted under its shadow. As a result,
most of the subsequent discussion took account of what were
taken to be the views of the members who had withdrawn. The
group did not by any means lose its influence on the conference
when it left.

There were many teachers working in the project who were
teaching in non-multi-racial areas, who had virtually no prior
knowledge about race relations and who knew intimately nobody
of a different racial background from themselves. The Archbishop Temple group were experienced and sophisticated.
Immediately before their withdrawal from the conference, there
were points where we believe it might have been possible for
myself as chairman to take an initiative to keep them in the
group by endorsing their experience as constituting a right
to leadership of the group. I did not do this because I did not
feel assured of their patience with people less skilled and
experienced than themselves. I believe I was right in this decision.

Finally, we believe that there is a crucial need for teachers
for whom race relations and racism are not central concerns of
their living to make a contribution within a general educational
commitment. Such a commitment is the necessary premise of a
project which sees itself in a service and supporting role. The
Archbishop Temple group seemed to have a commitment to the
elimination of racism which was stronger than and overrode
their commitment to teaching. Accordingly, the context of their
action must be seen as, in the broadest sense, political. In the
project we were concerned only with the educational contribution to that overall political objective.

We do not mean to suggest that political action on racism is unimportant: on the contrary, we do not believe that the political problem of racism can be delegated to the schools as if they were the means to solve problems that society will not face politically. This project seems to demonstrate that the appropriate contribution of education to interracial respect is limited though important. Probably, its contribution to the elimination of 'institutional' racism is marginal; but it is a consideration of the contribution of education which is necessarily the common ground for a diverse group of teachers.

Another aspect of the Strategy B conference is that it was the occasion of our attempting to negotiate with the teachers their role as co-researchers within the project. Since the major continuity between the Humanities Project and the present project is in the concern for teachers studying and researching their own work, this is an important matter; but we shall defer its full discussion for a few pages until we have described the Strategy A conference parallel to that of Strategy B reported above. This Strategy A conference was held at the University of York from 12 to 16 July 1973.

We have said that we had some difficulty in recruiting Strategy B schools for the project in terms of schools or LEAs not wishing to participate. Our difficulties were even greater in Strategy A, the Humanities Project strategy, no doubt as a result of the publicity attending the Schools Council's veto on publication of the project's collection on race relations, widely known as the 'race pack'. The result of this difficulty was to produce a group that was, on the whole, rather experienced in HCP, that was inclined to find its approach convincing, that was fairly clear about aims, and that did not require training in the method. Accordingly, there was much less work to be done on teaching in the Strategy A conference, and more attention was given to the role of the teachers in the research and to the assembling of teaching materials.

At the end of the Humanities Curriculum Project, the project team had a rather substantial archive of box files full of materials on race relations from which the teaching collection had been selected. This archive included those materials that had been in the vetoed race collection, though they were not identifiable (except that a couple of teachers in the conference had taken part in the previous experiment). During the first two days of the conference the teachers worked through this archive, making comments and suggestions towards a new collection for the new experiment.

Strategy B teachers had already tried to anticipate their needs for teaching materials at their own conference.

At that time, we hoped to produce two sets of teaching materials, but this proved over-ambitious both in terms of time and in terms of finance. In the end we produced a single compromise collection. Some experimental schools used a good deal of our materials, some a little, a few none. Some schools used materials already available to them (including the UNESCO ASPRO project) and some made their own. There is no sense in which this project can be regarded as testing teaching materials.

The other main issue addressed by the Strategy A conference was the role of the teachers in the total research framework. Discussion of this was fed by a paper prepared by Bob Wild, which I reprint here.

THE INVISIBLE MAN: AN ESSAY IN EDUCATIONAL RESEARCH

Bob Wild

Summary: This paper attempts to explore the relationship between teachers as research workers and professional research workers who co-operate with them. Both are seen to have a part to play, and fruitful collaboration is felt to rest on the development of a common language and a mutual strengthening of the research position. In this way it is hoped to build towards a tradition of educational research which will benefit all concerned.

This paper can pretend to be no more than a particular application of a more general one presented by another author (Schutz, 1964). The general paper reported attempts to study the typical situation in which a stranger finds himself in trying to interpret the cultural pattern of a social group which he approaches with the intention of familiarizing himself with it. It is interesting to note, in the context of the present project, that the exemplar of the stranger chosen is that of the 'immigrant'. It might be argued therefore that the paper presented here can be read at two levels, albeit unintentionally. Its overt purpose is to make clear to the reader the dimensions within which research in school takes place so that such research can be meaningful for both teachers and research workers who take part in it.

A useful starting point is the school and the culture within which the teacher finds himself. It is possible to regard the school as a small society which manifests many of the features of a wider society outside. Such a perspective calls attention to the structure of the school, its formal and informal organization, hierarchies, as well as the values, norms, rules, traditions, ceremonials and so forth, which constitute the school culture. Some might argue that the term 'society' should not be limited to an institution such as the school; others focus on the classroom as the reality of the school society. It does not seem necessary to argue the point here, but rather to note a more important fact. To look at the school as a society makes one realize that no two schools are alike. Each has a particular style, attributable to teacher-background, pupil-background, the philosophy

of the headmaster, tradition, past events, local influences
and so on. This cultural reality presents a different aspect
to the external researcher and to the teacher who acts and
thinks within it.

In his effort to be scientific and keep what he is studying pure, the professional research worker is frequently
afraid of stepping into the culture of the school. This casts
him into the role of onlooker. He is disinterested in that he
intentionally refrains from taking part in the network of
plans, means-and-ends relationships, motives and chances,
hopes and fears, which the teacher within the school uses
for interpreting his experiences of it; the research worker
hopes to observe, describe and analyse a particular process
taking place in the classroom and/or the school. To do this
he might wish to be all-seeing and thereby invisible (as
suggested in the title of this paper), or to be able to fit
into the skin of an actual participant. As these extremes
are unlikely to be realized, the researcher must compromise. He may, if he so wishes, get over the problem of con-
taminating the situation by sitting behind a one-way mirror
and observing what is going on in the classroom. He might
also feel that participation is far more worthwhile provided
that he does not compromise himself by furthering the action.
To avoid this he will respond in a non-directive way - in
other words, he will be a participant but not an actor. In
all this the teacher is rarely considered as a researcher.
Though he provides information for the professional research,
he does not *actively* direct his efforts. Reasons why this is
not satisfactory will be contained in the argument developed
in this paper.

The teacher within the school experiences its culture primarily as the medium within which he lives and only secondarily as something to be described and analysed. It may be
that description and analysis is clearly relevant to his
action; but caught as he is in the situation, it is difficult
not to settle for intuition. He is likely to single out those
elements of the situation which may serve as ends or means
for the realization of teaching aims or social contact. His
interests, in a sense, will radiate from his needs. This implies an immediate area which the teacher has 'knowledge
of', surrounded by a further area which he has 'knowledge
about'. For example, in day-to-day terms the teacher may
not be over-concerned with the educational philosophy of
the headmaster. Yet the desire to innovate within a particular part of the curriculum may make this of paramount
importance to those concerned. Then 'knowledge about' will
quickly change into 'knowledge of'. Each situation will
generate its own viewpoint. The research worker coming
from outside and attempting to look at the total institution
may feel that a particular teacher's viewpoint at a particular
time exhibits both incoherence and contradiction. For

example, at every point in the day demands are made upon
the teacher from all sides. The headmaster may wish a
particular group of pupils to become examination candidates;
the pupils themselves may feel unlike work due to a previous
games lesson or because it is the last period in the day. The
teacher is in the position of having to make a decision. It
may seem to be a choice of pleasing either the headmaster
or the pupils. In fact, his response is likely to be governed
by more complex considerations. His self-image as teacher,
his status in relation to others, previous experience during
the day, how he feels at that point, his future intentions,
as well as many other possibilities, are likely to play a part.
In retrospect, shorn of the reality of the situation, the
teacher's action may seem to lack a consistency and to be
downright contradictory. A teacher who has opposed examinations in a staff meeting appears as a 'crammer' in a given
classroom situation. From what has been said, it suggests
that the teacher in the society, as for that matter like the
individual in any society, is liable to have a system of
assumptions and perceptions relative to his own needs.
Some of these assumptions will be shared to give the school
the quality of a society. Anyone lacking too many of these
shared assumptions is likely to find himself outside of the
school culture. Without containing meaning accessible to
other teachers, statements become socially incoherent and
communication breaks down. On the other hand, broad
familiarity with the folklore of the school allows many teachers to make 'of course' assumptions.

The research worker approaching the school from without
does not have the security of a ready-made set of assumptions fashioned and worked out within the culture of a
particular school. He becomes essentially the man who has
to place in question nearly everything that seems to be
unquestionable to the members of the approached group.
To him the cultural pattern of the particular school does
not have the authority of a tested system of everyday
responses. To be sure, from the research worker's point of
view the school has a special tradition and background, and
this may be made accessible to him. But he has never himself experienced what it is like to be a part of that culture,
or to learn as a full member something of its history and
traditions. Whatever role the research worker takes up, he
is essentially a newcomer. In order to interpret what he
sees, the research worker is likely to rely heavily on past
experiences. These may be as either a teacher or a pupil,
involving all the tricks the memory plays. He is therefore
likely, at least initially, to place his own reality upon that
of the school. This must gradually be transformed if useful
interaction is to take place. For a time the researcher must
translate school meanings into his meanings, until he has
learnt the language. But, as he will soon find out, to speak

the language of the school is one thing, to interpret it is another. The difference between the two stages of understanding is familiar to any student of a foreign language. It is the difference between the passive 'knowing' of a language and its active mastering as a means for realizing one's own acts and thoughts. Any group may be unwilling to initiate a newcomer into its habits and assumptions, so the research worker is likely to undergo a phase of pseudo-familiarity and pseudo-intimacy. In his attempt to define the situation his uncertainty and hesitancy will seem bewildering to those who long ago internalized the norms and ritual of the school. The obviousness of most actions to the well-established teacher will make the question 'Why?' seem almost impolite. The answer is likely to be 'Because that is how it is done'.

It must not be inferred from what has so far been said that any criticism is being levelled at teachers. The points raised are immediately applicable to any social grouping, though, as one might expect, details will differ. Were a teacher to research a research unit, there would be a reversal of roles of 'teacher' and 'researcher'. What is important is that the situation in which the study takes place is fleshed out so that further discussion may be more meaningful. It readily becomes apparent that the school situation is extremely complex. The peculiarities of each school make any drawing of generalizations, except about the importance of particular variables, an almost impossible task.

Before going on to consider the implications of what has been said so far in terms of our present project, it seems useful to review briefly approaches to curriculum research. The most widely held view is that a curriculum is a proposal to be evaluated by measuring in behavioural terms the realization of objectives. These objectives are pursued through the materials and methods used in the classroom. Curriculum research then becomes evaluation employing psychometric tests. Wherever possible, laboratory-like conditions are produced and variables limited. This approach, in its classical form, consists of a pre- and post-test sequence with the 'treatment' in between. Frequently, other schools not directly involved are brought in to serve as controls.

In a more elaborate form, a longitudinal design measures change over a period of time. In the last few years many of the weaknesses of this approach have received public expression. All that need concern us here is the inadequacy of discrete measurement to reveal the complexity of classroom processes. Nevertheless, such measurement may allow the research worker information about the pupil which he would not otherwise be able to obtain, and at the same time provide a certain level of generalization about behavioural

change. It now seems that emphasis is shifting somewhat in
curriculum evaluation from a model based on before-and-
after measurement to one resting on description and por-
trayal. This gives a more accurate picture of what happens
in individual schools implementing various curricula.
Reports, descriptions, etc., supplement or replace standardized tests. It is responsive to the various audiences
it might be written for, for example decision-makers and
teachers. As an approach it would seem to have much to
offer, but it still separates the researcher as curriculum
designer from the researcher as evaluator. The retention
of the idea of a programme or product to be tested rather
than the classroom and teaching to be explored means that
the model is based on outcome rather than on the generation of further insights.

In conclusion, one can begin to feel one's way towards
a research design suitable for use in schools at large,
with particular reference to this project. The complexity
and individuality of each school has already been noted.
A given school will place its own stamp on any innovation
introduced into it. At the same time, the innovation will
serve to further develop the particular characteristics of
that school. The initial need of research in schools would
therefore seem to be to describe as fully as possible the
implementation of a particular teaching strategy against
the background of that school. In other words, research
should be directed towards schools rather than across
them.

It is at this point that the need for the teacher as an
internal researcher becomes most apparent. As previously
shown, the professional research worker is a newcomer
or stranger to the reality of each school. To put it more
bluntly, he is ignorant. In the light of what has already
been said, it is hard to see how it could be otherwise. This
would seem to place a responsibility upon the teacher as a
researcher. Without his taking upon himself this role, the
effectiveness of much that is done would seem to be severely
curtailed. The teacher has ready access to what is happening in his school. Lacking a developed research tradition,
the teacher may feel too hard-pressed and involved to make
sense of it. Also, each person's interpretation of a particular situation can, by definition, be no more than partial.
The external research worker by his very position is bound
to become a systematizer - in order to make sense of the
school reality for his own sake as well as for that of others.
The teacher as internal research worker, and the member
of the project team as external research worker, would
therefore seem to compensate for each other's shortcomings
and, more important, to deepen understanding of the process being observed. It allows the innovation to be perceived
from two standpoints, within and without. To achieve this

requires that a common language be developed between the two research workers. This places great emphasis on the use of regional meetings to forward this end. Benefits accrue to both parties in the undertaking. The development of one's research capacity as a teacher is an important way of establishing greater control over one's classroom. Similarly, increased knowledge of the classroom gives the person concerned with curriculum design greater understanding of the variables involved in teaching.

This paper was worked on in the Strategy A conference and came to be the basis for Bob Wild's relationship with the teachers in both Strategy A and Strategy B. There are some novel features of Wild's approach which are important for research work, in particular his refusal to enter the classroom he was studying for observation. Instead, he worked from tape-recordings of class work and data gathered by the teacher, supplemented by teacher and pupils discussing or being interviewed about their work. In this research strategy the audio-recording is supplemented by the perceptions of the participants. Emphasis is laid on the experience and perception of the people involved in the classroom process, and not on some notional objective social reality to which their experience is a response.

More immediately relevant at this point is the idea that the teachers were developing their own understanding, principles of procedure and techniques of teaching about race relations by the adoption of a research stance. We can see no alternative to this procedure for the teacher. It is not possible to pass on a prescription for teaching about race relations that can override professional judgment. And the best way to strengthen professional judgment is to adopt a research stance. Our advice is that teachers use the information that the research can give to repeat in their own school the experiment conducted by the teachers in the experimental schools. Of course, this is not easy. Teachers work under great pressure. But it is to be hoped that they will judge the extra effort of taping and discussing their work to be possible at least for the first year of teaching about race relations.

Now it is time to turn to Strategy C. The ten schools involved in this drama strategy came together for their conference in Newcastle-upon-Tyne in December 1973. They were to teach, as a general rule, through improvised rather than scripted drama. Dorothy Heathcote, of the Newcastle-upon-Tyne School of Education, who is well known for her work in this field, acted as consultant to the conference, and an evaluative report of the proceedings was commissioned from Tony Higgins of St Mary's College, Strawberry Hill. This report is a substantial document too long to quote here, but it is available for consultation at CARE.

Interestingly enough, the drama teachers who took part in the conference declined the task of formulating aims or notes or principles of procedure. They took the view that the tradition of teaching through improvised drama could not be caught in that way; but, by working within the conference through improvised drama and discussing the issues that the work raised, they defined their stance as clearly as they felt was useful.

Early in the conference, teachers were invited to say what was characteristic in drama, and what kinds of aims might be possible in teaching about race relations through drama. Some responses were as follows.

The aim is to structure living situations which carry tension within them and to bring those tensions to the surface. By bringing them to the surface, it carries a hope that you may come to terms with it. Drama is not a panacea...its very essence is tension.

In drama, often the children take over, and often the situation develops without the teacher. He must allow it to do so, so that the understanding of the group develops. In most drama, the aim is to develop understanding through a situation which the children then explore.

Drama can put people in the other person's situation. For example, we can subject the majority to the pressures which the minority would normally undergo, which may be a way of developing understanding. It gives the threatened the opportunity to take over the role of threatener.

Most discussions are teacher-controlled, and there is the possibility of repressing what the child wants to express. This should not happen in drama. You step back a little. You allow it to be child-controlled for a time.

Discussion allows an emotional buffer. You can always make your words push back a bit. In drama, you're at risk, and have to solve a problem or make a decision. You're not concerned with promoting the emotional buffer. You say what you think. You do what your reaction is. This is a much more valuable thing than what happens when you speak - that is tailored, because most people are insecure enough to think about what they say before they say it.

(Quotations from conference report)

If drama could expose and explore tensions, help children to get into other people's shoes, allow children to be spontaneous, explore issues not as issues but as embodied in situations, what problems, then, had to be faced? Was there, for

example, a contradiction between the principle of distancing
and the principle of spontaneity, of allowing the children to
take over and develop the situation without the teacher? How
often and to what extent would they take over, and what safe-
guards were needed when tension was exposed? Was the role of
the teacher in drama always and necessarily a participatory one,
which would allow him to make moves from inside the drama to
control emotion or tension before it got out of hand?

The conference report records the following topics and issues
of discussion - among many others.

(1) In racially mixed schools an 'uneasy truce' might have been
achieved. Would work in drama re-open the tensions? What kind
of risks were there in the work? What kind of commitment were
drama teachers prepared to make?
(2) The school was only one of the influences on young people.
Would work in school be robust enough to withstand prejudice
within the community?
(3) Should drama concentrate on prejudice in general or on
prejudice in race relations in particular?
(4) The relationship between drama and emotion; the power of
drama to release and help people encounter tensions; the potential of drama to help people get inside other people's shoes.
(5) It was suggested that, whereas in discussion students
might work on *issues*, in drama students would work through
situations. In drama, the teachers generally provide a framework and students provide the content.
(6) The need to preserve individuality of style and approach
in drama - 'There are as many different ways of doing drama
as there are people in this room.'
(7) The extent to which drama could work on political aspects
of race relations (institutional racism) as opposed to the psychological aspects of race relations.

It is worth drawing particular attention to the degree of
tentativeness that filters through these issues. We think this
was reflected in the teaching of the drama strategy in a good
many cases, and that in some schools the concentration was
on prejudice in general with race relations being represented
only in so far as the development of the work, as it followed
its own logic, tended to bring the racial theme in. Certainly
there was some reserve about pulling the pupils on to the
territory of race relations if they do not enter it naturally.

The brief accounts of Strategies A,B and C that we have given
above are intended to provide both information about the experimental development that took place within the research project,
and a starting point for discussing the problems and issues
involved in teaching about race relations, the better to plan
such work.

3 THE DESIGN AND LOGIC OF THE RESEARCH

Lawrence Stenhouse

Research is learning by systematic inquiry. In its pure form
the research act is motivated and shaped by the needs of such
inquiry. We do something because we want to find something
out.

The primary reason for the teachers with whom we worked
teaching as they did was not a research reason, but an educational one. Their classrooms were shaped by educational rather
than research aims.

Our job in the project team was to design a research from
which they and we learned as much as possible from their educational actions. This meant that we had to respond to educational
actions in a spirit of systematic inquiry. Working in this way,
with action that has to be justified in professional rather than
primarily in research terms, is a characteristic of action
research. We had to work alongside teachers, respecting their
educational aims and professional judgment, but trying ourselves to learn as much as we could for a wider audience about
the 'Problems and Effects of Teaching about Race Relations'.
We wanted to ensure that the participating teachers had the
best possible opportunity of learning too. Both their needs and
our own meant that it was part of our job to support them as
they developed a research role alongside their main role of
teaching.

How does one design a research to capture educational acts
in a spirit of inquiry? One way is to attempt to cast them in
the form of an experiment: another is to observe them carefully and record them. An experiment is shaped to sharpen the
bearing of observations on certain questions, and if possible
to enable observation to be expressed as measurement. Naturalistic observation responds to the natural shape of events and
attempts to portray them in a way that makes them open to
people who did not have first-hand experience of them. We
tackled our problem from both ends, using both experiment
and descriptive case studies. In experiment we are fishing
for generalizations; in case study we are portraying experiences that while they do not offer general laws, can be applied
to the new situations we meet as all thought-through experience can.

We shall look first at the problem of experimental design in
our action research context.

Let us begin by bringing to mind a pattern of classical
experimental work in the psychological laboratory. A group of

people is divided into two apparently comparable groups,
called an 'experimental group' and a 'control group'. The
experimental group is given some treatment whose effects interest us and the control group is not. The control group might
be called a 'comparison group'. The performance or condition
of the two groups is measured or observed before the experimental treatment is given to the experimental group and then
again after the treatment. Any difference that is observable
in the two groups after the experiment but not before is taken
to be the result of the experimental treatment. This design can
be expressed thus:

	Time
Experimental group	O X O
Control group	O O

Where O = observation or measurement and X = experimental
treatment.

This sounds very simple, but there are a number of problems
that must be overcome if reasonable conclusions are to be
drawn from such an experiment. For example, the experimental
and control groups must be comparable with each other; the
experimental treatment must be consistent throughout the
experimental group; the measuring instrument must be consistent for both groups; the control group must not be exposed
to any chance treatment relevant to performance on the measures; and no contextual conditions likely to affect the observed performances of the groups must bear on them during the
experiment. These conditions are difficult to meet, but unless
we succeed in meeting them the results we are comparing inside
our experiment will not really be comparable.

The problem of the comparability of experimental and control
groups concerns our ability to make statements about the effect
of an experiment. We compare an observation or a measurement
result in a group where we have mounted an experiment with
one in a group where we have not, and attribute any difference
to the experimental treatment. For example, we might compare
the effects of a new reading programme with the effects of an
established reading programme in schools. If we did so, it
would be important that the two groups taking the programmes
were comparable in all the variables relating to performance in
reading. This problem of comparability within the experiment
is crucial to our making valid statements about what has happened in the groups we have observed. It is an aspect of the
problem of internal validity.

Internal validity can best be ensured by conducting the
experiment 'under laboratory conditions'. This is because a
laboratory is designed to enable us to control the variables that
may, if uncontrolled, destroy comparability.

However, a laboratory is a privileged place in this respect, and often the effects we get there do not generalize reliably to real settings. Unless we are testing a theory, which brings together a lot of differing observations and makes sense of them, we shall usually find it difficult to generalize the effects observed within a laboratory experiment to the rough-and-ready conditions of real life. The laboratory is useful (and currently too neglected) in educational research, but it is for clarifying and refining theory. This is because it is difficult to generalize the results of the laboratory experiment by predicting the results to be expected outside the experiment, in a target population that concerns us in the real world. The problem of generalization to situations outside an experiment is that of external validity.

One could tackle this problem by making the laboratory more and more like the world outside. Educational laboratories might simulate real classrooms.

This observation makes it obvious that an alternative procedure is to conduct experiments outside the laboratory altogether and in real classrooms. Even then, if we have experimented in a limited number of classrooms, we must ask: is what we have discovered applicable to other classrooms in other schools? For example, all the schools except one in the present project are state comprehensive or secondary modern schools; so we would apparently be on thin ice if we attempted to predict from our results what might happen in teaching about race relations in public schools. Thus, the problem of external validity is raised even in classroom-based experiments. Such experiments may be called field experiments; and in their classic form in agriculture they were literally that: fields, such as most readers will have seen, where one fertilizer or strain of seed is tried out against another to see which is best.

The theory behind field experiment is that we can represent the contextual variables by sampling in such a way that they 'cancel out' into a blurred background against which we can get our experimental observations into focus. We want a sample of people and institutions and environments that is representative of the target population to which we want to generalize, or in which teachers want to apply, our results. We want our experimental schools to tell us about other schools out there in the system.

In order to create such a representative sample, however, we should have to know already the distribution of all the relevant contextual variables in the target population and to build them in the same proportions into our sample population. This is an impossible condition to meet. Therefore researchers generally try instead to draw random samples, that is, samples constructed on the principles of chance. The definition of a random sample is: a sample so selected from a larger population that each unit in the larger population has an equal and independent possibility of being selected.

Now, the main argument for random sampling is this. No
properly representative sample can be drawn, but so long as
the sample is drawn by chance rather than by judgment, it is
possible to use the mathematics of probability to assess the
chances of a difference observed between an experimental and
a control group being due to differences between the samples
rather than between results of experimental treatments.

We can observe a difference and calculate, for example, that
there is only one chance in twenty of its being an artefact of
sampling error (0.05 level of significance), or that the chance
is merely one in a hundred (0.01 level of significance). Such
calculations of significance are computed in our experiment,
but in the last analysis they are weakened as we depart from
random sampling, as we always do in field research in education. This is partly because we cannot control schools and
teachers and pupils, and hence cannot select them randomly
and then ask some to follow our experimental procedure and
others not.

We necessarily work with 'opportunity samples', which are
'naturally assembled collectives such as classrooms, as similar
as availability permits' (Campbell and Stanley, 1963, p. 217).
Having lost randomization, we need to consider very carefully
the sample that opportunity has made available to us. We do
this in our next chapter.

Our design is apparently one of experimental and control
groups using opportunity samples. Within this limitation on
sampling, we appear to be concerned with internal and external
validity. But what is the experiment about?

The conventional expectation is that it is to test which of
three ways of teaching about race relations is best. This is
emphatically not what we are attempting to do. Walker and
Schaffarzick (1974), surveying all the American studies they
could find that attempted to compare curricula in these terms,
conclude:

> The difficulties we experienced in trying to interpret the
> results of these studies led us to question the wisdom of
> designing and conducting comparative experimental studies
> of different curricula. Studies which locate the distinctive
> outcomes of different curricula and studies which determine
> the long-term school-related and life consequences of these
> different outcomes would seem to be more useful both to
> policy-makers and scholars. Such studies require that a
> great deal more research be directed towards creating mea-
> sures of a variety of outcomes other than achievement that
> commonly appear in claims made for and about curricula.
> (p. 109)

We agree with this view, the more so because we are concerned
primarily with teachers as an audience and only secondarily
with policy-makers and scholars. We do not think we have got

as far along the road that Walker and Schaffarzick point out as we might have done. This is partly because we have had to address some rather general questions.

The first of these is: does teaching about race relations tend to make the overall situation with regard to interracial attitudes worse rather than better? This is an important question, and one on which opinion has been divided. Stemming from it is another question: are there some particular ways of teaching about race relations that are liable to do damage? Of course, we can face this question only within the context of the teaching styles mounted in this project; and even then it is a difficult one.

We also hoped to pick up from the experiment some indication of trends of attitude among adolescents and to look for consistencies of result that might lead us towards theory; but these matters will be discussed later.

One theoretical line we might have hoped to pursue was closed to us by the constraints of action research. It would have been of great interest to compare the results of a non-authoritarian approach like that of the Humanities Curriculum Project with an authoritarian approach to teaching about race relations. Of particular interest would have been the relationship of these approaches to the reactions of pupils who differ in their attitudes towards school and teachers. However, as will be clear from the previous chapter, our Strategy B teachers did not in effect take an authoritarian stance, and this possibility was consequently lost to us, since it would have been quite improper for us to attempt to persuade teachers to adopt an authoritarian stance against their better judgment.

The adoption of respect for professional judgment in the classroom as an ethical basis for the research also prevented us from pressing our teachers to conform to rigid specifications of teaching, and hence the experimental treatments were not tightly controlled.

The limitations we have described are pretty well universal in field experiment in education. Such limitations suggest that we should be wary of over confidence in the validity of predictive generalizations drawn from our sample and purporting to apply to other schools and other classrooms.

So many variables, including some within the control of the teacher, are at work in teaching situations that it seems impossible to tease them out statistically in a way that has meaning for action (Cronbach, 1975). And quite clearly, in respect to teaching about race relations, different factors are at work in, say, a multi-ethnic school in urban Birmingham and an ethnically homogeneous school in Lincolnshire. Inferences drawn from the study of a sample can be applied only precariously in the school system as a whole.

Snow (1974) offers a useful lead here when he points out that, though a sample may not be representative of a pre-specified target population, a careful analysis of the sample itself may provide a good judgment of the target population to which it could generalize. He is still thinking in the classic terms of generalization. His point is even more striking if we cast the problem in terms of application of the research to a specific case: that is to say, one's own.

Such an application may be an inference from a sample to one's own case or from another case to one's own case.

Whenever a uniform policy or practice has to be executed throughout a population – of schools, classes or pupils – this shift from generalization to application will be seen as a weakening of the relevance of research to practice. However, in England at least, the general assumption is that schools should adapt to their own situations by differentiating their practice. This is particularly true of a problem like teaching about race relations, where the context and conditions of the teaching vary significantly. In such situations, and given such assumptions, generalizations that are merely couched in terms of probability will always be less favoured than applications based on informed professional judgment. That is why our research is primarily aimed at informing – and, in the longer run, strengthening – the professional judgment of teachers.

We hope to provide the information that will allow a teacher to judge whether his situation would fall within a target population represented by the situations sampled in the research. But we also want to put him in a position to judge that some particular situations within the sample cast light on his own, either because of a similarity or because of a contrast which clearly defines features of the teacher's own case.

This illumination of one's own circumstances by access to the experience of others depends upon the possibility of recognizing similarities and differences between other cases and one's own. Such recognition depends upon the existence of portrayals of experience, and this is the role of descriptive case studies in the present project.

Our measurement results document some problems of teaching about race relations, but they tend in their nature to provide data about effects. The title of our project, 'Problems and Effects of Teaching about Race Relations', expresses our belief, formed on carefully assessed experience in two other projects, that the documentation of the problems encountered by good teachers is a better basis for improving one's own practice than the documentation of best practice. Imitation is not the road to better teaching.

The principles underlying the three strategies are principles of navigation, not courses to be followed. We must, as Walker and Schaffarzick (1974) suggest, escape from the literal root meaning of 'curriculum'; must 'stop thinking of the curriculum as a fixed race course and begin to think of it as a tool, apparently a powerful one, for stimulating and directing the active learning capacities which are ultimately responsible for the achievement we want from schools' (p. 109).

Navigation is such an intellectual tool for the mariner. He needs charts, and we have done what we can to survey the overall features of the area of teaching about race relations. He also needs hazards and channels marked, and our case studies go some way towards providing lighthouses and buoys as an aid to navigation.

4 SAMPLING

Lawrence Stenhouse, Gajendra K. Verma and
Robert D. Wild

In this chapter we describe how the LEAs, schools, teachers
and pupils who took part in the experiment came to do so. In
terms of our case study approach, we might say quite simply
that we shall be concerned with how we gathered the schools
that were our cases. In the second part of the book we describe
some of these cases so that the reader can compare them with
his own, or with other cases with which he is familiar. A book
of classroom transcriptions drawn from other cases in the project has also been published (Sikes, 1979).

However, as well as our descriptive case studies, we conducted a programme of measurement, using tests we shall describe in the next chapter. Tests and test results do not give
you any basis for judging whether the cases are or are not
like your own. If they indicate what is likely to happen in your
own case, they do so not because you can apply them by exer-
cising judgment, but because to a useful extent they generalize.
But such generalization depends on the schools (and LEAs,
teachers and pupils) in the experimental project being like a
'population' of schools (including yours?) that did not take
part. To put it another way, they need to be a representative
sample. Trying to choose schools so that they are a representative sample is called 'sampling'.

There are two classic problems of experiment to which sampling is a response: maximizing the probability that experimental
and control groups within the experiment are comparable
('internal validity'), and maximizing the probability that our
sample group within the experiment is representative of the
population outside our sample to which we wish to generalize
('external validity') (see pp. 30-1 above).

From our standpoint in this experiment, a random sample of
forty state secondary schools might best be gathered by assigning a number to every state secondary school in Britain and
then selecting our sample by reading off the first forty numbers
from a table of random numbers. Similarly, a random sample of
pupils or teachers would best be approximated by numbering
all pupils and all teachers and then employing the same technique of selection.

As we have already mentioned, no experiments in real educational settings approach random sampling at all closely. The
present one comes closer than most, but falls far short. It is
worth noticing some of the difficulties.

In most educational experiments we are concerned to sample

schools, teachers and pupils. In order to do this randomly,
each would have to be sampled independently of the others.
To sample schools and then sample pupils in them is to lose
randomization in the pupil sample, because only the pupils in
our sampled schools and not those in all schools have a chance
of selection. We shall return to this problem later, but it is
worth noting here that in educational research only survey
work can hope to approximate random sampling at all closely.
Experiment, which is necessarily of limited scale and which
cannot control the selection of individual pupils for class-
taught treatments, cannot come near to random sampling procedures.

Furthermore, in Britain at least, a random sample is impossible to draw for an educational experiment because participation in any such experiment rests upon a policy decision. The
experimenter is not and cannot be responsible for policy
because he is not accountable: decisions rest with the LEA,
the school and the teachers. They must agree to participate.
This means that the sample is inevitably self-selected to some
degree, and this is a systematic bias. One would expect differences between those willing and those unwilling to participate
in experiments, particularly since a distinction has already
been drawn between early and late adopters of innovations
(e.g., Rogers and Shoemaker, 1971, 176-88).

Clearly, we are a good distance from the possibility of drawing random samples in an experiment of the sort we are reporting here, but given our area of concern, this is something we
have to live with. Here is Snow (1974) facing this problem:

> There are three steps in making inferences from empirical
> data. One step requires generalization from the observed
> sample of students to the accessible population from which
> it was drawn. A second step requires generalization from
> the accessible population to the target population with which
> one is ultimately concerned. The third step interprets the
> meaning of the generalization with respect to the substantive
> phenomena under study. The first two steps are statistical;
> they rest on the assumption of random sampling of students
> from populations. In other words, the sample is assumed to
> be representative of the accessible population, which in turn
> is assumed to be representative of the target population.
> But random sampling is rarely attained for the first step and
> never for the second. Usually neither population is even
> adequately defined or described.
> As pointed out by several previous writers (Lindquist,
> 1953; Cornfield and Tukey, 1956; Bracht and Glass, 1968),
> the investigator need not be overly troubled by these
> statistical steps, particularly the first step. He can at least
> generalize from his sample to a hypothetical accessible popu-
> lation *like those observed*. Regarding the second step, Bracht
> and Glass (1968) note that it

can be made with relatively less confidence than the
first jump. The only basis for this inference is a
thorough knowledge of *the characteristics of both populations and how these characteristics relate to the dependent variable of the experiment.* (p.6)

Thus, the key to generalization in both steps is thorough
description of student characteristics. (p. 270)

In fact, we would seem to need to describe LEAs, schools
and teachers as well as students, since a problem of sampling
arises in each case. This seems a tall order, particularly since
the characteristics of the total population related to attitudes
towards race relations are not well understood. The procedure
we propose to follow is to describe the way our sample was
drawn, relating our procedures to Snow's sampling strategies
for quasi-representative designs.

Our original intention was to draw a sample of forty-five
schools distributed as three groups of fifteen among three
different teaching strategies A, B and C. In the event, after
considerable problems in gathering our sample, we ended up
with fourteen schools in Strategy A, sixteen schools in Strategy
B and ten schools in Strategy C, where late notification of funding and staff illness interfered with recruitment of schools.

Our hope was to draw a sample of schools for each strategy
which would, so far as possible, represent within it the range
of variables we judged likely to be relevant to teaching about
race relations. However, we did not try to represent these
variables in the same proportions in our sample as in the total
population. We could not have attempted this within samples of
manageable size. Attempting to get the broadest possible
representation of variables, we recognized as we did so that a
variety of interactive effects among the variables would mutate
them in such a way as to leave prediction of their operation in
situations outside our experiment to the judgment of those
familiar with those situations. Thus, the teacher reading this
will have to estimate what is likely to happen in his own school
and class, using our report to inform - but not to override -
his judgment.

Our previous experience of gathering a sample of schools
from all over the country was in the context of the Nuffield
Foundation and Schools Council Humanities Curriculum Project
in 1967 (Verma, 1980, pp. 239-54). Then, the Schools Council
wrote to all local education authorities inviting them to express
an interest in taking part in the trial phase.

In the project reported here we again followed the assumption
that initial approaches should be made formally through the
LEA; but, since experience had shown that LEAs whose offers
were not taken up felt that they had been rejected after taking
the trouble to sound out schools, we decided in our case to
approach only a limited number of LEAs which would be likely

to give us the sample we wanted.

It is worth reproducing here the letter and enclosure we sent to the chief education officer of each LEA, not merely as documenting the approach we made, but also as a means of summarizing the project for the reader.

Dear Sir,

The Social Science Research Council Race Teaching Project: Participation of Schools

The aim of the Project is to investigate the problems and effects of teaching race relations to adolescents.

Several different patterns of teaching are likely to conduce to greater racial tolerance; but it is evident from previous research that some teaching intended to reduce racial prejudice can reinforce it. It seems clear that teachers will welcome support in developing effective methods and materials to handle this difficult but important topic. This project is intended to provide a sound basis for suggestions to teachers.

For the purposes of the research design we intend to study two teaching strategies, both of which we expect to be generally speaking successful, though each will throw up different problems. We shall produce materials to support the teachers in each case.

One of these strategies will follow from the work of the Humanities Project. The overriding aim will be 'to develop an understanding of the problems of race relations', the assumption being that such an understanding will tend in general to promote interracial tolerance. Teachers will be asked to take the role of neutral chairman in the discussion work which will be a main feature of this method. Since there are a large number of schools already engaged in the Humanities Project, comparatively little development work will be needed.

The second strategy will take a more positive stance than that of the Humanities Project, the aim being 'to combat racial prejudice'. In this case the premise will be that interracial understanding is often blocked by prejudice – in the strict sense of the word – and that it is appropriate for the school to provide experiences that attempt to break up that prejudice, and open the way for thoughtful judgment. The teacher, of course, will not be asked to adopt a neutral role.

The two strategies do not seem to us logically contradictory, but for experimental purposes we wish to develop them in different schools, at least initially.

In order to match samples, and because of the greater length of development work involved, we wish first to recruit the schools following the second strategy. Our hope is to find four clusters of four schools within easy reach of each other, and to recruit three (or possibly four) teachers in each.

Since the schools will be sharing the responsibility for development, and not simply trying out a curriculum, it is important that each should have a group of able and committed teachers who would be likely to be in sympathy with the aims of the teaching strategy they are developing.

I am writing to you to ask whether you would be willing to support us in working with a school in your authority, and if so, whether you could suggest one (or up to three) schools which would in your view be suitable. Since the sample should include a wide range of situations, it is not necessary that the schools should be racially mixed.

I have set out in the attached paper a general description of the pattern of work of the Project so far as we can anticipate it, and have attempted to define the nature and extent of the commitment a local authority would be taking on if it decided to support the participation of a school in the Project.

If you decide that you would be prepared to work with us on this development, perhaps you could let me have the name of the member of your staff I should contact. I shall then arrange for a member of the team to visit him within the next three months to discuss the selection of the school and the administrative arrangements which are necessary.

Yours sincerely
Lawrence Stenhouse

These are excerpts from the paper which accompanied the letter:

PROVISION NEEDED ON THE PART OF LOCAL AUTHORITIES AND SCHOOLS FOR PARTICIPATION; AND WHAT BENEFITS THEY WILL GET

MANAGEMENT OF EVALUATION

Pre-tests will be run on pupils in the Autumn Term 1973. Post-tests will be run early in the Summer Term 1974. Approximately six tests will be used and testing will require two mornings in each school, not exceeding two hours each morning. It would be a very great advantage if local authorities could make available on these mornings a school psychologist (preferably the same administrator for both pre- and post-tests) to administer the tests, or assist the Project in enlisting the co-operation of a psychologist in a college of education who would take on this task.

WHAT IS ASKED OF A LOCAL AUTHORITY PARTICIPATING

(1) The nomination of a member of the advisory staff of the authority who will act as contact and will give some support to the school involved.
(2) Possibly to release a psychologist for four mornings to administer tests during the session 1973-4 without payment, or co-operation in arranging for test administration by a member of staff in a college of education.

WHAT IS ASKED OF A SCHOOL PARTICIPATING

(1) Timetabling in half-classes for 45-60 pupils in fifth (or fourth) year 1973-4.
(2) Timetabling three experimental teachers during 1973-4 for one free period each week, *at the same time*, so that they can hold a weekly planning meeting.
(3) Provision of a tape-recorder for each of three teachers.
(4) Provision of some storage for materials.
(5) Readiness to keep records of the work.
(6) Readiness to grant interviews to a case study worker.

WHAT THE LEA AND THE SCHOOL GET

(1) A group of three teachers skilled in teaching race relations as a basis for development in the area.
(2) Strong support for school and teachers in meeting difficult teaching problems.
(3) Free materials for both teaching strategies up to about £30 cost per school.

We took similar steps to those used in Strategies A and B in inviting participation in Strategy C - teaching about race relations through drama. In short, the initial approach in gathering experimental schools for each of the three strategies was through LEAs.

Our general intention was to keep complete records of the process of collecting schools for our sample, but we fell short. As will be apparent from the account that follows, we had considerable difficulty in gathering the experimental schools we needed. Thus pressures of action built up, and there was less time for record-keeping than a tidily successful recruitment of schools might have left us. Responsive improvisation in the face of difficulties in getting schools meant that leads were taken - or declined - as a result of telephone calls about other matters, conversations at conferences, chats over coffee. Some of these may not have been properly recorded, and as a result there is probably a margin of error in the record of rejections: some LEAs may not have been approached because we had heard that such an approach would be unlikely to be welcomed; and these cases are not recorded as rejections even though they involve implicitly the same principle of selection.

From our records, we can say that we received twenty-two negative responses from LEAs. By no means all of these gave reasons for declining. Among the explanations offered were:

(1) 'in view of other commitments';
(2) educational reorganization; ROSLA; involvement in Schools Council Projects in eight subject areas;
(3) 'For a number of reasons we are unable to participate in the project';
(4) LEA circularized schools about the project and left them to contact us direct: no contact made;
(5) 'A number of factors have influenced this decision, not least the problems that some of the schools approached felt in coping with the timetable arrangements';
(6) 'At present there is no school within this Authority which is so committed and able to devote a significant proportion of its energies in this way';
(7) 'From our point of view, this project could not have come at a more inopportune time; we are very much involved with the reorganization of schools in the Borough this year....it will be virtually impossible to set up a team as you have in mind at any particular schools in the Borough';
(8) 'I do not feel that it would be reasonable for me to ask schools in this Authority....Reorganization of education in (name of Borough) was begun in September 1972, and schools are already involved in a good deal of adjustment to their organization and curriculum';
(9) 'I do not feel that I can commit any of our secondary schools at this late stage in the proceedings, as a considerable number of them are already involved in other areas of research and investigation. In addition, we are in the throes of the reorganization of our secondary education for September 1973, and so our teachers are heavily committed';
(10) '...but we are faced by a financial cut-back within the LEA which prevents us from sending teachers to conferences: we would therefore, be unable to comply with one of the requirements of participating LEAs';
(11) 'owing to reorganization'.

No doubt some LEAs declined to take part in the project because they were opposed in principle either to teaching adolescents in schools about race relations or to implying support for such teaching by participation. Others may well have distrusted the particular research team involved, since two of its four members had taken part in the earlier experiment in teaching about race relations conducted within the Humanities Curriculum Project which had acquired some notoriety in the press. No LEA cited these reasons for not wishing to participate, but conventionally they might well regard it as better not to make them explicit. We have some verbal evidence in two cases that a desire on the part of advisory services to participate was vetoed at CEO level.

There were instances of schools and LEAs that were not multi-racial dismissing teaching about race relations because 'there is no problem here' - this in spite of the fact that schools in such areas often teach about modern Britain in social studies. Race relations can apparently readily be seen as a parochial 'problem' rather than as a feature of national life.

On the other hand, two LEAs approached us and asked to participate, the initiative coming at advisory level. Information of the existence of the project had been picked up 'on the grapevine'. We responded to their initiative.

A further complication was that some schools approached us directly asking to participate and we recruited other schools through informal contact before approaching their LEAs. Thus some LEAs were brought into the project via schools.

In all, twenty-four LEAs took part. They were: Birmingham, Bournemouth, Derby, Derbyshire, Fife, Halifax, Hillingdon, Huntingdon, ILEA, Ipswich, Leeds, Lincolnshire, Luton, Manchester, Merton, Newcastle-upon-Tyne, Newham, Northampton, Nottingham, Reading, Teesside, Warley, Wembley and West Riding. It will be clear from the fact that we had forty schools that some LEAs had more than one school involved. In two cases both schools were Strategy C. In all other cases where there was more than one school, more than one strategy was represented, but no LEA had all three strategies.

The pattern of recruitment of LEAs is set out in Table 4.1.

Table 4.1

	Invitation to LEA (1)	Approach from LEA (2)	Invitation to school (3)	Approach from school (4)	Total (5)
Strategy A	6	2	4	2	14
Strategy B	10	2	1	3	16
Strategy C	6	2	2	–	10
Total	22	6	7	5	40

What can we say about the sampling of LEAs? Perhaps we must ask why sampling of LEAs matters at all. The answer is twofold. First, LEAs represent social and geographical areas; and second, they have a substantive effect on schools through policy. Clearly, Birmingham and Bournemouth are two quite different physical and social environments, and it is partly through the LEAs that we get diversity of context in our sample. Equally, our LEAs differ in the amount of freedom, attention and support that they give to schools, and there is evidence that this is important for experiment in education (Rudduck, 1976; Humble and Simons, 1978).

We cannot claim that our LEAs are a sample representative of all those in the country. For one thing, no one possesses 'a thorough knowledge of both populations and how these characteristics relate to the dependent variable of the experiment' (see p. 38 above). But we think we can say that their distribution suggests 'a good assortment', and offers, one might judge, a good coverage of relevant variables. Bias is most apparent in terms of LEA attitudes. We are not able to generalize to LEAs likely to turn down participation in this project. On the other hand, the diversity of recruitment revealed in Table 4.1 appears actually to strengthen our coverage in this respect as compared with a sample gathered entirely by response to invitation.

Nevertheless, the reader will have to exercise judgment in deciding how far our experience is relevant to his own. What we have tried to do here is to provide some material on which judgment can be exercised. The data offered here, however, must be set against the reports of sample loss that follow below.

At this point we must attempt to provide information that will make it possible to judge our sample of schools. Table 4.1 can give us some. From it we can tell that schools, like LEAs, were recruited in different ways. Some were chosen by LEAs: this applies to the twenty-eight schools in the first two columns. Some were invited by us: this applies to the seven schools in column (3). And some approached us and asked to participate. The schools invited by us were selected because of the personal connections of members of the team or - particularly in Strategy A - because the Centre had worked with them before.

This is far from a random selection procedure, but in fact diversity of recruitment might be judged an advantage, once it has been accepted that randomization is not possible.

As we recruited the schools, we tried to include in our sample a spread of variables that we judged might be relevant. For example, we aimed to include schools in differing environments and of different sizes and types. We saw it as very important to include a variety of multi-racial schools and of non-multi-racial schools. We were concerned not simply with multi-racial schools but with teaching about race relations in humanities, social studies and drama in all types of school. At the point of selecting the schools, we were not able to influence where the teaching was placed in the timetable or the number of teachers involved.

Both the schools selected by the LEAs and those selected by us are likely to have been in some sense 'good' schools, though there must be some doubt about both our judgment and that of LEAs (Rudduck, 1976; Humble and Simons, 1978). It would be safest to assume that our sample of schools does not include schools that are confronting the most serious environmental problems with the most limited teachers. We have generally been working with competent teachers in competently run schools.

We believe that one or two schools may have been constrained to enter the project against their better judgment because of the pressure exerted on them by the mere fact of being chosen by the LEA.

We see no way, using the normal channels to LEAs and schools, of securing a true random sample of schools. Indeed, we believe that in an action programme to use a true random sample would be unethical, since it would inevitably mean including schools quite incapable of meeting the demands of educational experiment.

We have seen how, in the first (double) level of sampling – that of LEAs and schools – some LEAs were chosen because of their schools and some schools were chosen through their LEAs. In the second level of sampling – that of teachers and pupils – a similar pattern was at work, though since it was internal to the schools we were not able to monitor the process closely. It is clear enough that some schools chose teachers, and (having already timetabled) assigned to the experiment pupils taught by those teachers, while others chose pupils (or courses and therefore the pupils taking them), and thus assigned to the experiment the teachers who taught them.

It follows from the selection of schools and the selection of teachers that our sample of pupils is an opportunity sample rather than a random sample. The size of the pupil sample and its distribution between experimental and control groups is displayed in Table 4.2. Control groups were drawn from those schools that could offer comparable pupil groups parallel to the experimental groups, but not being taught about race relations. Not all schools had such comparable parallel groups, and consequently these schools had no control groups.

Table 4.2 Sizes of experimental and control groups by strategy and school

	Experimentals	Controls
Strategy A	58/26/40/11/29/16 24/13/22/29/20 N = 288	14/65/9/7/8/8/17 N = 128
Strategy B	33/30/34/30/34/44 35/40/23/12/20/22 27/19/23 N = 426	12/14/33/15/62/10 20/15/13 N = 194
Strategy C	30/19/43/26/18/17 31/45/24 N = 253	11/16/13/8/16/18 13/7 N = 102

NOTE: One school (18 experimental, 8 control) has been dropped from Strategy A in this sample because it was discovered that experimental and control groups were confused in the school. Results by pupils in earlier tables were not adjusted as the results of the school would minimally work against the observed trends. One school in Strategy B (25 experimentals, no control) has also been dropped because of irregularities of test administration. Again, pupil samples were not adjusted, the results on the General racism, Anti-Asian and Anti-black scales all being in the direction of the reported trend (GR 19.14 17.79, t = 1.02; AA 7.25 7.00, t = 0.34; AB 8.18 7.43, t = 1.14).

There is a case for arguing that our sample of pupils and of teachers rests on a kind of teacher-pupil bonding. In almost all the schools in this experiment, as in the majority of schools in this country, any expressly social, moral or practical education offered to pupils between the ages of fourteen and sixteen (with the possible exception of a small-time allocation to religious studies) is confined to pupils not being presented for GCE O-level. Almost all the pupils in our sample were CSE candidates or non-examination pupils, and the CSE candidates were generally following Mode III syllabuses. In the head's mind as he selects teacher and pupils there is probably a bonding associating certain teachers with these pupils and these pupils with certain teachers. So it may well be that our sample is one of teachers timetabled to teach humanities, social studies, integrated studies and drama to the CSE bands and below, and known to be enthusiastic about this sort of work.

If the reader is a teacher, he will recognize the groups of teachers and pupils we are trying to identify, and basically the project is about them, largely because the O-level bands are generally too occupied with examinations to give time to such work. Our O-level sample is too small to draw conclusions, but our general impression is that it would be a better starting hypothesis that O-level pupils will be like the groups we have included than that they will be unlike them, both in the problems they raise and in the effects they manifest.

All the teachers except one involved in the experimental teaching were white, as are the vast majority of teachers in this country; the experiment may be said to concern the problems and effects of such teachers teaching about race relations. Strategy B had a preponderance of male over female teachers, whereas participation of the sexes was more or less balanced in the other strategies. We have no way of accounting for this.

Table 4.3 sets out percentage distribution of ages by strategy of those teachers for whom we have information. The distribution in Strategies B and C is remarkably similar. The weight lies between twenty-five and forty-five with a fair number of beginners brought in and a small number of senior teachers. (In Strategy C the weight lies between twenty-five and thirty-five rather than between thirty-five and forty-five, and our table does not reveal this.) In Strategy A there are fewer beginners and more teachers over forty-five. We can think of three possible explanations of this, but have not been able to confirm them, so we offer them only as help towards analysing the situation in the reader's own school. First, the greater seniority may be the result of the participation of teachers who came into the Humanities Project five years ago and have 'aged in the strategy'. Second, race relations as a theme may have seemed more central to HCP than to social studies or drama, and hence more integrated into a teaching team (i.e., involving senior members as well as junior). Third, the neutral chairman role may seem to some schools too demanding for beginning teachers.

Table 4.3 Distribution by age of teachers in the three strategies

Ages	Strategy A, n = 32 (35) % in age group	Strategy B, n = 39 (43) % in age group	Strategy C, n = 22 (23) % in age group
Below 25	3	18	18
25-45	69	72	73
Over 45	28	10	9

N.B. Information on age not available for all teachers (total number in each strategy in brackets).

So far as status is concerned, the distribution is not dissimilar in Strategies A and B. In both, the sample is fairly senior, with half or more than half the teachers in posts of some responsibility and heavy involvement of deputy heads or heads of department. In Strategy C heads of drama departments were invariably involved if they existed. The results in this project relate to teaching by mature teachers, often with posts of considerable responsibility, supported in some cases by teams including younger members.

In Strategies A and B there was a wide spread of subject background with weight in English, history and geography and, in Strategy B, some in social studies. In Strategy C most teachers had had specialized in-service training in drama or drama training as a component in their initial training.

An unfortunate omission is that we did not obtain details of teachers involved with the control groups. Since these teachers do not see themselves as participating in the experiment, it is not easy to ask them for details, and the act of doing so may influence their treatment of the controls. Also, since the controls are not being taught about race relations, it is perhaps difficult to know which teachers of those they meet to monitor!

There is another point about our samples of teachers that is worthy of mention, though it is necessarily a matter of our judgment only. Strategy A and Strategy C teachers had in common skills of a particular type - in discussion work and in drama. Strategy B teachers had less common ground in skills, but some of them had more specific interest and knowledge in the area of race relations.

We have now given an account of our sampling in respect of
pupils, LEAs, schools and teachers. We have not achieved
random samples, but we have, we think, come as near as any
experiment of this kind does to that desideratum. However, we
have also made it clear that we do not expect individuals
enmeshed in their own situations to be able to make wise decisions based on generalizations expressed as probabilities. Each
reader must ask what there is in his own situation that eludes
the general account we have given of those sampled by the
project. It will then be necessary to exercise judgment about
the possible consequences of those characteristic factors and
to monitor the situation carefully.

Conventional experimental design calls for an attempt to
stabilize the operation of contextual variables by sampling and
then, within the context, to control directly an experimental
variable. In the present case, the experimental variable would
be, one would expect, the teaching strategy.

We want to argue that, at the level of complexity – that is,
the level of verisimilitude or 'representativeness' (Snow, 1974)-
at which we are working, teaching cannot be a controlled
variable, but must be sampled.

We have empirical evidence, though it is difficult to present.
The project has had access to tape-recordings of teaching from
a majority of classrooms in our sample. From these recordings
it is clear that in each strategy there is a range of styles and
that there is overlap among the strategies. Thus, not all Strategy A teachers maintain a strictly neutral role; some Strategy
B teachers are rather neutral; some discussions in the context
of drama could well be from Strategy A or B; and so forth.

We do not regard this as the result of a regrettable failure on
our part adequately to control teaching as a variable. Indeed,
a widespread criticism of the Humanities Curriculum Project
strategy of discussion (though not one we accept) is that it is
too controlling, involving as it does a formalization of the
teacher's role as chairman of a discussion. Three years of
research went into producing criteria that constitute a kind of
behavioural specification for neutral chairmanship. We hold
that, if Strategy A does not show the characteristics in observed
practice of a rigorously controlled variable, then:

(1) it must be extraordinarily difficult to establish strict control
of teaching as a variable; and
(2) results based upon such control are likely to be of restricted
external validity, since the controls cannot be achieved in the
natural settings within which the results need to be interpreted.

Our examination of classroom tapes indicates that in none of
the strategies is teaching consistent enough to support the
claim that teaching style has been a controlled variable.

Accordingly, we have to accept that each strategy constitutes
a sample of teaching styles with a central tendency and varying

degrees of deviation from that norm. No doubt the central
tendency derives partly from the existence of the strategy
specification as a verbal statement. This is most true of Strategy A, least true of Strategy C. But it is also the product
of a cultural tradition set up in each case by the initial strategy conference attended by teachers before the experimental
teaching began, and continued and modulated by subsequent
contacts.

If this position is accepted, then we face the question, to
what extent are the teaching within our project and the cultural
tradition that supported it representative of the world outside
the project? This is a very difficult question to answer, and we
can only offer our judgment for the reader's criticism.

None of the teachers in the project was willing to take a
strongly authoritarian stance, nor did it occur to any to employ
techniques such as behaviour modification, conditioning or
brain-washing. Thus, the teaching in the project is relatively
non-authoritarian, in the sense that the normal sanctions of
classroom authority (punishment, ranging from rebuke to corporal punishment: reward, ranging from praise through marks
to prizes) have not been used to attempt to enforce tolerance
or respect (if that is possible) or to eradicate prejudice. We
think we have a fair selection of the range of teaching
approaches that 'appeal' to the students rather than attempt
to coerce them or place them under duress. The appeal may
be to moral or political reason or to moral or political sentiment.

We have not described in detail the notion of 'appeal' (though
it would be an interesting one to analyse) because we believe
that teachers who are concerned about whether their own positions are represented in the project will recognize in what we
have written a rough-and-ready but robust and realistic definition of our boundaries. We are, after all, describing a reality
too complex to be conformable to principles.

The cultural traditions of the project are less likely to be
found outside it than are the classroom styles, yet they have
probably been important in sustaining teachers through difficulties and in making for quality within any given style.
These traditions are in the main the product of teaching within
the context of a national project with a sense of pioneering,
of sharing a conference experience before teaching and anti-
cipating a conference experience after teaching.

At their strongest, the traditions could be described as
research-based teaching – the development of understanding
and of effectiveness through the systematic study of one's
own teaching. Certainly, if one wishes to utilize the results of
this project this is the prime desideratum: that one study for
oneself 'the problems and effects of teaching about race relations', using the work of the project as a point of departure.
This is easy to write; but it is extremely demanding in practice.

Accordingly, it is important for local advisers and head
teachers to do everything they can to provide teachers centre-

based and school-based support in order to achieve something
of the co-operative working and commitment characteristic of
a national project. The response called for is local projects in
preference to solo enterprises.

The point at issue is that we do not believe that sampling
can support predictive generalizations about problems and
effects to a target population of situations, and thus can
exempt the people in those situations from the need to exercise
careful judgment.

What sampling can do is to catch a wide range of variables,
sketch a universe of probability, and thereby document a
potential. By doing this we provide a framework for development work based upon the judgment of individual situations.
That development work must be self-critical and self-evaluative
if it is to yield well: it must be research-based.

This project has been engaged in research as a basis for
localized research and development. This seems to us the
obvious role of project research in curriculum and teaching;
but the position taken does not seem to be widely understood.
It is this attitude to the utilization of our research that, above
all, the teacher group in the project are concerned to disseminate.

This discussion of sampling should enable you to judge the
representativeness of the measurement results and to some
extent to relate your experience to the experience of the project. It does not invalidate or supplant judgment of your own
experience, but, we hope, supports it.

5 MEASUREMENT

Lawrence Stenhouse and Gajendra K. Verma

In Chapter 3 we explained the design of the present experiment. This design called for observations to be made before and after the experimental treatment. 'Observations' here does not simply mean 'watching', but rather 'gathering empirical data'; and just as physical scientists use instruments such as ammeters or weighing scales to provide measures of things we cannot see, so behavioural scientists have their own instruments. Psychometric tests are less directly validated (i.e. proven to measure what we want them to measure) and less reliable (i.e. proven to give us the same measure whenever the same amount is measured) than are most instruments used in the physical sciences. Hence, we have to pay much more attention to the problem of selecting our tests. It's easy to open a can with an efficient can opener: it's only when there is no can opener that we have to consider what instrument to use to try and get at the beans!

In this chapter we shall be concerned with the selection of our instruments - the psychometric tests. There are hundreds of instruments to choose from, and it is also possible to design instruments of one's own. The question facing us was 'which ones should we use?'

Now of course the answer to this question depends upon what problem we are trying to solve; and our aim was to document the problems and effects of teaching adolescents about race relations. It is as well to keep this in mind. We were not attempting to discover which of our strategies was most effective in combating racial prejudice, because we had no expectation that this was an answerable question; but there are still many who will expect us to arbitrate among the strategies, and even ask that we should. We believe that this pressure is a dangerous one. We have tried to make it possible to detect cases or strategies that give cause for concern, but we have not followed the statistics that would best support comparison. We have also concentrated in our choice of instruments on our main concern: to illuminate 'the problems and effects of teaching about race relations'. This is the position in the light of which we now turn to consider the problem of selecting tests.

In the field of research and development in curriculum and teaching, the best-known response to the problem of choosing tests is to adopt the so-called 'objectives model' in one's experimental design. This involves the researcher in getting the teachers to state their teaching aims in such a way as to define clearly for him what tests would be appropriate to measure the achievement of such aims. Such measurable aims are generally called 'behavioural objectives' or 'intended learning outcomes' because they define in precise terms the behaviour of which the student will become capable as a result of his learning on the experimental course.

Let us take an example (drawn from Bloom et al., 1956, pp. 75-87). The teacher of chemistry says that his aim is to teach a knowledge of principles and generalizations. Pushed to list the principles and generalizations he wants his students to know, he says he would like them to be able to recall some generalizations about common metals and he specifies these. A test item is written: Which of the following generalizations concerning the common metals are true?

(1) Most of the metals form only one insoluble salt.
(2) All the simple salts of the alkali metals are soluble.
(3) The metals of the alkaline earth group are precipitated as carbonates.
(4) The alkali carbonates are insoluble in water.
(5) Many of the heavy metal sulphides are insoluble in neutral or slightly acid solution.

This is really no more than a carefully organized examination. Such tests employed within this framework are known as 'criterion-referenced' tests, since their validity is underwritten by the criterion provided by the teachers' specifications of objectives.

In a research or evaluation setting built on the logic of the objectives model, the battery of tests used may include, in addition to the criterion-referenced tests derived from the specifications of objectives, other tests intended to provide measures of side effects, that is to say, effects that occur even though they are not consciously aimed at by the teachers. The hunch or hypothesis that these effects may occur is the researcher's, rather than the teacher's.

Now, it may well appear, since we had in our battery both tests of inter-ethnic attitudes and other tests, that we followed this objectives model. But in fact we have rejected it. The teaching in this project had no objectives in the strict sense. We did not push the teachers beyond the consensus of broad aims in each strategy to detailed consensus about objectives or intended learning outcomes. Within the very general aims of each strategy, there was divergence of teacher intention and teacher set. This is confirmed by the study of classroom process in the descriptive research programme. As we explained in the previous chapter, we sampled a rather wide range of teaching about race relations in order to probe its problems and effects. We were not testing a way of teaching, or a collection of teaching materials.

We need to look closely at the implication of our position for the selection of tests. In this experiment the researchers were responsible for choosing the tests without reference to the teachers to provide criteria by specifying objectives. Since criterion-referenced tests based upon the objectives formulated by other teachers in different situations would have low validity here, it was apparent that we could not use criterion-referenced tests. We got into this position without regret. For several reasons we preferred norm-referenced tests; but since this was to swim against the tide in the area of curriculum and teaching, some explanation of our preference is required.

We have explained the principle of criterion-referenced tests, which are, in effect, objective examinations. Norm-referenced tests are constructed on different principles.

The test constructor may be taken to be interested in devising a measure in a certain area such as, for example, race relations. From common sense or from theoretical work in the field, he makes up test items which look as if they bear on this area and then, by administering the test and subjecting it to 'item analysis', he selects the best items and discards the least good. 'The "best" items are those which are shown to be measuring the same attribute, to be at the right level of difficulty and to discriminate effectively between those with high ability in the quality measured and those with little ability' (Nisbet and Entwistle, 1970, pp. 87-88). Nisbet and Entwistle offer (in Chapter 8 of their book) an excellent simple introduction to test construction that will be of help to any reader without experience of testing.

In designing a norm-referenced test we are after a test that measures the same thing throughout, is pitched at the right level (for age or ability), and discriminates between the people who take it, spreading their scores out so as to highlight differences in their performances.

There is a problem of validity. 'The validity of a test is a measure of how well it tests what it is intended to test' (Nisbet and Entwistle, 1970, p. 90). In the present context the problem is rather acute. For example, we might construct a test that clearly measures a consistent attribute within the area of race relations, but we should be hard put to it to say in everyday words what that factor is or how much of the complexity of race relations we have caught in our test. Each of the tests we report the results of is printed in the Appendix, and data on reliability and validity are given there.

More controversial is the question of whether tests used in research on curriculum and teaching should be constructed (as norm-referenced tests are) in such a way as to spread the scores out into a distribution. Those who follow the objectives model argue that, since (in their view) curriculum and teaching should have goals, it is mastery of such goals that should be measured rather than the relative performance of individuals. Norm-referenced tests are tests to throw up the distribution of individual differences by concentrating on items that differentiate individuals. In short, norm-referenced tests maximize the variability among those tested, while criterion-referenced tests focus on specified learning behaviours and minimize inter-subject variance.

It is our view that it is appropriate to explore the effects of curriculum and teaching on the distribution of individual scores, and we are confirmed in this by work of Dahllöf (1971), which showed how significant differences of effects express themselves by pupils' exceeding the criteria built into criterion-referenced tests. Such effects can be picked up only by norm-referenced testing.

Accordingly, we opted for norm-referenced tests wherever possible and for the following reasons, among others:

(1) We were sampling teaching over a range of styles rather than controlling teaching by a curriculum specification.
(2) We believe that the effects of teaching manifest themselves in distributions and criterion-referenced testing by masking effects in the upper range of the distribution misrepresents effects (the criterion acting as a ceiling).
(3) Criterion-referenced measures tend by their nature to be situationally referenced, and hence do not easily lead towards generalization across experiments. They have a poor range of validity because they seek high validity at the expense of comparability (see Walker and Schaffarzick, 1974). We need public and widely used measures in research, and, for all their shortcomings, norm-referenced measures approach this desideratum more nearly than criterion-referenced measures.

Having decided in favour of norm-referenced measures, we preferred those that already had some currency (Nisbet and Entwistle, 1970):

Where it is possible to choose between using a standardized test in research and making up one's own test, the advantage obviously lies with the standardized test. It is economical to take advantage of the work of others in preparing an accurate and discriminating instrument; the standardized test is likely to be much more reliable (and probably more valid) than a home-made version; and research which is based on nationally available material can more readily be assessed and replicated. (p. 77)

Since we would want to stress the importance not simply of internal validity (the fit between test and teaching in the project), but also of external validity (the fit between the test and teaching about race relations in the target population), we would certainly endorse the claim for more validity tentatively put forward by Nisbet and Entwistle.

Selecting tests on this logic implies departing from the

procedures of formulating one's hypotheses or anticipations verbally and then trying to test them. Instead, one adopts the procedure of casting one's hypotheses in terms of tests. Not 'pupils who don't like school may be expected to...' but 'scores on the ABC alienation from school scale are expected to correlate with...'. Compromise is necessary here. If we go too far in one direction we find ourselves looking for our shilling under the lamp simply because the light is there; but we can go too far to the other extremes, and find ourselves feeling about for the shilling when, if we cared to change our position, we could find it reflecting the lamplight.

However, the fact of the matter is that, in research on teaching in naturalistic settings, particularly when, as in the present case, we have a central concern with attitudes rather than with attainment, we have so little reliable theory that hypotheses are hard to come by. Our reaction to this was to use testing less to test hypotheses derived from theory, more in an exploratory and speculative mode. We were trying to build a theory from the study of practice, not turning to the study of practice to test a theory. In our heads were such phrases as 'it will be important to be assured that this variable is not shifting', or 'it would be suggestive if there were a correlation of y with x'.

Let us review progress in this chapter so far.

We have rejected the objectives model for experimental design in research in curriculum and teaching. Distinguishing between criterion-referenced and norm-referenced tests, we have explained why rejection of objectives has pushed us towards norm-referenced tests, and why we believe this to be a good direction in which to be pushed. However, this leaves us with a wide range of choice of instruments and so far no principle on which to make that choice.

First, we shall discuss the selection of tests in the area of race relations and then go on to consider the selection of other tests.

Our position is that there exist no satisfactory tests of inter-ethnic attitudes or perceptions, and for these, among other, reasons:

(1) There is an acute problem in direct validation: how are we to establish that the behaviour sampled in the testing situation correlates with behaviour outside it? Particularly, how are we to predict from present test scores the reaction of a person who has not yet encountered people of other races to later encounters still to come?
(2) There is a lack of well established theory about inter-racial attitudes and perceptions and a consequent problem in establishing a rigorous theoretical basis for test construction.
(3) Most tests are so structured that they are not satisfactorily multi-ethnic. Either all or some respondents are faced with

some questions not applicable to their racial identity. In this
case the tests are usually appropriate only for white respondents. It might be held that, since the majority of respondents
in this experiment were white, this is not a great disadvantage
technically; but it is important that the bias should not be
offensive to other respondents.

(4) Within a large-scale experiment such as we are reporting
here, it is essential to use easily administered and easily scored
group tests, and this pushes us to relatively crude measures.

Given this position, our policy was to use a number of tests
of established reliability that had been employed in a variety of
other experimental contexts, even though this meant accepting
a pretty precarious validity. We would use them as 'straws in
the wind'. The tests would not offer our reader an adequate
and valid measure descriptive of what he (or common consensus)
takes to be the structure and climate of interracial attitudes
and perceptions. But if all our tests went one way, he might
expect a (non-existent) highly valid test to point in the same
direction. If all the straws behave as if there is a south-west
wind, we shall expect our sailing boat to do so too.

A further element in the situation was the existence of a
steering committee for the present project, which participated
quite strongly in the design of the test battery. The SSRC
grant was made on condition that such a steering committee was
set up, and its functions were stated in the following terms:

> the project will be expected to refer to the steering commit-
> tee on all substantial matters arising from the research
> including the presentation and balance of the materials used,
> the preparation of teachers for the neutral role, details of
> the research design and analysis and the social and political
> implications of the research.

It is fair to say that the major area of early divergence of
view between the project and a majority of its steering committee was in the selection of tests, and that the project felt that
it should modify its intentions in order to secure the support of
the steering committee. The situation is an interesting one from
the point of view of the management of educational research,
and three points are worth making here.

(1) The steering committee would have preferred the project
not to use tests in the area of interracial attitudes and perceptions. After much discussion, it rather grudgingly accepted
only the Bagley-Verma version of the Wilson-Patterson Scale.
The steering committee strongly criticized these tests, both on
research grounds by disputing their reliability and validity,
and on the social and political grounds that either they could be
capable of influencing pupils towards undesirable attitudes
(social) or that, even if this were not true, it could be seen as

being true (political). Since the two-pronged attack (from different members of the committee) was virtually impossible for the project to resist, the committee as a whole felt that the social and political risks were not justified in relation to tests that it felt the project had difficulty in justifying convincingly on research grounds.

(2) The steering committee also pushed us towards (and helped with) the designing of new tests. The design of new tests in this difficult area was not contemplated in the proposal, and no provision of time or resources was made for it. (Our estimate is a minimum of two years to design a test of inter-ethnic attitudes that would be more satisfactory than those in existence.) The tests designed within this project are therefore to be regarded as improvisations.

(3) Looking back on the debate now, it seems to us that a problem was created for the steering committee because the project could not communicate the rationale and justification of its experimental design concisely to others (as one must do in a committee situation). The present design could be understood in the autumn of 1972 only as the response of research intuition to problems encountered in the Humanities Curriculum Project, which were not, and could not be, shared between the project and its steering committee. Had we been able to write this chapter at the beginning of the project, our dialogue with our steering committee might have had different outcomes. As it was, we were not then as able as we are now to explain our reluctance to use criterion-referenced tests in this research.

Against this background, we now turn to describe the selection of tests of inter-ethnic attitudes for our battery.

The project proposed the following battery:

(1) the Bagley-Verma Test;
(2) the Semantic Differential;
(3) a version of the Bogardus Social Distance Scale;
(4) an Information Scale.

The rationale for this choice was that each of the first three of these tests was relatively well standardized and had been widely used, while each was constructed on a different rationale. They were thus collectively good 'straws in the wind'.

However, the steering committee rejected all three of these tests for the reasons given above. Nor would it accept the substitution of a stereotype test, in spite of the argument that, after the post-testing, any possible effects the test might have had could probably be neutralized by teaching about the test, basing such teaching on a development of the example provided in the Penguin Connexions volume, 'Foreign Faces, Foreign Places'. However, in the face of strong arguments from the project, the committee did ultimately agree to include the Bagley-Verma Scale, which its sub-committee on measurement had already rejected.

At the same time, the steering committee pressed the project to produce tests of its own, arguing for a closer logical link between the trend and content of the teaching and the test battery. Time was very short and any tests would be in the nature of improvisations.

Two members of the project team, L. Stenhouse and G.K. Verma, each produced a test, and Professor E.A. Peel, a member of the steering committee, produced a third. Under the pressure of designing these tests the team was unable to find time to design the Information Scale, and it had to be dropped.

The L.S. Discussion Questionnaire (see Appendix) asked respondents to imagine that they were present at a discussion in which two differing views were being taken by two different people and to indicate which view they regarded as 'more right'. The test was constructed merely from recollection of such situations and had no empirical base in the Humanities Project discussions. The test was constructed by assembling items under six heads or sub-scales: attitude towards the British; acceptance of people of other races; competition for apparently scarce resources; subordination/superordination; optimism/pessimism; and political policy. The items can readily be assigned to sub-scales by scanning the test, which is printed in the Appendix.

The Picture Description Test devised by G.K. Verma was a return under the pressure of the circumstances to develop the Situations Test which had been used in the Humanities Project. We had originally dropped this because of scoring difficulties, and the revision is less ambitiously projective than the original. The test was scored for perception of racial content in the pictures on a five-point judgmental scale, from no perception of racial content to strong emphasis on racial content. In the event, this test is not felt to have contributed enough to be reported here.

The short test contributed by Professor Peel was in form similar to the interpretation exercises with which children are already familiar in school. The passage was selected from among the teaching materials offered by the project to schools, and the questions monitored both the students' understanding of the passage and their views about the situation. This building of a test from the teaching materials would certainly seem to us the most promising form of criterion-referencing, concentrating as it does on content rather than objectives, though there are problems in the present case because the teachers were offered the materials for support but not asked to use them. Many of them did not or hardly did so.

Unfortunately, a printing error overlooked in proofreading in one of the five questions in the test could not be corrected before the test administration. Again, the results are not reported here.

In summary, the project secured the inclusion of the Bagley-Verma Scale alone of the instruments it proposed in the area of interracial attitudes. It improvised two other questionnaires and dropped the Information Scale in order to secure time to do this. Professor Peel contributed a further questionnaire. None of these improvised tests – which were prepared with the greatest haste – was standardized before use.

In a sense we fell between two stools: one, the pursuit of reliability and public currency at the expense of case-tied validity; the other, the pursuit of intra-experimental validity at the expense of reliability and public currency. The technical point is an interesting one, but perhaps even more so are the social issues raised by measurement in the area of interracial attitudes. We think that our measurement programme has made an important contribution to understanding the problems of teaching about race relations; but we cannot avoid the conclusion that, if measurement is to be an important element in research in this area, work is needed in the area of test development.

We used six contextual tests, two rather general and four sampling various areas other than achievement which might be expected to offer a prospect of interacting with interracial attitudes.

The two general tests were Cattell's High School Personality Questionnaire and Brimer's Wide-span Reading Test. Cattell's High School Personality Questionnaire is a wide-ranging general personality questionnaire with English as well as American norms. It has been widely used, though in recent years in particular its validity has been questioned. In the Humanities Curriculum Project Evaluation there were a number of significant differences between experimentals and controls on sub-scales of this questionnaire. So long as one avoids giving too much independent weight to the results of this test, we think it is valuable as a means of monitoring possible effects in a wide area of personality because of the range of factors it attempts to cover.

It is not possible to find an equally well standardized and wide-ranging test of the changes in achievement that may be in process during an experiment. We believe that there is a need to develop a general test of school achievement in order to monitor school effects in experiments on curriculum or teaching. Faced with the lack of such an instrument, we chose to use the Brimer Wide-span Reading Test. We actually believe this to be more an index of linguistic achievement than a pure reading test (if such exist outside the diagnostic field), but that suits our use. We are more interested in the relation of linguistic achievement than of reading to our other variables. The test purports to cover the age range seven to fifteen.

It remains to describe briefly the four tests chosen because of the apparent possibility of their interacting with tests in the area of interracial attitudes.

Coopersmith's Questionnaire is designed to measure the self-esteem of adolescents. It seems clear that there is a possibility of pupils' self-esteem being affected by work in the area of race relations, and the point does not need to be laboured.

The questionnaire, Aspects of School Life, is designed to measure pupils' liking for and interest in school, and the Verma-Sumner Questionnaire to measure attitude towards school authority. The school's capacity to influence attitudes in any area might be supposed to be related to the attitudes towards school life and school authority of the pupils concerned.

The fourth test chosen as relating to our centre of interest was the Himmelweit-Swift version of Adorno's F-Scale of Authoritarianism. Previous research and theoretical discussion has linked authoritarianism with hostile and prejudiced interracial attitudes.

The battery of instruments that emerged from this selection was pretty formidable, and two half-days were needed to administer it. We asked for comments from test administrators, and, while some were surprised by the degree of application to task of the pupils, others noted cases of tiredness or impatience.

We have tried to express in this chapter the reserves about testing of this kind held by ourselves and by others, particularly our steering committee. Methodology and design in research is - or should be - hypothetical and tentative. The paper 'Problems of research in teaching about race relations' (Stenhouse, 1975) puts forward the view that, in research in curriculum and teaching in naturalistic settings, where quantitative observation depends upon eliciting responses to group pencil-and-paper tests with all their shortcomings, measurement should be used as an exploratory instrument and its results made the basis for speculative reasoning or situational verification. This is not a familiar beaten track - the aspiration of measurement has been proof or falsification of hypotheses - but we hope to go a little way towards justifying our position by the contribution to understanding made by some later parts of this report.

TECHNICAL NOTE ON THE STATISTICAL PROCEDURES USED
TO ESTIMATE SIGNIFICANCE OF DIFFERENCE BETWEEN PER-
FORMANCE OF EXPERIMENTALS AND CONTROLS

The design of this experiment may be classified according to
the scheme offered by Campbell and Stanley (1963) and now
widely accepted as a point of reference as Design 10 (Non-
equivalent Control Group Design) or, if one took a more optimistic view of our sampling, as Design 4 (Pre-test-Post-test
Control Group Design).
On Design 4 they comment (Campbell and Stanley, 1963):

Even though Design 4 is the standard and most widely
used design, the tests of significance used with it are often
wrong, incomplete, or inappropriate. In applying the common 'critical ratio' or t-test to this standard experimental
design, many researchers have computed two t's, one for
the pre-test-post-test difference in the experimental group,
one for the pre-test-post-test gain (difference - L.S.) in
the control group. If the former be 'statistically significant'
and the latter 'not', then they have concluded that the X
(experimental treatment - L.S.) had an effect, without any
direct statistical comparison of the experimental and control
groups. Often the conditions have been such that, had a
more appropriate test been made, the difference would not
have been significant (as in the case where the significance
values are borderline, with the control group showing a
gain almost reaching significance). Windle (1954) and
Cantor (1956) have shown how frequent this error is.
(pp. 192-3)

In order to provide the fullest possible information, these t-
values are given in the tables in this report.
Campbell and Stanley continue:

The most widely used acceptable test is to compute for each
group pre-test-post-test gain scores and to compute a 't'
between experimental and control groups on these gain
scores. (p. 193)

This is the test used in the present experiment and given in
the final column of each table.
However, Campbell and Stanley continue:

Randomized 'blocking' or 'levelling' on pre-test scores and
the analysis of covariance with pre-test scores as the

covariate are usually preferable to simple gain-score
comparisons. Since the great bulk of educational experiments show no significant difference, and hence are frequently not reported, the use of this more precise analysis
would seem highly desirable. (p. 193)

In deciding to use t-test on gain scores we bore in mind the
following.

(1) These remarks by Campbell and Stanley:

Not to be confused with this ideal (assigning matched pairs
at random to treatments) is the procedure under Design 10
of attempting to compensate for the differences between the
non-equivalent experimental and control groups by a procedure of matching, when random assignment to treatments
is not possible. If in Design 10 the means of the groups are
substantially different, then the process of matching not
only fails to provide the intended equation but in addition
ensures the occurrence of unwanted regression effects. It
becomes predictably certain that the two groups will differ
on their pattern scores although independently of any
effects of X, and that this difference will vary directly
with the difference between the total populations from which
the selection was made and inversely with the test-retest
correlation.

The situation leads again to the use of covariance, but:

Recent cautions by Lord (1960) concerning the analysis of
covariance *when the co-variate is not perfectly reliable*
should be considered, however. Simple gain scores are also
applicable but *usually* less desirable than analysis of covariance. Application of analysis of covariance to this Design
10 setting involves *assumptions (such as that of homogeneity
of regression)* less plausible here than in Design 4 settings
(Lindquist, 1953). (p. 219, italics ours)

and:

On the one hand, there is a situation in which the experimenter has two natural groups available, e.g. two classrooms, and has free choice in deciding which gets X, or
at least has no reason to suspect differential recruitment
related to X. Even though the groups may differ in initial
means on O, the study may approach the experimentation.
On the other hand, there are instances of design 10 in
which the respondents clearly are self-selected, the experimental group having deliberately sought out exposure to
X (true of many of our teachers though not of our pupils -
L.S.) with no control group available from this same popu-

lation of seekers. In this latter case, *the assumption of
uniform regression between experimental and control
groups becomes less likely....*(p. 220, our italics)

(2) The assumptions underlying analysis of covariance contain
those underlying analysis of variance, and among these Glass
and Stanley (1970) cite:

$Xij = M + \&j + e\ ij$

i.e.,
an observation can be thought of as the simple sum of
three components: one reflecting the overall elevation of
the measurements (M); a second reflecting the increment
or decrement on the dependent variable resulting from all
observations taken in group j being exposed to treatment
j; and a component e ij that comprises things usually
referred to in the behavioural sciences as 'individual differences' and 'measurement error', among others. Various
ways exist in which assumption 1 can fail to be met. *One
is that the effect of treatment j is not the same, &j for all
persons exposed to the treatment.* (pp. 369-70, our italics)

The data reported in Chapter 8 below suggest a diversity of
treatment effects that might be termed 'incremental change
effects' and 'polarizing change effects'. This is also relevant to
the problem of uniformity of regression.

(3) Analysis of covariance almost inevitably invites comparison
between strategies. But inter-strategy effects, even if one is
sceptical of our general case against such comparisons, are in
this case confounded with teacher-group effects (e.g., Strategy A teachers are all trained in their pedagogy; Strategy B
teachers are more interested and informed in the area of race
relations). Under such circumstances we believe that the
researchers have some obligation not to follow procedures that
will tend to mislead.

(4) Given reservations (1) and (2) above and our general position that the quantitative results are sufficiently in doubt to
require confirmation by teacher judgment possibly supplemented by testing under application in classrooms, we are
convinced that analysis of covariance would both suggest
greater precision in the data than we would wish to claim, and
appear to remove the possibility of replicating our results from
the grasp of most teachers. The t-test is easy to apply in classroom and school experiments.

6 RESULTS THROWING LIGHT ON THE BACKGROUND TO THE TEACHING

Lawrence Stenhouse and Gajendra K. Verma

In the previous chapter we described a number of tests included in our battery that were measures not of racial attitudes, but of a sample of other variables such as might be affected by teaching or the experience of schooling. In the event, we found that none of the tests except those of inter-ethnic attitudes showed consistent patterns of difference between experimental and control groups.

Of course, we are discussing now general trends across the sample of schools. Individual pupils or individual schools showed measured effects in areas other than race relations associated with the experimental procedure. Individual pupil results are disregarded here, but teachers will be aware that, for example, strong motivation associated with interest in the topic of race relations may be likely to lead to gains in reading performance for a particular student.

One test, the Catell High School Personality Questionnaire, which had yielded results of some interest in the evaluation of the Humanities Curriculum Project, picked up no changes consistent enough to invite interpretation in the present experiment. Accordingly it is not reported.

What we report in this chapter are the scores on a number of tests or scales that show similar (though not usually significant) shifts in both experimental and control groups. This consistency of shift seems to disclose more about the influence of school or environment or about attitude to school than about the effects of teaching about race relations.

Such effects should throw some light on the general context in which the teachers worked. It seems worth attempting to sketch this context, using the clues picked up from the measurement programme and our judgment of the weight of the case study evidence, before going on in the following chapters to report the changes in scores on tests of inter-racial attitudes.

Since our interest here is in school or environmental effects, our unit of sampling is clearly the school, not the individual pupil. Thus, we have taken as our data the school mean scores and not individual pupil scores. This ensures that schools with large samples of pupils do not influence the results in proportion to their sample size. The results reported in this chapter are, in short, means of school means.

This lowers the size of the sample from the number of pupils to the number of schools. Samples as small as those we are then dealing with reduce the possibility of the results achieving statistical significance. Of the results reported in this chapter, only those on the Brimer Wide-span Reading Test meet formal criteria of significance.

In the case of the Brimer Reading Test, across all three strategies in both experimental and control groups the tendency was towards improvement in scores from pre-test to post-test means, and some of the gains reached significance (not tabulated, but see Figure 8.7). Deteriorations in mean score were recorded in two experimental and two control groups in individual schools, but these were not statistically significant. (In the case of the individual school result sample 'size' is, of course, the number of pupils.)

On the whole, we can conclude that most schools in the experiment were achieving mean gains in reading performance for their (generally non-academic) pupils over the term of the experiment. This is not a result that can be taken for granted. Our schools in this experiment seem on the whole to have been successful - sometimes modestly so - in improving the basic language skills of their pupils.

The scores on a number of other tests show trends that, while not significant, seem consistent enough to be of interest. These tests are:

(1) the Coopersmith Questionnaire, designed to measure self-esteem;
(2) the questionnaire, Aspects of School Life, designed to measure pupils' liking for and interest in schools;
(3) the Verma-Sumner Questionnaire, intended to measure attitude towards school authority.
(4) three of the four sub-scales of the Himmelweit-Swift version of Adorno's F-Scale of Authoritarianism:
(i)   authoritarian view of society;
(ii) authoritarian view of parental control;
(iii) attitudes favouring conformity and the status quo.

The fourth sub-scale of this instrument ('jaundiced view of life') did not show any consistent trends.

We shall deal first with the tests of attitude to school life and attitude to school authority. It is our impression from examining these tests that it is not as easy to distinguish between them as their description might imply, but that each is certainly a measure of favourable or unfavourable attitude towards school. And in each case, the higher the score, the more favourable the attitude.

At all points in Tables 6.1, 6.2 and 6.3, the results suggest that attitudes towards school may be becoming somewhat less favourable, and if this trend (which is consistent, but does not reach significance) is given credence, such deterioration appears to be a consistent background to the experiment. Teachers working in race relations - as indeed all the teachers working with the pupils in our sample - may be struggling with groups of adolescents who are disaffected from school and tend to reject what school has to offer them. At the same time, it must be remembered that this appears to be an endemic condition of schooling (see for example 'A Social History of Education in England' by John Lawson and Harold Silver, or Washington Irving's 'Legend of Sleepy Hollow').

Table 6.1 Strategy A: Results of some background tests. Means of school means and standard deviation (in brackets)

	Experimental, $n = 11$			Control, $n = 8$			Diff. of diff.	Trend
	Pre-test mean (s.d)	Post-test mean (s.d)	t-test diff. of means	Pre-test mean (s.d)	Post-test mean (s.d)	t-test diff. of means		
(1) Self-esteem* (Coopersmith Questionnaire)	18.09 (3.49)	17.92 (2.75)	0.128 n.s.	18.37 (6.21)	17.72 (3.31)	0.273 n.s.	n.s.	Towards higher self-esteem
(2) Attitude to school life (Aspects of School Life)	56.37 (2.71)	53.98 (4.65)	1.52 n.s.	59.67 (2.89)	56.55 (3.39)	1.99 n.s.	n.s.	Less favourable (but more variable) attitude
(3) Attitude to school authority (Verma-Sumner Questionnaire)	77.78 (3.82)	75.63 (5.34)	1.101 n.s.	79.31 (5.48)	77.11 (5.78)	0.781 n.s.	n.s.	Less favourable attitude
(4) Authoritarian view of society (Himmelweit-Swift F scale)	28.10 (2.83)	27.61 (2.66)	0.419 n.s.	27.68 (2.87)	27.33 (3.16)	0.232 n.s.	n.s.	Towards less authoritarian view of society
(5) Authoritarian parental rule (Himmelweit-Swift F scale)	14.76 (1.56)	14.37 (1.15)	0.68 n.s.	14.20 (1.11)	13.86 (2.18)	0.413 n.s.	n.s.	Towards less acceptance of authoritarian parental rule
(6) Pro-conformity and status quo (Himmelweit-Swift F scale)	15.74 (1.07)	15.79 (1.61)	0.105 n.s.	14.65 (1.51)	14.21 (1.51)	0.531 n.s.	n.s.	No consistent trend in this strategy

* On this test the lower the score, the higher the self-esteem.

Table 6.2 Strategy B: Results of some background tests. Means of school means and standard deviation (in brackets)

	Experimental, n = 15			*Control, n = 10*				
	Pre-test mean (s.d)	*Post-test mean (s.d)*	*t-test diff. of means*	*Pre-test mean (s.d)*	*Post-test mean (s.d)*	*t-test diff. of means*	*Diff. of diff.*	*Trend*
(1) Self-esteem* (Coopersmith Questionnaire)	19.78 (4.07)	18.90 (3.97)	0.513 n.s.	18.20 (3.13)	17.42 (3.93)	0.44 n.s.	n.s.	Towards higher self-esteem
(2) Attitude to† school life (Aspects of School Life)	55.45 (3.68)	53.89 (3.86)	0.97 n.s.	57.84 (5.62)	56.44 (6.21)	0.47 n.s.	n.s.	Less favourable attitude
(3) Attitude to school authority (Verma-Sumner Questionnaire)	77.89 (4.90)	76.94 (4.75)	0.461 n.s.	80.23 (7.41)	78.77 (9.47)	0.346 n.s.	n.s.	Less favourable attitude
(4) Authoritarian view of society (Himmelweit-Swift F scale)	28.61 (3.11)	27.53 (2.52)	0.899 n.s.	27.93 (2.56)	26.63 (1.90)	0.116 n.s.	n.s.	Towards less authoritarian view of society
(5) Authoritarian parental rule (Himmelweit-Swift F scale)	15.27 (1.53)	14.58 (1.69)	1.005 n.s.	14.92 (1.72)	14.27 (2.40)	0.631 n.s.	n.s.	Towards less acceptance of authoritarian parental rule
(6) Pro-conformity and status quo (Himmelweit-Swift F scale)	15.94 (1.54)	15.40 (1.60)	0.806 n.s.	15.64 (1.71)	15.13 (1.75)	0.589 n.s.	n.s.	Towards less acceptance of status quo

* On this test the lower the score, the higher the self-esteem.
† Test spoiled in one school, hence for this test, experimental n = 14, control n = 9.

However, although history would suggest that conscription into schooling is burdensome for the majority, the present experiment does not in fact confirm that suggestion. Our sample is not representative of the majority. Most schools tend to assign social education programmes to those below the average in attainment. Most schools tend to embark on experimental

Table 6.3 Strategy C: Results of some background tests. Means of school means and standard deviations (in brackets)

	Experimental, n = 7			Control, n = 6				
	Pre-test mean (s.d)	Post-test mean (s.d)	t-test diff. of means	Pre-test mean (s.d)	Post-test mean (s.d)	t-test diff. of means	Diff. of diff.	Trend
(1) Self-esteem* (Coopersmith Questionnaire)	18.08 (2.79)	18.48 (1.86)	0.403 n.s.	22.07 (3.18)	22.11 (3.72)	0.231 n.s.	n.s.	Towards lower self-esteem
(2) Attitude to school life (Aspects of School Life)	56.35 (4.40)	55.96 (2.82)	0.253 n.s.	56.29 (5.30)	54.87 (6.09)	0.498 n.s.	n.s.	Less favourable attitude
(3) Attitude to school authority (Verma-Sumner Questionnaire)	79.71 (4.07)	77.04 (7.16)	1.111 n.s.	73.38 (7.84)	70.61 (9.21)	0.652 n.s.	n.s.	Less favourable (but more variable attitude)
(4) Authoritarian view of society (Himmelweit-Swift F scale)	27.09 (1.28)	26.63 (1.92)	0.674 n.s.	26.45 (3.03)	26.40 (2.88)	0.338 n.s.	n.s.	Towards less authoritarian view of society but control rather stable
(5) Authoritarian parental rule (Himmelweit-Swift F scale)	14.81 (1.27)	14.01 (1.56)	0.132 n.s.	13.24 (1.32)	13.14 (1.33)	0.1509 n.s.	n.s.	Towards less acceptance of parental authority
(6) Pro-conformity and status quo (Himmelweit-Swift F scale)	15.43 (1.06)	15.47 (1.32)	0.0625 n.s.	14.95 (1.16)	15.11 (1.67)	0.1927 n.s.	n.s.	Towards more acceptance of status quo

* On this test the lower the score, the higher the self-esteem.

programmes with pupils below average in attainment. Both factors worked to make our sample heavily biased in that direction. There were some schools in our experiment working with genuinely mixed-ability groups and some working within CSE frameworks, but many mounted the experiment in non-examination groups.

However, it could be argued that to teach about race relations with generally disaffected pupils, whose attitudes towards school are deteriorating and whose achievements in the eyes of the school are modest, is the crucial test. Presumably, the counter-argument would be that pupils primarily motivated towards examination results would resent any consideration of attitudes that diverted them from cognitive goals, and thus teaching them would present different but important problems. This is not tested within our experiment, but it is quite possible for a teacher working in the area of race relations with academic streams to monitor such a reaction.

There is no doubt in our minds that these test results are confirmed by the very considerable difficulties teachers are observed to have in shaping adolescent attitudes. We are, of course, reiterating - particularly for the reader who is not engaged in classroom teaching - what most teachers know: adolescents who are not high achievers academically pose taxing problems in the area of attitudes, and the credibility of school to them is not strong enough to give teachers much assistance.

Less predictably, the Coopersmith Questionnaire, where lowering of score indicates rise in self-esteem, suggests that self-esteem may be growing rather than diminishing in this group of pupils. One might reasonably conjecture that the school does not provide the reference point for this development, which may well therefore be associated with a growth of independence of the school. Such a diagnosis of the situation would, we think, be confirmed by many teachers' experience. However, the trend does not show in the control group in Strategy C. Thus, hypothesis 2, which we draw from these scores, is only marginally preferable to its contrary and is not significant where it does show.

The scales indicating an authoritarian view of society and an authoritarian view of parental control show slight but consistent trends across all groups towards a less authoritarian view. This test was included mainly for its likely relationship to inter-racial attitudes (see Chapter 9), and it is not easy to interpret per se. One might suppose that it indicates a relaxation of authoritarian control over adolescents by society and parents in the face of the young people's aspirations. But of course we are dealing only with a mean.

Finally, there is no consistent result on the scale measuring attitude towards conformity and the status quo, where a high score indicates that the respondent is favourable to conformity.

It is not easy to summarize the results of these tests, particularly since the trends are not strong. Our hypotheses are thus speculative:

Hypothesis 1: In non-examination or CSE groups, teachers are liable to encounter a hardening of unfavourable attitudes towards school among adolescent pupils.

Hypothesis 2: Adolescents in such groups show some trend
towards higher self-esteem and presumably confidence.

Hypothesis 3: Adolescents in such groups show a tendency
towards a less authoritarian view of society and
a less ready acceptance of authoritarian parental
control.

It is important to bear in mind that the growth of youth
unemployment has substantially changed the social context of
adolescent school students since 1974, when the present experiment was conducted.

7 THE GENERAL EFFECTS OF TEACHING ON INTER-RACIAL ATTITUDES

Lawrence Stenhouse and Gajendra K. Verma

A widespread assumption underlying all education is that the teacher's intentions – or 'objectives', as they are called when couched in terms of outputs of students' behaviour – are likely to be promoted rather than undermined by his teaching. We do expect that when a teacher spends a term teaching pupils French or mathematics or reading they will know more or be more competent as a result. It may be otherwise in at least some cases when we are dealing with attitudes rather than achievements. Notoriously, some pupils taught Shakespeare at school are put off Shakespeare for life.

On these grounds alone it is pertinent to ask: what is the effect of teaching about race relations upon inter-racial attitudes? Although Strategy B teachers set out to improve attitudes, they might not succeed. The argument for checking up is stronger in Strategy C, where aims were less clear. Still stronger is it in Strategy A, where the aim was to promote understanding of acts, situations and issues in race relations with the assumption that attitudes are influenced by understanding.

Such research as exists in Britain (our assumption being that American results do not necessarily generalize to the British situation) reinforces the need to check effects on attitudes as far as we can. In a limited experiment in a further education setting in London, Miller (1967, 1969) reported that inter-racial attitudes worsened after, and apparently as a result of, teaching about race relations aimed at improving attitudes.

On the other hand, a larger experiment conducted within the Humanities Curriculum Project measured small but consistent gains in mean scores of tolerance in a sample drawn from six schools. The effects were associated with a particularly heavily researched and supported teaching style, namely, discussion under 'neutral chairmanship'. The result did not offer much help to those who did not wish to work in this style or lacked the training to do so. Nor was it dramatic enough to suggest that teachers ought to adopt the style in order to teach about race relations (see Verma and MacDonald, 1971; Bagley and Verma, 1972; and Verma and Bagley, 1973).

Cautionary advice has been offered to teachers by various committees or bodies concerned with education for a multi-racial society. The DES paper on the Education of Immigrants (Department of Education and Science, 1971) has this to say:

There are positive things schools can do in the face of the
need to prepare pupils for life in a multi-racial society.
This certainly does not call for direct teaching in primary
schools and probably not in secondary schools. The inclusion of 'Race Relations' as a separate subject on the timetable would be misconceived and probably self-defeating,
except perhaps as a Sixth Form study. Education to counter
racial and colour prejudice and promote healthy race relations need not be separated in any way from the normal content of the curriculum. A great deal can be done through
the normal teaching of history, geography, literature,
science, indeed most subjects, to develop the attitudes of
mind essential for sound race relations and to create an
atmosphere of reason and tolerance within which relevant
topics can be profitably discussed. A number of subjects
allow of specific teaching about immigrants' home countries.
It is equally important to ensure that newly arrived pupils
are taught about life and customs in this country. Some
definite teaching on different cultures, religions and backgrounds needs to be undertaken. Differences in colour
need to be freely recognised and discussed, certainly by
the more mature pupils. In this way misunderstandings
and misconceptions can be cleared up. Older pupils, too,
can be helped to understand the fallacy of holding stereotyped ideas about their coloured companions and to
appreciate how prejudiced attitudes are formed. Much can
be done to counteract the formation of stereotypes by
encouraging pupils in all subjects to test generalizations,
to formulate their own judgements and not to assess individuals in terms of preconceived ready-made value judgements on the category of people to which they belong.
Opportunities need to be sought for inviting immigrant
adults to visit the school and talk to pupils about their
own culture and ways of life. Some schools have found the
appointment of an immigrant teacher of considerable help
in developing healthy race relations. (p. 12)

There are a number of points worth taking up from this advice.
Considerable reserve is expressed about the teaching of
race relations as a specific subject or direct teaching of race
relations. We find this difficult to interpret. It seems unlikely
that 'race relations' would occupy a specific slot on the timetable, and therefore unlikely that this is the possibility about
which reserve is expressed. The second passage points to
what can be done in 'history, geography, literature, science,
indeed most subjects'. The omission of mention of social studies,
humanities, civics and sociology is perhaps significant, since
these are curricular areas in which race relations is likely to
feature as a named topic in syllabuses. Accordingly, we may
suspect that it is direct teaching of race relations within these
subjects that troubles the DES. The present experiment

attempts to test the hypothesis that such direct teaching is deleterious.

We are not able, except in the case of drama, to test the assertion that a great deal can be done through the normal teaching of a wider range of school subjects. In drama we have looked at the situation of improvised drama in multi-racial schools, where the theme can hardly be kept out, and in non-multi-racial schools, where the theme is usually introduced by the teacher.

It is perhaps worth reporting that in our experience by no means all multi-racial schools teach about immigrants' customs and backgrounds, and we encountered no non-multi-racial school that did this before the experiment. It has not fallen within the brief of this project to explore the problems and effects of such teaching or to provide materials to support it; but there is a clear need for research and development in this area, particularly since casual evidence that it is difficult to interest native British children in this type of study suggests that, unless materials and presentation are of very high quality, effects may be negative rather than positive in terms of inter-racial attitudes. However, this is a theme we cannot pursue here.

Two other points are worth taking up from these statements. One is the DES point about the formation of stereotypes. We have only unsystematic evidence on this since, as is reported above, we were unable to secure the support of our steering committee for our using a stereotype test. The other is the implication that a disposition 'to test generalizations, to formulate their own judgements' may transfer from other areas of study to race relations. We have fragmentary evidence on this point, which we shall discuss later in this chapter.

We shall look first at the effects on interracial attitudes of teaching about race relations in the present project. Did the teaching do more harm than good?

We must remember that our only established test, the Bagley-Verma Opinion Questionnaire, provides us with only an indicator of shift rather than an adequate descriptor. Our case rests on its use as a straw in the wind, on the unlikeliness of a whole range of attitudes and behaviours shifting in a direction counter to shifts recorded on the test. With this in mind we may consider the implications of Table 7.1. It has to be remembered that this table is a very generalized result. It reports the effects of the sample of teaching strategies on the sample of pupils (both described in Chapter 3 above). At this level we can make the following generalizations.

(1) The experimental sample - that taught about race relations - shifted towards tolerance over the period between pre-test and post-test. In two cases, the scales for anti-black and anti-white, this shift was at 0.01 level of significance. In one case, the general racism scale, the shift was at 0.05 level of significance.

On the anti-Asian scale the shift was sufficiently small to be likely to be due to chance errors.
(2) The control sample – that not taught about race relations – shifted in all cases towards intolerance. In one case, that of the anti-Asian scale, the shift was significant at 0.05 level. In the other cases the shift was sufficiently small to be likely to be due to chance errors.
(3) In all cases, if we judge tolerance as a desideratum, those taught about race relations did better (judged by mean pre-test and post-test scores) than those not taught about race relations.
(4) In the case of the scales for general racism, anti-black and anti-white attitudes, teaching about race relations appeared to produce positive shifts towards tolerance; but in the case of the scale for anti-Asian attitudes, teaching about race relations held attitudes more or less stable while failure to teach about race relations was associated with statistically significant shifts towards intolerance.
(5) Although numerical equivalence of scores between anti-Asian, anti-black and anti-white scales is precarious, there is an implication that anti-white prejudice is low – not surprising, given the overwhelming preponderance of white pupils in the sample.

Table 7.1 Pre-test and post-test scores on the Bagley-Verma Scale for total experimental sample (all strategies) and total control sample and significance of difference between shifts in experimental and control as calculated by t-test. Means followed by standard deviations in brackets.

(a) Subscale within Bagley-Verma scale	(b) Experimental Sample n = 992			(c) Control Sample n = 430			(d) Significance of difference of difference in (b) and (c)
	Pre-test	Post-test	Direction of shift, t-value means	Pre-test	Post-test	Direction of shift, t-value means	t-value for difference
(1) General racism	15.91 (9.54)	15.31 (9.81)	↓ 2.38*	16.81 (9.96)	17.22 (10.29)	↑ 0.90	2.04*
(2) Anti-Asian	6.18 (4.01)	6.09 (4.57)	↓ 0.70	6.24 (3.94)	6.70 (4.22)	↑ 2.36*	2.29*
(3) Anti-black	7.30 (4.96)	6.86 (4.83)	↓ 3.34**	7.85 (4.90)	7.89 (5.17)	↑ 0.15	1.85
(4) Anti-white	3.43 (1.96)	3.26 (1.96)	↓ 2.75**	3.13 (1.77)	3.25 (2.51)	↑ 0.91	2.24*

In interpreting these results it must be remembered that it is
relatively easy to get levels of statistical significance on samples
as large as these. Shifts of scores are really quite small. This
often leads to the question, 'Are the statistically significant
shifts educationally significant?' In our view, the recognition
that the test is merely an indicator invalidates this question.
The test is not criterion-referenced with respect to teaching
objectives (and such criterion referencing is not logically possible, we argue), so the question is: 'Are educationally significant shifts likely to be correlated with statistically significant
shifts on the Bagley-Verma test?' Our position is that the
hypothesis that they are is stronger than the hypothesis that
they are not.

We emerge from a consideration of Table 7.1 with the hypotheses that:

Hypothesis 4: Direct teaching about race relations in the age
range 14-16 will tend to have positive rather
than negative effects upon interracial tolerance
as compared with not teaching about race relations.

We can add:

Hypothesis 5: In the case of attitudes towards Asians, there is
a particularly marked negative trend of attitude
in groups aged 14-16 not taught about race relations.

Hypothesis 6: This negative trend tends to be moderated rather
than accentuated by teaching about race relations.

The next step we propose to take is to analyse the results by
strategy (A,B or C), and by racial background of pupils. We
should note in passing that, ignoring race of pupils, the same
tabulation of data (not displayed in this book) as adopted in
Table 7.1 would yield broadly similar results for both Strategies
A and B. All experimental scores would show increases in
tolerance, all controls decreases in tolerance, and the significance of the difference between experimental and control
would be 0.05 in both strategies for scales on general racism,
anti-Asian and anti-black scales. Differences on anti-white
scale fall below 0.05 level. In the case of Strategy C, all experimental scores show increases in tolerance, but so do the general
racism and anti-black scores in the controls. None of the differences between experimental and control reaches significance.

Our reason for analysing by race of pupils as well as by
strategy is that it would appear that the test has a different
meaning according to the race of the respondent. We set out in
Table 7.2 the scores of white students on the general racism,
anti-Asian and anti-black scales on Strategies A, B and C.
Reading for Strategies A and B, we find that all experimental

groups improve and all control groups deteriorate. In Strategy A the difference of performance of experimental and control groups judged by t-value for difference of shift is significant in all cases at 0.01 level. In Strategy B the equivalent differences are significant only in the case of the anti-black scale, and this at 0.05 level.

Table 7.2   Pre-test and post-test scores on the Bagley-Verma Scale by strategies and controls on individual strategies, together with t-test values and significances: white pupils

Strategy and sample numbers	Sub-scale within the Bagley-Verma Scale	Experimental sample			Control sample			Significance of difference ** – 0.01 * – 0.05 t-value for difference of shift/ experimental and control
		Pre-test mean and (s.d.)	Post-test mean and (s.d.)	Direction of shift t-value for difference of means	Pre-test mean and (s.d.)	Post-test mean and (s.d.)	Direction of shift t-value for difference of means	
Strategy A: Experimental: 266 Control: 126	(1) General racism	17.24 (10.05)	16.51 (10.25)	↓ 1.71	16.06 (9.66)	17.61 (10.49)	↑ 2.11*	2.83**
	(2) Anti-Asian	6.45 (4.13)	6.40 (4.21)	↓ 0.26	5.93 (4.02)	6.89 (4.50)	↑ 2.72**	2.70**
	(3) Anti-black	8.06 (4.81)	7.48 (4.74)	↓ 2.48*	7.76 (4.48)	8.47 (5.12)	↑ 1.76	2.87**
Strategy B: Experimental: 349 Control: 193	(1) General racism	17.25 (9.61)	16.17 (9.78)	↓ 2.27*	17.42 (9.93)	17.87 (10.58)	↑ 0.72	1.91
	(2) Anti-Asian	6.46 (3.96)	6.38 (5.41)	↓ 0.29	6.06 (3.77)	6.74 (4.36)	↑ 2.74**	1.77
	(3) Anti-black	8.35) (5.01)	7.52 (4.53)	↓ 3.23**	8.20 (4.71)	8.41 (5.09)	↑ 0.69	2.47*
Strategy C: Experimental: 242 Control: 92	(1) General racism	14.68 (9.07)	14.32 (9.49)	↓ 0.54	17.72 (9.92)	17.25 (10.20)	↓ 0.46	0.09
	(2) Anti-Asian	5.77 (4.11)	5.47 (4.06)	↓ 1.06	6.61 (4.14)	6.87 (4.24)	↑ 0.64	1.08
	(3) Anti-black	7.20 (4.54)	7.07 (4.66)	↓ 0.39	8.08 (4.86)	7.97 (4.90)	↓ 0.21	0.03

We have already argued that our experiment does not justify comparison of the performances of the strategies. However, there may be those who find that argument difficult to accept. It is therefore important to point out that it is particularly clear that no comparative judgment of effectiveness of strategy emerges from the results reported in the previous paragraph. The apparent advantage in Strategy A occurs entirely because

of greater deterioration in the control groups than in Strategy
B. Strategy B results in the experimental groups show greater
improvement than the equivalent results in Strategy A. If one
were to argue that this showed Strategy B to be more effective,
the argument could be countered on the grounds that, since
control groups were drawn from within the experimental schools,
the evidence is that on the whole Strategy A schools may have
been contending with greater prejudice. Even this is speculative, since control groups were not available in all schools.

We conclude that results on the Bagley-Verma general racism,
anti-Asian and anti-black scales for white pupils taught by
both Strategy A and Strategy B support Hypotheses 4, 5 and
6.

We can add:

Hypothesis 7: Strategy A and Strategy B are both moderately
effective in combating inter-ethnic prejudice,
and the data give no basis for prescriptive
discrimination between them.

Hypothesis 8: Schools will be wise to adopt whichever strategy
accords with the context of teaching and the
skills of the teachers involved.

Strategy C shows no marked advantage of experimental over
control groups. Although all experimental scores show increases
in tolerance, these increases are small. In the case of the
general racism and anti-black scales the margin between experimental and control groups as judged by t-values, though it
favours the experimental, is quite tiny. Only in the case of
the anti-Asian scores is the advantage marked. If we were to
take the results at this level, then they might lead us to the
following hypotheses:

Hypothesis 9: Teaching about race relations through improvised
drama does not lead to overall deterioration in
inter-ethnic attitudes.

Hypothesis 10: Schools would be unwise in general to rely solely
on drama as a medium of teaching about race relations if their objective is to maximize improvements in attitude.

However, there are some features of the Strategy C situation
that are out of line with those of the other two, and each of
these might tend to depress readings of the effectiveness of
the strategy.

(1) The pre-test scores for Strategy C experimental groups are
appreciably lower than the pre-test scores for the experimental
groups in the other strategies, and this might be expected to
leave less room for improvement (in more technical language, we
are concerned with regression effects).

(2) The pre-test scores for Strategy C control groups are appreciably higher (except in the case of the Strategy B anti-black score) than the pre-test scores for the control groups in the other strategies, and this might be expected to leave more room for improvement. (In more technical language, again, we are concerned with regression effects.)

(3) In Strategy C the control groups do as a matter of fact improve on the general racism and anti-black scales whereas they deteriorate in Strategies A and B. The control group on the anti-Asian scale deteriorates only slightly as compared with the control groups in A and B. We feel that we cannot rule out the possibility that some of the Strategy C control groups may have been taught about race relations elsewhere in the school, nor can we at this stage verify this.

(4) We also face the problem that teaching through drama might be expected to influence pupils in a more affective or imaginative, less cognitive and judgmental, key than Strategies A and B. It is entirely possible that the Bagley-Verma test is not a good indicator for drama work.

(5) There is some evidence that the organic nature of the development of a programme of improvised drama meant that the racial theme was more fitfully present in the work than in the other strategies and that certain strands in the introductory conference for Strategy C might lead teachers to work on prejudice in general rather than on racial prejudice. That is, the drama strategy was less direct in its approach than the others.

Clearly, it is important to attempt to understand better the range of effects that drama may have. This would best be done through intensive small-scale experiments, which could be conducted by teachers, perhaps with clinical evaluation, which might well be available from universities, colleges or community groups.

As we have already observed, our project, given the sample it was able to attract, is largely about the problems and effects of white teachers teaching about race relations to white pupils (in both multi-racial and non-multi-racial schools). This is of course the majority situation. Thus, as Table 7.3 shows, the samples of black pupils are regrettably small. Nevertheless, some hypotheses emerge, though they are weakly supported:

Hypothesis 11: Both before and after teaching, black pupils have markedly lower scores for racism and for negative attitudes to other races than do white pupils.

Hypothesis 12: There is some evidence that for black pupils teaching about race relations may increase general racism, anti-Asian and anti-white scores, though these remain (where comparable) lower than those of white pupils. (In our sample this trend does not show in the anti-Asian scores in Strategy B or in the general racism or anti-Asian scores of Strategy C.)

In short, there is some fragmentary evidence that teaching about race relations may increase the negative scores of black pupils, still leaving them much lower than the scores of white pupils. In no case does this trend reach statistical significance, but it is repeated often enough to draw our attention. And it probably accords with common-sense expectations. Low-prejudiced black pupils will harden in attitude a little as a result of teaching about race relations. If the white pupils (representing the majority society) show high prejudice, a black reaction is probably to be expected.

Table 7.3 Pre- and post-test scores on the Bagley-Verma Scale: black pupils

Strategy and sample numbers	Sub-scale within the Bagley-Verma Scale	Experimental sample			Control sample			Significance of difference ** – 0.01 * – 0.05 t-value for difference of shift/ experimental and control
		Pre-test mean and (s.d.)	Post-test mean and (s.d.)	Direction of shift t-value for difference of means	Pre-test mean and (s.d.)	Post-test mean and (s.d.)	Direction of shift t-value for difference of means	
Strategy A: Experimental: 15 Control: too small to use	(1) General racism	10.00 (6.99)	10.79 (4.60)	↑ 0.76	–	–	–	–
	(2) Anti-Asian	5.07 (4.01)	5.86 (2.85)	↑ 1.39	–	–	–	–
	(3) Anti-white	4.36 (1.59)	5.21 (0.94)	↑ 1.75	–	–	–	–
Strategy B: Experimental: 50 Control: too small to use	(1) General racism	13.44 (6.38)	13.65 (9.07)	↑ 0.25	–	–	–	–
	(2) Anti-Asian	6.96 (3.31)	6.52 (3.60)	↓ 1.05	–	–	–	–
	(3) Anti-white	4.37 (2.03)	4.52 (2.17)	↑ 0.54	–	–	–	–
Strategy C: Experimental: 15 Control: 10	(1) General racism	10.07 (6.39)	9.73 (4.91)	↓ 0.22	8.20 (2.93)	10.00 (3.29)	↑ 1.54	0.98
	(2) Anti-Asian	6.40 (3.63)	5.73 (3.11)	↓ 0.72	6.10 (2.26)	5.40 (1.36)	↓ 1.66	0.03
	(3) Anti-white	4.00 (1.46)	4.20 (1.90)	↑	5.00 (1.41)	5.90 (1.87)	↑ 1.54	0.86

Table 7.4   Pre- and post-test scores on the Bagley-Verma Scale: Asian pupils
(Insufficient numbers in control groups and in Strategy C to
provide a base for comparisons)

Strategy and sample numbers	Sub-scale within Bagley-Verma Scale	Experimental sample		
		Pre-test mean and (s.d.)	Post-test mean and (s.d.)	Direction of shift t-value for difference of means
Strategy A: Experimental: 15	(1) General racism	8.83 (4.74)	8.83 (4.93)	0.00
	(2) Anti-black	3.00 (2.45)	2.67 (1.97)	↓0.45
No control	(3) Anti-white	3.92 (2.18)	5.42 (1.85)	↑2.21*
Strategy B: Experimental: 40	(1) General racism	10.30 (5.02)	9.73 (6.27)	↓0.62
	(2) Anti-black	4.24 (3.71)	4.00 (3.73)	↓0.41
No control	(3) Anti-white	5.65 (2.16)	5.41 (2.02)	↓0.66

In the case of Asian pupils, the tendency is towards greater
inter-racial respect in all cases except Strategy A Anti-white
(Table 7.4). However, the numbers are so low in the Strategy A
sample that doubt must be cast on this result in spite of its statistical significance. It could clearly be the result of a reaction to
one or two teachers. Probably the safest hypotheses are:

Hypothesis 13: Both before and after teaching, Asian pupils
have significantly lower scores for racism and
for negative attitudes towards other races than
do white pupils.
Hypothesis 14: Unlike black pupils, Asian pupils appear not to
increase racism and prejudice scores between
pre-test and post-test.

The picture here is of a group that is confronted by considerable and increasing racial prejudice against itself becoming less
rather than more prejudiced towards others. Perhaps Asians

do not have the same reaction to the experience of racial prejudice and discrimination as do black pupils. If this is so, a
cultural factor is presumably at work.

So much for the general trend of results when we regard the
pupils as our sample. But there is a case for arguing that,
because schools were the unit at which the critical sampling
decisions were made, and then pupils were chosen because they
were in schools that were chosen, the sample should therefore
be treated as a sample not of pupils, but of schools. There is
much to be said for this view.

Accordingly, in Tables 7.5, 7.6 and 7.7 we present results
on the general racism, anti-Asian and anti-black scales of the
Bagley-Verma Test by strategies using the school as a unit.
The raw data for these tables are the mean scores of the
schools. This, of course, greatly reduces the sample numbers
for each statistic. Moreover, in some cases the control group
in an individual school can be rather small (see Table 4.2
above).

For the moment the supplementary data from Strategy A at
the foot of each of these three tables can be ignored.

The results support the hypotheses put forward earlier in
this chapter, though the t-test figures, influenced as they are
by the small sample, show that the trends fall far short of
statistical significance. So far as general racism scores are concerned, all strategies show decreases in racism in the group
taught about race relations. In Strategies A and B, parallel
control groups showed increases in general racism scores, but
in Strategy C the control group, like the experimental group,
showed decreases. In fact, these decreases were greater than
those in the experimental group. We are not able to account for
this result in Strategy C control groups.

On the anti-Asian scale the results are slightly different.
All control groups increase in anti-Asian attitudes. Experimental
groups in Strategies B and C show decreases in anti-Asian
attitudes. The Strategy A experimental group shows increases
in anti-Asian attitudes but these are of a much smaller order
than those in the control group, which are the highest among
the samples. Thus Strategy A shows the same trend here as
B and C.

Taken by school, all experimental and all control groups in all
strategies show a decrease in anti-black attitudes. In Strategies
A and B the magnitude of the decrease is greater (as measured
by t-value) in the experimental than in the control groups,
though only slightly so in the case of Strategy A. In Strategy
C, however, the control group has the advantage, though it is
slight.

On the whole, therefore, the results on the Bagley-Verma
Test analysed by school support the hypotheses derived from
the analysis of pupil scores. The slightly better performance of
the control group as compared with the experimental group in
Strategy C on the general racism and anti-black scales raises

Table 7.5   General racism pre-test and post-test scores on the Bagley-Verma Scale by schools (unit: school means) and by strategies with controls by individual strategy, together with t-test values and significances

| Strategy and sample numbers | Experimental groups | Experimental sample | | | Control sample | | | Significance pre- and post-test difference comparing exp. with control |
		Pre-test mean of school means and (s.d.)	Post-test mean of school means and (s.d.)	Direction of shift and t-value for difference of means	Pre-test mean of school means and (s.d.)	Post-test mean of school means and (s.d.)	Direction of shift and t-value for difference of means	
Strategy A: Experimental: 11	Exp. with parallel control	18.54 (5.71)	18.12 (5.12)	↓ 0.145	17.26 (2.64)	18.58 (3.92)	↑ 0.739	n.s.
Control: 7	All exp.	17.32 (6.25)	16.98 (5.87)	↓ 0.132				
Strategy B: Experimental: 15	Exp. with parallel control	17.93 (2.87)	17.01 (3.15)	↓ 0.648	17.34 (3.93)	17.61 (4.17)	↑ 0.141	n.s.
Control: 9	All exp.	16.35 (3.34)	15.69 (3.87)	↓ 0.500				
Strategy C: Experimental: 9	Exp. with parallel control	14.14 (2.22)	14.00 (2.99)	↓ 0.106	16.61 (4.83)	15.88 (3.37)	↓ 0.351	n.s.
Control: 3	All exp.	14.54 (2.40)	14.47 (3.13)	↓ 0.053				
Strategy A without schools 18 & 19 Experimental: 9	Exp. with parallel control	20.92 (4.13)	19.42 (4.14)	↓ 0.628	16.74 (2.48)	17.18 (1.37)	↑ 0.380	n.s.
Control: 6	All exp.	19.40 (4.72)	18.74 (4.84)	↓ 0.293				
School 18, Strategy A		8.60	10.30	↑ 0.96	20.37	27.00	↑ 1.67	1.06
School 19, Strategy A		7.42	7.79	↑ 0.30				

and reinforces doubts expressed earlier. Again, the result is difficult to explain. However, the margins are small, the appropriateness of the test to drama is doubtful and the judgment that Strategy C generally had adverse effects would not be a reasonable one.

Table 7.6 Anti-Asian pre-test and post-test scores on the Bagley-Verma Scale by schools (unit: school means) and by strategies with controls by individual strategy, together with t-test values and significances

Strategy and sample numbers	Experimental groups	Experimental sample			Control sample			Significance of pre- and post-test difference comparing exp. with control
		Pre-test mean of school means and (s.d.)	Post-test mean of school means and (s.d.)	Direction of shift and t-value for difference of means	Pre-test mean of school means and (s.d.)	Post-test mean of school means and (s.d.)	Direction of shift and t-value for difference of means	
Strategy A: Experimental: 11	Exp. with parallel control	7.14 (2.37)	7.45 (1.88)	↑ 0.271	6.44 (1.20)	7.31 (1.92)	↑ 1.017	n.s.
Control: 7	All exp.	6.66 (2.50)	6.76 (2.33)	↑ 0.097				
Strategy B: Experimental: 15	Exp. with parallel control	6.96 (1.36)	6.80 (1.18)	↓ 0.267	6.17 (1.46)	6.64 (2.04)	↑ 0.562	n.s.
Control: 9	All exp.	6.37 (1.67)	6.35 (1.71)	↓ 0.032				
Strategy C: Experimental: 9	Exp. with parallel control	5.92 (1.53)	5.62 (1.42)	↓ 0.406	6.58 (1.06)	6.61 (0.85)	↑ 0.062	n.s.
Control: 3	All exp.	6.04 (1.48)	5.78 (1.42)	↓ 0.380				
Strategy A without schools 18 & 19 Experimental: 9	Exp. with parallel control	7.86 (1.53)	7.83 (1.75)	↓ 0.032	6.33 (1.28)	6.61 (0.57)	↑ 0.489	n.s.
Control: 6	All exp.	7.89 (1.51)	7.78 (1.72)	↓ 0.144				
School 18, Strategy A		2.80	5.20	↑	7.12	11.50	↑	
School 19, Strategy A		2.75	2.71	↓				

There is nothing in the results considered by schools to disprove the hypotheses we put forward on the basis of the results considered by pupils.

We turn now to the supplementary data on Strategy A schools, which are presented at the foot of each of Tables 7.5, 7.6 and

7.7. When we looked at the data by school we discovered two anomalous schools which may show a similar pattern. Both have extremely low prejudice scores both before and after the teaching, but the scores rise between pre-test and post-test. Even so, the general racism post-test scores are the lowest in Strategy A, and are lower than all scores in Strategy C and all scores except those of two schools in Strategy B.

Table 7.7 Anti-black pre-test and post-test scores on the Bagley-Verma Scale by schools (unit: school means) and by strategies with controls by individual strategy, together with t-test values and significances

Strategy and sample numbers	Experimental groups	Experimental sample			Control sample			Significance of pre- and post-test difference comparing exp. with control
		Pre-test mean of school means and (s.d.)	Post-test mean of school means and (s.d.)	Direction of shift and t-value for difference of means	Pre-test mean of school means and (s.d.)	Post-test mean of school means and (s.d.)	Direction of shift and t-value for difference of means	
Strategy A: Experimental: 11	Exp. with parallel control	8.39 (2.64)	7.98 (2.51)	↓ 0.298	8.84 (1.28)	8.72 (2.43)	↓ 0.116	n.s.
Control: 7	All exp.	8.04 (2.83)	7.77 (2.39)	↓ 0.242				
Strategy B: Experimental: 15	Exp. with parallel control	8.48 (1.28)	7.78 (1.61)	↓ 1.021	8.24 (1.85)	8.12 (2.46)	↓ 0.117	n.s.
Control: 9	All exp.	7.42 (1.75)	7.02 (1.71)	↓ 0.633				
Strategy C: Experimental: 9	Exp. with parallel control	6.42 (1.49)	6.33 (1.48)	↓ 0.135	7.42 (3.01)	7.04 (2.37)	↓ 0.281	n.s.
Control: 8	All exp.	6.71 (1.65)	6.61 (1.63)	↓ 0.129				
Strategy A without schools 18 & 19 Experimental: 9	Exp. with parallel control	9.10 (2.02)	8.48 (2.35)	↓ 0.490	8.19 (1.12)	7.84 (0.75)	↓ 0.636	n.s.
Control: 6	All exp.	9.02 (2.20)	8.49 (2.10)	↓ 0.523				
School 18, Strategy A		4.10	5.00 ↑		10.25	14.00	↑	
School 19, Strategy A		4.17	4.79 ↑					

When these schools are withdrawn from the Strategy A sample, the remaining results become quite close to those in Strategy B, and Strategy A shows small improvements on the anti-Asian scale for the experimental group. In other words, these schools, which after deterioration still have extremely low prejudice scores, are pulling a considerable weight towards an increase in prejudice in the total strategy score. There is an apparent paradox in this situation: the least prejudiced groups are counting against a measure of success in teaching.

Each of the schools concerned had only one experimental group. The two teachers working with these groups are among the most experienced Strategy A (HCP) teachers, and both are extremely effective neutral chairmen. In school 18, which is in a multi-racial area where the non-white population is predominantly Asian, the teacher is a man. In school 19, which is in a non-multi-racial area in Scotland, the teacher is a woman, who is teaching within the Scottish rubric 'Guidance', i.e., small-group teaching sessions with a purpose related to counselling or pastoral work.

The anomaly is that, in both teachers' groups, mean racism scores rise between pre-test and post-test, but even after the rise remain very low indeed. Their pupils rate among the least racist in the whole experiment after the teaching, even though they were even less racist before it. In the case of school 18 (though not in the case of school 19) we have a parallel control group drawn from within the same year of the same school, and it has very high racism scores which increase between pre-test and post-test. But there was, so far as we can ascertain, no incident in the multi-racial area outside the school or in the life of the school outside the class teaching, which would suggest itself as an explanation of the increase in racism in both experimental and control groups.

One possible explanation of the results would be the hypothesis that the general influence of context was conspiring to worsen racism throughout the school during the period of teaching. The experimental teaching might then be seen as fighting this trend better than the control.

A second factor is the phenomenon known as 'regression to the mean', a statistical trend which might in any case lead us to expect extremely low scores to increase and extremely high ones to decrease. This would lead us to discount to an extent the increase in racism in the experimental group and to emphasize (more warily) the increase in the control group.

Having considered the evidence we have of the actual teaching in the classrooms, we wish to offer for consideration another explanation. Past work under a very competent HCP teacher has made the students open-minded or liberal when they approach any new topic. Their initial disposition is not to take strong views until they have had more chance to examine the issues. Almost inevitably, the discussion of evidence attacks the implied 'optimistic liberalism' of such a stance and

leads to a more realistic, less idealistic, view of the issues.
Even after that racism, as measured by our test, remains low.
Accordingly, we offer these hypotheses:

Hypothesis 15: Experience of the discussion of controversial
issues in the light of evidence and under a
neutral chairman can lead to a position of 'open-
mindedness' which transfers to new issues not
previously tackled. (The characteristics of this
'open-mindedness' are not at present described,
merely suggested (indicated) by trends in
scores.)
Hypothesis 16: Experiences in other styles of teaching may also
transfer.
Hypothesis 17: Transfer of open-mindedness will tend to produce a situation in which low racism scores on
pre-test will harden somewhat, but remain low
on post-test ('idealism/realism shift').

These hypotheses are speculative in the extreme, particularly
since there is some evidence of the students in school 18 showing impatience with the test. Nevertheless, we believe that the
line of speculation is well worth following.
So much for the shifts in scores recorded by our pre-test/
post-test measurement programme. We have used as a measure
of these shifts the Bagley-Verma Test, which was in fact the
only standardized test of racism included in our battery. If we
compare the results of the Bagley-Verma test with those of one
of the unstandardized instruments we used, the L.S. Questionnaire, we think we can throw a little light on the nature of
racist attitudes in our society.

Table 7.8   Correlations between L.S. Questionnaire and Bagley-Verma Test
by sub-scale (pre-test data)

	Bagley-Verma Test			
L.S. Questionnaire	*General racism*	*Anti-Asian*	*Anti-black*	*Anti-white*
Attitude towards the British	0.01	0.10	0.02	0.23
Acceptance of people of other races	- 0.29	- 0.19	- 0.29	- 0.26
Competition for scarce resources	- 0.45	- 0.44	- 0.45	- 0.10
Subordination/superordination	- 0.55	- 0.47	- 0.53	- 0.07
Optimism/pessimism	- 0.15	- 0.13	- 0.14	- 0.26
Political policy	- 0.46	- 0.37	- 0.46	- 0.28

Details concerning the L.S. Questionnaire are provided in the
Appendix. Briefly, it is a scratch instrument with the particular
design problems of alternative choice tests, but it has a reasonably convincing face validity, and internal analysis would allow
us to give some credence to its sub-scales. Clearly, we should
not push analysis of the results on this test too far, but it does
seem worth offering figures for the correlations of the sub-
scales of the L.S. Questionnaire with the sub-scales of the
Bagley-Verma Test. In reading Table 7.8 it is important to
bear in mind that, since positive scores indicate tolerance in
the L.S. Questionnaire and racism in the Bagley-Verma Test,
negative correlations confirm the relation between the two.
Among these correlations, a number are high enough to catch
the eye. They are those between the racism scales of the
Bagley-Verma, other than the anti-white scale, and the sub-
scales of the L.S. Questionnaire called 'Competition for scarce
resources', 'Subordination/superordination' and 'Political
policy'.

The specific items representing 'Competition for scarce
resources' in the L.S. Questionnaire are as follows:

A It is wrong for people to come here from overseas and take
jobs from British people.
B If people did not come here from overseas, Britain would be
short of people to do jobs which are important for this country.

A Many immigrants work too hard, and this does not help the
British worker getting better wages and conditions.
B British workers and those from overseas work well together
on the whole and the immigrants have helped the British worker
to go for better wages and conditions.

A We probably don't do enough for children from overseas in
our schools.
B Our efforts to help children from overseas in our schools
could easily make things worse for British children.

A Immigrants who come into this country take up houses that
should really go to Britishers.
B It's silly to draw distinctions between Britishers and immigrants when it comes to housing: anyone who is trying to
work hard and bring up a family deserves a house.

The specific items representing 'Subordination/superordina-
tion' in the L.S. Questionnaire are as follows:

A There is no reason why a white man should not accept a
black man as a supervisor or boss.
B It is better in this country that white people should be
supervisors or bosses.

A   There is a real need for more black and Asian policemen in
Britain.
B   On the whole it is wrong to employ people as policemen
unless they are British.

A   For an Asian or West Indian, the best way to establish yourself in this country is to make money and get yourself a really
good house and car.
B   It's not a good idea for an Asian or West Indian living in this
country to buy too expensive a house or car; it just offends
people.

A   British troops ought to fight just as well if they were led
by a black officer.
B   You couldn't really expect British troops to fight as well if
they were led by a black officer.

The specific items representing 'Political Policy' in the L.S.
Questionnaire are as follows:

A   Immigrants expect too much of Britain.
B   Britain could well do more to help immigrants.

A   The British have made a lot of money out of Africa, India
and the West Indies and they have a duty to people from these
lands.
B   The British did a lot to help Africa, India and the West
Indies and people from these countries should be grateful for
this.

A   The British government spends too much money on helping
countries overseas and not enough on the needs of this country.
B   The British government should do everything it can to help
countries that are not so well-off, even if it does mean a few
sacrifices.

The political policy items seem to us too few, too indeterminate
and too close to the other scales to tell us very much in terms
of correlation, but it does seem reasonable to see the other correlations as hinting at factors at work in racism in Britain.
Hence:

Hypothesis 18: One element in racism seems likely to be a per-
                 ception of people of different races as competitors
                 for scarce resources.
Hypothesis 19: One element in racism seems likely to be an
                 unwillingness of white people to accept the
                 appropriateness of black people being placed in
                 superior authority relationships to white sub-
                 ordinates.

We made an attempt to discover what might be the state of racial attitudes after a lapse of time by administering a re-test on some of the battery, including the Bagley-Verma Test, almost a year after the teaching. Unfortunately, the results were vitiated by sample loss. In Strategy A the original experimental sample of 298 (all races) was reduced to 135, and the control of 128 to 31; in Strategy B the original experimental sample of 426 was reduced to 98 and the control of 195 to 25; and in Strategy C the original experimental sample of 253 was reduced to 73 and the control of 102 to 28. (These sample figures take account of cases excluded from later analyses of the original sample because scrutiny of their tests led to the conclusion that they had not completed or had frivolously completed the test: experimentals: A,8; B,13; C.4; controls: A,3; B,3; C,1.) There is evidence that sample loss is systematic. For example, whole schools have dropped out, leavers have been lost, etc. And when the pre-test and post-test scores of the post-test sample are extracted, they differ a good deal from those of the original sample.

Table 7.9:   Results of second post-testing, a year after treatment with severe sample losses (figures for original sample in brackets) expressed as mean scores on the General racism, Anti-Asian and Anti-black scales of the Bagley-Verma Test. Students of all races included

Strategy and sample size	Experimental sample			Control sample		
	Pre-test	Post-test	Post-post-test	Pre-test	Post-test	Post-post-test
A GR	15.85(16.53)	15.06(15.91)	15.48	19.55(15.56)	18.90(16.86)	16.94
135(288) AA	5.96 (6.29)	5.86 (6.27)	5.99	7.45 (5.81)	7.71 (6.64)	7.10
31 (128) AB	7.30 (7.56)	6.82 (6.98)	7.02	9.26 (7.39)	8.71 (7.88)	7.52
B GR	15.85(16.49)	13.86(15.69)	12.90	14.36(16.81)	13.96(17.71)	13.36
98 (426) AA	6.40 (6.39)	5.23 (6.32)	5.29	5.32 (5.97)	5.08 (6.68)	5.24
25 (195) AB	6.76 (7.51)	6.12 (7.00)	5.44	7.04 (7.93)	6.48 (8.23)	6.12
C GR	12.77(14.11)	12.68(13.94)	14.03	17.29(16.79)	17.46(16.12)	15.36
73 (153) AA	5.63 (5.69)	5.03 (5.49)	6.05	6.36 (6.56)	6.64 (6.67)	6.29
28 (102) AB	6.01 (6.63)	5.96 (6.45)	6.33	7.89 (7.62)	7.86 (7.20)	6.89

Had these scores supported our hypotheses, we should not have reported them because of these weaknesses; but they do not and so we feel it important to report them however precarious they may be judged to be. They are presented in Table 7.9 where the sample sizes and scores of the original group tested are recorded in brackets. The first point we must make is that there is every reason, comparing the sample sizes and scores between original and residual sample, to expect irregularities of results as large as those recorded here as a statistical artefact. Second, if one were able to obtain reliable figures, there would be an acute problem in relating these to a short period of experimental teaching a year earlier. Not only do we hypothesize from our previous results, both with experimental groups and with control groups, that attitudes in our population are constantly on the move, but we may also expect that school experiences or events in the social context shared by whole groups may have influenced attitudes. Given all this, we think the statistics in Table 7.9 virtually worthless as a basis for judgment.

However, it would be unwise to assume that gains in tolerance achieved in school will persist in the long term. Racism cannot be cured by educational action on the part of school teachers, though they can make a contribution. Accordingly, we suggest:

Hypothesis 20: The effects of teaching about race relations to adolescents in schools are not likely to be persistent in the long term without reinforcement.

Hypothesis 21: The influence of school and social context is not likely to reinforce interracial tolerance in the absence of actions or policies actively designed to do so.

8 EDUCATION AND INDOCTRINATION

Lawrence Stenhouse and Gajendra K. Verma

Can we penetrate behind the gross statistical trends towards
improvement of interracial attitude reported in the previous
chapter and find in the texture of these results anything that
speaks more clearly to the judgment and experience of the
individual teacher? Can we present our data in a way that can
inform the life of the classroom?

If we regard our tests of inter-ethnic attitude as analogous
to opinion polls, we might examine the results in terms of
'swing', a little after the manner of election broadcasts. The
analogy is not perfect, but it will serve. The shift in scores
on the Bagley-Verma Test and the other tests we used to
take observations in the area of interracial attitudes is more
like an opinion poll swing than it is like an increment in attainment - that is, in knowledge or in skills.

However, we cannot be content merely with information about
a general swing. In elections people are concerned with the
results of voting and not with the opinions of individual voters.
The general trend is the focus of interest. But in education
we are, by definition, concerned with the individual.

Accordingly, we want some way of displaying our results
that indicates swing, but at the same time exposes to scrutiny
the effects within that swing on individual cases. This is what
we have attempted in Figures 8.1 to 8.6, where we have displayed the distribution of arithmetical pre-test/post-test differences on the general racism scale of the Bagley-Verma Test
for experimental and control groups by strategy.

It is important to be quite clear about the nature and deriva-
tion of the scores plotted on these histograms. If a student
scored 14 in the pre-test and 10 in the post-test, since high
score is intended to indicate high prejudice, his swing suggests
a lessening of prejudice. His score on our histogram will be
-4; that is, post-test less pre-test score. Minus scores indicate
a lessening of prejudice. If, however, the student, having
scored 10 on pre-test, scores 14 on post-test, his pattern of
scoring suggests an increase in prejudice. His score on our
histogram will be +4. Positive scores indicate increase in
prejudice.

Our histograms refer only to the general racism scale of the
Bagley-Verma Test; but the pattern of results is the same in
each of our attitude tests. Since all the attitudinal scales illustrate the principles we wish to discuss, these will serve as
exemplars.

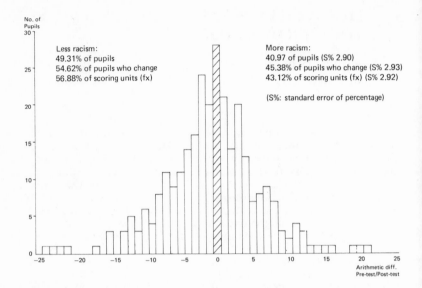

Figure 8.1: Histogram of differences between pre-test and post-test scores on general racism scale of Bagley-Verma Test, Strategy A experimental: n = 288 (4 scores excluded)

Note: These histograms were produced subsequent to the processing of the data; their first draft was based on computer print-outs giving pre-test and post-test differences. The results were so striking, especially in the cases of large swings, that the senior author felt that he must examine, individually, the pre-test and post-test scripts of all the subjects. In this examination he found a small number of scripts where large swings could have been due to gaps in the candidates' responses to items in the test, to patterns of response which seemed to indicate frivolous intent, or the like: these patterns were excluded from the analysis on the judgment that they were 'spoiled papers'. The effects of the excluded scores on the results as a whole being marginal, the data were not recomputed.

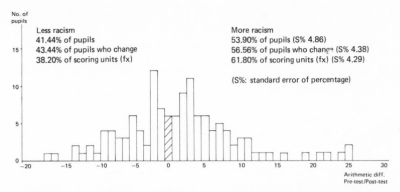

Figure 8.2: Histogram of differences between pre-test and post-test scores on general racism scale of Bagley-Verma Test, Strategy A control: n = 128 (1 score excluded - see note to Figure 8.1)

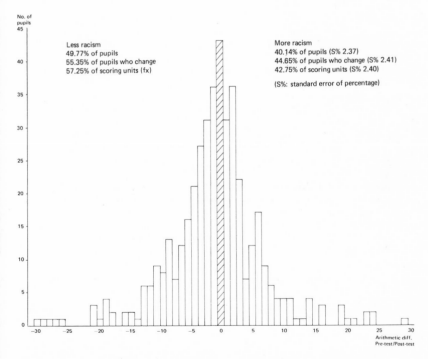

Figure 8.3: Histogram of differences between pre-test and post-test scores on general racism scale of Bagley-Verma Test, Strategy B experimental: n = 426 (7 scores excluded - see note to Figure 8.1)

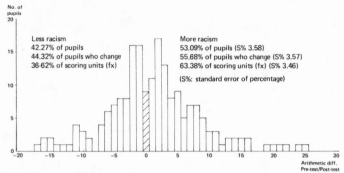

Figure 8.4: Histogram of differences between pre-test and post-test scores on general racism scale of Bagley-Verma Test, Strategy B control: n = 194 (2 scores excluded - see note to Figure 8.1)

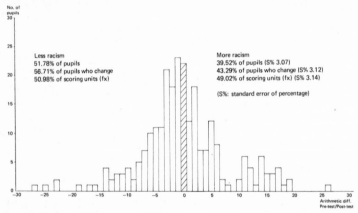

Figure 8.5: Histogram of differences between pre-test and post-test scores on general racism scale of Bagley-Verma Test, Strategy C experimental: n = 253 (2 scores excluded - see note to Figure 8.1)

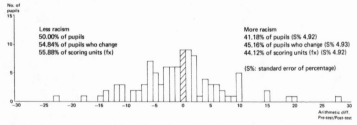

Figure 8.6: Histogram of differences between pre-test and post-test scores on general racism scale of Bagley-Verma Test, Strategy C control: n = 102 (1 score excluded - see note to Figure 8.1)

In considering the results we have to bear in mind two problems associated with the test. The first is our reserve about its validity. If the reader has a clear concept of what he means by racial prejudice, we cannot claim that the general racism scale measures this. He will have to ask himself whether a measurement that was valid in terms of his concept would, like our other attitude scales, conform to the pattern we shall discuss. The second problem is related to the way the test is constructed: it is what is termed 'norm-referenced'. And norm-referenced tests of the kind used are designed to generate difference between students. That is to say, they will tend to throw into relief the differences recorded in our histograms because of the way they are constructed. Some might even go so far as to argue that the measured differences occur because of the way the tests are constructed rather than because of what actually happens to the students.

In our view, these shortcomings can be faced only by considering our results against a broad context. In particular, it is important to assess whether the hypotheses to which they may incline us chime with philosophic analysis and with sociological and psychological theory as well as with the practical professional experience of teachers.

With this introduction, let us look at the histograms themselves. As in the results discussed in the previous chapter, the Strategy C data are different in trend from those for Strategies A and B. We shall discuss A and B first, and relate the C results to these later.

It will be helpful to start by looking at Figures 8.2 and 8.4, the histograms showing improvements and deteriorations in the scores of the control groups drawn from seven of the Strategy A schools and nine of the Strategy B schools. These are the individual difference scores for groups of students who are not being taught about race relations in their curriculum: the school is leaving this topic out of their studies.

In each case, the results are remarkably similar. Around about 4½ per cent of the students register no change of attitude; about 53 per cent become more prejudiced; and about 42 per cent become less prejudiced. About 38 per cent of all scores are on the improvement side of the histogram; about 62 per cent on the deterioration side. The range runs from -17 to +25 in both cases. The histograms appear to hint at a bipolarity: instead of one peak, there are two, at -2 and +2 or +3, but this is too uncertain a result to build much upon it. (As an indication of the error factor, we quote standard errors of percentages (s%) (Ferguson, 1976, p. 156).)

If we are to believe this result, students in the fourteen to sixteen year age range are likely on the whole to be in process of becoming more rather than less racist if they are not taught about race relations. What could account for this? It could, of course, be an artefact of our experiment, an effect to be found only among students not taught about race relations in schools

where race relations is being taught. We do not ourselves
think this a likely hypothesis. Among more likely ones are that
the general influence of our society, if not counteracted by
the school, conduces rather to the growth of racism than to its
eradication; and that the general curriculum of the school
(presumably from its choice of and handling of content) has a
similar effect. Probably both social context and school contribute to interracial attitudes.

The histograms for the two experimental groups of Strategies
A and B, shown in Figures 8.1 and 8.3, are also remarkably
similar. Each peaks at zero, that is, no change. Between 49
and 50 per cent of all students become less racist; between 40
and 41 per cent become more so; and the weight of scores is
balanced in the same direction, approximately 57-43. But the
range of scores is somewhat higher in Strategy B than in Strategy A.

If we turn now to Figure 8.5, the histogram of pre-test/post-
test differences for Strategy C experimental group, we find it
not so very different from the equivalent histograms for Strategies A and B. The balance of numbers of pupils is, in fact,
more favourable, almost 52 per cent becoming less racist and
only 39½ per cent becoming more so. It is the balance of scores
that shows up less well, being almost 50-50, and this is due in
the main to thirty-two pupils registering 10-19 increments in
racism score while only nineteen show decrements in this range.
It is difficult to know how much weight we should give to this
or how to interpret it, but it remains true that the overall
pattern would not lead us to avoid teaching about race relations
through drama, though it might make us hesitate in view of the
Strategy A and B results to use that technique alone.

The histogram that falls most out of line is Figure 8.6, for
the control group of Strategy C. This, in fact, shows improvement of attitude comparable to the experimental groups in
Strategies A and B. We are not able to account for this performance of the Strategy C control group. We have speculated
as to whether some of these groups were being taught about
race relations outside drama in social studies, history or
English, but we feel unable to confirm this reliably at this
distance of time.

Taken by and large - and allowing for our usual reservation
concerning Strategy C - these histograms tend to confirm
Hypothesis 4 in the previous chapter: direct teaching about
race relations in the age range 14-16 will tend to have positive
rather than negative effects upon interracial tolerance as compared with not teaching about race relations. But they also
throw into relief another result, which invites further discussion and analysis: in all cases a substantial proportion of students - a majority in the Strategy A and B controls, a minority
in the other cases - increase their racism scores between pre-
test and post-test. How are we to view this?

There are teachers who will feel discouraged by the implica-

tions of these results, because they had hoped - or even expected - that all or almost all students would become less racist in
attitude as a result of teaching. We think this is not a realistic
expectation, but we want to explore the problems in this area
at some length.

The exploration can start from a passage in Krathwohl, Bloom
and Masia's 'Taxonomy of Educational Objectives in the Affective
Domain' (1964). This handbook, on testing the attainment of
behavioural objectives in areas of affect and attitude, contains
in Part I a discussion likely to be useful - if critically read - to
any teacher concerned with the theme of the present book.
From it we draw these paragraphs:

> The authors of this work hold the view that under some
> conditions the development of cognitive behaviors may
> actually destroy certain desired affective behaviors and
> that, instead of a positive relation between growth in cogni-
> tive and affective behavior, it is conceivable that there
> may be an inverse relation between growth in the two do-
> mains. For example, it is quite possible that many literature
> courses at the high-school and college levels instill know-
> ledge of the history of literature and knowledge of the
> details of particular works of literature, while at the same
> time producing an aversion to, or at least a lower level of
> interest in, literary works. Clearly there is need for con-
> clusive experimentation and research on the relations
> between the two domains. Here, again, the specificity
> which a taxonomy can introduce into both domains is likely
> to reveal conditions under which one conclusion is sound
> as well as point to situations where the opposite conclusion
> is tenable.
>
> Perhaps one of the most dramatic events highlighting the
> need for progress in the affective domain was the publica-
> tion of Jacob's *Changing Values in College* (1957). He sum-
> marizes a great deal of educational research at the college
> level and finds almost no evidence that college experiences
> produce a significant change in students' values, beliefs,
> or personality. Although he has been criticized for his
> methods, definitions, and assumptions, his critics have
> not responded by pointing up changes in the affective
> domain which he had overlooked. Jacob's work has stimu-
> lated a considerable amount of soul searching at the college
> level and is undoubtedly responsible for an increase in
> interest and research in this area. We must pay our respects
> to Jacob for increasing our own determination to complete
> this Handbook. (p. 20)

The authors remind us that our experience of teaching school
subjects should show us how difficult it is to attain uniformly
desired changes of attitude. We know that people commonly
learn about literature and music, history and science, from

teachers earnestly desiring that their students should come to
enjoy and value their subjects, and yet the positive results
they would like to see are not consistently achieved. Schools
have never won the minds of all their pupils to the values
endorsed by their teachers, and it would be unrealistic to
expect that the influence should be that much greater when
the values are intensely held by teachers and of great social
importance.

However, it could well be suggested that liking or disliking
music or history is in the last analysis a matter of taste;
whereas racism is a moral defect, and demonstrably so. From
this it could be argued that as teachers we should do everything in our power to eradicate it.

Let us turn back to Krathwohl, Bloom and Masia (1964):

> the distinction (is) frequently made between education and
> indoctrination in a democratic society. Education opens up
> possibilities for free choice and individual decision. Educa-
> tion helps the individual to explore many aspects of the
> world and even his own feelings and emotion, but choice
> and decision are matters for the individual. Indoctrination,
> on the other hand, is viewed as reducing the possibilities
> of free choice and decision. It is regarded as an attempt
> to persuade and coerce the individual to accept a particular
> viewpoint or belief, to act in a particular manner, and to
> profess a particular value and way of life. Gradually educa-
> tion has come to mean an almost solely cognitive examination
> of issues. Indoctrination has come to mean the teaching of
> affective as well as cognitive behavior. Perhaps a reopen-
> ing of the entire question would help us to see more clearly
> the boundaries between education and indoctrination, and
> the simple dichotomy expressed above between cognitive
> and affective behavior would no longer seem as real as the
> rather glib separation of the two suggests. (p. 18)

We agree in wanting to avoid the glib separation between
cognitive and affective. The issue of indoctrination is too complex to be dealt with adequately in this book, but it seems
worth giving our view.

It is sometimes argued that indoctrination occurs whenever a
teacher attempts to promote a particular belief, view or attitude
and that indoctrination inheres in this intention on the part
of the teacher. We believe it more reasonable to reserve the
concept of indoctrination for those cases in which the desire to
promote certain views is carried to such a length that the
teacher is prepared to attempt to evade the judgment of those
he is teaching rather than to appeal to their judgment. And for
us this characteristic appeal to the judgment of the taught is
the criterion of an educational procedure, and that which dis-
tinguishes education from indoctrination. Whether an appeal to
judgment is simply an appeal to rationality we doubt, since we

believe that judgment involves the acceptance of responsibility for decisions, beliefs or attitudes which carry us beyond – though they do not negate – the rational. There is a reasonableness of emotion that is not entirely the servant of rationality.

What is critical is not the teacher's beliefs or his desire that his pupils should share them, but the procedural principles he adopts in his teaching, the appeal to judgment rather than the attempt to disarm it. Both Strategy A and Strategy B teachers seem to agree in appealing to pupils rather than coercing them. The difference is that the Strategy A teacher uses evidence to pursue understanding on the assumption that the pursuit of understanding will lead towards better attitudes, while the Strategy B teacher pursues better attitudes, hoping to increase understanding on the way.

We further believe that it is a good deal more difficult to indoctrinate even young children than most people appear to assume. In the case of adolescents, our view is that indoctrination can scarcely be accomplished without the considered techniques of propaganda, censorship and brainwashing. Of the latter, Snook (1972) writes:

> Brainwashing is a comparatively new term. Despite the emotions it arouses, it does not seem to refer to any new or mysterious process. Basically it involves the use of all known methods to change a person's pattern of thinking and feeling: conditioning, anxiety, fear, indoctrination, distortions, drugs, group analyses, enforced isolation – all are used in a massive attempt to change a person's outlook. (pp. 107-8)

Our estimate, based on what we know of the use of brainwashing in politico-military contexts, is that, even in the face of such massive attempts to change an outlook, some persons are likely to resist successfully, and that this minority is more likely to develop hostility than to develop indifference to the outlook desired.

Nevertheless, it remains true that a brainwasher would regard a situation in which the attitudes of a random selection of the whole population moved uniformly in one desired direction as satisfactory from his point of view. An educator, however, faces a paradox. If he values a particular attitude or outlook – love of literature, scientific curiosity, Christian commitment, respect for people of other races – then he will wish to promote that attitude. However, if he also values the process values of education, he will want to appeal to the judgment of his students and not to subvert it. Accordingly, he is bound to accept that, if his educational values – or the sanctions of his society – preclude brainwashing, then the expected outcome of teaching intended to promote a desired value, attitude or outlook must be a histogram with the broad characteristics of those in Figures 8.1, 8.3 and 8.5 above.

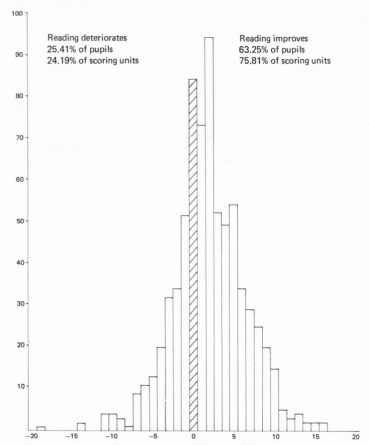

Figure 8.7: Histogram of differences between pre-test and post-test scores on Brimer Wide-span Reading Test, full sample: n = 732

It is worth comparing these histograms with parallel presentations of results in cognitive areas. Unfortunately, we have run no tests of straightforward, cumulative, cognitive attainment in this project. The nearest we have is the Brimer Wide-span Reading Test, which is attempting to measure performance in a cognitive attainment likely to be fairly heavily influenced by affective and attitudinal factors. But Figure 8.7, which presents the histogram for pre-test/post-test differences on this test, nevertheless provides an instructive comparison with those we have already considered. In this histogram the proportional distribution of pupils is 63-25 as compared with 49-40 in

Figures 8.1 and 8.3, while that of scores is 76-24 as compared with 57-43. All sets of scores of this sort are, of course, subject to a degree of error.

Given the reading test scores as an index of the effects of education on a heartland cognitive skill in which there is a long teaching tradition, we think that our results in the area of race relations are encouraging rather than discouraging; and we believe that anyone with his feet on the ground and realistic expectations will make a similar judgment.

However, the situation revealed by our histogrammic presentation of the results does call into question the application of behavioural objectives in attitudinal areas. If a behavioural objective is to be reasonably realistic, it must be a statement of the anticipated outcome. If this position be accepted, then the aim of promoting inter-racial respect or tolerance or undermining prejudice (or indeed any other aim in the area of values or attitudes) would translate into a specification of outcomes couched in terms of swing: to produce, as a result of teaching, a situation in which more students are moving in the desired direction and fewer moving in the undesired direction than would be the case without such teaching, the criterion being pre-test/post-test differences in score on any valid measure.

We find inescapable the paradox that we would be alarmed on educational grounds if the values, attitudes or outlooks of all our students moved in the direction desired by the teacher. In it is expressed the basic principle that education is primarily concerned with increasing pupils' powers, and that such an aim is incompatible with the aim of coercing attitudes. This is because an increase in powers necessarily involves an increase in the power to criticize instruction. The dilemma is that so acutely posed by 'A Clockwork Orange': moral action is free action. And the school is ultimately concerned with moral action.

We believe that this analysis of the situation, though it is inescapable, is not generally faced honestly. To the extent that it is not, the teacher may be held accountable for the results of his teaching in quite unrealistic terms. He may be expected quite to eradicate racism from his classroom. Under the pressure of such an expectation, the stress and anxiety of grappling with the expression of institutional racism in the attitudes of his pupils - at best considerable - become intolerable. He feels himself without support, and involved in a dishonesty forced on him by the inability of those in authority to face the truth. It is a situation parallel to that experienced by many men on leave from the trenches in the First World War. There is a similar disparity between the heroics and the realities of teaching.

The temptation may be to brush the whole subject of race under the carpet, failing in social studies, literature, creative subjects, history or geography to notice that ours is a multi-racial society and that this does raise issues and pose problems. We feel that this head-in-the-sand attitude is not defensible -

in any school, not only in multi-racial schools – and that the pattern of our control groups tends to support our view.

However, teachers who do face the reality of race relations have got to be assured that the nature of the problem they face is understood. In particular, they have a right to expect understanding support from heads, advisers and inspectors. And they ought to work in mutually supportive groups if possible.

We hope that this research report presents the situation dramatically and clearly enough to enable teachers to work on race relations without the nagging anxiety that the reality of the situations they are dealing with is not understood by colleagues and by members of the community.

All the evidence suggests that the school can make a worthwhile contribution to the improvement of racial attitudes, but that it can only ameliorate, not adequately counter, the influence of racism in society. If teachers encounter and have to work with the effects of institutional racism in their classroom – as they frequently and inescapably do – they cannot be held responsible for the full range of responses of their pupils. In the end, the school, which cannot remedy or avoid the forces of society that bear on it, cannot be held responsible for the reform of society and the adult world.

On the basis of this chapter, we offer the following hypotheses:

Hypothesis 22: Teaching about race relations through the strategies studied in this project can, and by and large will, lead to more students moving in the desired direction (less racism) than in the undesired direction (more racism) on a measure of racism.

Hypothesis 23: When teaching about race relations meets the educational criterion of appeal to the judgment of those who are taught, as opposed to adopting the stance of brainwashing, a fairly substantial minority of those taught will, during teaching, shift attitude in the undesired direction.

Hypothesis 24: The experience of the teacher in the classroom in the face of racism as expressed by some of the pupils is likely to be sufficiently taxing to make it necessary to define explicitly the support and interest of figures of authority in his/her school and school system and to make provision for mutual support to be offered within a group of teachers sharing the problem.

In addition to these hypotheses as stated above, we are prepared to go further and state 22 and 23 as general hypotheses applicable beyond the area of teaching about race relations:

Hypothesis 25: Teaching about any subject or topic in association with which an attitude or outlook is valued
by the teacher (i.e. there are affective as well
as cognitive aims) can tend to lead to more
students moving in the desired direction with
regard to attitude than in the undesired direction.

Hypothesis 26: When such teaching meets the educational criterion of appeal to the judgment of those taught,
a fairly substantial minority of those taught
will, during teaching, shift attitude in the
undesired direction.

In short, we believe we have here the basis for a general
hypothesis much wider in application than the field of race
relations in which we have worked. Teachers of literature will
find that, while most students may develop favourable attitudes
during their teaching, a substantial minority will develop
unfavourable attitudes.

We think that most teachers will recognize this: their experience will confirm our hypotheses. But it is not something that
the teacher finds it comfortable to keep in the forefront of his
consciousness or to reflect upon; and it is an especially uncomfortable thought in an area such as race relations, where the
values at stake seem so important both ethically and politically.
Yet it would be sociologically naive to believe that education,
even if it were deployed on a more thoroughgoing scale than in
this experiment (a few hours a week for a term), could shortly
solve the problems of race relations and racism in our society.
However, within its limitations, it may make an indispensable
contribution, and perhaps over the years the most important
of any agency.

9 THE SCHOOL: UNIT OF DECISION-MAKING

Lawrence Stenhouse and Gajendra K. Verma

In Chapter 4, where we discussed sampling, we pointed out that, since the primary sampling decision was taken at the level of the school, it could be argued that we should be thinking in terms of a sample of schools rather than a sample of pupils. Thus, in Chapter 7, where we presented the general trend of our results, we set these out not only for samples of pupils in each strategy, but also, in Tables 7.5, 7.6 and 7.7, for the samples of schools.

In taking up this thread again we want to stress that the school is normally the unit of decision-making. Indeed, we would go so far as to suggest that it should be: no teacher or department should enter the field of race relations without some consultation at school level. The major decision - whether or not to include race relations in the humanities, social studies, sociology, English, history or drama curriculum - will normally be made by a school or by a department after consultation within the school. In most cases, following on that decision, pupils will not be selected individually for courses involving teaching about race relations but rather will be assigned to them in groups as a result of the timetabling process. A consideration of the results by school is thus pertinent to the pattern of decision-making as it is likely to be found in practice.

However, when we look at the results by school, we must bear in mind that we have reduced our sample size to the number of schools in the experiment. And the sample is not, we imagine, representative, even within the limits of its size: the motives for entering an experimental project of this sort are probably rather different from those for taking race relations into the curriculum on an everyday basis.

Formally, if the schools were a true random sample, the logic of sampling would suggest that the sample of pupils would become less random and hence less representative by being chosen through their schools. However, given that the schools were not a random sample, we believe that the sample of pupils is likely to be more representative of a national population of non-academic adolescents than the sample of schools is representative of the schools of the nation: this because differences among schools attributable to different types of pupil and environment appear much better covered than differences attributable to heads, staffs and institutional variables.

Thus, it seems better to look upon each school as a case in itself than to lump all the school results together in a way that masks their variability from school to school. With this consideration in mind, we display in Tables 9.1, 9.2 and 9.3 the results for each school expressed as differences between pretest and post-test mean. This is the school equivalent of the results expressed graphically for pupils in Chapter 8. It is, that is to say, an index of swing.

Table 9.1 Differences between pre-test and post-test school means for experimental and control groups on the General racism (GR), Anti-Asian (AA) and Anti-black (AB) scales of the Bagley-Verma Test: Strategy A

(1) School code	(2) Experimental GR	(3) Experimental AA	(4) Experimental AB	(5) Control GR	(6) Control AA	(7) Control AB	(8) Comment code (see text)
03	- 1.83	- 0.35	- 1.22	–	–	–	C
07**	1.58	0.54	0.31	- 0.86	0.21	- 0.71	G
09	- 0.22	0.55	- 0.9	2.11	1.45	1.09	A
10*	- 0.63	- 0.18	- 1.54	–	–	–	C
13	- 0.85	0.37	- 1.29	- 0.89	- 0.56	- 0.67	D
17	- 2.5	- 1.17	- 1.78	–	–	–	C
- 18	1.7	2.4	0.9	6.63	4.38	3.75	B
19	0.37	- 0.04	0.62	–	–	–	D
29	- 3.42	- 1.75	- 1.67	2.0	0.87	- 0.25	A
31**	- 0.12	0.77	0.65	0.34	0.5	- 1.16	D
32**	- 1.61	- 0.7	- 0.83	- 0.07	- 0.77	- 0.38	A
39*	1.2	- 0.5	1.05	–	–	–	D
Mean of Strategy A controls (individuals)				(1.3)	(0.83)	(0.49)	

* 5-25% non-white

** over 25% non-white

In these tables column (1) gives the code standing for the name of the school. When the school has over 25 per cent non-white pupils, the code carries a double asterisk; when it has over 5 but below 25 per cent non-white pupils, it carries a single asterisk.

Columns (2)-(4) carry the difference between pre-test and post-test means for the experimental groups, a minus quantity representing an improvement in interracial attitude, a plus quantity representing a deterioration. Differences for the general racism, anti-Asian and anti-black scales of the Bagley-Verma Test are given.

Columns (5), (6) and (7) show the comparable results for school control groups where these exist. At the foot of the column are the control groups' mean differences for the strategy.

Table 9.2   Differences between pre-test and post-test school means for
experimental and control groups on the General racism (GR),
Anti-Asian (AA) and Anti-black (AB) scales of the Bagley-Verma
Test: Strategy B

(1) School code	(2) Exper- mental GR	(3) Experi- mental AA	(4) Experi- mental AB	(5) Control GR	(6) Control AA	(7) Control AB	(8) Comment code (see text)
01	- 3.51	- 1.6	- 2.57	- 1.75	1.43	- 1.34	A
02	0	- 0.67	- 0.10	2.43	1.22	1.43	A
04**	1.04	0.10	0.24	–	–	–	E
05	- 2.27	- 0.34	- 0.97	–	–	–	C
06*	- 2.00	1.29	- 1.30	0.55	0.34	- 0.52	D
08	1.09	0.30	0.07	- 5.4	- 1.2	- 2.33	G
09	- 2.89	- 0.22	- 1.97	2.11	1.45	1.09	A
11	- 1.58	- 0.48	- 0.53	–	–	–	C
14**	- 0.33	0.39	0.91	–	–	–	D
15	- 2.25	0.17	- 1.42	–	–	–	C
20	- 0.39	0.05	- 0.22	- 1.15	0.86	- 1.43	F
21	- 1.77	- 1.32	- 1.19	1.59	1.04	0.59	A
24*	0.19	0.37	0.60	4.93	1.07	1.65	B
30*	3.79	1.27	2.16	–	–	–	E
33	1.00	0.43	0.38	- 0.83	0.83	- 0.08	G
Mean of Strategy B controls (individuals)				0.90	0.71	0.30	

*   5-25% non-white
**   over 25% non-white

The final column contains a comment code which can be translated as follows:

A   Experimental scores improve and are better than controls.
B   Experimental scores deteriorate, but are better than controls.
C   Experimental scores improve: no control for comparison.
D   Indeterminate cases.
E   Experimental scores deteriorate: no control for comparison.
F   Experimental scores improve, but less so than controls.
G   Experimental scores deteriorate and more so than controls.

In terms of these codes, cases coded G and F may reasonably
be held to be cases in which teaching about race relations has
been disadvantageous; and cases coded E may need to be re-
viewed. We propose to examine the table for each strategy in
turn, providing where possible additional information about
cases where teaching appears to have been deleterious.

In Strategy A only school 07 seems to have a result that sug-

gests that the experimental teaching probably did more harm
than good, and this impression is confirmed by the school's
results on the L.S. Questionnaire.

Table 9.3 Differences between pre-test and post-test school means for
experimental and control groups on the General racism (GR),
Anti-Asian (AA) and Anti-black (AB) scales of the Bagley-Verma
Test: Strategy C

(1) School code	(2) Experimental GR	(3) Experimental AA	(4) Experimental AB	(5) Control GR	(6) Control AA	(7) Control AB	(8) Comment code (see text)
22	0.46	0.03	- 0.15	–	–	–	D
23	1.37	0.10	0.37	- 2.0	- 0.09	- 0.73	G
25	0.62	0.45	- 0.14	- 2.81	- 0.81	- 2.15	G
26	- 2.11	- 0.46	- 0.77	- 1.15	0.31	- 0.46	A
27	- 1.45	- 0.78	- 0.17	- 3.38	- 1.12	- 0.25	F
34	1.71	- 0.76	0.47	2.13	1.43	1.19	B
35	- 0.04	- 0.66	- 0.33	- 1.05	0.22	- 0.67	D
36	- 1.22	- 0.24	- 0.58	1.31	0.15	0	A
37	0.04	- 0.04	0.42	1.14	0.14	0	D? B?
Mean of Strategy C controls (individuals)				(- 0.67)	(0.11)	(- 0.42)	

The case study data yield illuminating information, though
we feel that there is a problem in presenting it adequately to
the reader in view of the need for confidentiality. However,
we can say that the school, which is heavily multi-racial, is in
an environment where racial issues are politicized and there is
a good deal of overt tension. Historically, there is some evidence of conflict among the staff on racial issues: that is, some
members of staff feel that others take racist positions, though
the problem is less acute than it was. Again, the tradition of
the school was authoritarianism in the face of a pretty intract-
able discipline problem.

Evidence from the tapes shows teachers at the authoritarian
end of the Strategy A continuum, probably in part because of
background problems of discipline. Pupils were difficult to
engage in discussion. They complained that the subject was
boring, which we interpret at deeper than face value. There
appears to be a desire on the part of members of the group to
protect one another.

Finally, the teachers became concerned about the work they
were doing within the project. There is evidence of cautious
evasion of issues on the tapes, and after three or four weeks
the teachers discontinued teaching about race relations. The

effects are effects of a programme of teaching abandoned.

Thus one can say that the situation was clearly a difficult one, and that the teachers knew it and felt that it was going wrong. (They would not be surprised by the test results.) On the other hand, the school did not teach through the term, and it can only remain uncertain whether it might have worked through a bad patch to an ultimate improvement. It must be extraordinarily difficult when one feels things have gone wrong to decide whether to drop teaching while they are in a mess or continue in the hope of an improvement.

In Strategy B schools 08 and 33 give cause for concern, as do 04 and 30. School 20, where general racism and anti-black scores drop less (but not significantly less) than those in the control groups, while the anti-Asian trend is held better in the experimental than in the control (but not significantly better), does not seem to us to cause concern. In those cases where the control group does better, tolerance increases in the experimental: where the control group does worse, there is in effect no deterioration in attitudes in the experimental group. This is the only school considered in this chapter that is also the subject of a case study: namely, Wild's study no. 3. It does not seem that the teaching was as disastrous in its results as the teachers feared.

School 08's results show a rather small deterioration of attitude in the experimental group which contrasts with exceptionally large improvements of attitude scores in the control group.

There is some evidence that this school may have entered the project partly motivated by rivalry with other schools in its locality, and that, once in the project, it felt some discontent with the attitudes and performance of the central team. Teachers from the school expressed disappointed and critical views at the conferences and in interview with the researcher. The research team did not have access to tapes of teaching, which were reported stolen. However, we do know that the course was heavily film-based with a minimal use of the materials provided by the project. Indeed, the school might almost be regarded as employing a fourth strategy - teaching by film. However, it must be said that conditions of morale in the school would mitigate against the strategy being realized at its strongest: that is, the case cannot be taken as evaluative of film-based teaching about race relations.

In the case of school 33, the results favour the experimental group on the anti-Asian scale, but favour the controls on the general racism and anti-black scales. The L.S. Questionnaire results show generally patterns associated with improvement of attitude in both experimental and control.

In this case we are dealing with an all-white school where the case study data run counter to the measurement results. With the exception of one lesson, which seemed to our researcher unduly risky, all the evidence seems to be of successful teaching. The teacher was a youth leader with very good contact with the pupils inside and outside school. He used materials from the UNESCO Aspro Project, which appears to be widely successful. He was extremely open with the pupils about the intentions of the experiment, and he took regular evaluative feedback from them. He was pushing towards tolerance, but gently, and he was always fair, honest and sincere with the pupils.

The evidence from the case study and the evidence from the measurement results being at variance with one another, the case is difficult to interpret.

In schools 04 and 30 the pupils' score on the Bagley-Verma Test deteriorate, but we have no control groups in the same schools with which to compare them. Both schools are multi-racial. The scores in 04 are not too distant from those for the means of the Strategy B controls, and case study data suggest both that the teaching was relatively well received and that the background of race relations in the neighbourhood was not entirely favourable. Our own judgment is that there is no great cause for concern. School 30 is more difficult to estimate. The school is an inner-urban multi-racial school in a difficult neighbourhood. Just before the project teaching began, the senior teacher involved wrote withdrawing from the project and citing: inadequate facilities, poor equipment in bad repair, inadequate typing and duplicating facilities, little time available for preparation and administration of the project, shortage of staff, large proportion of probationary teachers, and failure of the LEA to provide extra funds for the project. This was interpreted by the LEA as an attempt to use the project as a political lever to secure advantages for school and department, and in the long run the team leader was persuaded to remain in the project. He assented with some reluctance.

Surveying all the schools in Strategies A and B in which test scores suggest that teaching about race relations may have had deleterious effects, we find only one case where both school and research team are surprised by the result. In all the other cases there do seem to have been factors that could be seen as warning signals - though they were seen too late.

The conclusion that it may be very difficult for teachers nominated by school or LEA to escape involvement in a project of this kind we find a very troubling one.

So far as the doubtful schools in Strategy C are concerned, we are not able reliably to throw light on their situations owing to the failure of the fieldworker in this branch of the project to produce reports, a deficiency mentioned earlier in this book.

10 THE CASE STUDIES OF SCHOOLS IN STRATEGIES A AND B

Lawrence Stenhouse and Robert D. Wild

In earlier chapters we have drawn only lightly on data from the field studies, which were a central feature of the project, using them mainly to entice the imagination of the reader to conjectural recreations of the real-life situations producing the symptoms picked up by the measuring instruments. Now we turn to the problem of how best to present these data to throw light on the problems and effects of teaching about race relations.

This is by no means easy to solve. The data are of various kinds. There are audio-tapes of work in classrooms produced by the teachers involved, together with written notes and commentaries, again by the teachers. There are written documents produced by the schools: brochures, hand-outs and the like. There are tapes of pupils discussing the work with no teacher present, with a teacher present and with a member of the project team present. There are taped interviews with teachers and others conducted by the field worker, Bob Wild, and there are taped conference sessions where teachers from different schools and strategies met in discussion. Altogether there are approximately one thousand hours of taped material.

These materials can be broadly classified into the documentary and the reflective. The documentary category includes all materials – almost invariably paper records – produced by schools as part of their normal functioning (cf. Webb and Webb, 1897, p. xi), and running records (normally audio-recordings in this project) of the school or classroom at work when the defined task is educational or administrative (not research or teacher development). The reflective data – in this case mainly recorded discussions among pupils, discussions among teachers at conferences or interviews with teachers – is second-order in that it consists of attempts by participants to reflect upon their experience either for the sake of developing their understanding and competence or at the prompting of research workers.

In handling such materials we are dealing not with events or happenings themselves but with evidence of happenings. Understanding such evidence implies interpretation of it, and there can be no such understanding that is, as one might say, interpretation-free. Yet all interpretation takes place within a framework of understanding. Thus, there is a dialectic between understanding and interpretation, each in turn adjusted to the development of the other. We have to sharpen progressively our ability to interpret and our capacity to build understanding related to interpretation.

It is particularly important to notice that the interpretation of case study involves concepts, that the reader's interpretation may be somewhat different in its conceptual map from that of the research worker, and that in this situation it is important to try to build a conceptual framework slowly. We are in fact inviting the reader to attempt to develop his own theory of schools and education.

All the paper data have been examined by Bob Wild, who has been responsible for this aspect of the present research; and all the taped material has been listened to by Bob Wild and/or Grace Wild and/or Frances Laws. A high proportion of it has been painstakingly transcribed. The result is a problem similar to that of the contemporary historian; so large is the stock of data that it is both difficult to organize in the mind of the research worker and difficult to reduce to a scale where it is at once manageable by the reader, true to the research worker's understanding and open to critical appraisal.

This problem is that of reducibility, and it is the central problem of presenting 'qualitative' data. Quantitative data are readily reducible, but there is quite a problem in giving them meaning in reference to human action. Qualitative data are rich and complex in meaning, but the problem is to reduce them to manageable proportions without losing their essence: density and ambiguity. Reading the summary of 'Bleak House' or 'Hamlet' in the 'Oxford Companion to English Literature' conveys nothing of the understanding of life offered by the originals.

The problem we are discussing is one common to all historians, and to all field sociologists and anthropologists. We argue that in essence it is how to transmit an understanding (the researcher's) of transactions and understandings (the researched actors') to a third party (the reader) in such a way as to convey the richness and ambiguity of the data and the texture of the researcher's judgment. The reader requires some apprehension of both in order to understand the presentation.

In sociology and anthropology one resort is to theory. The professional sociologist or anthropologist addresses fellow-professionals by means of a theory, which serves to characterize the basic judgmental framework of the researcher and allows the professional reader to elucidate and criticize the understanding provided by applying the theory to other cases, either at the level of reviewing his experience or at the level of systematic verification.

In this project we are primarily concerned not with sociological or anthropological (or psychological) theory, but with educational theory, that is, with the understandings of the person who acts qua teacher or educator rather than of the person who acts qua sociologist or anthropologist. Educational theory grounded in careful study - as opposed to educational theory disputing ideals - is extraordinarily undeveloped, and is a very minor element in the teacher's (and the educational theorist's) understanding of professional experience. And it is to that understanding that we address ourselves.

What we hope is that teachers will be able to make helpful assessments, relevant to their own situations, of the problems and effects of teaching about race relations. What we offer in succeeding chapters is a group of presentations by Bob Wild and Jon Nixon of some of their insights and understandings acquired in the study of a mass of data. We introduce this with an account of Bob Wild's view of his task - and of the reader's - which is intended to support an understanding of the presentations based on careful judgment. What follows, then, is his.

Rather than attempt to express my approach to case study through a definition, I propose to offer as an introduction a brief snatch of case study material and to sharpen definitions as we go along. The material is selected from a school to be presented in more detail later:

TEACHER: Before break you got together in pairs to exchange your views on mixed marriage, so Mary and Sarah, would you like to start, saying what you as a pair decided upon perhaps?

MARY: We are going to discuss a talk about a coloured girl aged 19, who wants to marry a white boy. The mother of the girl is coloured too.
'Mother, I have something to tell you.'

SARAH: Mother speaking.
'Come on then, speak up.'

MARY: 'I am going to get married to a white boy.'

SARAH: Mother again.
'Well, what is the matter with that? A white boy is just as good as any other kind of person. I am not a prejudiced....'

TEACHER: 'Mm.' Mary (slight pause to allow Mary to speak if she wishes) 'So, can I take it that the views, um, of the two of you are that mixed marriage presents no problems?'

Our qualitative data are concerned with individuals in particular situations. We are involved in the study of small behaviours, and the key concept for organizing these data is interaction. Use of this concept focuses attention on the patterns created by individuals in their attempts to relate in the classroom, at staff meetings or elsewhere. This gives case study a spatial flavour, since interaction implies a field of interplay. But one must not think of it as static space, for an important feature of interaction is transience.

This transience of interaction suggests a parallel with the theatre. Sociologists frequently use the term 'actors' for individuals and speak of enactment within a social context. Like a play, as Aristotle defined it, interaction has a beginning, a middle and an end, and usually finishes before nightfall. To make sense of interaction and the form it may assume requires that one carefully bear this in mind. To this end case study within education might be regarded as a 'sociology of occasions' (Goffman, 1972, p. 2 and passim).

A second feature of the brief extract quoted above might be the sense of familiarity that it offers. We may all feel that we know what it is about. The practising teacher in particular is likely to feel that he or she can smell the classroom smell, see the blackboard and hear the pupils clattering in after break to take up the task set them by the teacher. To the more cynical it may seem that the teacher has employed the time-old device of divide and rule by giving the pupils the onus of the work, in order to catch his breath within a busy day. If we are not teachers, we have none the less been to school. It all seems therefore to be quite straightforward and commonplace. But this appearance is deceptive, and should not be taken to be equivalent to 'readily penetrated and understood'. The behaviour of animate subjects as opposed to inanimate objects is familiar enough but difficult to understand in an analytic or predictive sense because of its particularity. The case study worker perceives unique aspects of a situation, and as a perception, not as a result of scientific analysis.

Perception involves interpretation. What we gain from the research worker is not reality itself, but methods that may be usefully employed in interpreting it. This opens up the possibility that case study, for all its engaging appeal to the recognition of reality, may be no more reality-orientated and commonplace than quantitative analysis. If this is so, why is case study so commonly perceived in simple terms?

The answer to this question lies perhaps in our familiarity with the raw data of case study. Though we are not consciously aware of it, we are of course constantly interpreting everyday situations in a 'qualitative' way. Our 'nativeness' (Cicourel, 1973) makes this seem second nature. In interaction we are constantly monitoring other people's responses, modifying our own, selecting suitable linguistic codes and so on.

I am claiming that it may be possible to be rigorous and disciplined in interpreting case study data rather than to see interpretation as resting on alternative creative styles. We may have been partially blinded to this possibility, I have hinted, because we already carry out some of the methods and procedures involved in our everyday dealings. What we must avoid is the error of tidying. The enemy of understanding is the tendency of many of us to equate rigour with orderliness (Ryle, 1960):

But then under the influence of the auditor's grave and sober voice he suddenly begins to wonder. Here everything in the life of the college is systematically marshalled and couched in terms which, though colourless, are precise, impersonal and susceptible of conclusive checking. To every

plus there corresponds an equal and opposite minus; the
entries are classified; the origins and destinations of all
payments are indicated. Moreover, a general conclusion
is reached; the financial position of the college is exhibited
and compared with its position in previous years. So is
not this expert's way, perhaps, the right way in which to
think of the life of the college, and the other muddled and
emotionally charged ways to which he had been used the
wrong ways? (p. 75)

Clearly, reading case study and judging it is not wholly
straightforward. We need to look for an approach that will
allow us to interpret case study data meaningfully.

It is hard to see, unless we simply want to be impression-
istic, how we can begin to interpret case study without reference to some form of criterion. Indeed, even to be impression-
istic suggests a model somewhere in the background. In everyday situations we are constantly measuring what happens
against our expectations.

As we have seen, case study data are concerned largely with
interaction and the patterns which that produces. It is not
surprising to find therefore that the frameworks that are used
to interpret them reflect this; i.e. they are usually structural
themselves. The quest, then, is for a suitable structure.

Since our professed attempt in this project is to generate
educational - not sociological, psychological, or philosophical -
theory, the actual educative process should define the theory
by which we attempt to investigate it. Though one may generate
an educational theory to interpret individual schools against
case study data, this is only the initial step. Experiences
within individual schools should then amplify or modify theory.
There should be a constant dialectic between theory and practice. What we need in a sense is a blue-print theory grounded
in and disciplined and developed in the light of actualities.
Again, there is no one pedagogic model. We may, for example,
take the teaching about race relations in our particular school
as the measure against which to set others. The alternative
method of interpretation offered here is based on the researcher's experience in analysing data across schools.

The construction of an educational model runs immediately
into a semantic problem. As in defining case study, one needs
to get inside the concept involved. To enter, we have to accept
terms so loosely defined that they may lead to misunderstanding
and even confusion about what is being said. Hopefully, the
terminology may reshape itself into a more meaningful whole as
one goes along. The reader will have to bear with this.

It is useful to consider, first, the school as an institution
which must constantly recreate itself anew. A total institution
might be seen as isolating the inmates from the wider society
in an almost complete sense. A school cannot do this. There may
be a wall round the school, but it contains a gate through which

pupils normally enter and leave on a daily basis. Again, the
pupils as clientele do not necessarily choose to attend. It is
very much a daily institution, and demonstrates much of the
impermanence which that suggests. Morning assembly is the
point at which daily re-creation begins. Lessons are meticu-
lously divided off from each other by bells. The importance
of bells in institutional terms might be explored elsewhere.
Pupils may be regimented from one classroom to the next.
Notices and notice boards proliferate. Playground duty, dinner duty and even bus duty serve to convince the pupils that
teachers, as representatives of the institution, are omnipresent.
Only towards four o'clock or on Friday afternoons do institutional patterns visibly weaken. This is as one might expect.
Homework may extend the identity of the school beyond its
walls. The teachers themselves are subject to pressures similar
to those experienced by the pupils. There are strict hierarchies
of responsibility, and the headmaster often seems omnipresent
in the staffroom, particularly at the end of break. Staff meetings and departmental meetings are natural expectations.

All this is said not as critical comment, but to indicate the
effort that the school needs to make in order to realize itself
within the constraints under which it operates. It may be
argued that schools have moved away from this image towards
one of co-operation and community, and this may be so at a
primary and infant level. But responsibility towards others as
a method of control and the need to show one's work to the
head teacher should not be understated. Certainly, empirical
evidence from schools at a secondary level would suggest that
the timetable may be regarded as the institutional mainspring.

What has not been mentioned so far is the task to which the
school as an institution directs itself. This may be defined as
attempting to provide within the classroom setting a situation
in which teaching or learning, or both, can be carried out
successfully. It is a pedagogic aim. It is almost one of attain-
ing pedagogical preparedness.

From our cursory consideration of the school as an institution we can postulate, somewhat crudely, stages of institutional
progress towards this end. At the lowest stage, a school that
lacks coherence and a sense of identity with the end may
demonstrate a number of disorders. Motivation on the part of
both the pupils and staff may be low, discipline poor and lessons
devoted to attempting to establish some sort of order. It may
be left to the individual to make of it what he can. Truancy and
staff turn-over may be high. At a second stage, the school may
feel that it has realized itself in institutional terms. It is what
the outsider might consider to be a well run school. The pupils
may be uniformed and well behaved. There is a relaxed atmosphere, and the various disciplines are well established. Tradition seems to be an important factor. Everyone appears to be
busy and to know what they are about. The third stage is somewhat more difficult to describe. In a way, it can best be per-

ceived by setting it against the second level. A school that
has developed a highly acceptable self-image may be reluctant
to meet change. To take an extreme example, if a school is
examination-orientated and wishes as many pupils as possible
to pass on to the more traditional universities, it already has
a framework within which it can find an institutional definition.
In such a situation knowledge may be perceived in a highly
factual and specialized way. To suggest that it is otherwise
would be to threaten the whole institutional framework. The
third stage, then, may be partly idealistic, but envisage the
school as being pedagogically open. In a sense all the three
stages are ideal types, in that they rarely occur in a pure
form. Because a school has problems of identity, it might be
pedagogically open to innovation, though perhaps unable to
sustain it. In the same way, a grammar school going comprehensive may have a well established traditional structure
within which an intrusion of non-academic pupils causes conflict. Also, a particular class studied by the researcher may
be atypical of the school as a whole. Nevertheless, these
stages, which for convenience we can refer to as those of
conflict, institution and pedagogy, do begin to provide us
with a workable structure, by means of which it may be possible to begin an interpretation of case study data.

To build such a structure further requires that we consider
another educational dimension which relates much more fully to
pedagogy. So far we have provided only a one-dimensional
model based on the school as an institution. It is now necessary
to look at the knowledge that enters the school and the way in
which it does so. As Stenhouse (1967) notes:

> What are we to say about the culture of educational groups?
> First, educational groups are formed as a matter of policy
> with the defined objective of initiating pupils or students
> into culture. Because society does not provide, as a matter
> of common experience, the group affiliations which would
> transmit all the cultural understandings we should wish,
> we form specialized groups to take over the task. Educators
> are responsible for controlling the experience of these
> groups. (p. 56)

Teachers in a sense, then, may be regarded, to use a term
taken from communication theory, as gatekeepers. Pedagogy is
essentially concerned with communication. To the educational
practitioner, himself trained within a particular discipline, this
may seem obvious. To the geographer, historian or mathemati-
cian, what he is about makes good sense. They would not quarrel with the general term 'culture' to cover these multifarious
activities. Yet things may not be as simple as they seem. The
teacher in a primary school is often bewildered by the inability
of certain children to grasp the chronological aspect of historical
events. It usually ends up by the pupils collectively, and under

the guidance of the teacher, painting a frieze which is finally
hung around the classroom. The pupils are then invited to
leave their desks or work places and make a journey through
time by walking in a defined way round the room chaperoned
by the teacher. Ignoring the skill of the teacher in handling
the situation, why should this be? It takes considerable mental
effort to realize that the problem in part may be created by
the teacher's view of knowledge. Why should isolated events
which occurred over a vast span of time be threaded together
in this way? How does one thread together events that happen
simultaneously but are discrete? What we are concerned with
is not so much events but the way in which historians interpret
them. To say that an Iron Age hill fort has been at the bottom
of the garden since one was a boy is a perfectly sensible statement, but it is not an historical one except in a loose sense.
Disciplines are concerned with interpretations; they are methods
of perception. As such they are highly abstract - so abstract,
in fact, that it takes considerable effort to make these interpretations available to the pupil. Visits to the 'real world' by
school groups are carried out in a highly formalized way. Reality in history, geography, science or religious instruction has
all the artifice of dramatic reality. Pedagogy is concerned with
communicating to the pupils methods by which they can make
use of these interpretations in making sense of the world
around and within them. Particular difficulty is likely to be
experienced when the school seeks to absorb a new area of
interest. Pedagogy has not only to communicate an interpretative structure, but also to construct it as it goes along. This
is particularly relevant when considering teaching about race
relations.

The two dimensions of our framework, the school as an institution and pedagogy as a process of construction, need to be
brought together into a composite whole in order to provide a
suitable model against which to attempt to understand what happens in schools and classrooms. The deficiencies of it as a
theoretical tool are not to be denied. Aspects of education such
as pastoral care, for example, are not included. Such a model
is also very difficult to visualize two-dimensionally. A way of
doing this might be to speak of educational co-ordinates or a
typology, and by using a matrix to make findings over a number
of schools representationally meaningful. Another method might
be by use of analogy. If education mirrors culture, and the
culture within which present schools developed was a colonial
one, might not the structure be fleshed out as an example of
internal colonization? This suggestion might seem to be rather
far-fetched, but would not be regarded as such by at least
one eminent historian. Here it is proposed to leave any possible
theoretical inference to others better qualified, and to see how
far what has been conceived, with all its inadequacies, may be
used to interpret practice. The purpose of such a model when
proposed was to do no more than this. In turn, a study of

classroom practice may lead us towards a more robust theory. The next four chapters are therefore devoted to studying aspects of teaching about race relations in the light of what has been said so far. For this purpose, reference will be made to four schools. Lesson extracts cannot be too lengthy, but it is hoped that they will be sufficient to allow the reader to make his own interpretation if he wishes to do so.

11 CASE STUDY 1: STRATEGY A

Robert D. Wild

It was a traditional girls' grammar school with a high academic reputation. As such, it attracted pupils from a wide area. Now it is in the process of becoming comprehensive, and as a result the catchment area has been reduced somewhat. The school is located on the outskirts of a large conurbation. An arterial road passes close by. Well kept parks give it almost the atmosphere of being within a green belt, marking off the city from the dormitory towns beyond. Housing is estate, both private and council. As population has moved further out from the conurbation there is a sense in which the estates, built in the 1920s and 1930s, have been left behind. Elsewhere, the phrase 'lacking a pulse' has been employed to describe this. The school is an imposing building, red brick and porticoed, within its own acres. Over a thousand pupils attend the school, of which only 5-10 per cent may be classified as coloured. These are mainly of Asian origin. There is some correlation between the comprehensive intake and the latter.

The headmistress is an imposing figure. To her, the school is her school. To make sense of what goes on in the school, therefore, one has to begin by considering the headmistress. This is no easy task, as she is an extremely complex person. Depending upon the viewpoint taken, she might be regarded as liberal and humane or as authoritarian and dogmatic. For example, her study is next door to the staffroom: this can be seen in terms of facilitating communication or as a means of keeping a watching brief on the activities of the staff. Similarly, all matters, both large and small, must proceed through the headmistress. One could cite examples ad nauseam. What is important is to realize how far the influence of the headmistress seems to permeate every aspect of the school. She seems to perceive her role in both a traditional and an innovatory way. While seeking to emulate all that is best in educational practice, there is the need to fashion it to fit her own situation as she sees it. Concern is with the individual and how best each may realize her potential. Academic studies are regarded both as a liberating force and as a means towards excellence. There is even an element of women's emancipation if not liberation. On one occasion the headmistress encouraged Muslim girls in the upper part of the school to read the Koran, something unusual for females in their culture. These are examples that have a bearing, however indirect, on race relations. In a wider sense, she is fully supportive of anything that will further the development of her

girls. At a personal level, she expects to know all her colleagues and pupils and for them, in turn, to know her.

The headmistress appears to be somewhat wary of influences
directly intruding from outside. Outsiders, she feels, do not
understand what is being attempted in the school. At the same
time, they may threaten to disrupt, particularly in terms of
academic excellence. As already suggested, the headmistress's
philosophy lays stress on individual worth. The sociologist
therefore, as a possible dehumanizing social mechanic, may be
seen to challenge the integrity of the human psyche. The
researcher in education, as far as he is perceived to be of this
kind, is likely to have difficulty in gaining access to the
school. In any case, the headmistress sees research as something which, in the order of things, should be undertaken by
the school itself, in order to better excellence. Yet at the same
time she is pleased to share her findings of what is going on
with outsiders. From what has been said, it will be seen, that
she is deeply committed to what she is doing at both a rational
and an emotional level. It is possible that her enthusiasm may
sometimes spill into too many areas at the same time, and that
the staff as a result are unable to keep up in the sense of
comprehending what is intended. In summarizing the stance
taken by the headmistress, it can be suggested that she perceives herself as a progressive educationalist, willing to innovate where necessary in order to maintain and broaden academic
standards.

Originally, four teachers were to be involved in the project.
In the event, two taught about race relations. Both teachers
seemed to embody the values expressed by the headmistress.
This may be partly because both held posts of responsibility
and one in particular worked closely with the headmistress in
the area of curriculum development. Teaching took place at the
fourth-year level. During the experiment an 'incident' took
place involving one of the teachers. In this context we are not
directly concerned with what happened, though passing mention
may be made. The incident took place in a fifth-year group
discussing truancy, not in a session directly related to the
teaching about race relations. Details are uncertain but seem to
involve the white majority of the class verbally attacking a
small group of Pakistani girls and the subsequent defacing of
a folder.

The brief quotation given on p. 112 in Chapter 10 represents
the opening of a lesson given by the other teacher and is directly relevant to what we are considering. In fact, the lesson, as
it replicates many others, is worth looking at in some detail. A
useful point to begin is from where the previous dialogue
finished:

TEACHER: Right. Let's hear all the views that you've all
    made....Would you like to say what your group decided?
PUPIL 3: First, the child would have to get the parent in a

good mood.

PUPIL 4: After that, ask questions about other people on race marriage, not alone. The mother or parent must either agree or disagree. In this case the parent agreed. The couple would have to decide where they get married and the guests might disagree. They might have to go to another country or get some consent. If they both, boy and girl, love each other a lot, the boy or the girl would have to change religion and be one religion. If they don't want to be separated, the parents can't do much about it, because if the girl and the boy love each other a lot the parents can't separate them at all. It, it would have to be settled and agreed with, the, both parents that they agree with the marriage.

PUPIL 3: If they agree, they can change their religion and live together. If the parents disagree the children might run away and live together without getting married, until their parents agreed to let them marry each other.

PUPIL 4: We agree with mixed marriage, we agree with changing religion, different costumes, different food and not eating meat or anything...agree with all the above notice.

PUPIL 3: No.

TEACHER: Right. Third group, would you like to start?

PUPIL 5: This is about a mother and her daughter discussing the twenty-year-old daughter's getting married to a Pakistani man and is putting the problems she'll have to take.

PUPIL 6: 'Mum, I've got to ask you for some advice.'

PUPIL 5: 'Go ahead then.'

PUPIL 6: 'But I don't know how to, how you will take it.'

PUPIL 5: 'Well, try me and see.'

PUPIL 6: 'Well, the problem is, I'd like to get married to a Pakistani boy.'

PUPIL 5: 'Well, how do you think it will work out? What about religion?'

PUPIL 6: 'I would learn Pakistani religion like my future husband had to when he was young.'

PUPIL 5: 'Do you think you would be happy?'

PUPIL 6: 'We shall have to try and see.'

PUPIL 5: 'Well the truth is, do you really love him?'

PUPIL 6: 'Yes, I love him very much.'

PUPIL 5: 'Would a white girl be allowed to live and associate with a Pakistani family?'

PUPIL 6: 'Well, I've been in there before and their parents like me.'

PUPIL 5: 'Would you have to wear a sari?'

PUPIL 6: 'I would take the responsibilities of...wearing them while in the street.'

PUPIL 5: 'Well, if you think that is best - that is, best for you well, there's nothing I can do to stop you from marrying him.'

PUPIL 6: 'Thanks a lot. Would you like to meet him?'

PUPIL 5: 'Yes. I'd like that very much.'

PUPIL 6: 'Well, I've just got one problem.'
PUPIL 5: 'And what is that?'
PUPIL 6: 'What is father going to say about this?'
PUPIL 5: 'Leave it to me....I will speak to your father and
  sort things out for you.'
PUPIL 6: 'Thanks mum.'

So far, the pupils are attempting to build towards the concepts used in race relations by reference to their own real or
supposed experiences. How their parents will react to the boy
who they eventually wish to marry is likely to be pertinent to
the thinking of girls of this age. Genuine love is seen as the
solvent to overcome all possible problems. The pupils are therefore primarily concerned with making their own feelings explicit
to themselves. The language indicates this. They are not liable
to conceptualize meaningfully in any other sense. Too great a
degree of abstraction is required at this stage. The issues that
race might provoke are nowhere approached. At best, superficial mention is made. Admittedly, one of the later groups
brings up the problem of the half-caste child resulting from a
mixed marriage, but what it might 'get called by the people'
is the only comment made. The teacher seems perturbed that
racial issues are not formalizing themselves within the group:

TEACHER: Right. Well I must say that I'm quite surprised with
  the results of these five discussions we've had, that few of
  you seem to see any great problems or, if you do see it, you
  don't express it very strongly. Now you've heard the views
  of everybody, would you like to comment on some of those
  views? Would you want me to run through summarizing?

(Long pause)

The discussion that follows is intermittent and shortlived. The
teacher then abruptly changes the structure of the session by
the introduction of written evidence. Explicitly, this is to
further the exploration of marriage between black and white:

TEACHER: OK, could we pause there. Um, would anyone like
  to comment on that section?
PUPIL 1: Her parents didn't like, um, mixed marriages.
TEACHER: But...
PUPIL 4: She didn't say that...just never met one....
TEACHER: Oh!
PUPIL 1: Just don't like him at all you see.
TEACHER: Where is that...where does it say they don't like
  him?
PUPIL 4: They don't, it, it doesn't say they don't like him,
  they're just kind, just they don't want to, like, have her
  marrying him.
TEACHER: Mmm. Would anyone else like to comment on that?...

saying that it doesn't say she doesn't like them, but there's this feeling that they don't like the Negro. Right...would you like to read?

PUPIL 2: 'Our pub...'

TEACHER: (prompting) 'Our public appearances'

PUPIL 2: 'Our public appearances were greeted with indifference in'

TEACHER: (prompting) 'university'

PUPIL 2: What?

TEACHER: (prompting) 'university'

PUPIL 2: 'University cities and the only place our...'

PUPIL 4: (prompting) 'partnership'

PUPIL 2: 'partnership'

PUPIL 3: (prompting) 'regularly provoked'

PUPIL 2: 'regularly provoked more than simple...'

TEACHER: (prompting) 'curiosity'

PUPIL 2: 'curiosity was in London. Possibly it was...'

TEACHER: (prompting) 'naive'

PUPIL 2: 'naive of us to hold hands in Notting Hill, but we only needed to visit friends...'

TEACHER: (prompting) 'there'

PUPIL 2: 'there to hear sh...'

TEACHER: (prompting) 'shouts'

PUPIL 2: 'shouts of assor...'

TEACHER: (prompting) 'assorted'

PUPIL 2: 'assorted'

TEACHER: (prompting) 'yobs'

PUPIL 2: 'Yobs, yobs go...'

TEACHER: (prompting) 'Go and — your own kind'

PUPIL 2: 'Go and — your own kind, and other in...'

TEACHER: (prompting) 'uninventive'

PUPIL 2: 'uninventive results'

TEACHER: (prompting) 'insults'. Right. ... Oh, you said you didn't want to read.... Would you like to read?

PUPIL 1: 'Gradually we incurred a freak novelty value in university society and were often invited to dinner by people who would never have bothered with us individually. We were always unofficially guests of honour on such occasions, the hostess invariably...' (pauses)

TEACHER: (prompting) 'invariably introducing us'

PUPIL 1: 'introducing us with a "Look what I've caught" sort of air. These dinner parties were usually embarrassing because of the clumsy tact with which any topical...'

TEACHER: (prompting) 'topic remotely'

PUPIL 1: 'remotely con, connected with race was considered unmensunable...'

TEACHER: (correcting) 'unmentionable'

PUPIL 1: 'unmentionable'

The session continues in this fashion for some considerable time before petering out. It has become a reading exercise rather than anything directly relating to race relations. Certain comments by pupils might, if taken out of context, seem to indicate an attitude towards prejudice, but given the lesson extracts above, their significance would seem to be slight. What does come over if the full transcript is read is the sheer tedium. As soon as one piece of evidence has been correctly read and a few points taken up, another is taken up and used in the same way. It is no wonder, if one can say this without losing a research position, that one pupil interrupts another reading with the exclamation 'it's boring'. The transcripts of other sessions and the teacher's own notes support the view that this one is fairly typical. The term started with an introductory discussion concerning the worthwhileness of dealing with race relations. The second session involved a piece of written work by the pupils defining such terms as 'prejudice' and 'race'. By the third session the pupils were already immersed in attempting to read a quite difficult piece of material. It is worth giving the teacher's own comments here:

Purpose of selection - a provocative article should produce issues.

Pupil response - the group read this right through although this took four periods (40 minutes each) with a week's gap in the middle. I thought the group very restrained, in view of the provocative statements, and I was surprised at the persistence with which they tackled the article, discussing sections as they read. In retrospect this section of work set the pattern....The pattern seemed to be restrained interest, a willingness to listen and a few strongly expressed outbursts, but all the time I had a feeling that the girls were not as direct as they had been in other...discussions on Sex and Family.

The session which then followed was the one from which extracts have been reproduced here. This was followed by an examination within CSE Mode 3. Again, to make reference to the teacher's notes:

1. Written work - prior to seeing 'evidence'. Should immigrant groups seek to integrate in their new country? Consider this in relation to religion and education.
2. Evidence and Discussion Session
    'Muslim's single sex row may spread from Bradford', *Times Educational Supplement*, 11.1.74.
3. Written work - arising from discussion which, unfortunately is very faint (further taping problems).
    (i) 'If they choose to come here they should mix with us.' Comment.
    (ii) 'If immigrant groups have their own schools

they will be better off. So will we.' Discuss
these comments.
(iii) Would such segregation help or hinder race
relations?
4.   Taped talks by individuals. (Most chose mixed
marriage.)
All this took ages.

By this stage in teaching about race relations the teacher
observes that interest within the group was flagging. The session following the examination was marked by discord. The
pupils were far more animated than before, at times noisy, but
the cause of this was less in terms of pursuing a topic than in
intimating a desire to do something other than race relations.
Pupils argued that to continue was unfair to the Pakistanis in
the group - 'everything we've done is against coloured people,
not done anything against white people'. How far this reflects
a growing awareness of racial issues or was done to protect
members of the group is an open question. It could also reflect
a sense of boredom and frustration felt by the pupils in
pedagogical terms. The latter is the suggestion offered here.
The result was a change of teaching style on the part of the
teacher. Improvised drama of a kind was used to explore a white
colonial situation. The numerical difference was stressed in
dividing up the group and the white minority protected their
interests by barricading themselves behind desks and chairs.
A later session involved going round the school interviewing
other pupils, mainly coloured, to get their opinions. This
produced an interesting essay by a Ugandan Asian who had
recently arrived in this country. Otherwise pupils did not
respond in any real sense to the questions posed by the group.
    How is one to interpret what happened with this particular
group in the school? The teacher had her own explanation to
offer:

There has been great pressure to examine mixed marriages
but I was disappointed in the group's response to this area
of study in view of initial enthusiasm. I think this may have
been my fault. The post-exam period was very busy and...
was being squeezed out of my preparation schedule by
marking 'mock' exams. Films, external speakers, would
have helped had I the time to organize this. The group discussions - threes and fours - which I tried produced rather
stilted responses.

Absence - Flu - Discontinuity.

In view of the composition of the group, the stilted response
is difficult to account for:

Six Asians - Pakistani and Ugandan Asians.
Two or three of these are voluble, articulate and very
willing to talk.

A half-caste West Indian/English girl - popular - ... -
strong sense of social justice.

These influences in the group have been strong voices
for moderation, balance.

Three of the white girls have since expressed a very
strong dislike of immigrants. However, of the three one
has been in hospital since January, one is indolent and
the third very shy in discussion and said little until
side 6.

The six remaining English girls include two regular
truants, one who is articulate, sensitive and rarely in
school. One articulate, moderate, liberal, etc. One very
silent, very shy.

One is tempted to fall back on the explanation that members
of the group were involved in an elaborate strategy to protect
each other. As the area is race relations, this has a certain
appeal. In research one is encouraged to doubt the obvious.
It may be wise to follow the same rule in interpreting data. From
the lesson extracts given here there is no real evidence to
support this explanation. The further knowledge that the teacher was attempting to use the Humanities Curriculum Project
approach in teaching is interesting. At the conference preceding
the experimental term, she showed perhaps greater emotional
commitment to this as an approach than anybody else present.
Yet the sessions with her group indicate almost an inversion of
the approach, in that discussion seems to be supporting evidence rather than evidence being impartially fed in to stimulate
discussion. One might argue that she was inexperienced in the
method, being trained only immediately prior to the experimental
term. This is true, and suggests that the group having only
had a term beforehand to develop the HCP methodology with a
possibly inexperienced teacher (in the method, that is) would
demonstrate procedural difficulties. This they do. Again, the
material on mixed marriages given by the project to the teachers
could be criticized on the grounds that the reading level
required was too high. The teacher herself made this point,
but surprisingly, in supplementing the pack from her own
sources, basically chose the 'Guardian' and the 'Times Educational Supplement' (see examinations). It is hard to understand why she should persevere with using difficult material
when she obviously knew that some of the group, at least,
had considerable reading problems.
Perhaps this is the point at which to return to our theoretical
model in the hope that we may attempt an interpretation, however fragile. To consider the dimensions of the school first,

it has much to offer in terms of excellence and is well aware of
the fact. Because of the headmistress and the traditions, the
school is highly conscious of itself at an institutional level. Yet
it seeks more than this. By researching itself it wishes to carry
its achievements further. In this sense the school believes itself
to be pedagogically open. But here a problem arises. Innovation
must not change the school; rather, the school must change
innovation. Pupils need to excel in the traditional disciplines in
order to realize themselves, and the headmistress must remain
the fulcrum of the institution. HCP may have been perceived by
the school as offering something of excellence to the less able
pupils. It might be more than that in the sense that the underlying educational values of the approach seemed to chime in with
those held by the headmistress. In any case, it is now useful to
consider the teacher with reference to what has been said. Given
the school background, it it likely that she wishes to lead the
pupils towards excellence. Her expectancies are therefore those
of a grammar school teacher facing a fourth-year class.

The other dimension of the model can usefully be brought in
here. It has already been suggested that the pupils are trying,
at a very simple level, to articulate to themselves and others
something of their feelings about race relations. It is done in a
personal and anecdotal way. They are seeking to develop the
linguistic and conceptual tools which will allow them to build
towards something that they do not understand. The pupils are
on the lower rungs of a conceptual ladder, so to speak. The
teacher seems to be elsewhere. Her expectations relate more to
fourteen-year-olds who have already had three years in which
to fashion abstracts as meaningful in the traditional subject
areas. She seems almost impatient with them for being unable to
speak in the right way and thereby bring up the right issues.
The evidence she selects, in for example the case of mixed
marriages, may not simply have been chosen for relevance: it
focuses on what the teacher would consider to be conceptually
correct. Hence the mismatch that runs through the extracts.
The pupils become increasingly bored and reluctant, while the
teacher pushes more and more material in, in order to realize
her intention. Eventually, the teacher is forced to cede to the
demands of the pupils.

This interpretation is no more than it pretends to be. How
far it may be useful to measure case study against such a model
is for the reader to decide. In any case, the example of one
school is hardly sufficient to reach any conclusions. We therefore move on to consider the next school.

12 CASE STUDY 2: STRATEGY A

Robert D. Wild

This school, like the previous one, is located on the outskirts of a large conurbation and has over a thousand pupils, of which about 10 per cent are coloured. Here similarities tend to fall away. It is a comprehensive school but has passed through the phase of being a secondary modern. The original building on the site began as a central high school in the 1930s. By becoming officially a comprehensive school in the mid-1950s it seems to have lost something of its earlier academic status. For ten years it functioned as a secondary modern school, despite the label. Only since 1967 has it begun to fulfil the comprehensive intention. Two further buildings erected on the site in the early 1960s have increased the facilities offered by the school. It takes both boys and girls and had at the time of the experiment developed a sixth form of approaching ninety students. The school as a unit is embedded in an extensive complex of pre-war council estate development on garden city principles with some private housing. Smaller developments and in-filling has occurred since the war. Inevitably, amenities are limited, shop footage, for example, being dependent upon the size of the various estates. For adults public houses strategically placed and social clubs offer some sort of community focus. A number of youth clubs attempt to meet the needs of the youngsters. There is a reasonably good transport service allowing quick access to the inner city and readily available amenities. From what has been said, it would seem reasonable to suggest that the school intake reflects a wide variety of parental backgrounds. Again, the coloured intake is less homogeneous than in the case of school A. It includes pupils of West Indian, African and Chinese origin as well as Asians. Quite a number are British by birth.

A conspicuous feature of the school is the social consciousness and conscience felt and expressed by senior members of the staff. This may in part reflect the school's own history and the multifarious needs of the area that it serves. A school that has both lost and gained academic status can be expected to show educational sensitivity: 'This school is now truly comprehensive for the first time and I see no reason why we shall not be compared favourably with any comprehensive school in the country.'

There are many clubs and societies in the school, which also has a particular interest shown in the Duke of Edinburgh award scheme. There is a well developed house system (up to the fourth year), and senior staff have been appointed to extend

pastoral care into the upper school, to oversee homework with
under-achieving pupils and to care for maladjusted pupils.
Nevertheless, the intake of more able pupils means that the
improvement of academic standards is a major concern, with
GCE entries beginning to vie with those for CSE. These facts
in themselves, however, do not fully explain the social consciousness expressed above. To attempt a fuller explanation,
one must delve deeper into the organization of the school and
make mention of certain personalities.

Where possible, responsibility for running the school is
given to the pupils. This is attempted through a school council
as well as by an executive committee in the sixth form which
has regular meetings with the headmaster. The purpose of
such councils and committees is something more than a gesture
in terms of public relations or in democratizing the school.
The deputy head, who was in fact acting head during the
experimental term, and the senior mistress believe that the
task of the school is to prepare the pupils - one might almost
say arm them - to meet whatever awaits them in the wider
society outside the school. Hence the sense of social consciousness which pervades the school. Hence the councils and so on.
At the moment the school is very concerned to develop mixed-
ability teaching in the first year with a view to considering
its extension to the second and third years. Again, the social
implications of this must be viewed not simply as a response to
an edict from above, or to educational fashion, but in terms
of the school's own declared purpose. Indeed, the school agreed
only to participate in the project because the improvement of
race relations was seen to have social implications. How far the
intention implicit in the approach might actually improve race
relations was left as an open question, but from the educational standpoint the school felt that it should be given a try.

It is interesting to note that, as in the case of school A,
the teachers involved were senior members of staff. Two were
heads of department and the third was the senior mistress
(owing in part to the illness of another senior staff member).
Before the experimental term, a letter was sent to the parents
of pupils likely to be involved, offering to withdraw any whose
parents objected. No objections were received. A meeting was
called to give the parents further information, but none
attended. The teaching strategy adopted with all groups was
that based on the approach of the Humanities Curriculum Project. Of the three groups that took part, one is of particular
interest here because of the way in which the composition of
the group seems to have influenced the form of the sessions
and ultimately the way in which race relations was perceived.
It must be emphasized that the deputy head did not consider
the group to be 'typical' of the school. To say what is typical
of a school is obviously very difficult. The audio-tapes of the
other two groups do not demonstrate the particular problems
associated with this group. Despite the possible atypicality of

the group, it does throw up certain issues which it would seem
a pity to lose if one is attempting to study the problems and
effects of teaching about race relations. Hence the choice, and
we hope that the reasons for it will become somewhat clearer
as we proceed. The best method of considering the group would
seem to be by starting with a brief personal sketch of each
member contributed by the teacher.

BARRY

A large, affable, easy-going individual. Dominant in the
group and highly sceptical about HCP methods. Impatient
with evidence and 'impartiality'. Enjoys provoking the
chairman, e.g. starting a petition to dispose of me - but
not very serious (I think!). Often makes provocative statements, e.g. 'All Irish are bastards', but in discussion
sometimes reveals more complex attitudes. Has very little
time for the girls in the group - or for a female chairman.
His mother is part German, and other members of the
group refer to this when retaliating to his teasing. An
Irish family live next door to him, which may have contributed to his violent prejudice against the Irish.
Attendance - 20/22

TIM

Pleasant manner - more serious and reflective than some of
the others - but not above joining in many diversions. Well
motivated towards HCP, and enjoys the discussions when
they go well (by our standards). He acted uncharacter-
istically when I had him on a 'chit' in a different group but
apologized at the beginning of the next HCP lesson - possibly under threat from the Head of House! He seems to me
much more tolerant than Barry, but sometimes gives way to
him in discussion.
Attendance - 20/22

PAUL

Aggressively self-confident with a rather condescending air
that upsets some of the group members. He is very domineer-
ing and is said to resemble his father in this. His family background is rather disturbed - as is indicated on some of the
tapes I think. His father is now very ill and he is clearly
anxious about this - he is often absent from school to help
...when his father is in hospital. He is given a lot of responsibility in the school which he sometimes abuses by being
rather violent (in my opinion). There is a violent antipathy
between Paul and Ann because of a fight between Paul and
Ann's boyfriend. This flared up in our very first discussion.
I am not sure how much of the anti-Semitism expressed in
the group is really just reaction to Paul's personality. I find
Paul difficult to control in discussion, because his opinions
annoy me and his manner can be obnoxious. Barry has

interpreted this as anti-Semitism on my part. Paul clearly regards me as a useless chairman.
Attendance - 12/22

JOHN
Small, lively - he was in the remedial class but he doesn't seem remedial to me. His father is African but John is white although his brothers and sisters are coloured. He vacillates between being completely silly and remarkably thoughtful and observant. His comments on the pupils' tape seem to me to be very honest and critical. He's very friendly with Brian and inclined to take part in a comic 'double act', to the detriment of the discussions.
Attendance - 19/22

BRIAN
A slight, sensitive-looking half-caste boy. He looks slightly oriental (hence the 'Paki' teasing) but his father is West Indian. He was in the remedial class and seems to me to be badly handicapped by poor reading and a limited ability to express himself verbally. As a result, he often reacts with frustration to controversial points arising in discussion - shouting 'that's tight!' or something and unable to say why. I had a lot of trouble with him at first, which I suspected was partly due to the subject matter of the discussions. He has been teased and taunted about colour in the past, I think. I got the Deputy Head to ask him if he wanted to come out of the group, but to my amazement he said that he didn't. He's gradually settled down, but still has spells of destructive activity.
Attendance - 19/22

SANDRA
Small, pretty but a bit bedraggled-looking. Likes to appear 'hard'. I think she's had a very difficult home life (I had her in my tutor group in the first year when she was thin and pathetic and desperate for attention). She's lively in discussion but often difficult and perverse. She has a strong sense of injustice and seems to me to be aggressively tolerant! When she objects to a prejudiced view she will (ironically) shout 'Don't be Jewish!'. She tends, like Brian, to explode violently when she can't explain what she means. She is very candid at times and on one tape explains why she truants from HCP sometimes. She has a reputation for being difficult and for 'giving cheek'.
Attendance - 10/22

CHRISTINE
Very rarely speaks and has never made a real contribution to discussion, but does express her opinions in written work. Sits between Amanda and me. She does not seem to

be embarrassed or bored, but just chooses not to speak!
Attendance - 14/22

MARGARET
A small, cheerful girl - a bit 'prickly'. Teased terribly by
Barry until she decides to be quiet. She seems to enjoy the
discussions and often makes gallant efforts to contribute.
She tries hard for a while and then gives up! I find it
very difficult to control this situation and get the boys
to listen. I have a similar problem with Joyce whom the
boys also will not take seriously.
Attendance - 13/22

ANN
Pretty girl with a 'tough' image. She was sent to us from
another school because of some misdemeanour. When she
decides to take part, she is a good issue-generator, but
frequently she's either apathetic and dormant or else silly
and actively destructive. She has a violent aversion to
Paul and this hostility has interfered with some of the
discussions. She's friendly with Sandra and Clare.
Attendance - 17/22

JOYCE
Very immature and childish girl. Rather odd (hides things
and calls out the fire brigade). She has spells of incredibly
silly behaviour, but for most of the time is quiescent. She
tries to contribute to the discussions but she is so incoherent that the others - especially the boys - will not listen
to her. Often, with prompting and interpretation, her
observations are very much to the point, but they are frequently ignored. She, like Brian, will say 'that's tight' and
then be unable to go any further. She has moods when she
won't do anything.
Attendance - 15/22

AMANDA
More 'lady-like' than the rest of the girls! Quiet-spoken
and rather reserved. She will contribute to the discussion,
but does not assert herself. She used to contribute more
but now the boys tend to tease her and make her blush
(Paul is said to 'fancy' her and I suspect that Barry does
too, and this seems to be why they tease her!). The boys
clearly exclude Amanda (and possibly Christine) from
their view of the girls as a load of nuts and scrubbers!
She is noticeably more mature and law-abiding than the
other girls.
Attendance - 18/22

CLARE
Attractive half-caste girl - father from Africa, mother Irish.

Said by some staff to have a 'chip on her shoulder' (!).
Before we started I was warned that Clare might be very
touchy about colour, because she had been in other situations. However, I didn't find this - apart from a tendency
to explode rather violently into colourful language - a common practice in the group! She introduced a fresh element
into our discussions - having a harder, more realistic (in
my view) attitude to colour problems - it was a pity that
her attendance was poor. (Her truanting was from school,
not just the lesson, like Sandra.) I don't think that the
subject matter of the discussions bothered her much after
the first few lessons. Whatever else was wrong with our
group, I do think we managed to defuse the personal hostility to some extent.
Attendance - 10/22

JANET
Aggressive and tough - possibly fairly 'delinquent'.
Partner-in-crime with Sandra and Joyce in various mis-
deeds elsewhere in school, I suspect. Poor attendance -
possibly partly because of her near-illiteracy (my view).
She did contribute to discussions as the group atmosphere
improved to some extent.
Attendance - 11/22

It will be seen that the group composition is diverse. Three
members - Brian, John and Clare - may be regarded as
coloured. Another boy, Paul, is Jewish. Barry has a German
mother and Ann was born in Iran. Almost half the group, then,
share cultural, if not ethnic, diversity. Yet it would be wrong
to see differences within the group simply in these terms. A
diagram of the seating arrangements (as chosen by the pupils
themselves) reveals further considerations (Figure 12.1).

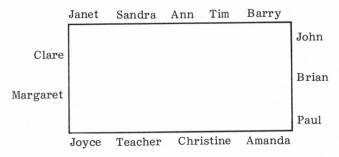

Figure 12.1

There is a distinct boy/girl division within the group. This
is not uncommon among fourth-year pupils in a school. Never-

theless, it does add another factor to an already complex situation. From the evidence so far provided by the profiles of
individuals and the seating arrangements we may attempt by
use of a sociogram to explore diversity even further (Figure
12.2). The sociogram suggests, as if we were not already
beginning to suspect, that the group is rent by animosities at
a personal level. The protagonists tend to face each other
across the table. It would not be going too far to suggest that
hardly anyone likes anyone else. Where they do, the feeling is
not always reciprocated. The dialogue between Barry and the
teacher is likely to provide the main axis of group dynamics.

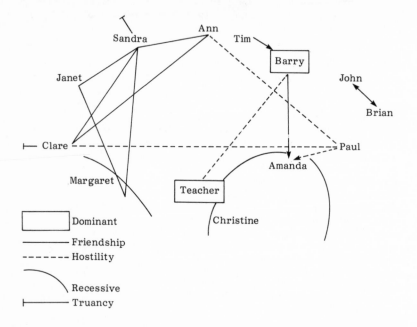

Figure 12.2

Barry, possibly because of his size and ability to vocalize, is
constantly making a bid for the leadership of the group. He
dislikes the girls and is able to out-vocalize all but the strongest personalities among them. Margaret and Joyce are thus
reduced to a state of frustrated incoherence. Inevitably, they
are likely to become increasingly recessive in terms of participation. The frequent absences of Clare and Sandra reduce
the possible contributions of the girls still further. Christine
and Amanda seem to feel misplaced in the group and hardly
contribute at all. In fact, later in the term they asked to be
removed from the group. This leaves Janet and Ann to take

the main brunt of the sarcasm instigated by Barry. Unfortunately, the teacher, besides being a head of department, is
also a female. This means that Barry is likely to resent her
both on the grounds of an authority position (and thereby a
challenge to his leadership of the group) and because of her
sex - she is likely, at least in his mind, to be in sympathy
with the girls. The boys show some ambivalence in their attitude towards Barry. Some, like Brian, may hope to usurp
Barry, but feel unable to do so. Paul certainly seems to feel
at least equal to Barry, but his manner sets the group against
him. Clare and Ann demonstrate a strong dislike, if not hatred,
of him. This really leaves John and Brian, both small and in
a sense inconsequential members of the group, particularly as
they have difficulty in vocalizing their feelings. To gain attention they are likely to resort to fooling about and disrupting
the proceedings.

To cope with a group of this nature would be a difficult task
for any teacher. Add the fact that the teacher is involved in
an educational experiment, and the task would seem to become
almost insurmountable. Certainly it is likely to stretch the
coping strategy of the teacher to the extreme. To attempt to
build group cohesion on the basis of realizing the needs of
the members of the group would seem to be a non-starter. Their
needs, as they would seem to perceive them, consist in scoring off each other. The reason for this may lie in the temporary
nature of the group, consisting as it seems to of problem pupils
from other classes. Indeed, the members, or at least some of
them, may see those sessions as cathartic - allowing them to
work out personal frustrations prohibited in other lesson situations. Add the absenteeism to the situation, so that group
composition is rarely constant, and the teacher's problems
become something that one would not envy.

To understand the implications of what has been said so far,
it is useful to look at an actual session and see how far the
conjectures made above are substantiated. For this purpose
extracts from an early session would seem suitable, in that the
basic framework taken up in later sessions is in the process of
being worked out. It should be noted that Sandra, Margaret
and Christine were absent from this session.

TEACHER: The second meeting of this group. We're going to
begin by looking at the minutes or the report on the last
meeting. I'll read them through and then if you want to
make any comment you can. Stop me if there's anything that's
not clear.
JANET: You haven't said what it's about, Miss.
TEACHER: Mm?
JANET: You haven't said what it's about, Miss.
TEACHER: Oh! HCP Race Relations. OK? Right. Report on the
first meeting. Can you look at these? While you look through
see if there's anything you don't, that you want to ask

about...

TEACHER: Report on the first meeting. The group members' records. That means it's for you to keep in your folder.

BARRY: Cor!

TEACHER: The following views and questions were raised by group members:
'What is race relations about?' which was raised by Ann.
Then suggestions which were made:
Other kinds of people - Jews, Pakistanis, etc.
Then somebody else asked, oh no, Ann asked 'What does prejudice mean?' And amongst the things that...

ANN: (interrupts) I never.

TEACHER: Well somebody did.

ANN: It was her.

TEACHER: Oh! It was Joyce. Right Joyce? (girls laugh) Then amongst the suggestions that were made were:
It's about other countries not getting on; people not liking other people, perhaps the Irish or the French, or English and Italians.

(inaudible comment)

TEACHER: Somebody said 'prejudice is stupid' and asked the group how they would feel if people were prejudiced against them.

(tape breaks)

TEACHER: Then somebody said 'all Jews have big noses', as we were talking about prejudice...

(interruption)

TEACHER: Somebody else asked 'Does it matter if they do; it's like coloured people having wide noses?'...Somebody said 'Countries don't naturally get on.' Somebody else disagreed and said 'That can't be true because countries depend on one another.' Someone said 'But surely Jewish means mean.' Someone else asked how could you find out if that was true. Someone said 'Well most Jews have money.' But someone said 'That's 'cos they work hard.' And then somebody else added 'Anyway people can be mean and not be Jews.'

ANN: Like these Americans aren't they?

TEACHER: Then the question was asked, 'What do immigrants have to do with race relations?' Someone said that they're the cause of all the trouble.

(comment: 'Yeh!')

TEACHER: Too much money has been spent on them...

BOY: (interrupts) They are.

TEACHER: But someone else said that they thought they worked for their money like anyone else.

(muttering)

TEACHER: Which of the things that were raised in the last meeting would you like to go on talking about? Are there any comments about what I've read out in these minutes?

BARRY: They're daft, Miss.

TEACHER: Can, can you go, can you explain what you mean, Barry?

BARRY: All this about Jews got big noses. Who said that?

CLARE: If you knew any Jews...

BARRY: Ann. Try her's for size.

ANN: No

BARRY: Miss, the Indians have got as bigger noses as Jews have.

ANN: Not like you...

TEACHER: Will you two listen please to the discussion that's starting?

(noise)

TEACHER: Now, what do other people think about what...

(noise)

TEACHER: What do other people think?

CLARE: All big heads are Jews.

BARRY: Immigrants are the cause of all the trouble. There!

TEACHER: Joyce, Joyce just said white people are the same as black. What do other people think?

AMANDA: Yes.

PAUL: I agree.

BARRY: Talk about the Irishmen.

TEACHER: Paul's just asked a question. Can you ask it a bit louder, Paul, so that the rest can hear?

PAUL: I can't be bothered now. I don't know, I've forgotten what I said.

BARRY: He ses, 'Why are some people white and some people black?'

TEACHER: Why are people, some people black and some white?

JOHN: Hah! Been in the sun too long.

CLARE: (laughs) Been in the country long enough.

TEACHER: What do other people think of that?

PAUL: It depends what countries they are though.

JOHN: Yeah. I mean some countries do, some countries don't.

BRIAN: Most of it's daft. Israel (mutters).

PAUL: It's only the Arabs that don't get on.

BARRY: The Arabs are...
PAUL: What about Sudan and Libya, who are joined, two coun-
   tries into one middle...
TEACHER: As an example of countries that do get on?
TEACHER: Can anyone think of an example? Paul's thought
   of an example showing that countries do get on. Can any-
   one think of an example showing that they don't?
JOYCE: They don't.
TEACHER: Well, can anybody suggest an example that might
   be evidence to support that?
CLARE: The Irish and the English don't.
BARRY: Well we don't like navvies.
CLARE: Shut your gob, you.

   (laughter)

TEACHER: Why do you say, why do you say that? What um,
   what evidence have you got to say that?...Well, right,
   then, anybody else suggest why Clare says the Irish and
   the English don't get on. What evidence can we...

TEACHER: Do other people think this?
BARRY: We have to send over the troops.
CLARE: You don't have to.
BARRY: Of course we do.
CLARE: You don't have to at all.
BARRY: You can't have England ignoring...
CLARE: You don't have to, do you?
BARRY: (inaudible)
CLARE: Oh shut your gob, you!
JOHN: Besides, if they'd keep to their own part of the country.
TEACHER: Do most people agree with John? John say, John,
   say what you were going to say so that people can hear it.
JOHN: England should keep to their country and the Irish to
   theirs.

   ('noise)

TEACHER: Do...but...

   (noise)

BARRY: What should happen is this, they should bring out all
   the English troops out of Ireland...
PAUL: I'll tell you another thing, there's Hong Kong. Doesn't
   it, Miss? Hong Kong belongs to England?

   (chatter)

JOYCE: Finish the Irish off.

(chatter - inaudible)

TEACHER: We've, when we were talking about, Sh - Ann, Ann
   do you want to add something?
ANN: No. (yawns)
TEACHER: When we were talking about war we got on to the
   subject of Ireland and we didn't have any evidence. Do you
   still want to see, urm, in race relations, to talk about the
   English and the Irish?
CLARE: Yeah
JOHN: Yes
BRIAN: Oh yes.
BARRY: Oh no, not the navvies.

(inaudible)

TEACHER: Joyce come on, listen.
ANN: Miss, can I say summat?
TEACHER: Yes, go on Ann.
ANN: Do you know those Ugandan Asians?
TEACHER: Just a minute. Shush!
BARRY: All the Ugandan Asians what come over to here make
   an army and send them over...
JOYCE: I'm thinking.
ANN: I know but they were...

(inaudible)

TEACHER: Let Ann come in, Clare.
ANN: Miss, he's interrupting me.
TEACHER: Yes, yes quite right. Paul, Ann was going to say
   something about the Ugandan Asians, if Clare wants to come
   in afterwards there'll be ample time. Go on, Ann.

(interruptions)

ANN: No other country would take them would they? So we had
   to take them.
JOYCE: Ah well said Clare.
TEACHER: What do other people think about what Ann said, 'No
   other country would take them'?

CLARE: What yer looking at me Tim for when anybody ses
   owt?
BARRY: (laughs)
CLARE: You heard...

(interruptions)

(interruptions)

TEACHER: Sh! Do people agree that there's a lot of prejudice against the Irish?
ANN: What's stupid about them?

TEACHER: Do other people think that Barry answered Ann's question? She wants to know why he doesn't like the Irish.
BARRY: ...for a start...

(interruption)

TEACHER: Go on, Barry.
ANN: They're just the same, aren't they?

(interruption)

ANN: I want to know my question.
TEACHER: Barry, try and make your ideas a bit clearer and then if John wants to come in afterwards...

(interruptions)

BARRY: Well you can see the difference can't yer?
VOICES: No we can't.
CLARE: You can see the difference in other people but not in Irish.
TEACHER: Can you give, can you give examples of, to make it practically clearer?
BARRY: They look a bit mad don't they?

(interruption)

BARRY: You never see an Irish Mick in, in an office, do you?
CLARE: Never see a chimp, do you?

(interruption)

TEACHER: Never see Irish - Sh! Now we agreed not to make fun, didn't we?
CLARE: I don't care.
TEACHER: You were saying you never see Irish people working in an office.
BARRY: No, they're always out - shovelling.
CLARE: Yeah, they're doing your dirty work, aren't they?
BARRY: I know. That's why, that's a difference.
JOYCE: They road sweep.
BARRY: All the buildings going up here...

JOHN: Every country is different from another.
PAUL: Not really...
CLARE: What do you mean, habits and that?

(interruption)

CLARE: Are you trying to tell me my mam's got dirty habits?
BARRY: Shut up.
CLARE: 'Cause she hasn't, mate.
TEACHER: Well look, if Clare...
BARRY: I know...
TEACHER: Clare's going to give you some...
CLARE: You shut up Tim, you big-headed...
TIM: We're talking about the Irish.
TEACHER: Yes, well we're discussing Clare, we're discuss-
  ing...
CLARE: Well, me mam's Irish isn't she?
BARRY: ...we didn't...
TEACHER: Well listen, we've agreed not to discuss people we
  know, haven't we? Now, if you wish to give examples of
  kinds of Irish habits you don't like, and Clare wishes to
  give us some information that she might know about the way
  the Irish behave, then we can. But we can't have people
  calling one another names.

(interruption)

TEACHER: There are too many people in this group who can
  be name-called against.
JOHN: You what?
TEACHER: Are you prepared, Clare, to, um, if you disagree
  with Barry and you think he's wrong then just explain why,
  giving your reasons rather than shouting.

(Clare interrupts)

She's quite, she's quite...

(boy interrupts)

CLARE: I still can't understand what's different about us.
TEACHER: Let's...
BARRY: Tell me...

(inaudible)

TEACHER: Janet thinks they're the same. Could you, could
  you say a bit more why? What makes, what makes you feel
  the Irish and the English are the same?
JANET: They are.
CLARE: Live in the same country, don't they?
JANET: They're the same.
BARRY: Oh shut up! If they don't know now they never will.
TEACHER: Well look, Barry...
BARRY: Get on with it.

TEACHER: You need to listen to their...

PAUL: eh - you know the Irish people that come over, um, to...
BARRY: How do you know?
TEACHER: Barry said the Irish are used to digging because they're navvies.
CLARE: They're what?
BARRY: I didn't say 'cause they're navvies. Yer daft.
TEACHER: Oh, sorry. Say what you said again, then, so that people can understand.
BARRY: They're used to digging now, aren't they, with the...
CLARE: Oh, aye!
BARRY: Thought they did (in) Ireland when they was over there, all this you know, like they don't use coal, they use that stuff called peat or summat.
CLARE: Just 'cause they're Irish they have to dig!
BARRY: They're used to it because of the bogs and in Ireland...
TIM: That's it.
TEACHER: Which part of Ireland are we, are we talking about? Are we talking about southern Ireland or northern Ireland?
BARRY: Londonderry.
CLARE: They don't even know themselves.
BARRY: Slums.
TEACHER: Which part were you really talking about, Barry, when you, or did you mean the whole of Ireland when you were talking about the peat and the digging?
BARRY: Oh, um...

ANN: Get Irish policemen and things like that, don't you?

(boy interrupts)

TEACHER: Ann said Irish policemen and Irish soldiers...

(interruption)

JOHN: Pardon?
TEACHER: Ann said you get Irish policemen and Irish soldiers.
BARRY: Not over here you don't.

TEACHER: We've got a bit off the point haven't we, of talking about the, um, Irish?
JOHN: Miss, no.
TEACHER: No, no explain why we haven't, why we're not off the point, John.
BARRY: ...they're the navvies aren't they?

(interruption)

BARRY: It's not bad wages, that navvying...
TEACHER: Do we agree that, are you saying that Irish people
earn a lot of money?
BARRY: Yeah. I am saying...

These extracts indicate something of the ground plan for later
sessions. In order to legitimize what the group is doing the
teacher is forced, in the face of the constant abuse and conflict, to seek a goal outside of the needs of the individuals
concerned. She looks outside of the group to justify what
they are about, so to speak. The group initially agreed to
do HCP, and further to consider race relations as a topic. In
the first session (as is normal in HCP) an agenda was drawn
up with a list of discussion points which it was anticipated
would form the basis for discussion in future sessions. Whenever group activities seem likely to disintegrate, the teacher
spells out the terms of legitimization to reinforce authority
and, she presumably hopes, stimulate progress. Hence the
semi-legal aspect of some parts of the session. The antipathy
between the boys and the girls is clearly indicated. For those
who expect prejudice to manifest itself simply in terms of
colour, the dynamics of the group suggest that this may not
always be so obvious. Race relations, at least in the early
sessions, is perceived in relation to the Irish and the Jews.
The reason for this would seem to be the boy/girl dichotomy
and the dislike of a particular member. Indeed, the obviously
black girl in the group suffers not because of her colour,
but because she is unfortunate enough to have an Irish
mother! Throughout the session Barry gradually builds up his
position as leader of the group by being both destructive
and constructive. The teacher is therefore left in the dilemma
of needing his contribution while, as a concomitant, having to
take his hostility. The other boys, with the possible exception
of Paul, are likely to vocalize their support for whichever of
the two seems dominant at a particular time. As for the girls,
the verbal onslaught they seem likely to incur may produce
silence, truancy and even a desire to stop the sessions, in
order to protect themselves at a personal level. How far these
suggestions, taken from a review of one session, are likely to
become realized is probably best demonstrated by reference to
the teacher's own notes.

SESSION 1
A lively but disjointed and undisciplined discussion started
when one pupil asked what race relations is....The discussion steadily deteriorated and became more disjointed as
individual members lost concentration. Considerable interest
obviously exists, but the group does not have sufficient
identity and cohesion to function properly. The aim was
partially achieved in that several potential issues were
raised and a divergence of opinion expressed. However,

the discussion was so disorderly (and the chairman's authority so precarious) that the lesson was very unsatisfactory.

SESSION 2
The discussion which developed focused on the question of prejudice against the Irish, which was raised by one of the dominant members of the group....I was so concerned with achieving some kind of disciplined discussion, and with preventing the most reluctant members from being too disruptive, that the context of the discussion suffered. Also, in trying to be neutral, I tend to become recessive in terms of content, yet still talk too much! For the next meeting I have prepared a structured questionnaire on the questions that the discussion raised in an attempt to get all of the group to consider them.

SESSION 3
Discipline was more difficult than on the previous occasion – but this is usually the case, as they are more unsettled on a Wednesday afternoon. Most of the group took the questionnaire seriously, but one member persistently refused to co-operate and was eventually excluded from the room (Brian). I did this because at the time I felt it was the only way in which we had a chance of getting a discussion started. I was so depressed by Brian's attitude, and my failure to change it, that I later asked the Head to remove him from the group. However, Brian protested that he liked HCP (which I cannot believe!). So next Monday is to be his last chance! The discussion was disjointed and undisciplined but it began to focus on the topic of jobs and appeared to suggest the issue: 'Does prejudice stop people getting jobs?' A printed sheet of some of the main points which emerged was prepared for Monday, and the questionnaires were 'marked' with comments such as 'thoughtful answers' added. Marking or checking written work seems to improve discipline and encourages them to take their work seriously. I try to put comments which are 'impartial' to content but not to degree of effort and application!

SESSION 4
The group made more of an effort to listen to one another, and at times managed to sustain a more coherent discussion than usual. The picture P17 was introduced in an attempt to diversify the discussion, but it appeared to reinforce the anti-Irish prejudice of some members. The piece of evidence no. 122 was introduced to question the view that several members held that coloured people found it easier to get jobs than the Irish – only extracts were used because of the length of the article. A food taboo

emerged when discussing whether coloured people could get
jobs in catering. Although discipline is still not good, and
pupils' attention varied – and although content was superficial – I felt that it was an improvement on previous sessions.

SESSION 5
The group had missed a previous session, so there was a
problem of lack of continuity. The previous discussion
had started on the topic of prejudice and jobs and the
group had talked about coloured teachers (amongst other
things)....The discussion suffered from the lack of a clear
issue. I wasn't using the evidence properly, i.e., 'as
evidence' in investigating an issue and as 'starters' they
were very ineffective. The general discipline was better
(but spasmodic absence by nearly all members means
that improvements in discipline can be temporary). Paul –
one of the dominants – was missing today, and also Joyce
– and this affected the group composition. The pace of
discussion was slower, but unfortunately it was not
reflective as well. The group were critical of the chairman
for not putting her opinions, and this was felt to be one
of the causes of the 'boredom'. I think that for next time
I will select a much more provocative piece.

SESSION 6
The discussion still sounded undisciplined and disorderly
but in fact most pupils seemed to make a much greater
effort to listen to what was being said and to contribute.
Brian and John, in particular, who rarely take part in
discussions, listened more closely and took part in some
of the exchanges. The part of the evidence that was used
effectively provoked discussion and the pupils seemed to
have some personal experiences on which to draw. At one
point I went into the stock room to get the pictures, and
the exchange that occurred when they thought I was out
of earshot was aggressive, revealing hostility between
Paul and Clare (who is a friend of Ann).

SESSION 7
The discussion began with the police issue, but Joyce's
question, 'What has discussing race relations got to do
with this?', generated more interest – eventually leading to John's question, 'Why do white people hate
coloured people?' It seemed, at the time, that this issue
would generate sufficient interest at the next session.
Barry criticized the chairman for lack of discipline – most
pupils wanted anyone who spoils the discussion to be
thrown out (unless it's them, I suspect!). They also felt
that the discussions weren't getting them anywhere.

SESSION 8

Pupils seemed to lack the incentive to discuss. The discussion was sporadic and desultory - interest flagged and concentration was limited. None of the items used sustained their interest. I think that they need some change of activity, although when asked, they all say that they would rather talk than do other forms of work. I think that I'll provide some structured worksheets for written follow-up work. I found last term that they could cope with this type of work and that it helped them to focus on particular issues. After the half-term holiday we will have films to act as stimuli. The first part of the discussion was reasonable while they were still discussing the police, although it became a discussion on prejudice (?) against the police, rather than against racial groups. The real collapse occurred when I introduced 32, in an attempt to focus on race hatred for our chosen issue, when members refused to even finish the piece! We then talked briefly about why the discussion had broken down.

SESSION 9

The composition of the group was entirely different from the previous week. The two aggressive dominants - Paul and Barry - were both absent, and girls outnumbered boys. The discussion was very slow, with an unusual number of silences - at times reflective, but more often just lethargic. Discipline was no problem (in the absence of Barry, Paul and Tim) but pupils were unwilling to make much of an effort and appeared bored and tired at times. There was a feeling on the part of several members that it was wrong to discuss race relations in a mixed group because it wasn't fair to the coloured or Jewish members of the group....The others didn't like talking about race when it affected their friends. Others disliked race because they found it 'boring'. In general, it was the content and not the method they objected to.

SESSION 10

Some chronic absentees had returned who were out-of-touch with both the group and the method. The aggressive dominants, Paul and Barry, wanted to talk, but wouldn't observe discussion rules....I then stopped the group after a confrontation with Sandra (a persistent truant) and Joyce - both of whom refused to do any work. The rest of the group settled down and worked on the sheet until the end of the lesson. I threw Sandra and Joyce out. (Joyce would not have acted like this without Sandra's example, I suspect.)

SESSION 11

Discipline poor - but better than previous session. I tend,

as usual, to dominate far too much in an attempt to hold the
attention of some members of the group - also in an attempt
to focus discussion on one point at a time - hardly successfully! The group was too small (only seven) to sustain a
proper discussion, anyway.

SESSION 12
Only seven pupils were present, which made proper discussion difficult and put too great a strain on the attention and
concentration of some, I think. Several issues arose in the
discussion, but I found it difficult to get them to discuss
at any depth. Once the group encounters a difficulty and
there is a pause, someone will introduce something different,
which the others pounce on, in order to escape - and I do
not have sufficient presence of mind or control to keep them
at it. I still dominate far too much in an attempt to hold
their concentration and divert them from other 'activities'.
We tended to stray from the general topic of race relations
in the USA.

SESSION 13
Only five pupils were present until half way through, so we
did not start until two more arrived. By the time we started,
no one felt like working - as is apparent on the tape. However, I thought it was better to do something, rather than
allow absenteeism to defeat us completely. (There is now
going to be a blitz on fourth-year absence, which should
help.) Some pupils seemed to have a fixed idea that the
Ku Klux Klan consisted of Negroes - which they had obtained
from an RMS (Religious and Moral Studies) lesson in the
morning! I tried to use the evidence as the 'authority' on
the nature of the Ku Klux Klan rather than telling the
group - but without much success.

SESSION 14
I felt that I could keep quiet during this silence because the
group were relatively passive (though fidgeting) after
Brian asked Barry to start it off....I don't know whether
this was because they are too dependent on me, because
of my poor technique, or whether they found the piece too
inaccessible. A reasonable discussion began between a few
members of the group, but most opted out for most of the
time - either listening, or engaging in mildly disruptive
activities - this put me off and I tended to lose the thread
of the discussion too easily. At one point they referred to
'Whicker Way Out West' and also to a news item referred to
in a previous discussion - but they were not very keen on
referring to the actual evidence. Sandra and others, after
remaining quiet for most of the discussion, began a vigorous
protest against the topic of race because in their view, it
always led to a discussion of war, and they didn't want to

discuss this.

SESSION 15
The kind of lesson that makes me feel like giving up teaching - instantly! The discussion degenerated into chaos after
an uneasy start. Reasons for this seemed to include the
return to the group of several absentees, who were out of
touch with recent work. Paul, in particular, represented a
problem to me, because of his aggressive manner and his
tendency to make loud pronouncements rather than trying
to discuss. His views are, as he claims, very prejudiced
(in my opinion) and these provoked the others into
retaliation, rather than leading to a reasonable discussion.
An interesting feature of the session was the group's refusal to consider the words of a pop song as 'evidence'.

SESSION 16
I don't think the lethargic start was very helpful. Perhaps
more directed questioning would have been better? ...The
lesson was much harder work for me than it sounds on
tape - I always felt that it was on the point of breaking
down, although in fact I think several of the group members were working quite hard (for them). Occasional lapses
into German/Paki insults went on between Barry...and
Brian....It was unfortunate that Paul was absent - since
he had really produced the issue. Clare produced a new
topic in this session, but it is quite likely that she will be
absent on Wednesday. This continual change of group
composition destroys continuity and makes improvement
more difficult.

SESSION 17
After the minutes, I proposed to my group that we should
read the evidence, suggesting that it might help us to have
a good discussion. We managed the first paragraph, but
they were so reluctant and inattentive that I stopped. I
asked them if they were willing to go on - and they said
'no', and chose to start a discussion based only on the
minutes. As usual, Wednesday was much harder work than
Monday, and after a tolerable start the discussion broke
down into casual chat. The question, 'Why are some people
coloured?' came up again (it had been raised much earlier
in the term). Some of the group - especially Clare - were
interested in this, but I was at a loss on what evidence to
use, or how to develop an inquiry into this. At one point
Barry criticized me - saying that I wasn't doing my job
properly as chairman - I wasn't asking enough questions.
The group frequently say this - and yet I feel that I ask
too many questions (but not the right ones!).

SESSION 18
(I'm going to attempt taping with a small group tomorrow
for use with the whole group on Monday.) I hoped to have
five members - Barry, Tim, John, Sandra and Clare -
whom I chose because I thought they would at least make
a serious attempt. Only Barry, Tim and John appeared,
which resulted in a 'boys' view'. They worked in my
stockroom - and all I told them was that they were to
discuss what we had done this term in HCP, giving their
opinions. They appear to have stopped the tape sometimes,
to discuss what they were going to say. I found their discussion on discipline very interesting - and similar to discussions that I've had in the past with my former two
groups. They always think that they should be sent out,
put in detention or hit. (The teachers that they referred
to on the tape - I forgot to tell them not to mention names -
are known as strict disciplinarians by the children.) I feel
that I can't exert that kind of discipline and still maintain
an atmosphere in which they will say what they really think.
I experienced the marked boy/girl polarization in my last
group as well - I wonder if I cause it? The attitude that
West Indians are all right, but Indians and Pakistanis are
not, seems to be very common here!

SESSION 19
Discussion cut short by fire drill (April Fool's Day). Pupils
reacted rather explosively to the tape, and what followed
was an argument rather than a discussion. Brian, in particular, was upset by a reference to him which he thought
was unfair. He brought up the point of absence interfering
with the discussion (unprompted by me!). Paul was offended
that I had not sent for him to make the tape. (I hadn't
sent for him because I thought he would dominate it too
much.) I was sorry that so many girls were absent, since I
had wanted a reaction to the view that the discussions
would be all right without the girls.

SESSION 20
The atmosphere of the discussion was not very serious -
last week of term. It was difficult to get them to talk about
the content of previous discussions, although they were
keen to talk about the group members and the chairman.
They are still convinced that item 2 was 'made up'. (Down
among Mr Powell's constituents.) They were very adamant
about giving detentions, lines, etc., for misbehaviour
(although one or two retracted later), but I'm still not
convinced it would be the answer.

So far, we have concentrated our attention on a particular
group in the school, because a detailed study of the personalities involved seemed to indicate rather strongly why the

sessions structured themselves as they did. It is suggested here that the teacher's notes serve to amplify conjectures arrived at earlier. The next step would seem to be to attempt an interpretation based on the theoretical model offered in a previous chapter, and from that to consider the implications for the teaching of race relations. Before going on to do that, however, it does seem important to consider briefly certain incidents in the sessions.

One of the pieces of material used contained, almost fortuitously, the statement that a police car ignored a fracas between a white taxi driver and a coloured bus driver, following some traffic mishap. This was interpreted by some members of the group as an indication that the police were afraid of the coloureds. This theme overflowed into the following session. Mention was made of the police – whether black or white – being afraid when they were outnumbered. Someone gave the example of a few police facing a miners' picket line. It was argued that some police hate black people and tend to pick on them. Evidence for this was the fact that there were more coloureds than whites in prison. By the third session conflict within the group had become to some degree externalized into an antagonism against the police in general, as is implied in the teacher's notes (see session 8). Though perhaps of marginal significance when considering the group, particularly in terms of dynamics, it is a feature that seemed to occur frequently across the schools involved in the project. It appears that racial tensions within a group or against 'them', in the case of an all white class, quickly disappears once attention becomes focused on the police. Dislike of the police (and thereby authority?) seems to become a superordinate goal inducing co-operation among pupils. It would be wrong to take this point too far, but its significance should be noted.

The second incident relates to the effect of the researcher on the situation that he wishes to study, though at first it may not appear to. In session 9 the teacher comments that several members of the group felt that it was wrong to discuss race relations in a mixed group because it wasn't fair on the coloureds or Jewish members of the group. Others didn't seem to like talking about race when it affected their friends. In the case of school A an attempt was made to suggest that boredom and frustration on the part of the pupils were related to similar factors. Again, in the session under scrutiny here, the teacher goes on to suggest in her notes that certain members felt bored with what they were doing. But no suggestion is being made that the same explanation will fit both cases. The reader is justified in feeling some scepticism at the apparent attempt of the writer to explain away for a second time possible signs of 'racial awareness' in terms of pedagogy. But these are pedagogical situations with which we are dealing. The reader is therefore asked to bear with the writer while he attempts to proffer an explanation of what he believes may have happened.

Then he is entitled to draw his own conclusions. Immediately preceding the session with which we are concerned, a member of the project team visited the school and interviewed a group of both fourth- and fifth-year puils, which included members of the immediate group. After discussing the merits of doing or not doing HCP, the interviewer then began to question the pupils about doing race relations:

INTERVIEWER: Right. What I was trying to find out was, um, first of all whether you think it's a good thing to talk about race relations in school?
BOYS/GIRLS: Yes.
INTERVIEWER: Now, why do you feel that? Do you think it's...

(silence)

INTERVIEWER: Do you feel that there's a problem in the school, um, itself, with the way people mix together and the way they treat one another...
GIRL 1: No, because...
INTERVIEWER: ...or do you feel there's not much problem in the school?
GIRL 1: Oh! You see, coloured people get treated the same...
INTERVIEWER: I see.
GIRL 1: ...except for Paki - Pakistanis, 'cos no one likes them.
INTERVIEWER: And, um, why do you feel it's good to discuss it, what's it do? I mean suppose I was to come along and say, um, it's got to be stopped, schools can't discuss things like that! How would you defend it?
GIRL 1: Could you just, um...
BOY 1: How would you what?
INTERVIEWER: How would you defend it?
BOY 1: I'd give you reasons.
INTERVIEWER: If you wanted to do it, how would you argue with me if I said...
BOY 1: I'd tell you what my reasons were...
GIRL 1: By saying...
INTERVIEWER: Well, suppose I say it just disturbs everybody and stirs up our society and...
GIRL 1: Well, if everyone enjoyed doing it they'd let you do it wouldn't they?
BOY 2: Well, if it disturbed everybody no one would want to do it, there'd be no difference...
INTERVIEWER: Sorry...Yeah.

(laughter)

The teacher was not present at this interview. One can only suggest how she may feel. In a sense, as her group was being interviewed by an outsider, the teacher may feel that in some

way her work with the group is being assessed - even that
she, in a sense, is being assessed. She is likely to become somewhat anxious about the outcome of the interview in terms of
what the school is attempting to do in the area of race relations
(this goes for the other teachers as well, one presumes). Her
response will be similar to any teacher in such a situation. She
will speak to individual pupils afterwards and even possibly
listen to the tape made of the interview, if it is available. The
next session, at least initially, is likely to be something of a
post mortem. The audio-tapes here support this suggestion:

TEACHER: What about questions about race, about the race
 pack in particular? Did he ask you things about the race
 relations pack and the work we'd been doing this term?
TIM: Mostly, if you liked it and that, you know, if it was all
 right.
TEACHER: What did people say?
TIM: I don't know because then the other people kept talk-
 ing about their mates, you know, different people.
TEACHER: You mean they didn't like talking, having to talk
 about...
TIM: Their mates, you know, and coloured people and that.
TEACHER: It made them feel awkward, did they say? Who said
 that?
TIM: (Name) and I forget their name, and this other girl
 in the fifth form.
ANN: (Name)
TEACHER: Did you agree? Do you feel like that too or, or do
 you not feel like that?
TIM: Not bothered.
TEACHER: What about other people? I think it was from Mrs
 (name) group where, um (name) in particular said that
 she was friends with (name) and she didn't...
ANN: Yeah.
TEACHER: ...like having to say things, um, or answer
 questions. Did she say on the questionnaire she didn't like
 having to fill in some questions about coloured people?
ANN: She didn't like having to read that, that question
 thing...
TEACHER: Yeah.
JOYCE: Well she, well with (name) sitting next to her she
 didn't know what to put in, you know, what to put down.
TEACHER: She didn't want to offend her?
ANN: She didn't want to offend her.
TIM: ...or else she'd have got her head kicked in.

 (laughter)

TEACHER: Do you think she really meant that, that she'd
 have got her head kicked in, or do you think she meant,
 you know, that she didn't want to offend (name)?

JOYCE: Well,...

TEACHER: What do we feel, what do you feel like in this group about, um, talking about, um, not necessarily coloured people, but perhaps, um, Jewish people or anybody who might have prejudice, Irish people? When there are people in the group who, um, might be offended?

TIM: It's hard, isn't it? 'Cos you're also talking about mates aren't you in a group?

TEACHER: Do you think people mind talking, you know what HCP, if, if we have a discussion that goes properly where people don't call one another names, right? I know it sometimes gets out of hand and we do get people calling one another names and shouting, but when we have a good discussion, or a good bit of a discussion where it goes properly, do you think it's all right then? Or do you think people probably still don't like it?

(pause)

TEACHER: What do you think Ann?

ANN: Oh, well. (sighs)

TEACHER: We ought to have Brian here, because Brian once said he didn't like um discussing race.

TIM: That's 'cos he's a half-caste, isn't he?

TEACHER: Well we've had Paul as well, and he didn't seem to mind talking about the Jews and prejudice against the Jews, did he?

TIM: Aye, but all he is, is half-Jew.

TEACHER: Did (name) say anything in the big, the discussion with, um,...

GIRLS: Not really much.

TIM: She kept quiet.

TEACHER: What, she didn't like doing race relations?

It is interesting to note that the teacher seems to have taken the possible 'fears' expressed by the interviewer to heart. In a sense, the beginning of the session is a natural re-run of the previous interview. Two authority figures, one external and the other internal, appear to be expressing doubts about the wisdom of doing race relations if the composition of the group is mixed. It is little wonder that the pupils respond as they do. Perhaps what it is important to learn from this is just how intrusive the researcher may be in his attempt to glean understanding, albeit unwillingly.

In developing an educational model to help us in interpreting particular case studies, we made mention of the fact that a group rather than a school might demonstrate conflict. This is what we are dealing with here. To say simply that the group is rent by dissension, as the evidence so far adduced would suggest, is not enough. One might question whether the group can be considered as a constant. Frequent absence makes each session almost a new start. The result is that at a group level members are unable to begin building towards the necessary degree of abstraction in order to interpret race relations. Both the language and the conceptual framework necessary are missing. Yet, paradoxically, the pedagogical approach offered by the teacher does seem to offer a way forward. So that, although the group is in a state of almost constant conflict, the procedure offered by the teacher embryonically contains pedagogical possibilities which might allow innovation. In the event, the material about race relations becomes ammunition for the settling of personal animosities. Where there are strong differences between members of a group or a class it would seem that materials used serve a secondary rather than a primary function. The materials can almost be about anything, war and race relations offering only two possibilities. What is being suggested is that group conflict may override content, so that, in the case of race relations, conflict within the group is likely to lead the members to perceive race relations to be about conflict. As many schools are likely to contain a group similar to this one, the importance of considering the instance in such detail would seem to be validated in terms of teaching about race relations. It contains implications that may be of value in guiding teachers. At the same time, it may indicate to the non-practitioner the complexity of the educational process. To conclude and make summary of what has been said, it is perhaps best to end with an extract from one of the sessions:

JANET: Why can't you change the subject, it's about war...
TEACHER: Pardon?
JANET: Why can't you change the subject?
TEACHER: Subject from what?
JANET: Summat else.
TEACHER: To what?
JANET: Anything, but not war.
TEACHER: Somebody tell Janet, Janet we haven't been doing war for a term. I know you've been away but we did stop war at Christmas.
JANET: I know, but we did war last term, didn't we?
TEACHER: Yes, we finished it at Christmas. We're not talking about war. It just happens that this is the Black Panther piece.
JANET: It's all like war, isn't it?
SANDRA: It's all with war, isn't it, it's all the same.
TEACHER: Don't (to boy tapping). Well if...don't. All right, pick another, pick another point in this piece to discuss, then, or suggest something we could go on to.
JANET: It's still war, isn't it?

13 CASE STUDY 3: STRATEGY B

Robert D. Wild

This school started life in the early 1950s as a junior high school. It had no academic pupils because they were 'creamed off' to the local senior high school. During its first few years there were about 750 pupils in four years. At the time of this study the school had grown into a six-year comprehensive of about 1,400 pupils and was expected to reach a maximum of 1,600 pupils in the late 1970s.

At the time of the race relations project, the school was in the throes of developing a fifth and sixth year. This involved preparation of an enormous number of academic courses. Also involved in the development was a new scheme of timetabling and a new course in geography in third and fourth years. As one of the two teachers was involved in timetabling and the other in developing a new course in goegraphy, it is clear that life for them was quite hectic.

There was a need at the time for new teaching methods as well as new buildings to cope with the larger school role, the greater bands of ability among pupils and the new academic levels required. The building programme was well under way, containing areas for both the physical and social sciences and also including a custom-built self-contained block for educationally sub-normal children. Obviously, the facts of new buildings and change of role have pedagogical implications. The possibility for experimentation and innovation was therefore very real.

Balanced against these considerations must be some awareness of the educational system with which the school operates. The school is in Scotland, and obviously the system is different in many ways to that in England. For information on the complexity of the historical background to Scottish education the reader is referred to the standard works. Nevertheless, it is appropriate to make some points here. Teachers in the school under consideration are normally appointed as academic specialists. In Scotland, university graduation has long been compulsory for secondary schoolteachers (except in practical subjects). To comprehend what is meant by 'academic specialist' is difficult for teachers in England, but no one in Scotland is in any doubt. High value is placed on academic activity, and this at one time offered the teacher professional status on a par with the lawyer and the doctor. Now there is a clear gap in status between the graduate teacher and the other professions, to the detriment of the teacher. Teacher-training in Scotland has always laid special emphasis on the method of presenting the specialism as well as accurate content. This usually meant in Scottish schools, beyond the second year, a certificate stream and a non-certificate stream. The non-certificate stream followed basically the same themes as the academic pupils but in a less demanding and more flexibly structured manner. This school has, ever since its early days, been famous for innovations. Many pilot schemes were tried and tested here, especially in science and technical subjects as well as 'work experience' and inter-disciplinary inquiry. A large number of the staff has been involved in development work leading to methods being adopted throughout Scotland.

In order to eradicate the natural divisions that arise between pupils who are deemed 'certificate' and those 'non-certificate', the school policy was to call every pupil 'certificate' by presenting everyone for at least English and arithmetic in the Scottish Certificate of Education examinations. As well as this, it became policy to allow pupils to elect to study six more certificate subjects over and above the two stated. The very ablest pupils could study seven subjects plus arithmetic, and the number of certificates chosen depended on the ability of the individual pupil.

Where pupils were studying, for example, only four certificate subjects out of the possible six, in the option groups, where they had no preferred certificate choices, they had non-certificate courses of a less demanding nature. To reach the non-certificate course the pupils 'bridged the gap' out of the certificate into the non-certificate areas and such pupils were known as 'bridgers' in the relevant option groups.

While the school was still developling, emphasis was of necessity laid on academic course developments. As a result, there grew a feeling that some 'bridgers' were not being as well treated as was possible. Because of this, there came the establishment, under the guidance of a committee, of a social and health education course, which it is hoped will have both relevance and purpose.

> The main tendency in Scottish Secondary Education has been a stress on the development of cognitive skills. The purpose underlying the implementation of a Social and Health Education programme is an attempt to achieve a shift of emphasis – an emphasis towards social, personal, vocational and moral development....The approach of the teacher should be based on the technique of 'Non-directive group counselling'. One aim of the technique is to enable the pupil to acquire those verbal and social skills necessary to enable him/her to participate in group discussions and to express ideas and feelings with some accuracy and intelligence. Another is to expose the pupil to views other than his own, to test his opinions against these, to have his own ideas criticized and to ensure that opinions strongly held can, where possible,

be consciously tested against known facts. The role of the
teacher is to act as a catalyst to the group and as a support to individuals. The teacher must be resourceful in
injecting fact and accuracy into discussions where these
are lacking.

It is in this area in the third year (the fourth year in English
terms) that the teaching about race relations has been located.
The pupils involved in the experiment we are reporting are
therefore 'bridgers' in the sense of the term explained above.
   The rector is very ambitious for his school. He positively
encourages the staff to go ahead and try out new ideas. As in
the case of social and health education, committees have been
set up for this purpose. His experience in journalism also
makes him sensitive to the importance of presenting a correct
public image of the school. Its catchment area has been described as 'mottled'. The school lies towards the periphery of
a medium-sized industrial town. The town has docks, and mining is carried out in the surrounding area. Many of the pupils
come from working-class backgrounds, some from the surrounding countryside and a few from dormitory estates. Except for
one or two individuals, the composition of the school is white.
   As might be expected, the teachers who took part in the
project were sympathetic to the notion of widening the curriculum to meet the needs of all pupils. Both were senior members of staff, one being the assistant rector of the school.
Both were academic specialists, but in order to differentiate
between them and at the same time preserve confidentiality, we
shall use the term academic specialist and assistant rector.
Previous schools were handled somewhat chronologically. In
the case of this school, a reversal of this procedure seems useful. The academic specialist in his report at the end of teaching
about race relations had the following comments to make:

   I felt this was the most disastrous piece of work I was ever
   involved in. My immediate reaction is that I cannot teach in
   a vacuum. These pupils have no experience of any facet of
   the race relations problem, and nothing I could do could
   replace this lack of experience. In the light of my own thinking, you cannot teach about race relations *until* there is a
   problem. This is contrary to most of the views I heard at
   Norwich.

   I feel that I maybe chose the wrong type of group to conduct the experiment with. These were a mixed ability group
   of 14-15-year-old boys. They ranged in ability from pupils
   taking six 'O' grades to those taking none. I have a very
   good relationship with the boys, but by the end of the
   experiment I found I was losing their confidence. I think I
   hammered the subject too much. If I were doing it again
   next session I would choose a group of greater ability or

maturity, e.g. sixth formers. I would also stretch it out
over the year, putting a one lesson module to them every
two or three weeks.

There were other problems outside the school. Firstly, the
Norwich Strategy B conference was in May 1973, while the
actual teaching experiment started in January 1974. The
gap between them was too long. Ideas and enthusiasm stirred up at the conference were largely dissipated by the
time the teaching began. Secondly, the teaching material
arrived very late - nearly the end of December 1973. This
did not allow much perusal to see what could be best fitted
into a teaching scheme. Thirdly, much of the teaching
material was too literate, too intellectual for the pupils
involved. Anything over one page long had to be disregarded. Fourthly, I was involved in the introduction of
a new syllabus into the SIII and SIV certificate section in
geography. This had been taking up a great deal of my
time.

This report is on the short side; there are no tape-recordings because I felt there was absolutely no tape worth
listening to and scrubbed them. I feel thoroughly dis-
heartened by the whole thing. I cannot do more than
repeat my conclusion - I feel that you cannot teach in a
vacuum. The pupils cannot appreciate race relations till
they are faced with a multi-racial situation of some sort.

By the time of the York Conference, which followed the experimental term, his position seems to have become even more
radical. He is no longer simply preoccupied with what went
wrong, but more with how the time could have been better
utilized:

We joined this experiment, but I feel that it is not what
we should have been really tackling in the school. I feel
that there are other things which are more important at
the moment in [our town]. Now, I can be shot down in
flames about this if you want. To my mind, at the moment
the environment question is much more vital in [our town].

The education of children to look at their environment, to
start worrying about it. [Our town] is one of those places
which dumps its raw sewerage in the sea, and so on. This
to my mind is the social education that I personally think
is important, because it's relevant to them. In our situation the race question, because of possibly a lack of social
mobility, is not too important yet....'What's this got to do
with us? Nothing. Why can't we get back to something that
we can be involved in, because this doesn't involve us.'

The assistant rector, at the same conference, used expressions such as 'a bit of a disaster' and the impossibility of teaching race relations 'in a vacuum' with regard to his own experience. The fact that these comments echo the earlier report may suggest that the two teachers have influenced each other in arriving at an overall conclusion. Both teachers, however, are convinced that each reached his own conclusion independently because of the different methods used. Naturally, they discussed the course as it went along, and possibly the discussions helped them to reach their individual but unanimous conclusion. But this is not really the issue here. The problem we have to tackle is that of arriving at some understanding of what may have led the teachers concerned to such a pessimistic viewpoint.

The two teachers involved worked under conditions that were hardly conducive to success. Most of the problems have been dealt with at the beginning of this chapter, but three more points need explanation. First was the fact that the school timetable had already been drawn up before the commitment to teaching race relationships had been made. This meant adding something new - which is normally difficult in a tightly structured timetable unless it is within a non-academic group. Second was the problem that the teaching material was very late in arriving - not until the session was five months old. This meant removing the chosen groups from the work they were already doing. Third was the problem of the academic specialist's group consisting of boys who were doing anything from two 'O' grades to seven 'O' grades: a real mixed-ability group, whose numbers fluctuated from week to week. The assistant rector's group consisted of a very small number of low-ability girls who 'bridged' out of every option group.

The ability range of the boys and the uniformly low ability of the girls (five out of the eight actually having suffered or suffering from some form of emotional disturbance) compelled the teachers to opt for a 'one-off' lesson. The majority of the pupils did not have good enough recall to be able to refer back to the previous week's topic.

Each lesson for both groups lasted fifty-five minutes, once a week. The organizational problem facing this teacher is best expressed in his own words:

> I am assistant rector at [our school], and simply because of circumstance all my teaching has to be geared towards the fact that I am always liable to get hauled out of my room in order to deal with one crisis or another. In fact, I think on one occasion I was in my office taking them for a talk about one or two things and I think in the space of ten minutes we had seventeen major or minor crises to be dealt with. So, this in effect means that my teaching of anything is below par, because it's got to be geared to the situation that, if I get hauled off, the class is able to get

on with some work. So it's basically book material. I
finished up limiting myself to the use of the pack but not
as neutral chairman [sic]. I was committed...the class
was chosen for its size quite deliberately.

The constraints within which the teachers had to work having
been described, it is now useful to consider the teaching itself.
There were obvious differences in the approaches used to some
degree relating to the practical considerations amplified above.
As the academic specialist notes:

I think this is correct. To change attitudes and the teacher
to be committed, now [my colleague] and I got two different
ideas about what we were doing from Norwich. [My colleague]
thought that he was to use nothing but the pack, whereas
I felt all was fair in love and war, that we were out to change
attitudes and use anything that we liked. Therefore, in my
course I included a bit of role-play, and very much weighted
the guided discussion with me expressing my viewpoint.
These were my two main themes.

It is unfortunate that the only evidence at hand for a study of
his lessons is lesson notes. Had the tapes not been destroyed,
they would have been likely to provide deeper insights into
the situation he encountered. Nevertheless, as the academic
specialist expressed such anxiety about the outcome, it is seemly
to begin considering his account.

LESSON 1

Intention
To teach a lesson about noise pollution but to introduce a
new element - prejudice - into the classroom organization.
Pupils with fair hair set on one side of the room with pencils and paper provided. Black haired, etc., pupils on
other side with nothing provided. Chalk and talk, question
and answer followed, involving only fair-haired pupils.
When black-haired pupils began to talk they were silenced
rudely, even threatened with punishment. Last fifteen
minutes, discussion on my behaviour.

Reaction
Pupils puzzled to begin with. Those favoured quite happy
with the situation. Those discriminated against wondering
why. Those discriminated against grew restless, then angry
when slapped down.
     My reaction - delight with progress of the lesson and with
the end product: fifteen minutes of discussion of what had
happened and the feelings of individuals during the lesson.
Total reaction - dislike of discrimination where it affects
them.

LESSON 2

Intention
A straightforward lesson on 'stereotypes'. I will go into
classroom and write on blackboard: 'Teenagers are long-
haired, dirty, scruffy, loud-mouthed, foul-mouthed,
lazy vandals.' I hope noisy discussion will follow.

Reaction
Pupils incensed. Only 'long-haired' was allowed to stand.
Then followed a discussion of the statement and how it came
into being. Then pupils made up a stereotype of teachers.
This was dissected to see if it fitted me - only 'old' was
allowed to stand.
   My reaction - very happy with the discussion.

LESSON 3

Intention
To start teaching a lesson on German treatment of the Jews
in 1930s and in World War II. Half way through lesson be
called away to 'phone. As I go out of the door (no work to
be left) I will say 'Ian Campbell, if there is any noise from
this room I will punish you.' Wait ten minutes...in store on
floor below. Go back up to room and try to punish Ian for
the noise which will undoubtedly follow.

Reaction
A boring lesson got the pupils restless. The lack of work
to do in my absence really stirred them up.
   Ian's reaction - anger, refused punishment, knew he was
guilty of making a noise but did not see why he should be
punished when rest were not. I explained that he was to be
a 'scapegoat' - I had been offended against and as I did not
have the energy to punish all twenty people in the class I
had chosen him to take the punishment.
   Reaction of the class - silence, no support for Ian at all.
All glad not to have been picked on.
   My reaction - the discussion of our behaviour brought
out a dislike of being the scapegoat, and shame for not
supporting him.

It is useful to pause here. So far, the comments in the lessons
given seem to be in sharp contrast to what his final report
would lead one to believe. From this point on disillusionment
seems to set in, at least on his part, and some suggestion of
this may be reflected in the diminution of comment. It is important to note that the modules that seem fitted to a 'topic'
approach have until now had no explanation given. The teacher
begins the next session by explaining the general intention -
that of dealing with race relations.

LESSON 4

Intention
To give a potted history of the British Empire. Discuss the
benefits enjoyed by British people of colonial trade and
development of new industry. Mainly the jute industry in
Dundee, which I know a considerable amount about. Discuss
why these industries were not developed to any great extent
in India/Pakistan during the British rule.

Reaction
An enjoyable lesson, not so much the content, but the
recounting of personal stories about Dundee. Disturbing
end to the lesson: despite the aim and content of the lesson,
one discerning (?) pupil voiced the opinion that the 'Pakis
should be sent back'. It was disturbing on two counts:

(a) the content was intended to raise sympathy for the
    exploited colonial peoples;
(b) the presence of immigrant groups in this country was
    never mentioned.

LESSON 5

Intention
To present the view of a 'Commonwealth of Nations'. To
emphasize our responsibility on account of c.250 years of
economic exploitation.

Reaction
A disaster. I came up against a brick wall. There was consensus that not only should no immigrants be allowed into
the country, but also those already here should be repat-
riated.

LESSON 6

Intention
To present the case of the Uganda Asians - having British,
not Ugandan or Indian/Pakistan, citizenship, because our
government gave it to them.

Reaction
Another disaster. No legal or moral argument carried any
weight. Discussion was one-sided. There was a hard line
taken: they felt India/Pakistan should have taken the
expelled Asians. We had no responsibility.

LESSON 7

Intention
To give factual information on where our immigrant population lives and analyse why.

Reaction
A good geographical lesson. But as far as the experiment
is concerned, totally sterile. The class enjoyed the map
work, but were a bit fed up with the subject. I will give
them a change next week.

LESSON 8 (with a full week's rest since Lesson 7)

Intention
To study the socioeconomic viewpoint that black people constitute the fourth class in Britain, below the white working
class.

Reaction
The discussion was lively but disheartening. I could not get
through the brick wall of unknowing prejudice.

LESSON 9

Intention
To study examples of discrimination from newspaper articles
in the pack.

Reaction
Disgust. I can argue the class round in circles but cannot
break down the prejudice.

LESSON 10

Intention
To find out how many immigrants these pupils know of in
their local area (actual numbers). To relate this to the
'They're taking us over' theme mentioned in the last lesson.

Reaction
The great brick wall came down. I got absolutely nowhere.

LESSON 11

Intention
To relate the Ulster situation in terms of prejudice to the
situation that could develop here, stressing the violence.

Reaction
This was an impassioned lecture. They listened to me quietly.
I left no time for discussion but left them to think it out
themselves.

By the conclusion of the lessons the teacher seems to have passed through the whole gamut of emotions. His reaction to the
first lesson was that of delight; the second he was very happy
with; while the third seems to have at least proved useful. The
fourth almost suggests bewilderment because the aim towards
which he was working seemed suddenly to be threatened. From
then on the term 'disaster' and 'brick wall' begin to be employed.
The final lesson seems to be an impassioned attempt at a final
breakthrough by dealing with a topic nearer home.
If the first teacher seemed surprised when he encountered
prejudice, the problem facing the second - the assistant rector
- seems to have been almost the opposite. His surprise consisted of the non-encounter with strongly held and prejudiced
views. Something of his frustration is suggested by the comments he made following only the second session. Part of the
blame is laid on the intellectual ability of the pupils and thereby
the demands made by the academic level of the materials. He
had chosen to use only the materials from the teaching pack.
As it turned out, these materials were far too difficult for these
girls. He had to spend much time sifting out short, obvious
items to match the ability level. His warning was against using
the whole pack unless the teacher has a very good, senior
class. This is made clear in his report. Yet behind this one
can sense his impatience to reach the 'take-off' point necessary
to realize the strategy:

There's one thing, it's definitely teaching in the raw. I
never realized just quite how many odd side noises you
get, what with documents being rustled, and bells ring-
ing in the background, and people trampling in wanting
things. It is definitely real classroom teaching. I have two
main problems at the minute. The first, something I mentioned in the lesson in fact, was that most of the girls are
very much on, as it were, on our side. They are opposed
to things dealing with race relations, or anti-racial, racism.
What I'm trying to do now is to get them to cast their minds
to a situation where they would be actively involved in
racial upsets. Most of them, however, have rarely experienced anything like this, and to be quite honest their
intellectual level isn't such as to be able to cast their
minds very far.
    The second problem is the problem about material. Many
of the texts that are provided in the pack are very long,
very detailed, very complicated and very intellectual.
Quite frankly, I think I am not going to be able to occupy
the next seven or eight weeks with topics on race relations.

The material is of such a high standard it is really beyond these girls. I would say that most of it demands an intellectual ability of something in the region of sixth-year studies. The pictures are good, the cartoons are good, but they don't provoke all that much in the way of discussion, and in fact, as you'll gather, I've actually had to tell them to take something home and read it for next week. Mostly because these documents are far too long to be read within the time available. I'm finding it's difficult, fascinating but difficult.

The problem facing the assistant rector is that of combating something that refuses to manifest itself. The task set by the strategy conference was to combat prejudice. If the pupils will not bring forth the prejudices that they as members of a prejudiced society are assumed to have, what can be done? Perhaps the assistant rector, by expressing prejudices, can make manifest what is presumably latent in the group. Once this has been achieved, the way seems open to begin the process of demolition by reference to available evidence. The danger of the approach lies in its subtlety. Admittedly, the role of the teacher as defined in the conference documents suggests that:

The teacher should be an example of a person critical of prejudiced attitudes and opinions held by himself and by society at large and trying to achieve some degree of mutual understanding and respect between identifiably different human groups.

Yet the documents referred to presupposed that the teacher's admissions would synchronize with those made by the pupils. If the teacher goes it alone, so to speak, he may be exposing himself to risk. As the assistant rector seems to have felt that the lack of response on the part of the group necessitated a pedagogical ploy of this kind, that is, the devil's advocate, the implications are worth following by use of extracts from a lesson:

TEACHER: National Front. Yes. In other words, they don't want the, um, black people to come in. Now, look at that one which says 'Britons First'. Now what two things are they obviously frightened the black people would take away?
GIRL 1: They would take over their jobs and houses.
TEACHER: Take over their jobs and houses. You remember last week I told you of a particular area where an aunt of mine stays?
GIRL 2: Bristol.
TEACHER: No, it begins with B, but it's not Bristol.
GIRLS: Birmingham.

TEACHER: Birmingham, right. You remember what I, I told
you about the bus journey?

GIRL 3: You see all black people and no whites.

TEACHER: All black people and no whites. Actually, I got
from the paper today a story about a coloured man from
Jamaica who had done very well in his job and he wanted
a good house. So, he went and had a look at an all-white
area and got a very nice house in a, up the end of a
street. He offered to pay the price that was asked for the
house, it was all set up, the lawyers and so forth all
agreed. When he went to pay the money he found that the
house had not been sold to him. Although agreements had
been made, all the other people in the street had got
together and bought the house from, directly from, the
man who owned it. Now why would they do that?

GIRLS: To stop the black people...

TEACHER: To stop the black people coming in. Is that fair?

GIRLS: No.

TEACHER: But....

GIRL 3: In a way it is.

TEACHER: Well, I was just going to say, let's say you are
all people who have houses in a white area and you found
that you, there was a black family going to come and live
in your street; would you just say 'Well, fair enough', or
what?

GIRL 1: I wouldna' bother.

GIRL 2: Neither would I.

GIRL 4: Neither would I.

TEACHER: What, can I, um....

GIRL 3: (laughs)

GIRL 1: She lives on a farm.

TEACHER: Lives on a?

GIRL 4: Lives on a farm.

TEACHER: Well, yes, all right, well, we won't know about
that, she lives on a farm, all right. Now...

GIRL 3: Even if I lived in a town I wouldna' bother then.

TEACHER: But what is the fear that people have about...

GIRL 2: In case the...

TEACHER: ...what happens in an area...

GIRL 1: the room...

GIRL 3: In case they take over too many...

TEACHER: They take over, they ruin the area. (pause) This
usually unfortunately turns out to be true, that an area
which is inhabited by all black people becomes, um, a bit
run down. Now this, then, is white people protesting,
right?...

TEACHER: Right. In other words, what do you think these
black people are trying to say?

GIRL 2: That everybody's the same.

TEACHER: Well, they're trying to say that everybody's the
same, but that's a sort of long-term view. They're protest-

ing about what?

GIRL 1: That they're get...they're not getting treated as well.

TEACHER: They're not getting treated fairly, right? They're not getting treated fairly. How do you think the two protests compare in number, size?

GIRL 2: There's more people against than for.

TEACHER: More people against than for. So obviously, then, you've understood that white people can protest against blacks. Black people can protest against whites, so I mean, it's not all a one-sided protest. There was an incident where in fact a Scottish doctor claimed that he was persecuted by Welsh people, now does that sound daft?

GIRL 1: Just different colour and they speak different.

TEACHER: Hm. Actually, I, I'm having a problem in a way, because you are all quite nice about it, you all think that race relations is bad, you know the anti-colour. It's mostly seeing you are against this racial business, but maybe if half the school was black you would think differently. I'm sure you would think differently, in fact. Now let's turn to something which will suit you lassies fine. Like fellies – coloured fellies. Right? 'The Negro in my life' (title of newspaper article the pupils are studying). What you, what I'd like you to try and do now is think of, um, you being deeply interested in a coloured lad.

GIRL 1: I was...

TEACHER: You were, were you? Good, good.

GIRL 1: (very quietly) He was quite nice, wasn't he.

TEACHER: Come on, slowcoach. Actually, you will see that there is, er, a different case on each side. One of them is 'The Negro in my life', obviously a girl, and the other side is 'White girl in my life'. So again we get the opposite points of view. What, what you must always try and do, um, when you're discussing anything, and something like race relations is extremely complicated, is to get both sides of it. What did you say about a fight, 'always takes two to have a fight'? You'd look a bit daft fighting with yourself, always takes two...

TEACHER: You see, we suffer from the disadvantage of not having a coloured problem here; it's dead simple. Therefore you are not fully aware of what it all means. Say, for instance, somebody asked me, 'Would you let your daughter marry a coloured man?' That would cause me a tremendous amount of heart-searching.

GIRL: (sighs)

TEACHER: It would. If you were parents and somebody said 'Would you let your daughter marry a Negro?' Would you?

GIRLS: (chorus of 'no's' and 'don't know's')

GIRL: ...I would become a Pakistani.

TEACHER: I wouldn't say that, I think I would say, if anything, with your name and with your colour and your face,

you definitely can't. Actually, there's an interesting little
thing here. There was a protest by women that coloured
shop assistants are not allowed to handle women's underwear.

GIRLS: (very amused and laugh)

GIRL: (inaudible)

TEACHER: Say it.

GIRL 4: America.

TEACHER: No. Hackney, which is in London. Some shop
assistants are not allowed to touch ladies' underwear in a
number of stores. Ladies' underwear, for some mysterious
reason, is taboo. It has some sexual or psychological taboo
that it is not to be touched by coloured shop assistants.
Comments?

GIRLS: Daft
   Stupid
   Daft
   Mental

TEACHER: But if you live in an area where white and black
detested each other, you know, you could see this feeling
simmering. And you went into a shop and a woman offered
you your undies, do you really think you could say 'Ah,
keep your dirty hands off'?

GIRLS: (chorus of 'no's')

GIRL 1: No. I couldn't say that.

TEACHER: What I've seen, not in ladies' underwear, like you
seem to have, I've seen in London, in one of Lyons Cafes,
which is a sort of universal snack bar place, a coloured
woman coming to pick up a cup and saucer. The cup was
empty of tea which the woman had been drinking, and the
black woman said, 'Have you finished?' and she said, 'Shove
off, you black ——.'

From the extracts it is clear that the teacher at this point is
walking a pedagogical tightrope. Though throughout he attempts
to spell out his intention, one cannot be sure how the group
is reacting. Any of the girls who express a tolerant point of
view are brought up short. The teacher suggests that whites
may fear blacks taking over their jobs and houses. Examples,
sometimes anecdotal, are cited. He admits that areas inhabited
by all blacks do tend to become 'a bit run down'. The teacher
actually says that they suffer from not having a colour problem in their town, though this has a different meaning when
seen in context. And so on. Tapes from other lessons indicate
a similar pattern. Many of the pupils will be aware that he is
trying to stir things up and provoke them into realizing some
of the problem aspects of race relations. Nevertheless, it is
just possible that one or two may perceive things in a different
way. If they lack the subtlety to follow the argument closely,
the teacher may simply seem to be mouthing sentiments that
they have heard elsewhere and which are anti-tolerant. If this

happened, his authority as a teacher might be misconceived, in that these factors give added weight to what he 'apparently' said. To say these things is to make the reader aware of the problems that pedagogy, and not only race relations, may throw up. It is nowhere suggested that in this situation the approach used did in fact produce unfavourable outcomes.

How far can the experiences of the two teachers be bridged? At first glance their experiences seem to lie at opposite ends of a spectrum. So with their responses, at least initially. In considering this school it is important to refer back to a statement made in an earlier chapter. There it was suggested that, where a school seeks to deal with a new area of knowledge, it not only has to communicate an interpretative structure but also to construct it as it goes along. In the cases of school A and school B, an interpretative structure was ready to hand, that of the Humanities Curriculum Project (HCP). Teachers using drama also had an approach, based on improvisation. The 'committed' teachers had premises, procedures and a role definition from their conference, but no tried methodology. Their task was both to construct the pedagogy and at the same time to implement it - in many ways a daunting task, especially when the teachers found themselves back in their own schools and frequently encapsulated in their own classrooms.

Mindful of these facts, it is now useful to have recourse to our theoretical model. The information at the beginning of the chapter would suggest that at an institutional level the school is pedagogically open. Indeed, it has need to be. Both the authority and the rector of the school were eager that teachers should take part, and would have liked members to be involved in at least two of the strategies. But perhaps a proviso should be entered here as we are dealing with the Scottish educational system. Both the teachers involved have had a background of academic specialization. It is interesting to note that in the social and health education report, already quoted from, emphasis is laid on the testing of opinions against facts, and that an important function of the teacher is to inject fact and accuracy into discussions where these are lacking. Something of this attitude seems to be implied in an article written by the two teachers involved in the project:

We were asked by Mr (X), the organizer of Social Subjects for (our) County, and Mr (Y), the rector of the school, to attend the Strategy B conference at Norwich in May. Using all available teaching materials, the teacher must be committed to removing racial prejudice from the minds of the pupils. He need not necessarily state his position at the outset, but he should do so when the moment comes, as it surely must, when a pupil says, 'Please sir, what do you think...?'

The implications drawn from this may be false. But they do suggest that the Scottish teacher may see his role, even in areas not directly cognitive, as more academic than his English counterpart. Accuracy and fact are expected of him by the pupil, and in turn he expects the pupil to reach the point of demanding this from him. If this is so, then the bridge between the academic specialist and assistant rector, as indicated at the York Conference, is possibly methodological rather than conceptual. An equally valid argument might be that the committed teacher cross-culturally believes that facts will out. If the pupils once grasp the facts, then they will tend to become more tolerant. In this case, both sets of factors may be operative. It does mean that the pedagogical openness of the school needs to be qualified to a certain extent.

Our real concern here is with the other dimension of the model, that of pedagogy itself. What has been said nevertheless has considerable bearing on any interpretation offered. The form of the lessons is surely limited by considerations of time and pupil choice. The content may also be limited by the academic expectations of the teachers. The academic specialist begins by using role play. In this way he deals with prejudice, stereotyping and scapegoating. So far so good - at least, that is what he seems to feel. Would it be stretching the evidence too far to suggest that he feels that these attitudinal facts have been established and now it is for him to correct pupils' misconceptions (or ignorance) in the area of race relations? Hence his plea in the fourth lesson because the pupils were not responding as he expected they should, particularly as 'the context was intended to raise sympathy for the exploited colonial peoples'. That the pupils may not have linked the role-play with the factual lessons on aspects of race relations does not seem to occur to the academic specialist. Both teachers, in fact, seem to control their groups rather tightly. From the tapes it is evident that the assistant rector is always leading the girls and directing the flow of the session. There is humour, but it is usually 'teacher humour', which any practitioner would instantly recognize. The assistant rector also seems to be impatient with the pace of the lesson and the lack of academic skill on the part of the girls in reading and absorbing academic fact. In reality, he is forced to do the thrashing around, making statements about housing (again), toilet habits, personal hygiene, the 'ropiness' of some foreign degrees and so on. It is as though both teachers are seeking to get their pupils towards some academic starting-line. If they can reach this in teaching about race relations, from then on they will have a well tried and trusted method to apply: that of eradicating ignorance by fact. Obstacles can then be surmounted, so to speak. That neither reaches the firm ground of ignorance and prejudice to be attacked seems to discourage them profoundly and lead in their minds to a sense of disaster. It certainly may not be that, given the magnitude of what they are attempting.

14 CASE STUDY 4: STRATEGY B

Robert D. Wild

The school is in a rural area. The village in which it is located is slowly becoming a dormitory settlement, if not a town, to serve a medium-sized market town some five miles away. The school, a mixed secondary modern with nearly 600 pupils, is sited within one of the new estate developments. What has been said so far suggests something of an urban or semi-urban orientation: what is missing from the impression being built up is a sense of the rural setting and relative isolation. Some of the pupils obviously come from the village; yet a large number live on farms remote from each other. The area is not one crossed by arterial routes between other parts of the country. Traditions and habits change less quickly here than in the cities. Many pupils may have little contact with each other outside the school. The school bus collects them at certain points in the morning and deposits them back there at night. Holidays may be spent working on the farm from which they come. Many of the pupils have never visited London or any other large city. The life of many is relatively self-contained and well-ordered. The expectation will be that as adults a high proportion will work in this, their native area for the most part. Some are likely to migrate from the area in order to seek job opportunities. The school and the area therefore possess certain peculiarities which need to receive our attention. The pupils are unlikely to have had much contact with foreigners, whether whites or coloured. There is in fact one coloured pupil at the school. It takes a long time for any stranger entering the area to be viewed as one of the community. The remoteness, then, has implications in terms of teaching about race relations. There may be both advantages and disadvantages to consider.

The potential problems of such an educational environment – both rural and remote – seem to have stimulated the local authority to be extremely sensitive to its needs. A new and progressive headmaster has recently been appointed. He is counterbalanced by the deputy head, a woman, who has a feel for what the community will tolerate. In building terms new amenities are being added to the school. At the beginning of the project controversy was raging over the pros and cons of having outward-facing units in the new science laboratory. The authority's enthusiasm for the project reflects its enthusiasm for the school as a whole. Its general desire to keep ahead in educational developments is also reflected in the participation, through a number of schools, in a Department of Education and

171

Science project at the same time. Nevertheless, while keen, the teachers actually to be involved in the teaching about race relations did feel it necessary to stress the apathy on the part of pupils sometimes to be met in rural schools, and that the material provided might prove too difficult in terms of reading level and content. The group chosen to take part was from the fourth year and comprised those not taking external examinations. In that sense, they were the lower-ability pupils. The group consisted of twenty-six boys and eleven girls, giving a total of thirty-seven in all.

The original intention was to use the three periods on a Tuesday afternoon for the teaching of race relations. This was within the humanities course. Broadly, the format was to have one teacher (of three) taking the whole group while the others observed. Then the large group was to be split into three smaller groups for discussion purposes. Finally, the small groups were to reassemble to compare their findings. In this all three teachers would participate as well as the pupils. However, as the course developed, the other four humanities periods on a Thursday morning had to be used also, in order to realize the programme. Added to this the fact that one of the teachers was ill for part of the term, thus affecting arrangements, and one can see that the teaching pattern increased in complexity. An interesting feature of the sessions was the difference demonstrated by the teachers when leading the discussion in small groups and facing the full group plus participant observers. The latter occasions seemed naturally to evoke a formal style.

TEACHER: So just the, put the ones in you can get, then, please. Quickly as you can. Then we want all pens down. Now, you're not to pick up your pen again until you're given the order to do so. Let's have all these pens down please. Now this next duplicated sheet, highly perfumed...
PUPILS: (groan)
TEACHER: ...got a lot of gaps in. Now you're not to try to, er, fill this in just yet please. So we want all these pens and pencils down on the desk, and don't pick them up again for a while.

In this school, as in the others considered, the teachers tended to be senior members of the staff. One, the leader, was head of the humanities and a linguist, the second, tutor to the upper school and a geographer, and the third, tutor to the upper school and a biologist. For convenience as well as confidentiality, we shall adopt a similar procedure to that employed in the previous school, by referring to them as the linguist, the geography teacher and the biology teacher. One period a week was set aside on the timetable as a preparation time for members of the team. The importance of this, given the complex arrangements, should be noted. In the last school studied the difficulty

of building from a conference blueprint towards an interpretation of race relations while at the same time communicating it
to the pupils was stressed. Concentration was therefore on
the pedagogical dimensions of the new theoretical model. The
teachers in this school are also using Strategy B, the committed approach, which provides an opportunity for further
exploration of the issues this strategy raises in practice.

In school D we shall therefore concentrate almost solely on
the pedagogical aspect and assess its usefulness by examining
teaching in action. In the institutional sense there would seem
to be parallels between the two schools. Both were eager to be
pedagogically open and yet contain something of the institutional
level in that the teachers concerned are all subject specialists.
The question posed as we consider the lessons and the programme intent is the degree to which the teachers respond to
the strategy demands and the degree to which they respond
to the needs of their discipline. The two may not necessarily
be incompatible. Given the backgrounds of the teachers involved
and the needs of the pupils they teach, what a committed teacher means may vary greatly from situation to situation. How
far we can begin to construct a profile of a 'committed' teacher
across situations remains to be seen.

The programme devised by the teaching team shows a broad
approach and follows very closely the guidelines laid down at
the strategy conference:

Since we lived in an area where there was next to no evidence of racial tension and the pupils encountered few
people of different race, we decided that the first part of
our programme ought to be informative rather than seeking particular views. We began by asking the children to
discuss their replies to seven questions aimed at finding
out their attitudes to people of different race. The questions were as follows:

(1) Who are the British?
(2) What is the difference between an immigrant and an
    emigrant?
(3) Which immigrant groups are the largest in Britain?
(4) Why do you think people leave their own country to
    come to live in Britain?
(5) Would you like to leave Britain and go elsewhere to
    live? If so, where would you go? If not, what things
    would make you want to stay?
(6) What do you associate with the following colours?
    Red, pink, white, brown, blue, black, yellow and
    brown.
(7) Would you mind having a foreign person living next
    to you?

Our next two sessions covered the history of early immigrants to Britain and the formation of the British Commonwealth. This was followed by an attempt to consider recent trends in immigration, the reasons for those trends and problems encountered. We used the BBC 'Scene' programme on Ugandan Asians to supplement the lesson. We visited the Commonwealth Institute as the next stage of the programme. Although extremely interesting, the pupils were overwhelmed by the wealth of information. A prearranged talk on the Caribbean proved helpful.

Having covered the background information, we moved on to a more detailed exploration of attitudes. We used as a starting-point the UNESCO material entitled 'What is Man?'. With the co-operation of the head and the staff of (name) School, a visit was arranged to allow the children to meet people of different races. For many, this was the first occasion that they had spoken to a coloured person. We used extracts from the pack as follow-up material to the visit, attempting to show the problems encountered by immigrants on entering the country and endeavouring to adapt themselves to the British way of life. The UNESCO Rumour Clinic idea was used successfully in that it showed big discrepancies between the first and last pictures. I thought this very good material in that it offered purpose and variety and the pupils could readily see the changes taking place and could see that the same thing could happen in everyday life. Drama was introduced to show an example of discrimination at work. The theme was 'A Room to Let', and the husband of the house was asked to choose which of three applicants would get the room. He did not see the callers, and made his decision on information given to him by his wife. The three people were a labourer from a nearby building site, a coloured student and a young mother. The husband chose the student, and according to ballot more than half the class would have done the same.

We reverted to the pack to provide examples of prejudice and discrimination in action and made attempts to introduce words such as 'stereotype' and 'scapegoat'. By now the end of the term was quickly approaching. It was decided that we should look at the wider issues of racial prejudice and we chose the USA as a suitable starting-point. To illustrate the situation existing there we used the 'Scene' programme on Los Angeles.

Our final sessions were stimulated by the excellent 'Scene' programme, 'Sportsmen or Politicians'. Inevitably, this raised the subject of Black Power, and we were able to use the materials supplied in the packs to reinforce this. The sporting theme also led us to South Africa, apartheid and the end of the term.

It is now useful to consider the implication of the programme
in some detail. The initial lesson was in fact done in small
groups. Concern was really with ascertaining who were the
British. As one might expect, and as the geography teacher
notes, the pupils did not see the question in terms of immigrants but along the known lines of English, Scottish, Welsh,
Irish, etc. Prompting was necessary to include other ethnic
groups in their considerations:

LINGUIST: There are some people living in the country now
who class themselves as British, who are British in fact.
And, but they've done it the opposite way round, (name),
to what you were talking about. It's not people from
Britain who've gone elsewhere, but it's people from elsewhere who've come to Britain. Now, what sort of people
would you consider in that group?

PUPIL 2: Are they the people like's been over 'ere, come
over 'ere for a, a little while and who didn't like it and who
got a diff, British passport to go back to over, to where
they was, was before. And that's 'ow they got the British
passport like that. Is that the way they do it?

LINGUIST: I suppose you could. (pauses) That's still not
quite the people that I'm thinking of. We can't add anything
to that list? How many people do you know then who live in
this country but are not English?

PUPIL 1: Sir, Asians.

LINGUIST: Asians, right.

PUPIL 3: Er, Africans.

LINGUIST: Africans.

PUPIL 4: Pakistanis.

LINGUIST: Pakistanis.

PUPIL 1: Indians.

LINGUIST: Indians. Anyone else?

PUPIL 5: Japanese.

PUPIL 4: Chinese.

LINGUIST: Japanese, Chinese.

PUPIL 4: Them from 'ong Kong.

PUPIL 5: They nearly own all our restaurants now, sir, don't
they?

PUPIL 6: Italy.

PUPIL 7: It's not fair for the French. French...

PUPIL 5: There's not many French, though, is there?

PUPIL: There ain't many.

PUPIL 6: They've got their own country, 'aven't they, to live
in?

LINGUIST: All right, (name)?

PUPIL 4: Ugandans.

LINGUIST: Ugandans, yeah.

PUPIL 4: Ukrainians.

Slowly, and at different rates, the group moved to cover the other questions:

LINGUIST: Now these are, um, are some of the people, then, who're living in this country. They're not necessarily all British, are they?
PUPIL 4: No.
LINGUIST: But they are some of the people who are living in this country. OK? Um, let's leave it there then, that question. Let's go on to no. 2. What is the difference between an immigrant...?
PUPIL 5: No, other way round.
PUPIL 3: An immigrant is a person what comes into England and an...
PUPIL 5: Emigrant.
PUPIL: Emigrant is a person what goes out.
LINGUIST: OK. So if you went to Australia to live, (name), would you be an immigrant or an emigrant?
PUPIL 8: An emi...I can't say the word.
PUPIL 5: Emigrant, emigrant.
PUPIL 8: An emigrant.
LINGUIST: So, you'd be an emigrant, would you? OK. We put that question in just to make sure that everybody knew the difference between the word 'immigrant' and 'emigrant'. 'Immigrant' means people who've gone into the country. 'Emigrant' means those people who go out. Which brings us to no. 3: Which immigrant groups do you think are the largest in this country?
PUPIL 4: What, them from different countries, do you mean?
PUPIL 2: Sir, the Asians.
LINGUIST: The Asians.
PUPIL 2: The West Indians. Indians.
LINGUIST: And West Indians.
PUPIL 7: Pakistanis.
LINGUIST: Yeah.

As the responses elicited from the other groups did not diverge dramatically from this one, it seems sensible to continue the lesson development as it took place within that led by the linguist for purposes of continuity. Of particular interest were the answers given to the question concerning the meaning of colours:

LINGUIST: Umm, white?
PUPIL 2: Electric.
PUPIL 1: Light.
PUPIL 4: Light.
PUPIL 3: Light bulb.
PUPIL 6: Life, life.
PUPIL 9: Paper.
LINGUIST: Life? Why life?

PUPIL 6: Because it's got colour, brightness and...
PUPIL 5: Electricity's life.
LINGUIST: Yeah, OK (name), what did you give for white
   on that? Well, what if you haven't got it written down,
   what would you, if I said to you what does the colour
   white mean to you, what would you say?
PUPIL 8: Daylight.
LINGUIST: Daylight?
PUPIL 9: Yeah, snow.
LINGUIST: Snow. All right, snow. Yeah, OK.
PUPIL 9: Paper.
LINGUIST: Blue?
PUPIL 2: Chelsea.
LINGUIST: Chelsea?
PUPIL 2: Yeah, football teams.
PUPIL 8: Sea.
PUPIL 9: The sky.
LINGUIST: Chelsea, sea, sky.
PUPIL 3: Chelsea, sea, sky.
PUPIL 4: They will say this afternoon, they'll see the sky.

   (pupils talk at once)

LINGUIST: Black?
PUPIL 1: People.
PUPIL 5: When it's dark.
PUPIL 8: Dark people.
PUPIL 5: Dark.
PUPIL 2: Night.
PUPIL 3: Death.
LINGUIST: People, death.

   (pupils talk at once)

LINGUIST: OK, um, next colour. Yellow?
PUPIL 3: Sun, sun.
PUPIL 1: Bananas.
PUPIL 6: Colour of our skin.
LINGUIST: Sun, bananas.
PUPIL 2: Moon, moon.
PUPIL 5: Stars.
LINGUIST: Moon and our skin.
PUPIL 8: Skin?

Then this led to the linguist probing how far they would accept
immigrants into their own area:

LINGUIST: No. 7. Would you mind having a foreign person
   living next to you?
PUPIL 8: Shall I read out...
PUPIL 9: If she was all right, sir. If she was a bit of crumpet.

LINGUIST: I think we've got to, we've got to decide, folks, that we're not going to all talk at once, because if we're all talking at once, we're going to get no result at all. You know, we're going to get just a blur over there. Um? Let's try and stop ourselves talking all together.

PUPIL 8: All right. I'll read out. Yes, if it was a French girl, but if it weren't, no.

LINGUIST: So, you wouldn't mind a French girl living next to you?

PUPIL 3: No.

PUPIL 8: Or Swedish, or Swedish.

LINGUIST: Well, I wouldn't either but, er,...

LINGUIST: Can, can we take that question any further?

PUPIL 2: Depends what sort, sir.

LINGUIST: It depends what sort?

PUPIL: It all depends, sir.

PUPIL 6: If it was a foreign like film star, or Pele, I wouldn't mind at all, but if it was an ordinary nig-nog, I'd boot 'im out.

(laughter)

PUPIL 7: What, what if it was Cassius Clay?

PUPIL 6: Oh, 'e - I said any sportsman or famous person.

Small points emerging from the other groups merit passing reference. In one the pupils seemed to be totally unaware that there were even European immigrants in the country. In the other group the teacher insisted on the pupils using respectful labels when making comment on people of other races. In many ways, the opening in which a broad approach was used to gradually focus in on pupils' prejudices would seem to offer much in allowing one to then determine future teaching strategy.

In contrast, the following lessons seem to revert to a much more traditional form. In the first instance this may in part be due to the absence of a team member which therefore may have resulted in some improvisation. The lesson appears to be taken straight from a textbook:

GEOGRAPHY TEACHER: This state of affairs lasted up to the late Bronze Age. Anybody know why an age should be called a Bronze Age?

PUPIL 1: Did they find bronze and make things out of it?

GEOGRAPHY TEACHER: Well, they made - they didn't find bronze because what is bronze? Bronze is...

PUPIL 2: It's an alloy.

GEOGRAPHY TEACHER: It's an alloy of tin and copper, isn't it? You get tin and you get copper and you put them both together and boil them up in a pot and it comes out as bronze, and you make things out of them. As you say, you

make implements and weapons and utensils out of bronze.
Good. That's about 400 BC. Now, we've come across these
letters, these letters BC in our history lessons before.
What do they mean?

PUPILS: (chorus) Before Christ.

GEOGRAPHY TEACHER: Yeh, that's right. We must stop for a
second and think about our time span in history because...
people looked back after a certain stage, they looked back
and then they made up a calendar from that head point, and
they took BC as a very significant thing, date, birth of
Christ, and they had time before the birth of Christ and
time after. Now, what's what letters do you use for after?

PUPILS: (chorus) AD.

GEOGRAPHY TEACHER: Yes, which mean what? What do they
stand for?

PUPILS: (chorus) Anno Domini.

GEOGRAPHY TEACHER: Good. And No. 4 now. Some of the
very first immigrants were the Iron Age people. Now, we've
had the Bronze Age people because they had weapons and
other things made out of bronze. These were called Iron
Age people because they used iron as their chief metal.
For weapons and so on. They lived in large groups or
tribes, and tribal wars were frequent. And all those people
together were called the Celts. That's what the Celts were.
Later tribes of Belgic people arrived and conquered large
areas of Celtic territory. So the Belgic people were also
'immigrants'.

The follow-up included work-sheets with appropriate blanks to
be filled in, a map of the migration routes taken by early peoples through Europe to the British Isles to be completed, and
an exercise on place names. The next lesson involved the whole
class being asked about the Commonwealth. They were required
to list the countries concerned and then locate them on a map.
The session ended by the pupils being divided into groups of
three or four and the giving out of work cards and outline
maps - 'the best writer copy out some information, the best
drawer do maps and the other colour in'. The theme of immigrant settlement in this country was dealt with in a rather
similar way by the geography teacher. An outline map of England and Wales was produced, with certain towns indicated
by initials. Using atlases, the pupils were expected to fill in
the names of the towns in full. These were towns having a large
number of immigrants. To be fair, the lessons were not all
concerned with map work, and this did tend to be regarded as
a practical piece of work set towards the end of the lesson in
order to reinforce what had gone before. The lesson dealing
with the arrival of immigrants had made use of a film concerning Ugandan Asians. At the beginning the teacher made a comment which may well have influenced pupil reactions in later
sessions. The suggestion indicated:

The big problem now that was beginning to arise was that they were in fact different colour, and by the time this afternoon is over I hope to have given you one or two examples which show that the fact that people have a different coloured skin is much more likely to create ill feeling than the fact that people are of a different nationality and of the same coloured skin.

Mention has already been made of the visit to the Commonwealth Institute. It is perhaps useful to reflect pupils' responses to the experience:

GIRL 1: We also went to the Commonwealth Institute, it is in London. I thought it was rotten because it was boring and there was not much to do. I would not like to go there again.

GIRL 2: And we went to the Commonwealth Institute and found that interesting. We saw a film, then looked round, and we met this man and his name was Mr Ali and he showed us some slides, and he had some clothes and different tools to show us and if we wanted we could try the clothes on.
I thought that was interesting because you would know what it felt like to wear the clothes the Indians and Chinese wear, and the other countries. I have learned a lot about relations, I didn't think it would be so interesting. But there is a lot of interesting things.

With the use of the UNESCO material entitled 'What is Man?' the discussion of prejudice began to assume a more open form, and the approach was less formalized once more:

LINGUIST: (reads from pupils' list regarding the characteristics of an Englishman)
'He does not like dark people.' Is that, that, that one goes, then?

PUPIL 1: Well, some of 'em do and some don't.

PUPIL 2: Some don't.

PUPIL 3: My dad does, but I don't.

(laughter)

LINGUIST: Your dad does, but you don't?

PUPIL 3: No.

PUPIL 4: I don't.

(pupils talk all at once)

LINGUIST: Well, one at a time then, please, because we're getting overwhelmed again. Go on, [name].

PUPIL 1: (   )

LINGUIST: What were you going to say, [name]?

PUPIL 5: Well, I was, er, I was going to say, er, these immigrants are being, er, shipped in now without you knowing,
an't, an't they?
LINGUIST: Well, are you talking of...
PUPIL 5: Well, they are, an't they? Because they're smuggling
immigrants into this country now.

(pupils all talk at once)

LINGUIST: Well yes, I think they are. Yeah I know that,
that...
PUPIL 6: And English don't like that.
PUPIL 7: This country, this country's gettin' over-populated
and they're still bringing more and more in.

(pupils talk among themselves)

LINGUIST: If you listened, if you listened to what we said
at the end of the lesson a week ago, there are in fact more
people who leave this country at the moment to live elsewhere than there are people who come from other countries
to live here, and this, this has been the trend since 1967.
So, I don't think you've, you're not quite true on that one,
that there are more immigrants coming than, than ever
because the, um,...

(pupils moan)

LINGUIST: So, um, you're talking about um, Pakistanis and
so on...
PUPIL 3: Yes.
LINGUIST: Supposedly being smuggled in?
PUPIL 5: Yeah they are.
LINGUIST: Yeah?
PUPIL 3: They'll over-run the country.
PUPIL 4: Sir?
LINGUIST: Yeah.
PUPIL 4: Englishmen must be kind because we always let 'em
Blackies come and live 'ere, but if we wanted to go and
live there, they wouldn't let us.
PUPIL 6: Like when they got chucked out...
PUPIL 7: Then what would 'appen?
LINGUIST: What would happen when?
PUPIL 6: If we got kicked out of 'ere?
PUPIL 7: Yeah. Where would we go then?
PUPIL 6: They wouldn't let us go and live in their countries.
LINGUIST: Well, surely haven't, surely we have lived in their
countries, haven't we?
PUPIL 6: I 'aven't.

(several pupils agree they haven't)

LINGUIST: No you boys, you boys...

(pupils carry on talking among themselves)

LINGUIST: But, er, to go back to another lesson or two, you
heard Mr [name] talk about the British Empire and, um,
how ships and people and armies from this country went
all over, well, lots of places throughout the world and set
up their own businesses, trading posts and so on there.
PUPIL 6: They 'ad to take the land.
LINGUIST: So you would prefer the, the Indians, Pakistanis
and West Indians to come here and fight us for it, and if they
won they could have it?

(some pupils assent)

Perhaps the most significant event in the course was a visit to
a school in the Midlands having a large number of coloured
pupils. As one of the teachers notes:

The session showed that the pupils enjoyed their visit to
[name] and that what for many was a first encounter with
a coloured person, was a successful one. I think that the
visit helped tremendously to make the children realize that
immigrants, etc., are not just people you read about and
see pictures about. It made the problems seem much more
real.

Full use was made of the trip in terms of studying the local
geography and industry, and a route map was constructed
by each pupil. But above all, the impact of visiting another
school seems to have been enormous.

The best trip we have been is to [name]. We went to
[name] school but one thing that surprised me that
was all of the boys could smoke there but we cannot
smoke here.

TEACHER: What sort of things did you talk about when you
were going round? Er, did any of you ask them questions
about how they got on in England?
PUPIL 1: No.
PUPIL 2: Football, we were talking about, weren't we mostly?
PUPIL 3: Yeah, football mostly.
PUPIL 2: Football, because, er, he was mad on it. The boy
who showed me and two of my mates around [name] school
was a second generation. He was born in [name], he was
just a bit bigger than myself. Nearly all the questions he
asked was about our school. There was one thing about
their school I did not like and that was the way they serve
dinner out.

Inevitably, the teachers were anxious to assess the effect of
the exercise in promoting increased tolerance:

LINGUIST: Would you like them to come, would you like to be
    all the time in the same school?
PUPIL 1: No.
PUPIL 2: No.
PUPIL 3: No.
LINGUIST: Why not?
PUPIL 4: 'Ow do you mean, sir?
LINGUIST: Well, er,...
PUPIL 4: Do you mean like to live in [name] and go to the
    same school as them?
LINGUIST: Well, if you, if you like, either you sort of go to
    live in [name] or perhaps, er, say a group of twenty or
    thirty families came to live within the [name] area so that
    they were coming to this school. So that you had, er, you
    had coloured people with you in school in about the same
    quantities as you saw yesterday? So we got, we got some,
    to some extent we got a bit the wrong impression yesterday.
    There wasn't quite, you'd probably have seen in the play-
    ground, although there was a lot of coloured people there,
    um, they, they were asked if they would like to come and
    meet you. So in fact we did meet, er, coloured people from
    all over the school, um, and there were a lot of, um,
    English people that we never probably even saw. Well,
    you saw them in the classroom didn't you? But er, um,
    you know if there were thirty folks, say, about that num-
    ber, came to, came to our school permanently, came to live
    in the area and came to school here, would you like that?
PUPIL 1: Wouldn't mind.
PUPIL 2: I wouldn't mind.
PUPIL 3: I wouldn't mind about coming here to live.
PUPIL 4: Wouldn't worry you really, once you got used to
    it.
PUPIL 5: Well, if they don't come 'ere and start trouble it'd
    be all right.
LINGUIST: But why should they start trouble?
PUPIL 3: Well, you never seen anyone making trouble yesterday,
    did you? No? Well, er...
LINGUIST: You wouldn't mind, [name]?
PUPIL 3: No.
LINGUIST: Do you reckon they'd start trouble?
PUPIL 3: No.
PUPIL 2: Not really.
PUPIL 4: No, not really. Once we'd got used to them. We'd
    do all right.
LINGUIST: So it's a question of living together?
PUPIL 2: Yeah.
LINGUIST: Now, [name], would you feel the same?
PUPIL 5: Mmm.

PUPIL 4: It'd be us lot would cause trouble at first. We, we would pick on 'em, wouldn't we? It would be us lot would do, causing the trouble.

LINGUIST: [Name], would you mind?

PUPIL 6: No.

LINGUIST: Now, what about, then, let's change the situation slightly. We, we'll accept them in the school, all right? And they'd be quite, quite welcome and you think...we might have a few difficulties to begin with but once we got to know them, as you were beginning to get to know them yesterday, um, then things would be OK. There would be people you'd like and people you didn't like so much, just as there are people you like and people you don't like so much in school anyway, aren't there? There are some people you like a lot better than others, don't you? So, you say you think it would be the same? Well, what, what would happen then, d'you think, um, if they came, if a group of them came to live next door to you?

PUPIL 1: Don't know.

LINGUIST: [Name]?

PUPIL 3: Wouldn't mind at all.

LINGUIST: You wouldn't mind at all?

PUPIL 3: No.

PUPIL 5: As long as you got friendly with them you'd be all right.

LINGUIST: But from yesterday, would you say that there's no reason why we can't be friends with them is there from...?

PUPIL 2: No.

PUPIL 3: Not really.

PUPIL 6: They was friendly enough with us.

It should be mentioned that at least one member of the team expressed concern that the gains which seemed to have been achieved might weaken considerably, given time.

Sufficient attention has been paid to the course to make the general structure accessible. To continue further might prove repetitious and boring to the reader. The role of the committed teacher in this school could conceivably be labelled innovatory-traditional. Throughout, there has been a constant interplay between the strategy delineated at the conference and the subject strengths of the teachers involved. Why this should be is an open question. It may be that the team saw advantages in building upon the known - their specialisms. On the other hand, they may have found innovatory methods required in a sense a retreat from time to time. The expectations and ability level of the pupils are important factors in such delibera-tions. How far we can define what we mean by a committed approach may not have been answered by a study of this school and the previous one, but we may be some way towards begin-ning to formulate such a definition.

15 INTRODUCTION TO THE STRATEGY C CASE STUDIES

Jon Nixon

Because of the various research stances I was forced to adopt, each of the following studies draws on a different range of data. In Case Study 5 I was writing as an observer who had access to tapes of the lesson, taped interviews with the teacher, a copy of the teacher's lesson plan and of the materials used, and my own observation notes; in Case Studies 6 and 8 I was working entirely from tapes of the sessions and from taped interviews with the teachers and (in the final study) with several pupils; while in Case Studies 7 and 9 I was writing up lessons I had myself taught and was therefore able to draw on a much wider range of data.

Case Studies 6 and 8 are largely descriptive; whereas 5 and 7 attempt an analysis and appraisal of the lessons being studied. Case Studies 5 and 7, however, tackle entirely different pedagogical problems: the first is of a single lesson and explores the structure of that lesson, while Case Study 7 is of a course of lessons and concerns itself with problems of continuity and progression within the course as a whole.

Each of the studies presented a different set of research problems. In the study of my own classroom (Case Studies 7 and 9) the problem was to ensure that I was giving sufficient evidence. Since I had access to a wide range of information which was not formally documented (concerning, for example, my own state of mind while teaching the lessons, the status of drama within the school, the personal history of individual pupils and the relationships within the group), it was all too easy to arrive at an interpretation that would have been unsubstantiated except to those with access to the hidden data. I had to remind myself that what I was interpreting was not the lesson I had perceived as teacher, but the lesson as conveyed in the sum of the data available.

In the study of the single session (Case Study 5), the chief problem was suspending my teacherly judgment. I tried, while observing, not to think what I would have done in that situation, but to appreciate the lesson for what it was. I found this difficult, as I was teaching full-time while writing the studies. More than once I had to check myself from attempting an answer to questions which as an observer I was only in a position to pose. I hope these checks do not appear to be an evasion. They are intended as a mark of respect to the teacher whose lessons I was observing and to the reader who must test each of my judgments against their own experience.

Studies 6 and 8, where I was working entirely from tapes of the lessons and from interviews, presented two problems. It was difficult, first, to gain a sense of participation in the lessons and, second, to be certain whether what was on the tape was of central importance or merely a peripheral occurrence picked up by the chance positioning of the microphone. Both these problems were partially eased by interviewing the teachers and listening to their reactions to the lessons. In this way I experienced, albeit vicariously, a gut reaction to the lessons and acquired an overview which allowed me to place the tapes in context.

The studies are presented in the order in which they were drafted. I was already working on the first two while teaching my own course of lessons and was therefore to some extent grappling in practical terms with the problems I found emerging in other teachers' lessons. There was a constant two-way passage of ideas between my own classroom and the studies I was working on. The work documented in Case Study 9 was carried out some time after the other studies had been drafted and was an attempt to utilize some of the insights culled from the previous work.

It is hardly surprising, therefore, that certain preoccupations run through all these studies. The problems of teaching about race relations through drama cluster in my mind round such practical considerations as the relationship between improvised drama and open-ended discussion, the variety of roles the drama teacher may adopt and the effect of these roles upon the pupils, the expectations of drama entertained by the pupils, the effects of timetabling and the suitability of the teaching strategies employed.

Finally, I must emphasize that my judgments are valid only in so far as they are informed by the evidence available. Where I have included my own analysis and appraisal I have tried also to include all the evidence upon which my interpretation is based.

16 CASE STUDY 5: STRATEGY C

Jon Nixon

It is an all girls, comprehensive school of 1,100 pupils towards
the eastern end of one of the London boroughs. The reputation
of schools in this borough declines as one moves eastward
away from the fashionable middle-class suburbs towards the
predominantly working-class catchment areas housing a high
percentage of Greek Cypriot and West Indian families. The
school building is old and red-brick: narrow corridors, small
rooms and a playground surrounded by twelve foot railings.
The only entrance is by a side gate which leads through the
playground, at the far end of which a large notice directs all
visitors to report to the school secretary.

The head of drama, whose lesson I had come to observe,
believes that good drama work takes time to develop. Almost
her first comment when we met was that two hours was not long
enough to explore the theme of race relations in any depth.
She is formal and seemingly conventional, both in her attitude
to visitors and in her relationships with pupils. The image that
many people have of the drama teacher as a flamboyant creature
of mood is hardly appropriate in her case. For she relies not
on charisma, but on patience, a cool nerve and the capacity to
listen. 'I try', she says, 'not to impose my own views on a
class, but to get them to think about both sides of the situation.'

By way of preparation she had made photocopies of National
Front and National Party leaflets to initiate a discussion among
the pupils; formulated a number of questions to maintain and
focus the discussion; and decided in broad terms what the
main phases of the lesson were to be. These she had jotted
down as

(1) discussion;
(2) discussion in pairs;
(3) group improvisations showing what it is like to be black in
a white community.

In the event, the second phase took the form of a large-group
discussion led by the teacher.

There were four leaflets, among them one issued by the
National Party only a few months after the organization had been
formed and entitled 'At last... someone who speaks up for the
British!' A National Front leaflet entitled 'Transport staff'
claimed that 480 busmen had been injured in assaults during

1974 and alleged that 'West Indian youths marauding around London in gangs' were responsible. Another National Party leaflet, addressed to those who 'want Britain for the British', advocated scrapping overseas aid 'to inefficient Afro-Asian countries'; withdrawing grants 'from deadbeats, hooligans and Communist trouble-makers at our universities'; and rooting out of public life 'all Communists and others who act to strengthen the Soviet Union, including those inside the Labour Party'. Finally, a National Front leaflet claimed that 80 per cent of muggings in Lambeth were by blacks; and that during nine months of 1974 black youths were responsible for 172 out of 203 assaults in Lewisham. The leaflet was entitled 'Citizens!' and ended 'Stand up for law and order - join the National Front'.

Entering the drama room, the girls were each handed a copy of one of these leaflets. They read them through and, having arranged themselves into three groups, began to discuss them informally. Each group comprised pupils of British, West Indian and Cypriot origin. When asked what her reaction was to the leaflet she was reading, a West Indian girl replied: 'Not to read any more'. Nevertheless, these small-group discussions continued for twenty-five minutes, during which time the teacher observed and rarely interrupted. In adopting this role she was deviating from her original plan, which had been to start the lesson with a large-group discussion and proceed to small-group work. Her reason for this change of plan, she said afterwards, was her realization as the pupils entered that each group needed, initially, to work at its own pace and in some degree of privacy.

At two o'clock the teacher called the pupils together for the large-group discussion in which she hoped to pose some of the questions she had previously formulated:

- What are your reactions to the leaflets?
- Are the allegations they contain true?
- Do you feel they are advocating law and order?
- What do you think about their proposals concerning repatriation?
- Who are 'the British'?
- Is there any evidence of racial discrimination in England?
- Why do you suppose some black people turn to crime?

All these issues were raised during the lesson, although not necessarily in the order shown or at this particular stage. The questions were not intended as an exhaustive list of topics to be covered in the time allotted, but merely as a useful checklist of possible areas to explore.

From the outset, the discussion was characterized by the absence of any radical disagreement among the group members. The following extract is typical of the way in which each pupil supported the other by echoing what had just been said. These verbal echoes served either to emphasize a point, substantiate an assertion or develop the line of argument of the previous speaker. The value of any contribution was measured in terms of the extent to which it expressed the unanimity of the group.

PUPIL: Miss, I think once they say 'Get the West Indians out!' they are going to start on the Greeks, the Irish...
PUPIL: They're trying to get all of them out, all immigrants out.
PUPIL: The English always like to have a scapegoat. First it was the Irish that they said were depending on the state. Then it was the Jews. Then they felt sorry for the Jews because everyone else was feeling sorry for the Jews; and then it was the Greeks, and then it was...and now it's the coloureds. They just need someone. They cannot blame it on themselves.
TEACHER: So do you feel, then, that the National Front are getting support because people want a scapegoat?
PUPIL: Because they...they're going to people and telling them 'Oh, look at him. He's doing better than you. He's foreign. You should be doing that job. He should be doing this.' Or something like that. They're bringing hatred.
PUPIL: Because no one can accept failure, and they need someone to blame.
PUPIL: And it's easy to blame someone that's not...
TEACHER: What sort of thing are they worried about, then, the people who support the National Front?
PUPIL: They're just worried about getting left behind.
TEACHER: As a country do you think?
PUPIL: No, they think the ones who are taking over...
PUPIL: Miss, in the programme they said that the white people, the majority that they spoke to, they think that the black people, immigrants, are taking over...
PUPIL: Even if they are taking over, they're not taking over by wanting to. It's just that, I dunno, it's just that in most important jobs, or really dirty industrial jobs that need to be done, it's always the foreigners doing them.
PUPIL: Yes, that's true.

As in the case of her pupils, the teacher reinforced the sense of group identity through a process of reiteration: with her first question she paraphrased what had just been said by repeating the term 'scapegoat'; with her second question she made explicit the link, which was only just beginning to emerge, between racial hatred and fear; while her third question, although it called forth one of the few contradictions within the discussion, was merely a modification, couched in the interrogative, of the preceding statement. Her handling of the discussion was, thus, one of the factors contributing to the insularity of the group.

If this insularity was the effect the teacher had hoped to achieve, one wonders why she did not use the discussion to

draw the pupils towards some understanding of how and why
they were reacting in such a way. If, however, it was not the
effect she was aiming at, why had she initially presented the
pupils with such a limited range of viewpoints? The provision
of literature expressing racial tolerance as well as racial hostility
might have given them the security within which to adopt a more
detached and quizzical mode of inquiry. For, given the manner
in which the lesson had been introduced, the pupils had little
alternative but to take up a defensive position. This is not to
say that the pupils in any way confused the views expressed
in the leaflets with the attitude of the teacher, but simply to
recognize that such leaflets would be bound to alienate any
multi-racial group of pupils irrespective of their teacher's
personal beliefs.

The swift consensus achieved by the group generated its own
distinctive, anti-racist humour, the purpose of which was not,
as with a racist joke, to draw a deliberately broad racial stereotype, but to point out the absurdity of such stereotypes ever
being taken seriously:

> When I went to Wales...an old lady come up to me, and she
> goes, 'Hello darling, you over from Africa? You come over
> here for teaching?' I goes, 'No, I was born in London.'
> She goes, 'London?' I goes, 'Yea...' She goes, 'Are there
> lots of you up there?' I goes, 'Yes there are quite a few of
> us.' She goes, 'You wasn't born here?' I goes, 'Yes, I was
> born here.' She goes, 'How old are you?' I goes, 'Fifteen.'
> She goes, 'You're big for fifteen.' She was so shocked. It
> was so funny the looks I got there.

The fact that this anecdote was punctuated with laughter tells
us something important about the experience and attitudes of
the pupils; for only those knowledgeable about, and tolerant
towards, the idea of a multi-ethnic community would appreciate
the humour of the story. To one who was as ignorant of second-
generation immigrants as the woman mentioned in the anecdote,
its point would be lost; to one who was as intolerant as, say,
a member of the National Front, it would be far from funny.
The humour, in so far as it relied upon a shared system of
beliefs and attitudes, was as context-bound as the racism it
sought to subvert.

A dissenting voice did emerge, however, from a white girl
who was viewed with some suspicion by the rest of the group.
She had only one friend, a black girl. For the first ten minutes
of the discussion the white girl remained silent. When she did
speak she delivered the following 'set speech', which was in
marked contrast to any of the other girls' contributions:

> I'm not sure that you can always believe statistics, because
> in the local paper not very long ago there was a chart which
> showed the amount of immigration coming into...and it said

that it was the highest in 1920, and that it has been going
down very rapidly ever since. Well, the trouble is that
with something like the National Front, with Communism,
or whatever it is, you're not always sure that you can
believe statistics, which I think tend to mislead people.
They say that 80 per cent of crimes are committed by
blacks. Well, they might be or they might not be.

Unimpressed by her lack of certainty, the pupils received
these comments with some embarrassment and hostility. It was
difficult to know from what the girl had said whether she was
casting doubt on the National Front statistics, on the figures
published in the local paper, or on both.
    A few minutes later she made a further attempt to gain a
hearing. Although she adopted a less equivocal tone, she was
still having difficulty finding her own voice.

PUPIL: May I suggest, this isn't my view necessarily, but may
    I suggest that desperate situations call for desperate mea-
    sures.
PUPIL: What sort of views has your dad got? I know he's
    National Front.

The tentative 'may I suggest', and the claim that the view being
put forward was not necessarily her own, suggest a degree of
uncertainty unique among the contributions to the half-hour
discussion. The question uttered in response went to the heart
of the matter. Placed in the awkward position of having to
mediate between her father's views and those of her own peer
group, the girl replied:

PUPIL: He says that blacks as a whole have got less reserve,
    by which he means, say, you get a classroom situation where
    a teacher yells at a girl. One of the coloured girls is more
    likely to stand up and yell back than, say, I would be. Now,
    he thinks that they have got less reserve, so that as a
    group they are possibly more excitable perhaps.
PUPIL: No, more able to stand up for their rights!

The final comment in no way denied the premise 'that blacks
as a whole have got less reserve'. Indeed, the premise was
tacitly assumed by the second speaker in order to argue a
different case: that the lack of reserve should be seen not as
excitability, but as an ability to stand up for one's rights.
    Half of the two-hour lesson had now passed. The teacher
initiated the final phase by telling the pupils

to work out in groups an improvisation based on the idea
of what it's like to be black in a white community, or maybe
not even as obvious as that: what it's like to be different.

She put a time limit of half an hour on their preparation, during which she once more observed their work, only occasionally intruding to cajole the sluggish and encourage the downhearted.

The change-over of activities seemed to fracture the lesson. The pupils found considerable difficulty in relating the ideas they had been exploring during the discussion to the problems they were now facing in their drama work. These problems were, in almost every case, formal: concerned with the development and rounding-off of the plot, or the follow-on from one scene to another. The theme of race relations became merely a hook on which to hang the drama, the pupils tending to rely on complicated story-lines rather than exploring the clash of values and attitudes implicit in their chosen situation.

The following extract, for example, is taken from an improvisation in which the mother of a white girl slams the front door in the face of the black boyfriend, whom the daughter has brought home to meet her parents.

BOYFRIEND: I don't trust them, you know I don't.
GIRL: They might be a bit abrupt at first, but they'll come round.
MOTHER: That's her.
GIRL: Mum, don't shut the door. Mum, open up.
MOTHER: Jennifer, get in here.
GIRL: Mum!
MOTHER: Take him away, he's a coloured man.
FATHER: I'm joining the National Front, didn't you know that?
MOTHER: This is a respectable neighbourhood, and I'm not having you going out...
GIRL: I don't care about respectable. Just because his skin's a different colour doesn't mean he's not respectable.
MOTHER: Now, listen, I'm warning you, you'll be packed off to Scotland now with me and your dad. Come on, pack your things.
GIRL: Where are you going?
MOTHER: To your Aunt's. Aunt Betty.
GIRL: I don't want to go, Mum, please let me stay.

As soon as the pupil playing the girlfriend tried to slow down the action and discuss some of the issues underlying what was happening, the pupil playing the mother initiated a new development in the plot whereby everybody was to set off for Scotland. The characters rushed from one activity to another without any opportunity to reflect upon the significance of the events that had overtaken them.

It may well be that the pupils were unable to explore the theme of race relations in any depth because they were unable to handle the drama form with any degree of subtlety. What they finally produced was a sentimental 'soap opera', in which the girlfriend, having alienated her parents by running away from home, asked her boyfriend to marry her, and, when he accepted, immediately announced: 'I must go back and tell my mum and dad. They may have softened up a bit'. Predictably, mother and father had indeed 'softened up', for as soon as they had heard that Alec was a doctor they had agreed to accept him as their daughter's future husband. The dramatic problem posed by the clash of values was immediately spirited away, and we returned once more to a cosy consensus by which, presumably, everybody lived happily ever after.

There may well be a correspondence here between the pupils' inability to value divergent viewpoints in the discussion and their inability to explore them through drama. The crucial question for the teacher is: how could she have helped her pupils to handle these two modes of discourse in such a way as to explore the racial theme more fully?

Perhaps the most interesting, and disturbing, of the three plays was that presented by a group comprising two black and three white girls, including the girl who had spoken up earlier about her father's views. In this short improvisation the girls turned the subject on its head to show what it might feel like to be white in a black community.

(Three white girls are sitting in their flat.)
1: God, oh my God!
2: What's up with you then? You know what blacks are like.
1: White coffee, please.
2: Are there any papers around?
3: Well, there's a Daily Herald somewhere. Black.
1: My God!
2: What's the matter now?
1: Black Prime Minister says, 'Get whites out of Britain.
   Britain for blacks. Black power in...'
2: Why don't we see if there's anything on?
1: Well, it does say something about a disco down here. It
   says 'anybody welcome'.

(The three friends are on their way to the disco.)

3: Come on, you lot.
BLACK GIRLS: (shouting) Black is power! Black is power!
3: Come on, it looks OK.
2: Well, it's white music anyway.
3: Can we get a drink?
2: Yea, over here.
BLACK GIRLS: (singing starts) Black is the colour...What
   are you lot doing here?
3: This is a white disco.
1: Come on, I'm getting out.
BLACK GIRLS: Move man, move.
1: Come, let's get home while we still can.
2: Yea.

BLACK GIRLS: I say, fellows get those white people out. We
  don't want them in, do we?
3: That was close.
2: How would they feel if we tried to push them out?
1: Come on, I'm going to bed.
2: Yea, I'm tired.

(Back in the flat, next day.)

3: Oh, what a beautiful black morning. (laughing) Get out,
  you white trash.
1: What can we do about it?
2: We can call the police.
3: It's worth a try.
2: Hello, is that the police?

(The flat later)

3: They've come. Oh God, they're bloody well black!
2: Oh God Almighty, what can we do? We must get out.
3: There's only one place to go and that's the West Indies.
  Everyone's going there.
BLACK GIRLS: Freedom!

Understandably, the class reacted strongly against the cynicism
of this piece. Its most disturbing feature, from my point of
view, was the willingness of the two black girls to assume,
within the play, roles closely corresponding to the stereotyped
view of West Indian life contained in the National Front and
National Party leaflets distributed at the beginning of the lesson.
    In one respect this improvisation was typical of all the drama
work produced by the pupils. For not one of the groups placed
at the centre of its drama a character whose prejudice became
the major theme of the work. The main characters were in each
case the victims, rather than the agents, of racial prejudice.
    During this lesson, then, two related problems emerged. The
first concerned the swift consensus achieved by the pupils,
who were united in their rejection of the extreme, racist views
put forward by the leaflets. As a result, they dismissed the
few divergent opinions which were expressed within the group.
The second problem concerned the use of easy stereotypes and
stock responses within the drama work. Racial prejudice was
presented as something that happens to 'us' as a result of the
feelings and actions of 'them'. Clearly, these two problems were
closely related, for each frustrated the teacher's intention 'to
get them to think about both sides of the situation'. The emer-
gence of the two problems would seem to confirm what the teacher stated at the beginning: that a session of two hours does
not allow enough time to explore with a group of pupils an issue
which, as she put it, 'is really close to them and impinges on
their lives'.

17 CASE STUDY 6: STRATEGY C

Jon Nixon

The mixed comprehensive school, on the fringes of a Midlands
city, stands in pleasant suburbs, but draws on a predominantly
working-class area. The majority of its 1,300 pupils come from
a large council estate nearby. Six per cent are immigrants.
Drama, like all subjects, is taught in ability bands up to the
end of the fifth year, but no examination in the subject is
offered. The drama department is staffed by two teachers, one
of whom had, at the time of the project, just returned to
teaching after a nine-year break. Each teacher agreed to monitor her work with a group of thirty fourth-year pupils,
although neither had previously been engaged in a research
project that involved any form of self-monitoring. At the
beginning of the term each group had only one forty-minute
lesson a week. This proved inadequate for the project, so
each group was timetabled for a further period and the teachers
given time after the lessons to write up notes and discuss their
work together.
   A sense of isolation soon developed in both teachers in spite
of occasional visits from the local authority drama adviser and
from members of the project team. Their chief problem, initially,
was that of re-defining their roles in order to work together
as a mutually supportive team, each helping the other to record
and to grasp the significance of what had happened in the
lessons. Although they shared a common approach to the subject,
they had to learn how to plan together, to observe each other's
lessons, and, perhaps most difficult of all, how to discuss each
other's work. In the course of an interview that took place half-
way through the term, the teachers talked about some of these
difficulties.

INTERVIEWER: Is it interesting working together?
TEACHER 1: Well, no, it has driven us potty, let's be honest.
   Because we feel we don't know each other as human beings
   any more. We don't talk to each other socially any more.
   We don't get enough time. I don't ask L. how she is or what
   colour she is going to paint her ceiling.
TEACHER 2: You see, we have done quite a lot of work in half-
   term and in the evenings trying to plan lessons. G. has only
   just had this lesson freed now. Normally, she has had to
   go off and teach...
TEACHER 1: Straight away, as soon as that is over.
TEACHER 2: ...which is very difficult. But now it has been

arranged, because we have had a lot of problems with this work; a lot has been done to get her free as we have had to get together to tape our comments after the lessons at night and at half-term. You see, we don't talk to each other any more about family and children and homes and the pleasantries...

TEACHER 1: We look at each other and think 'ah! ah!'...

INTERVIEWER: What would be the difference between the present situation if you weren't in the national project? I mean, if you decided that you were going to work on this yourselves, and make the decision entirely yourselves?

TEACHER 1: We wouldn't care about making mistakes. We wouldn't care if the kids reacted in what we felt was the wrong way.

INTERVIEWER: Might you have done it yourselves?

TEACHER 2: I might have done it on my own or you might have, and we would have said to each other: 'Hey, I've got something interesting going. How about you having a go?'... Or 'What are we going to do this week? I'll tell you what I did last week and it went down very well...'. We would probably have done it that way, I think; much more generally.

Their own expertise, as teachers and researchers, developed throughout the term as they talked through their classroom problems and shared one another's insights. To suggest that they had an easy passage, however, would be misleading. For they were being asked to be innovatory twice over: first, by introducing into their classroom a controversial issue rarely treated explicitly in schools and, second, by extending their professional role to include that of researcher. The pressure under which these teachers were working was therefore considerable; a point to be borne in mind throughout the following brief description of the lessons that emerged from their partnership.

The course of lessons began with the pupils exploring in groups the problems facing two young people of different racial origin who have started going out together. Each of the groups prepared an improvisation in which the boy visits the home of his girlfriend. At the beginning of the second lesson the pupils were told to act out a conversation between the couple some time after the visit. The following extract shows two English pupils acting out a conversation between a Pakistani boy and an English girl. Much to the amusement of his classmates, the boy assumed a heavy, stereotyped accent.

GIRL: Ali, I was ever so sorry about when you came to our house on Sunday. It was just that our dad lost his job, you see, and he can't find another one anywhere. That made him seem worried and on edge.

BOY: You sure you not telling me lies, Deborah?

GIRL: No, of course not.
BOY: My daddy is chief executive Green Shield Stamps.
GIRL: Oh, is he really? I'd love to meet your dad.
BOY: He's a bit stuck-up at the moment.
GIRL: Oh, what a shame!
BOY: When I get married he will give £10,000 away and a
    new house.
GIRL: Oh, that's nice.
BOY: Maybe we can get your daddy a job.
GIRL: Oh, do you really think so?
BOY: Yes.
GIRL: Well, what about coming round to our house one Sunday
    and discussin' it with my dad?
BOY: That'd be very nice.
GIRL: Oh, good.

In order to be accepted, the black boyfriend had to have a
superior social position to the white girl. One group, for example, prepared an improvisation in which the girlfriend's parents,
on realizing that their daughter's Pakistani boyfriend was a
doctor, switched from an attitude of antagonism to one of positive approval.
    When each group had shown its work the teacher initiated a
further improvisation in which the girl returned home after
seeing the boy.

MOTHER: You're here at last are you? Half past eleven!
GIRL: Oh, it's only quarter of an hour late.
MOTHER: You've been out with him again. I told you.
GIRL: Oh, what's wrong with that?
MOTHER: The neighbours 'll start complaining, that's what's
    wrong.

The mother's reaction provoked the comment from one member
of the group that she might well have been equally disapprov-
ing of a punk-rocker as a boyfriend for her daughter, on the
grounds that he too would start the neighbours complaining.
    A week later the teacher discussed with the class why the
visit had failed. Each group then prepared an improvisation
involving a second visit. When these improvisations had been
shown to the rest of the class, the teacher asked the groups
to describe what had happened. The ensuing discussion included
the following contribution from one of the girls in the class.

It's not only really coloured people, Miss, that they're prejudiced against. Sometimes, if you've got a southern person
from down South and a person from the North comes, and
it's sometimes the same with them. The family doesn't like
her, so they don't give her a chance. And they talk about
her or him behind the daughter or the son's back.

Her comment was an attempt to relate the drama more closely to her own experience and thereby extend her understanding of prejudice. By so doing, she may well have deepened the experience for the whole group. For hitherto the pupils seem to have operated at a fairly superficial level, showing little inclination to reflect upon the issue with any seriousness. As the teacher herself pointed out, this may well have been a result of her own inexperience in leading class discussions.

Starting the next session at some distance from the racial issue, the teacher asked the pupils to prepare an improvisation in which 'two ordinary, English people' were talking about their forthcoming marriage. Only when these improvisations had been performed did she ask them to explore a similar situation involving an English and a Chinese person.

GIRL: Are you going to ask me now? We've been going out with each other for six years.
BOY: Well, Kung Fu, my darling, I haven't got much ackers on me at the moment.
GIRL: What do you mean by this?
BOY: Money, I mean.
GIRL: Money. Well, we could go to China.
BOY: I'm not living in China.
GIRL: Why not?
BOY: I don't like the cooking.
GIRL: I can cook.
BOY: I suppose you can...My mother can cook quite good.
GIRL: I don't like her beef broth what she cooks.
BOY: She does a beautiful beef broth.
GIRL: I like rice.
BOY: Well...I think we should live in England myself, if we do get married, that's if; I think we should.
GIRL: Well, I think we should.
BOY: Live in England?
GIRL: Yes.

The pupils were told to prepare a final improvisation set in a pub or a youth club. One member of each group was to tell the others about the recent engagement.

GIRL 1: Oh, that Chinese food, I can't stand it!
GIRL 2: It's horrid!
GIRL 3: Hi girls, you'll never guess.
GIRL 2: What?
GIRL 3: I'm engaged.
GIRL 1: Who's the lucky fella, girl?
GIRL 3: Wong Chu.
GIRL 2: Wong Chu?
GIRL 1: That chinky Chinaman from down the road?
GIRL 3: What about him?
GIRL 1: I mean, if you love him you can't do very much about it.

GIRL 3: Well, I do love him and we're going to get married. There's the ring.
GIRL 2: Oh, isn't that lovely!

Some of the conflicts and tensions developed by the pupils throughout these series of improvisations were picked up by the teacher and used in the next session. Working in the same pairs, the pupils were to imagine that they had been married for a month and that they were having their first, serious quarrel.

BOY: Oh, God blimey, I'm not eating that chinkyman food. You bleedin' take it back and give me a plate of fish and chips, English food! No more o' that foreign junk. If I don't get my fish and chips I'll go and fetch it myself.
GIRL: Go and fetch it then.
BOY: And I won't come back.
GIRL: You what?
BOY: Chicken food!
GIRL: I'll go and get you some bread and butter then.
BOY: Oh, no you don't. Fish and chips!
GIRL: You can go and get it yourself.
BOY: I will.
GIRL: Go on then.
BOY: I will.
GIRL: Go on.
BOY: Right then, I'm going down pub.

Lacking the knowledge necessary to structure their work round more subtle, cultural differences of attitude and upbringing, the pupils could only present the domestic conflict in terms of a clash between two crudely drawn images of the British and Chinese ways of life: fish and chips and 'chinkyman food'.

At the beginning of the next session, the pupils were told that they would be working in pairs. They were to imagine that they worked in a factory. For twenty years they had done the same job until, one day, the boss came along and told them that they were to change jobs. The pupils were to discuss this situation in the role of the two workers. During the second half of the lesson the pupils worked in groups of five. They were to imagine now that three members of each group had worked together for a long time. The manager had appeared with a school-leaver and informed the three that one of them must be transferred. It was the duty of the other two to make the newcomer familiar with the job.

MANAGER: Morning, girls.
GIRLS: Morning, sir.
MANAGER: Just popped in to tell you that one of you's going to have to change your jobs.
GIRL 1: I'm not. I don't see why I should.

MANAGER: Well, you've got to decide it between yourselves.
GIRL 2: Well, we're not changin', are we girls?
MANAGER: I've got a new student coming in this afternoon...
   You've either got to go in the postal department or the
   cooking department.
GIRL 3: I've been there and I don't like it.
MANAGER: Oh, come on, you've got to...
GIRL 2: I'm not. I'm not.
MANAGER: Alison, come on.
GIRL 1: They're not a friendly lot over there.
GIRL 2: How dare you!
MANAGER: Well, you're leavin' in a week.
GIRL 1: Oh, I suppose I'll have to anyway.
GIRLS: Goodbye...
MANAGER: Well, here's the new girl.
GIRL 2: Holy Joseph, look at that!
MANAGER: Well, show her the ropes.
GIRL 3: Hello. This is the machine that you work. This is
   how you do it: you pull the lever, press the button, push
   the lever up. All right? Will you try it? Pull the lever! This
   one! That's it. Push the button down as you do it. Push
   the lever again. That's right. And you've got to do that
   much quicker than you're doing it. A hundred and fifty
   times a day.
NEWCOMER: I can't do it.
GIRL 2: Well, you'll have to learn, won't you?
MANAGER: How's the new girl getting on, then?
GIRL 2: Well, I don't know really.
MANAGER: What about getting her an easier job, then?
GIRL 3: We tried to help her. We've been very nice to her,
   but she just doesn't know how to do it.
MANAGER: Well, let her have the job for another day or so,
   until she learns the ropes.
GIRL 2: Why can't Alison come back? She'd do it much better.
MANAGER: All right, I'll see about getting Alison back.
GIRL 3: Right.

At no point during this lesson was the racial issue raised by
either the teacher or the pupils. This would seem to have
resulted, in part, from a conscious decision taken at about
this stage of the term. For, in the interview with the teachers
already quoted, the suggestion was made that 'if you do
ordinary drama of human relations in the sense that you are
not going to talk about race...it tends to come up on them
personally instead of being structured into the drama'.
   A similar approach was adopted initially the following week.
The teacher asked the pupils why some young people leave
home. The pupils replied that it was because of arguments at
home, because they were 'fed up' or perhaps because their
parents were re-marrying. She told them to act out, in pairs,
a telephone conversation between a landlord and a young

person who had just left home and was looking for somewhere
to live. A further improvisation was then set up in which the
pupils worked in groups of four. One person was to act as
the landlord and three as applicants. The landlord had to show
them round and decide which to accept. Only after these
improvisations had been performed did the teacher make specific
reference to the racial issue:

> When you go on to do the next thing that I want you to do,
> I want you to imagine that you have people coming to see the
> flat who are of different races, different nationalities. Can
> you think of any problems that you'd face in looking for a
> flat which you haven't touched on?

A short discussion followed. The pupils then began their preparation, which was cut short by the bell marking the end of
the lesson.

When the class re-convened a week later, the teacher read
to the pupils a poem by Wole Soyinka entitled 'Telephone Conversation'. After discussing the poem they returned to the
improvisation that they had begun to prepare at the end of the
previous lesson. One of the groups prepared a piece which
prompted the following exchange between teacher and pupil:

TEACHER: What nationality were you?
PUPIL: Pakistani.
TEACHER: Pakistani. And did you really think that Pakistanis
   made stew out of spiders?
PUPIL: I don't know.
TEACHER: You don't know.

It is difficult to know whether the pupil's admission of ignorance is genuine or merely thrown in for the amusement of his
classmates.

During the final session the pupils prepared an improvisation
in which friends at school discuss the rumour that a black
family are to move into the neighbourhood. The pupils then
acted out a conversation between the neighbours.

NEIGHBOUR 1: Oh, hello...
NEIGHBOUR 2: Hello.
NEIGHBOUR 1: I've got something to tell you.
NEIGHBOUR 2: Have you?
NEIGHBOUR 1: You know that house...
NEIGHBOUR 2: Yes.
NEIGHBOUR 1: Coloureds are moving in.
NEIGHBOUR 2: Coloureds?
NEIGHBOUR 1: Mm...Do you know what?
NEIGHBOUR 2: What?
NEIGHBOUR 1: They smell...Do you know what else?
NEIGHBOUR 2: What?

NEIGHBOUR 1: There's twelve of 'em.
NEIGHBOUR 2: Twelve!
NEIGHBOUR 1: Mm...Do you know summat else? They eat curry in bed.
NEIGHBOUR 2: Curry in bed!
NEIGHBOUR 1: They sleep on the floor.
NEIGHBOUR 2: Sleep on the floor!
NEIGHBOUR 1: Mm...It stinks! 'orrible! AND they do black magic.
NEIGHBOUR 2: Black magic!
NEIGHBOUR 1: Mm...black magic. So what we going to do about it?
NEIGHBOUR 2: Like what?
NEIGHBOUR 1: I hadn't thought of that actually.
NEIGHBOUR 2: Have you ever spoken to a coloured person?
NEIGHBOUR 1: No. In fact, I don't even know what one looks like.

This exchange was met with laughter, not because it trivialized the issue, as had been the case in some of the earlier work, but because it defined what was for the pupils the key problem: their own ignorance of people of other races. The prolonged period of playing with stereotypes, of assuming heavy accents and exchanging racist jokes, may well have been a necessary prelude to more thoughtful work. For their humour could be seen as a continuum, at one end confirming prejudice and at the other confounding it with a flash of insight. In the later, more thoughtful, improvisations the pupils did not abandon the humorous; they used it to inform and shape their drama so that laughter sprang from its very structure.

After the lessons had been taught the teachers were interviewed a second time. The following extract from this interview suggests something of the complexity and strength of their response to the term's work.

TEACHER 2: I mean, honestly, didn't we hate the whole, blummin' thing? We did, you see. We hated....It was a nightmare! You've no idea!
TEACHER 1: We stirred up so much 'aggro'...
TEACHER 2: With ourselves, you know; I think a lot with ourselves as well.
TEACHER 1: And with the kids...
TEACHER 2: They didn't like doing the project.
INTERVIEWER: Why?
TEACHER 2: Don't know.
TEACHER 1: Brought out all their...
TEACHER 2: Because they didn't want to face that they felt any prejudice. You see, in this school before I don't think there was really any consciousness of race at all. Was there, really? We didn't have enough coloured kids.
INTERVIEWER: Did they feel the problem was being imposed

upon them to some extent?

TEACHER 2: Yes, this was the whole point really.

INTERVIEWER: Did you feel that the problem was being imposed
upon you?

TEACHER 1: Yes.

TEACHER 2: In a way...Yes, I said I felt that suddenly...I
mean, I always thought before I was never prejudiced and
I still think I'm not, but suddenly I was aware of things
within myself and it was the same for the kids. They became
aware that inside them there was more than they'd ever
thought about. I mean, you can say it's a good thing to
bring it to the surface. It is, if you know how to handle
it. But it takes a great deal of patience and time on the part
of the teacher.

TEACHER 1: Which we haven't got.

TEACHER 2: You know, which you haven't got in a big school.

'It was a nightmare!' Such exclamations, scattered throughout
the interview, articulate the teachers' own doubts as to whether
they had measured up to the task. The nightmare was their
own fear of failure. Other memories - 'suddenly I was aware of
things within myself and it was the same with the kids' - recall
their sense of importance of the work in which they had been
engaged.

Although this account has given a very limited view of individual lessons, it has, I hope, revealed the structure of the
course as a whole. The topic was kept alive by careful sequenc-
ing of the drama; the pupils holding the 'story line' in their
minds from week to week. This was achieved without the teacher
relinquishing the traditional role of initiator or instructor. The
pupils were encouraged to fill out the detail, but the teacher
defined the framework of action. She did so by means of a
limited number of teaching strategies: some discussion but, in
the main, small-group improvisations shown to the rest of the
class.

18 CASE STUDY 7: STRATEGY C

Jon Nixon

There were three of us: one fully qualified teacher and two
student teachers. One of the students was a drama specialist
in her second year at the Central School of Speech and Drama,
and the other, a graduate of English completing his Postgrad-
uate Certificate of Education (PGCE) at Cambridge. We were
working within an independent drama department of which I
was the head. The other fully qualified member of the department was timetabled elsewhere and therefore not directly
involved in the teaching of this particular second-year group.
Situated within a predominantly working-class area of inner
London, the comprehensive school drew on pupils of many different racial origins: English, West Indian and Cypriot mainly,
with some Asians. The proportion of black to white pupils,
within both the group and the school, was about three to one.
Members of the drama department enjoyed slightly reduced
class sizes of twenty, rather than thirty, which was the norm,
because of the nature of the subject and the limited facilities
available. A classroom, situated some way from the main body
of the school, had been converted into the drama studio. Since
it had to act as a form room and on occasion as a teaching room
for other subjects, it was furnished with tables, chairs and
lockers. Consequently, space was limited.

Few plans had been made prior to the commencement of the
course. Brian, the PGCE student, had expressed a wish to see
some drama work, and as a result had been invited to join in
the lessons. Maria, on the other hand, was obliged to attend,
as drama was her main subject. Both began as observers.
Primarily, a clear brief was given them concerning what aspects
of the lesson to observe and make notes on. Soon, however,
their roles were extended to include that of teacher as well
as observer. Neither of the two student teachers was involved
as fully as I had hoped in the planning of the lessons. I took
responsibility for initiating new phases and expected Brian
and Maria to respond appropriately. Their role cannot have
been an easy one.

I also took responsibility for documenting the lessons. In
addition to recording on tape what actually happened, I wanted
a record of what the various parties thought had happened and
what they thought was the significance of what had happened.
This involved monitoring the pupils' and student teachers' viewpoints as well as my own. Occasionally, early on in the course
of lessons, a pupil was asked, or volunteered, to act as an

observer and make notes along with Brian and Maria. A more successful way of monitoring pupils' viewpoints, however, was by interview. We experimented with three different forms: the pupil interviewed by a student teacher; by a complete outsider visiting the school; and by another pupil in the same group. Each of these methods, we found, highlighted different issues.

As soon after each lesson as possible I noted down what seemed to me to have been its main phases. Before the lesson I defined my objectives and decided on how best to involve Brian and Maria. Rarely did I teach from a clearly formulated lesson plan. I knew how I wanted to begin and where I wanted to go to, and had mapped a few alternative routes; but each lesson turned on the unexpected. For the innumerable, quick decisions that comprise each teacherly act were in this case a response to ideas and suggestions thrown out by the pupils. Several days after the lesson, having had time to study the various notes and tapes, I wrote more generally about what I saw as the key problems to have emerged.

In order that the progression within the course may be perceived from the outset, I shall present my own weekly record at this point. This does not include the more reflective comments added later. Each lesson was eighty minutes long, lasting from 11.15 am to 12.35 pm.

LESSON 1
Class arrive and sit at tables. I explain how tables have to be moved back. They move them back and form a circle of chairs. For about ten minutes I check their names against my list and try to memorize them. The pupils test my memory. We play movement games; moving around and freezing; creeping up on someone whose back is turned. Back into circle. We discuss what drama means to different people, then play a very quiet, watching/listening game. I tell them to discuss in groups of three or four the sort of drama they have done in the past. At about 12.15 we are ready for the large-group discussion. Most of the talk is anecdotal – about past drama lessons.

LESSON 2
As pupils enter I ask them to put the tables back and form a circle of chairs. Games: walking without touching one another; shaking hands with every member of the class; creating tableaux of everyday situations. Back in a circle I hand out copies of a map and unroll a length of blank paper on the floor. Gillian volunteers to write down suggestions. Discussion about what map shows. Interest begins to flag fairly quickly. Break up into same groups as before to fill in census forms. Each group is a single household. It's about 12.10 now. I explain that we've been finding out about the roles we are to adopt and the situation we are to work within. They are now to prepare short plays showing

a memorable event in the life of their household. I give each group the choice of acting the play out or telling it in the form of a story. All choose former.

LESSON 3
Pupils slow in arriving. I introduce Brian and Maria and ask if one of pupils will also make notes. Adewole volunteers. I put the map and the list of suggestions from last week's discussion in the centre of the circle and ask the pupils to mark where their homes are. Adewole joins in to say he is a judge. Anthony says he is a scientist, and Colin a chauffeur. Gillian is a student and there are two nurses. I initiate role-play set in a supermarket, a school and a factory. This continues till about 12.05. I ask whether they can think of any situation in which all the inhabitants of Hometown (the name now generally agreed upon as most appropriate) would find themselves together. 'Party' is suggested; this quickly followed by 'Jubilee'. I tell the pupils that I will be entering in the role of a newcomer at some point during the party. They begin acting. I take the part of a very quiet-spoken, nervous person who is hungry, homeless and without money. Anthony offers me a home, food and cash. I break the improvisation and tell the pupils that each household is to be provided with a folder. Everyone is to write a letter about an interesting incident in Hometown.

LESSON 4
Pupils enter and sit on chairs in circle. Brian and Maria also sit in the circle this week. I narrate the story so far, adding that the families have made a decision to leave the country on account of rising unemployment in that area. I tell them that it is the night before their departure. In their family groups they are to choose one household article 'of sentimental value' that they want to take with them. Back in the circle I explain that we are going to act out the voyage and that Brian and Maria will be my 'officials'. Pupils are ushered out of classroom. I tell them that when they re-enter the room will be a boat. I begin to allow them in one by one. (From this point on I only communicate with the passengers through Brian and Maria.) Passengers to take a blanket from the pile and sit down three feet from one another. I tell Brian and Maria to check their baggage. I ask Brian to ask Anthony what he has in his bag. Turns out to be family album - the article of sentimental value which they chose to bring with them. I confiscate it. All members of the family owning the album are segregated. Passengers told they can ask me questions by writing them down. Brian and Maria carry out 'routine medical inspection' of all pupils not writing down questions. Questions collected in. Pupils divided: those who posed questions are put on one side, while the

rest are fed. I break the improvisation and ask pupils to
return to chairs. What is the place like that we are going
to? Hot. Near sea. Is it an island? Yes. Is it a real place
or a make-believe place? Make-believe. What sort of people
live there? No-one lives there. The story begins to fall
into place: there was a ship-wreck, but the passengers
managed to get to an island. They survive off the natural
produce. I ask each family to write the story of the voyage
starting where I left off at the beginning of the lesson.

LESSON 5
Class enter and sit on chairs in circle. I briefly remind
them that they are on the island and ask them where they
live and how they feed and clothe themselves. Adewole
says they eat potatoes which someone carried ashore from
the wreck. Each family begins to make a home using chairs,
tables and blocks. Brian and Maria enter as 'outsiders'.
They speak very quietly to the pupils and tell them that
they must leave because this is holy ground. Some pupils
gather round; others, notably the Lee household, start
to build defences using the tables. Pupils go back to their
homes. A lot of talk. Brian and Maria stand with big slo-
gans written on paper – 'Go back home!' and 'Stop muck-
ing about with our island!' Members of the Barnes household go round trying to organize a meeting. By 11.40
they are beginning to bring their chairs into a circle for
a meeting. 'Who is the chairman?' asks someone. Anthony
says there are to be three: the leaders of each household.
He calls on each person to say what he/she thinks ought
to be done. No one has any ideas except Jackie: 'Drive
them off the land!' Anthony says that they could offer
to 'give them science'. 'We've got to respect their religion, haven't we?', says someone else. At 11.55 Brian
and Maria enter the meeting. They want the pupils to go
and live on the marshes. Anthony: 'You have to understand that we are human beings, as well.' I break the
improvisation and say that each household is to produce
a short play designed to show that its culture could be of
value to the 'outsiders'. The Barnes household shows
hinges being put on a door, fishing nets being made and
used, and books being read; while the Scotts and Lees
display their medical skill.

LESSON 6
Sitting in the circle I ask the pupils if they want to continue with last week's work. Marcia says 'No', adding that
she doesn't want to work with Adewole. Adewole also wants
a change. Anthony looks confused. I place five photographs
in front of them. The boys led by Adewole seem interested
in one photo and the girls led by Marcia in another. I take
a vote and Adewole's faction wins. I ask questions about

the photograph. We establish that the building in the background is a prison, that the two white men are visitors and
that the two black men in uniform are warders. I ask for
volunteers to act out the arrival of the visitors at the prison. Marcia and a few other girls want to be warders.
Anthony and John are the white visitors. They act out the
scene as the rest of the class watch. I break this at the
point when the white visitors are about to enter the prison.
I tell Marcia and her warders to organize the rest of the
class as the inmates of the prison. This she does by
separating the black pupils from the white. Brian and
Marcia also act as warders. I explain to the class that we
are going back to the point when the white visitors arrive;
but that this time we shall run it on and show their tour
of inspection. I establish that the white visitors are English
journalists. Each pupil is then told to write a newspaper
report which appears as a result of the journalists' visit.
At 12.15 Brian calls the pupils to him. He says that he has
a confession to make: he is not really a prison warder, but
a government spy. He calls on the governor of the prison
(Marcia) to justify her policy of racial segregation and on
the journalists and prisoners to give a report of prison
conditions. These six lessons were taught consecutively.

By an unfortunate set of circumstances, the remaining lessons
were, with one exception, abandoned as a result of unexpected
closures and clashes with special school functions. I shall not
deal here with the single lesson which we did manage to teach
in the second half of the term, for it took place more than a
month after the lessons just outlined and was, therefore, very
much a one-off session.

We shall now look at the course of lessons in more detail,
prising open some of the problems barely touched on in this
preliminary account.

Since none of the teachers involved in the project had taught
this particular second-year group before, it seemed appropriate
to begin by asking the pupils what they expected from drama.
This we did in the first lesson. The following snatch of conversation is taken from the large-group discussion which formed
the final phase of that lesson.

TEACHER: Would you like to tell us what sort of things they did
    last year?
ANGELA: Games mostly.
TEACHER: What sort of games?
ANGELA: Two people sat in the middle of the room and they had
    this bunch of keys, and the rest of us had to try and get
    the keys, and they had to touch us. They were blindfolded.
TEACHER: I see. Did you enjoy that game?
COLIN: Yes, we did.
TEACHER: Well, what was the point of it?

COLIN: We had to come in close and quietly get the keys.
JOHN: There was only one person in the middle and everyone
sat round. The teacher pointed to somebody and only one
person went up to get the keys.

The response to my question, 'What was the point of it?', I
found of great interest. For the value of the experience, as
far as the pupils were concerned, had been intrinsic to the
game (i.e., 'to come in close and quietly get the keys');
whereas, to my mind, if the experience had had any value
whatsoever, this had been extrinsic to the game (i.e., learning to work together, operating a rule system, etc.). The
pupils' remarks confirmed my opinion that they had had little
experience of the kind of drama which, in so far as it may be
used to explore ideas and reflect upon large, social issues,
is in itself of educational value. I resolved, therefore, to come
at the theme of race obliquely, allowing the pupils to approach
it in their own time and on their own terms.

   This involved selecting an aspect of the racial issue that was
neither highly topical nor charged with emotion. Since very few
of the pupils were first-generation immigrants, I felt that the
theme of 'immigration' would be sufficiently remote from their
own experience while at the same time providing a useful point
of reference. In order to explore effectively through drama
what it is like to be a member of a minority, immigrant group,
I felt we should have to start at least one step back from the
racial issue, with the pupils building a fictional homeland, from
which in a subsequent phase of the drama work they would
'emigrate'.

   This process of 'building' began with the second lesson. The
initial large-group discussion, from which the following extract
has been taken, was based upon a map of an unspecified urban
area. Copies of this map had been handed to the pupils at the
start of the lesson.

ANTHONY: Is there a railway line down there?
TEACHER: I don't know. I was wondering that myself.
MARCIA: It don't look like a railway line to me.
LINDA: It's a motorway.
CLAUDIA: What do you mean, 'it's a motorway'?
JOHN: This isn't a real map, is it?
TEACHER: Yes, it is.
ANTHONY: It's a railway. Those are the tracks on it.
TEACHER: Is there anything else it might be other than a
   railway or a road?
MARCUS: It could be a flyover, sir.
MARCIA: Flyover?
RAYMOND: For all you know it could be a runway.
ANGELA: Here we go again!
LINDA: It's a motorway and that's it!

I felt ill at ease during much of the discussion, for the pupils seemed unsure of what I wanted them to do with the map. After all, why do people usually consult maps? Because they have lost their way or are studying regional geography, perhaps; but rarely, as I pointed out in the lesson, because they want to make up a play. Yet, that is what I was asking these pupils to do. Questions such as 'This isn't a real map, is it?' revealed a genuine confusion concerning the nature of the task they were engaged in.

Not knowing how they were expected to 'read' the map, they were not sure to what authority they should appeal in the case of a dispute. They were looking at the map as geographers; asking what a certain symbol was intended to signify. Had they been looking at it as dramatists they would have asked what the symbol could be made to signify. Would it be in the best interests of the drama, in other words, if the line on the map were to represent a railway, a road, a canal or a rainbow? As it was, I must have appeared to many of the pupils to have been encouraging them to be incompetent geographers.

Brian, who observed this discussion, made two comments: 'Are the kids transposing their own area upon that of the map?' and 'Perhaps the more thoughtful kids are finding it difficult to get into this discussion.' The first comment was interesting simply because it was posed as a question. Had I been less confused about what I wanted the pupils to do, his question would have been a statement. For the discussion ought to have been an attempt by the pupils to transpose their own area, in terms of locality and personal experience, upon the map, and thereby upon the fictional world they were creating. The second comment pointed to one of the results of the confusion, namely that the thoughtful pupils were likely to have been more confused by the assignment than those who took it at face value.

The process of building belief in character and situation continued throughout this session and the next. The discussion having ended, the pupils filled in census forms, thereby forming themselves into family groups and establishing the roles they were to adopt over the next few weeks. Four other strategies were employed: prepared improvisation, role-play, large-group improvisation with the teacher working 'in role' with the pupils, and creative writing emerging from the practical work. Since I was trying to show how drama may be a form of 'thinking-not-yet-finished', the stress was upon work performed not for an audience, but for oneself. The following transcript shows the loosely woven form some of these improvisations took. This particular piece of work was produced in response to my instructions to act out a memorable event in the life of the family group.

MOTHER: It would be a nice day to have a picnic, don't you
    think so, Terry?

FATHER: I don't know.
MOTHER: Well, it's Sunday and there's nothing to do in the
    house - let's have a picnic.
FATHER: If you say so.
MOTHER: You'd like that, then?
FATHER: OK, Let's go.
MOTHER: Michelle, go and get the...
DAUGHTER: Oh, all right, all right...
MOTHER: Right. You lot go and get changed while we make the
    sandwiches. Come on, Michelle.

FATHER: How much will it be if we go to the forest?
TAXI DRIVER: Oh, it won't be very much.
FATHER: How much?
TAXI DRIVER: About £1.50.
MOTHER: And drive carefully.
TAXI DRIVER: All right, madam. First stop?
MOTHER: The forest. We haven't got all day, you know,
    hurry up!
DAUGHTER: This is a nice car - four seats.
TAXI DRIVER: Madam, what time shall I come back for you
    tonight?
MOTHER: About 9 o'clock.
TAXI DRIVER: Right.
DAUGHTER: Be careful you don't crash the car, they're
    very expensive.

FATHER: I'm going fishing.
MOTHER: Wait a minute, wait until we've had lunch, then
    you can go. Right, this is lunch.
FATHER: On the floor?
DAUGHTER: Yes, it's on the floor, it's a carpet.
MOTHER: Michelle, behave yourself, and don't eat like a pig.
    Remember your table manners. You may not be at home,
    but I still would like you to eat up with good manners.
FATHER: Don't use them big words! (laughter)

MOTHER: Right. You can go fishing now. Me and Michelle
    will go climbing. We enjoy climbing.

(The daughter falls)

FATHER: Why don't you fetch a helicopter?
TAXI DRIVER: Emergency!
MOTHER: By the time you get help she will be bloody dead!
FATHER: Help me get her into the helicopter.

The evident lack of polish, as shown in the unsophisticated
shifts of scene ('Right, this is lunch'), the partial slipping of
role ('Don't use them big words') and the clumsy ending in
which the 'deus ex machina' takes the form of a passing

helicopter, hardly mattered. What did matter at this stage was that the pupils should be allowed to create for themselves a fictional context in which they could breathe freely. For until they had learnt to relax and play together there was no hope of deepening their drama work.

Such a context had to allow each pupil some measure of privacy. Drama can be a frighteningly public activity for many pupils. By occasionally asking them to work independently, I hoped to give the pupils the opportunity of feeding in ideas, experiences and feelings which they might not want to declare openly. Anthony, for example, in one of the written assignments constructed an event that never found its way into any of the practical sessions.

> Dear David,
>   Yesterday something terrible happened. I was walking along the road and I saw something happen so quickly I didn't believe it. A man with a gun walking along the road shooting every child in sight. I quickly hid. He didn't see me. But I was so scared. You are the only person I could tell. Do you know what I could do? If so, please write back soon.
>
>   Anthony

By granting his assumed character this secret existence, Anthony was adding an entirely new dimension to his drama work.

But what about race? The whole pattern of the term's teaching centred on the belief that, without first establishing a fictional framework within which to operate, no worthwhile exploration of the racial issue could take place. The family groups were established to develop more reflective work. These sub-groups were sufficiently stable to survive outside the drama lesson, as two of the pupils pointed out when interviewed by a visitor to the school who had observed one of these early lessons.

VISITOR: Now you're all in different families in there. The Scotts, the Lees and the Barnes, is that it? Do you have a feeling about your family in there? Do those people become special to you?

RAYMOND: We all live in the same house.

VISITOR: But you're not in a family?

RAYMOND: Two are my parents.

MARCIA: When we're in the class, not in drama, it sort of still carries on, as if we are all a family.

VISITOR: Does it really?

MARCIA: Yes. We say 'go away Scott', and when we are in class Dionne, she's my daughter and her name's Michelle, she goes, 'hello Mum' and it's beautiful. And the others ask us what's happening, and we have to tell them, and

they kind of like to put themselves in it as well, not as
family but as friends.
VISITOR: So just to kind of sum it up, how do you say, to
somebody who was only concerned with what you learned,
what would you say you learned in drama?
MARCIA: I'm not the only person in the world, there is other
people, and we should all pull together and be as one,
because I've learnt all sorts of things about other people,
outdoors, and what their feelings are like.

The balance between the areas of learning described here by
the pupils – such as the sense of wellbeing, the ability to work
together, interest in how other people think – and the areas
of learning we hoped to work towards – such as the intellectual
and emotional grip upon certain issues – is a delicate one. In
performance or stage-play drama the plight of a few individuals
stands out; in this more loosely structured drama there is
greater equality among the players, but the issues or dilemmas
are not so sharply delineated. The problem of finding a focus
was therefore a crucial one.
     At the beginning of the fourth lesson I initiated a significant
shift in the action of the drama work. The pupils were informed
that the Barneses, the Scotts and the Lees had decided to
emigrate. The voyage by boat was acted out with Brian, Maria
and myself taking the part of the crewmembers intent upon
making the trip as unpleasant and degrading as possible for
the passengers. By the end of this improvisation I had two
options open to me: either to inform the pupils where the voyage
was leading, or to let them decide for themselves. I chose the
latter. During the ensuing discussion the pupils concocted a
fantastic story of shipwreck on the high seas followed by a
miraculous escape to a desert island.
     The loss of Hometown was not strongly felt. Left to define
their own Strangetown, the pupils constructed an ideal which
seemed romantically more attractive than Hometown. Whereas
the latter had been 'like a little industrial town', their new
abode was to be a sun-drenched island where they would live
in bamboo huts and feed off mangoes and pineapples.
     The following week Brian and Maria once more worked 'in role'
with the pupils; this time as natives of the island upon which
the Barneses, Scotts and Lees had settled. The pupils were put
in the position of having to negotiate with and justify their own
way of life to the natives. That evening after school Adewole
and Anthony recorded a conversation about these last two lessons.

ANTHONY: And then one day we all decided to emigrate.
ADEWOLE: Yes. We didn't know where.
ANTHONY: We didn't know where, but we were going to emigrate on this ship. I paid for first class to go on the ship
and I think so did the Scotts and the Lees, but we were

all put in the same room. When we got on there we were told
we had no rights at all...

ADEWOLE: ...other people, there were three of them, one
lady...yes, there were three of them, the Captain and one
lady and a man, and they were very very strict and we had
to have...for dinner we had dried bread and cold milk. I
don't know what the hell that was supposed to be, but we
had it. And then we had to sit down in our blazers and
things like that. Oh, disgusting!

ANTHONY: They confiscated the Barnes family's personal
goods, and they made them sit away from everyone else, and
they didn't give the Barnes a receipt for it, and after quite
a while, when the ship sank, everybody, including the crew,
I think, got on to the island.

ADEWOLE: Everybody survived, everybody swam.

ANTHONY: Yes, everybody swam. We all tried to save a few
things...

ADEWOLE: Yes, and we did, like potatoes. We saved things
that we didn't really need, but now we know that we do
need them, so that was just an instinct.

ANTHONY: We all woke up the next day on the beach - you
know, like you see in the films and we went searching
around...

ADEWOLE: We didn't know where we was...

ANTHONY: And we found three, really nice, you know, quite
good caves. It was a lucky thing they were there.

ADEWOLE: Yes, three of them, just for three families too,
the Barneses, Lees and Scotts - the Barneses lived in one,
the Scotts lived in one and the Lees lived in one - but they
were quite untidy and...

ANTHONY: Cold?

ADEWOLE: Yes, cold and uncomfortable and everything like
that. So I think we had to...we built our furniture and we
had to hunt for food...

ANTHONY: Yes, we stayed in there for quite a while until we
settled down...after the first few days, we thought we had
settled down - we started to build our own houses.

ADEWOLE: Yes, the caves or the huts were a bit uncomfortable...

ANTHONY: We made them out of cane and palm leaves and
things like that.

ADEWOLE: Yes. Just like you see on Robinson Crusoe...

ANTHONY: Yes, because I'm a scientist and Wally's a doctor,
and we know all different things about the earth, and how
to get water - irrigating and things like that...

ADEWOLE: Yes, it was better for a scientist.

ANTHONY: And after the first week - four days after the
first week these two strangers came. We didn't know there
was anybody else on the island and apparently we were
living on...holy ground...their holy ground...

ADEWOLE: Yes, that's what they said...and we tried to

persuade them and said 'No, this, this whatever you call it...
this holy ground is not only for you because our ship was
shipwrecked and then we came on this island which we
thought was deserted', and tried to explain everything to
them but they couldn't really understand our language so
clearly and they started saying...and this and that...
ANTHONY: Yes. They thought we were mad...
ADEWOLE: Yes, and when we tried to explain that our ship
    had sunk they said...they didn't really understand.
ANTHONY: They didn't know what a ship was...
ADEWOLE: Yes...they hadn't got no respect for other people.
    They just told us to get off their holy ground and go to...
ANTHONY: Yes. They wanted us to live in a swamp...
ADEWOLE: Yes, swamp. So they had the good part and we had
    the bad part. They didn't realize that we were human beings
    as well as they were.
ANTHONY: Then after that we stopped for a while and we made
    up a play about how we could get them to respect us as
    human beings. Like, we show them something good, that if we
    helped them to do it, they probably might let us stay and
    respect us. Everywhere on the island seemed to be holy
    ground to them, and there was quite a few of them they say.
    So we have to try and show them like fishing, we can show
    them fishing, we can show them reading, we can show them
    the English language, we can teach them many things.

The narrative is in part being retold and in part discovered as
the boys tease out the implications of their drama work. Shaping the account from within their assumed roles, they grasp in
hindsight the significance, the form, of what they enacted. Yet
at the same time they are detached, aware of the account as
artefact and of themselves as makers: Anthony's comment, 'like
you see in the films', and Adewole's reference to 'Robinson
Crusoe' suggest a degree of conscious craftsmanship. Their
account is a corporate effort at grasping the inner structure,
the significance, of their drama work. Thus, although during
much of the account Adewole and Anthony seem to have been
preoccupied with practicalities, a more general issue was now
beginning to emerge: the encounter between an 'immigrant' and
an 'indigenous' culture. My chief concern in preparing for
the sixth and final lesson of half-term was to enable the pupils
to perceive this issue clearly and explore it as fully as possible.
   The lessons began with my asking the pupils whether they
wished to continue with the work they were involved in. By
so doing I must have seemed to many of the pupils to be casting
doubt on the most appealing aspect of the work: the sustained
story-line, with the opportunities it afforded for developing
roles and deepening commitment. My question allowed dissension
within one sub-group to dictate the mood of the class. For
neither Adewole nor Marcia wanted to continue working together.
Being strong personalities, they swayed the opinion of the class

in favour of change.

The pupils were then shown five photographs. The boys, led by Adewole, were most interested in one, and the girls, led by Marcia, in another. I asked them if they wanted to work as one large group, in which case we would have to choose one photograph to work from, or in several groups, in which case each group could choose its own. Marcia was adamant that the class should work as one large group. We took a vote on which photograph to use and the one that Adewole was backing won. The girls began to grumble, but I reminded them that it was they who had wanted to work as one large group. Marcia found a way of compromising without losing face. She outlined a plot of which the two photographs, her own and Adewole's, depicted different scenes. It was not a serious suggestion: just a token gesture. The rest of the class took it as such. No one contradicted her.

The drama that resulted was set in a prison. Anthony and John took the part of two white visitors, roles that were later defined more precisely as foreign journalists; while Marcia took the part of the governor of the prison who segregated the prisoners according to their racial origins. She justified this policy of segregation on the grounds that it prevented riots. Although more obviously related to the racial issue than the previous weeks' work, this lesson operated at a fairly superficial level. By changing the dramatic context at this stage we had also changed the focus; so that it was now a different problem we were trying to explore. The process of building belief in the roles and the situation was contracted into the space of half an hour.

Towards the end of the lesson we tried to focus the work by setting up a discussion which was led by Brian in the role of a government official.

BRIAN: Guards, will you make sure there is absolute silence in this room please? Madam? Madam? Will you sit down please. Excuse me, are these members of your staff? Right. I'm taking this unprecedented step of calling you all together like this, because I've a confession to make. For the past six months, you've all known me as a warder, in this prison. In fact, I'm not a warder at all. I've been working for the government inspecting the conditions in this prison. The recent visit by these journalists brought the matter to a head, and I feel it's now time to reveal my true position. The government for the past few years has followed a policy of racial segregation. Blacks have been separated from white. I have noticed that in this prison it is still the case, despite the fact that the government has changed its policy. I noticed that whites were kept separate from blacks all the time. Now this is no longer...Guards, can you maintain silence please at the back? Thank you. I would like to call upon the Governor of this prison to justify the continuation of this policy of segregation, to explain why she carried it out. Would the Governor, please, like to take the stand? And speak to everyone.

MARCIA: Well, when this prison was first built, we had segregation. Right? It was blacks in one half and white in the other and when the new law was passed we tried to bring them both together. The white and blacks wouldn't get on. There were fights and there were riots, so we just decided they should be segregated again. We can't have the discipline of the prison broken down just because the blacks won't eat with the whites and the whites won't work with the blacks. They won't stay in the same cells and so we just segregated them again and made them as the way they were. Unless you want to make the prison all white or all black it's just going to have to stay the way it is.

ANTHONY: You talk of them as if they're oranges.

MARCIA: Do I? I've been the Governor of this prison for quite a long time and I've seen the riots and fights that have been going on and it's best for the prisoners.

ANTHONY: It would help the prisoners to get along together if they are put together.

BRIAN: I would just like to point out that I invited along the two English journalists who first came to the prison. You've probably read some of the reports that came out in the national papers as a result of their finding. I feel at this point I would like to ask one of them to back up his report. So perhaps, sir, you would now like to reply to that formally.

ANTHONY: When I came to this prison, I found out some of the prisoners seemed to be not very well at all. The cooking conditions, I might add, were extremely bad.

BRIAN: Excuse me, sir, might we just confine this conversation to the matters of segregation, which is what my government is most interested in?

ANTHONY: With regard to the matter of segregation, or, as I've just said splitting the blacks from the whites, not segregation (sounds too much like an orange to me).

MARCIA: Because you are one!

ANTHONY: I find that this segregation (so-called) is not very good. If you split the blacks from the whites you're going to find that the bonds that split them apart become stronger all the time. You should have, in fact, kept them together. Well, let them do certain things together at first until they begin to become friends.

MARCIA: Fight together.

BRIAN: The Governor would like to answer that point.

MARCIA: When the act was passed, we put all the prisoners together, right? And we shared the cells with blacks and whites. One morning, nearly every single morning, there was riots. There was fighting.

ANTHONY: You've just said the prisoners, the black prisoners,

shared a cell with the white prisoners. You don't do that at
first, you say they're just next door to one another - well,
not next door, just a few cells away.

MARCIA: We sort of just put them all together, but it won't
work. They've been apart for so long that they couldn't
take being together.

BRIAN: I feel at this point it might be useful if we heard from
some of the prisoners themselves. At first from a coloured
prisoner and perhaps from a white prisoner. Prisoner Adewole,
would you like to talk to us?

ANTHONY: May I just say one thing first? Which is - tell your
warders not to stop him from saying anything, because he
was the one that was found in that little hole.

BRIAN: Right, Prisoner Adewole.

MARCIA: You weren't sent here to be petted up, you were
sent here to be punished.

ADEWOLE: The warders treat me like pigs and she, the Govern-
or is a...

BRIAN: Thank you, Prisoner Adewole.

MARCIA: No, let him say it!

BRIAN: Prisoner Adewole? How do you feel about being
separated from all the white prisoners.

ADEWOLE: I don't mind.

BRIAN: Do you feel that this is the right thing to do?

ADEWOLE: I suppose so. There's riots every day and fighting
every day. What else can they do?

BRIAN: Thank you. Sit down. Perhaps we can have some
comments from a white prisoner, say, Bobby? We have no
white prisoner who is prepared to speak?

ANTHONY: I believe this might be because the warders are
influencing the prisoners.

MARCIA: That is an allegation. Explain yourself. Influencing
the prisoners in what way?

ANTHONY: The prisoners may be afraid of the warders.

MARCIA: Well, what have they got to be afraid of? There is no
strong evidence. That is accusation. Have you any proof?

BRIAN: Right, at this point, I would like to state my government's case. And to outline what my government's policy is
going to be in the future. Following recent newspaper reports
in newspapers throughout the world, my government has
been placed in the extremely embarrassing situation. Now,
whether our nation likes it or not, the rest of the world
favours a non-racialist policy. It favours a situation where
blacks and whites must be allowed to mix in all parts of the
community, including our prisons. Now, following recent
newspaper reports, the government has been put in a very
precarious situation. Our stated policy has not been carried
out in one of our own prisons. Segregation has continued.
Now, in future, this segregation is not going to apply in any
of our prisons. There will be no riots, no violence and I
expect our prison warders to be able to control their

prisoners. That is what they are here for.
MARCIA: Well, there's only two.
BRIAN: Governor, I would like you to state how you are going
to apply my government's instructions.
MARCIA: The whole prison will be used. White prisoners will
eat with black prisoners. They will share everything and if a
white or coloured prisoner does not want to share - they'll
have 24 hours solitary confinement!

The banter with which the lesson had begun was obviously
finding its way into the discussion. I suspect, for example,
that Anthony's association (or was it genuine confusion?) of
'segregate' with 'segment' (and thereby with orange) was more
an act of one-upmanship than an attempt to develop the drama.
Marcia, on the other hand, in her conversation with Anthony,
slipped out of the role only once, when she replied 'Because
you are one!'. It was Adewole who seemed least able to put to
one side, or integrate into the drama, the previous conflict.
For his insult hardly made dramatic sense when viewed against
his general agreement with Marcia that racial segregation ought
to continue. Moreover, his reasons were much the same as hers:
'there's riots every day and fighting'. He seemed not to understand that within the context of the drama it was his dislike of
her views as the governor, rather than of her behaviour as
Marcia, that was of significance.
Nevertheless, embedding the discussion within the context of
the drama proved to be an effective way of handling disagreement while at the same time allowing the plot to develop. It was
a method we had used before, of course, notably when the
pupils were put in the position of having to negotiate with
Brian and Marcia, who had taken the role of natives on the
island. In each case the method allowed the teachers the opportunity of guiding the discussion from within (e.g., 'Excuse
me, sir, might we just confine this conversation to the matter
of segregation...') and maintaining discipline (e.g., 'Guards,
will you make sure there is absolute silence in this room,
please?') without appearing heavy-handed. Its advantage over
other methods of handling discussion in the drama classroom
is obvious if we consider the uneasy start I had when discussing the map. For the problem with all discussion work in drama
is how to value divergent viewpoints when progress with the
plot demands action based on consensus. The strategy whereby
teacher and pupils discuss an issue 'in role' goes some way,
I believe, towards solving this problem.

19 CASE STUDY 8: STRATEGY C

Jon Nixon

The three consecutive sessions we shall be looking at in this study formed part of the activities of a school drama club which met on a weekly basis. No independent drama department existed within the school, but drama was used as a teaching method within the English department, one of whose members had special responsibility for developing the use of drama across the curriculum. This member of staff also organized the extracurricular drama work. 'Extracurricular' may be misleading in this context, for the work undertaken during the three sessions had developed from issues raised in class. The pupils who attended the sessions did so because they wanted to explore their ideas more fully through improvised drama.

There were about twenty pupils in the group. These were mainly in the second and third years, although a fourth-year boy and a sixth-year girl were also present. An interesting aspect of the work was the way in which the older pupils helped, and assumed responsibility for, the younger ones. Because the sessions took place outside school hours, the pupils were able to overcome the usual constraints imposed by the school's organizational structure. Since the practice was to stream all pupils in the first three years for all subjects, the drama session afforded a rare opportunity for the pupils to work together regardless of age and ability.

The school was a seven-form entry comprehensive school numbering 1,200 pupils and 77 teaching staff, and situated in north London. Seventy per cent of the pupils were first- or second-generation immigrants. Of these, 45 per cent were Jamaican and 45 per cent Gujerati-speaking Hindu, mainly from East Africa. Other minority groups included Chinese, African (mainly Nigerian), Pakistani and other West Indians. A large percentage of the Jamaican pupils had been born in England or had come over when very young, whereas most of the Asian children still had memories of East Africa. The Asian pupils were further isolated by being, in the main, middle-class in a predominantly working-class area. It is hardly surprising, therefore, that racial aggression within the school was usually directed against the Asians by both the whites and the West Indians.

Within the drama group there were three Indian pupils, three West Indian girls, an Italian boy and one white South African boy. The remaining six pupils were of English origin.

Shortly after the final session the teacher was interviewed

about the work. In the course of this interview he was asked
what he had been trying to achieve through the drama.

> The first thing I was trying to do was to get the kids actually
> to understand the notion of prejudice. That was the first
> thing. The second thing was to take a look at the power of
> rumour. I had already touched on this issue with the class,
> as opposed to the group, before the sessions began.

The key word was 'understand', implying the prime importance
of the pupils' mental grasp of certain concepts. No mention was
made of enabling the pupils to work together, to initiate ideas
for the group or to develop the ideas of others; of what might
loosely be described as the area of social learning frequently
associated with necessarily group activities such as improvised
drama. This may have been because the teacher was working
with a well motivated group of pupils who were there of their
own free will. Unlike teachers working within school hours,
he was not, during these particular sessions, struggling
against the compulsory nature of schooling, and may therefore
have been assuming a greater degree of co-operation and
involvement than usual.

The sessions may be briefly described.

The rostra were put at one end of the room and the pupils
divided into two groups. One group, comprising the Uplanders,
was to remain on the rostra and the other, the Downlanders,
on the floor. The teacher established an 'age-old dislike'
between the two groups. This manifested itself in rumours that
the others were 'bossy' and 'smelly'. Each group decided on
its own form of government. The Downlanders were urban and
fully industrialized, the Uplanders rural and underdeveloped.
Each relied upon trade with the other. Feeling between the two
groups ran so high that war eventually broke out. It was
decided that the Downlanders would win because, although few
in number, they had more sophisticated weapons. The Downlanders, therefore, had to decide how to rule over the defeated
Uplanders. A governor was appointed, border-guards established, and access between the two lands denied. In the mean-
time, an Uplander threw something at one of the guards. A
lengthy trial ensued, at the end of which it was decided to
punish the offender 'extra strong' so as to deter any other
would-be rebels. A sentence of ten days' hard labour was
finally passed on him because, according to the judge,

(1) we don't like him;
(2) he perjured himself in court; and
(3) we ought to make an example of him.

The Uplanders retaliated by kidnapping the governor and
demanding weapons in exchange for his life. At this point the
teacher interrupted the drama work and initiated a discussion.

The following transcript is of part of the trial scene. Unlike much of the drama work that took place in the course of the three sessions, this was highly structured. The structure, however, was not imposed from the outside by the teacher, but emerged from the formality of the enacted situation.

The scene began with the prosecutor dominating the action by posing mainly closed questions to the first witness:

PROSECUTOR: Border-guard, please step forward. Did you, on the 29th March 1932, observe the defendant throw a stone at you from the other side of the border?
BORDER-GUARD 1: Yes.
PROSECUTOR: Did it hit you?
BORDER-GUARD 1: Yes.
PROSECUTOR: Where?
BORDER-GUARD 1: Here.
PROSECUTOR: Your left cheek or your right cheek?
BORDER-GUARD 1: My right cheek.
PROSECUTOR: You may sit down. Oh, have you any questions?
DEFENCE COUNSEL: No.
PROSECUTOR: You may sit down.

His cross-examination of the second witness followed a similar pattern, to the extent of once more patronizing the defence counsel by asking him if he has any questions. This time, however, he has.

PROSECUTOR: You may sit down. Second border-guard, please step forward. Did you observe the defendant throw an object at your fellow guard?
BORDER-GUARD 2: Yes.
PROSECUTOR: What was it?
BORDER-GUARD 2: Not too sure.
PROSECUTOR: Did it hit him?
BORDER-GUARD 2: Yes.
PROSECUTOR: How do you know it hit him?
BORDER-GUARD 2: I saw it.
PROSECUTOR: Did he hold his face? Did he shout? Did he scream? Are you sure it hit him?
BORDER-GUARD 2: Yes.
PROSECUTOR: On which cheek did it hit him?
BORDER-GUARD 2: The right.
PROSECUTOR: The right cheek. You may sit down, unless... any questions?
DEFENCE COUNSEL: Yes. If you saw the accused throwing the object, how come you don't know what it is?
BORDER-GUARD 2: Well, it's a small...it was quite small...
DEFENCE COUNSEL: Can you tell us about it?
BORDER-GUARD 2: No.
DEFENCE COUNSEL: Then how do you know what cheek it hit him on?

By the time the accused is questioned, interaction between the
pupils involved in the scene has increased considerably. The
drama has developed into a game where the prosecutor tries
to show some inconsistency in the story of the guards. The
point of the game, as far as the guards are concerned, is to
edit what they are saying so as to corroborate one another's
accounts.

PROSECUTOR: So you're in your house eating a banana. What
  day was this?
ACCUSED: The 29th March.
PROSECUTOR: The 29th March.
ACCUSED: At 7.35 precisely and 10 seconds.
PROSECUTOR: Well, this incident happened on the 23rd March.
ACCUSED: It happened at 7.35, 29th March.
PROSECUTOR: How do you know it happened at 7.35 on
  29th March?
ACCUSED: That's when I's eating my banana and all of a
  sudden two of your guards come in and arrested me.
PROSECUTOR: On the 29th March?
ACCUSED: 7.36–7.37. But I started to eat my banana at
  7.35.
PROSECUTOR: And they came and arrested you at 7.30?
ACCUSED: Yes.
PROSECUTOR: So you were eating your banana after they had
  arrested you?
ACCUSED: Yes.
PROSECUTOR: But you could not have been eating the banana
  while the object was thrown across the border.
ACCUSED: The banana was thrown over on the 23rd March.
  I then took it and put it in the cupboard, and ate it on the
  29th March at 7.35.
PROSECUTOR: After the guards had arrested you?
ACCUSED: Before the guards had arrested me.
PROSECUTOR: But the guards arrested you at 7.30.
ACCUSED: The guards arrested me at 7.37. I should know,
  I've got a digital watch. Look!
PROSECUTOR: So the guards arrested you at 7.37.
ACCUSED: Yes.
PROSECUTOR: Exactly?
ACCUSED: About that.

One of the characteristics of this kind of drama, where all the
participants share responsibility for developing the plot, is
its capacity for generating as many meanings as there are
people involved. For some of the pupils it was a play about
war and for others a play about how to win an argument; it
was about justice for some and the workings of a law court
for others; and for some, no doubt, it was, as the teacher had
hoped, about the nature of prejudice and the power of rumour.
The problem for the teacher was how to focus upon the desired

area of learning without losing the interest of those pupils for whom the drama meant something quite different.

The teacher tried various means of achieving this focus. The improvisation he set up was such that the issue of racial prejudice was likely to emerge at some point in the course of the three sessions. Setting up an improvisation in the hope that certain predetermined themes will come to the fore is rather like calculating the course of a biased bowl: one can never be sure of hitting the jack. The teacher tried to reduce this element of chance by guiding the drama once it had been set in motion. This he did by assuming various roles as occasion demanded. Sometimes he would take the part of a quiet bystander and sometimes that of an interviewer, prodding the participants with questions. At no point did he adopt a key role, such as judge or advocate. He remained, rather, in the position of an umpire who, although not affecting the outcome of the match, defines the state of play and is the final authority in the case of contention. The teacher's silence throughout most of the trial scene was not a result of his having opted out. As one of the pupils who was interviewed afterwards said: 'We came to him with all our problems and told him what we were doing.'

Adopting a more traditionally instructional role during the final discussion, the teacher tended to present the pupils with ready-made judgments about the racial issue. His questions were posed with the obvious intention of drawing out a 'moral', so that the discussion became a sort of epilogue, a ritualistic closing of the drama form. In the following extract, for example, his comments leave the pupils in no doubt as to what he considers to be the acceptable attitude to racial prejudice:

TEACHER: Was there any justification for your saying 'they're different' at the very beginning of the first session?
PUPIL 1: No.
TEACHER: None whatsoever. What did you do when you were trying to point out differences?
PUPIL 1: We said they were smelly.
TEACHER: Yes, yes. Did you have any grounds for that?
PUPIL 2: Yes, their smell was different from ours. They ate curry.
TEACHER: Right, fine.
PUPIL 2: And it was a different smell and not a nice smell to us.
TEACHER: Yes...But is it fair to say that because it was different it would be wrong?
PUPIL 2: No.
TEACHER: Right.

One wonders to what extent the shift to a more obviously committed role in this final discussion may have confused the pupils and had an inhibiting effect upon their exploration of the racial issue.

The problem for the teacher was how to forge a link between the play the pupils were actively involved in at that moment and the universal issues he wanted them to reflect upon through the drama. He was aware that the trial sequence had only partially solved this problem:

> The trial became too important. We started to wax eloquent a bit and get bogged down in pseudo-criminal procedure, and we lost the basic thread that we were trying to isolate. All sorts of issues emerged about bananas being thrown and who had done the dastardly deed. So the play became about something other than prejudice or rumour at that point. It was difficult to bring it back.

The final discussion, therefore, became something of a salvage operation: an attempt to make explicit the connections that the teacher had hoped might occur during the improvised drama work.

20 CASE STUDY 9: STRATEGY C

Jon Nixon

A problem highlighted by the previous studies is the difficulty
many drama teachers had in approaching the issue of race
directly. The majority of lessons I taught and observed explored
the issue by analogy. Indeed, the one teacher who with her
fifth year pupils did tackle the subject head-on, when interviewed after the lesson added the cautious footnote:(1)

> On the whole I think pupils in the first and perhaps second
> year are fairly innocent. Obviously, if it does come out of
> a lesson then I'll discuss it with them. But I won't impose
> it on them as being a problem. Because I think when you
> discuss something like that you're saying 'This is a problem'.

Clearly, it was felt that we were working in an area where it
was incumbent upon everyone to tread warily.

The reason for this tentative approach had to do with the
circumstances within which drama teachers so often have to
work. With perhaps no more than an hour a week with any one
group it is extremely difficult to create an atmosphere of
mutual trust in which contentious issues may be raised frankly
and openly. Under such circumstances it seemed not only the
safer, but also the wiser course to go in sideways, letting the
pupils make their own links between the enacted situation and
what they saw as the underlying issue.

The disadvantages of such an approach are, however, considerable. How can one be sure, for example, that pupils involved in an improvisation set on a desert island and concerning,
say, an encounter between the indigenous population and
unexpected arrivals from over the seas, are relating this to
their own experience of racial prejudice? Such work may be fun,
but the extent to which it fulfils the teacher's aim of enabling
the pupils to explore the issue of racial prejudice is questionable.

This nagging worry concerning the genuine educational value
of much of the work I had been involved in, prompted me to
search for a more direct approach to the subject. Quite by
chance I came across a couple of articles (23) which outline
certain techniques associated with psychodrama. I ought to point
out that at this point I had read very little in this field. My
knowledge of Moreno's work was limited to the extract included
in John Hodgson's book (4), a monograph written by one of
his clients (5) and my experience of attending a single psycho-

drama session.

Nevertheless, I decided to give it a try. I selected two small groups of older pupils (a fourth- and fifth-year class) and taught them parallel courses of lessons. Because they were both CSE groups I met them for two eighty minute sessions each week and had, therefore, built up a good working relationship with them. I could also rely upon the pupils being fairly well motivated, since all of them had opted for drama. Space will not permit a detailed comparison of these two courses, but it is worth noting in passing that there were often significant differences in the way in which the two groups tackled identical tasks.

In this study I shall be looking in detail at only one session: the initial fourth-year lesson.

Of the eight pupils who were present the four girls and one of the boys, Marcus, were of West Indian origin, and another boy, Theo, of Greek origin. The only materials used were copies of Wole Soyinka's poem, 'Telephone Conversation'.(6)

The lesson began by my giving out copies of the poem, introducing it briefly and reading it aloud:

> The price seemed reasonable, location
> Indifferent. The landlady swore she lived
> Off premises. Nothing remained
> But self-confession. 'Madam,' I warned,
> 'I hate a wasted journey - I am African.'
> Silence. Silenced transmission of
> Pressurized good-breeding. Voice, when it came,
> Lipstick coated, long gold-rolled
> Cigarette-holder pipped. Caught I was, foully,
> 'HOW DARK?'...I had not misheard... 'ARE YOU LIGHT
> OR VERY DARK?' Button B. Button A. Stench
> Of rancid breath of public hide-and-speak.
> Red booth. Red pillar-box. Red double-tiered
> Omnibus squelching tar. It was real! Shamed
> By ill-mannered silence, surrender
> Pushed dumbfoundment to beg simplification.
> Considerate she was, varying the emphasis -
> 'ARE YOU DARK? OR VERY LIGHT?' Revelation came.
> 'You mean - like plain or milk chocolate?'
> Her assent was clinical, crushing in its light
> Impersonality. Rapidly, wave-length adjusted,
> I chose. 'West African sepia' - and as afterthought,
> 'Down in my passport.' Silence for spectroscopic
> Flight of fancy, till truthfulness clanged her accent
> Hard on the mouthpiece. 'WHAT'S THAT?' conceding
> 'DON'T KNOW WHAT THAT IS.' 'Like brunette.'
> 'THAT'S DARK, ISN'T IT?' 'Not altogether.
> Facially, I am brunette, but, madam, you should see
> The rest of me. Palm of my hand, soles of my feet
> Are a peroxide blond. Friction, caused -

Foolishly, madam – my sitting down, has turned
My bottom raven black – One moment, madam!' – sensing
Her receiver rearing on the thunderclap
About my ears – 'Madam,' I pleaded, 'wouldn't you rather
See for yourself?'

The pupils listened intently, laughing at the line 'but madam, you should see/The rest of me' and again three lines later at 'has turned/My bottom raven black'.

As soon as I had finished reading Jane said 'I didn't get all that' and Clara 'I didn't get any of it!' Excited talk followed. Several pupils were obviously confused as to what the phrase 'Button B, Button A' meant. Having cleared up this confusion, I asked: 'What can you tell me about the landlady?'. Voices in unison replied 'Prejudiced!' Jane and Marcus both noted the change of tone towards the end of the poem. It was not like a 'normal' conversation, commented Jane, because the African did not ask about such practical matters as the price of the room. I pointed out that the poem recalls only the final part of the conversation. Jane asked about the phrase, 'omnibus squelching tar', and then with the help of Marcus pieced together her own interpretation of the passage.

The discussion centred on the text of the poem: questions of interpretation, of the meaning of specific words and phrases and the tone of certain passages. Thus, the poem served the useful function of providing an initial focus for the work. It is perhaps significant, however, that the two pupils who had the most to say during the discussion were the more literate of those present. Veronica, who said nothing, is only just able to write her own name.

I wound up the discussion by preparing the pupils for an improvisation in which the African, having just had the telephone conversation recorded in the poem, goes round to see the landlady. What sort of an attitude might he adopt, I asked, when making the visit. Three suggestions emerged:

(a) he very much wants the flat and is willing to be both polite and humble in order to get it (Nina);
(b) he still wants the flat, but is prepared to speak his own mind (Jane); and
(c) he is no longer bothered whether he gets the flat or not, but is determined to satisfy his own feelings (Marcus).

I took the part of the landlady and we ran through each situation with Theo as the African's 'ego double'. Warning him against saying too much I explained that his task was merely to voice the more significant, unspoken thoughts of the character he was shadowing.

Two important strategies were introduced during this phase of the lesson: that of the teacher in role and of the 'ego double'. The former I adopted in order to be able to raise problems from

within the drama. By maintaining an obstructive, unsympathe-
tic persona I hoped to prevent any premature resolution of
the problem posed by Soyinka: The strategy of the 'ego double'
was used as a way of enabling the pupils to reflect upon the
situation in more depth. I had hoped that Theo would provide
a sparse sub-text which would reveal the underlying issues of
the drama work. But I was clearly expecting too much. They
would need preparing much more fully in the use of this strategy if they were to see it as anything other than a gimmick.

Nevertheless, much excited chatter and laughter ensued as
we brought our chairs back into a circle to talk about the
work. I quickly initiated the next phase: 'Has anyone here
ever been in a situation where they felt they were being treated
differently because of the colour of their skin?' This question
was met with silence. Eventually, Robert started to tell us an
anecdote about how the police 'picked on' him and his mate
because of the length of their hair. I pulled him up, saying
that there are many reasons why people may be made to feel
different, but that at the moment we are considering differences
of colour. Nina (quietly): 'You can't really explain that though.'
Theo began to tell how a policeman called him 'a Greek bubble
and squeak' because he was wearing a badge with 'Stuff the
Jubilee!' printed on it. I returned to Nina's comment. She
explained that usually discrimination cannot be 'proved' – it
is a 'feeling'. This comment seemed to strike a chord. Jane
went on to tell how once she had this 'feeling' on walking into
a Wimpy Bar full of white people in an area where there were
very few blacks. This was followed up by further examples
from Marcus and David. Nina: 'People never say anything, they
just look at you.'

To introduce the final phase I asked Jane if we might use her
experience in the Wimpy Bar as the basis of a group improvisation. She agreed to this. I said that if possible I wanted one of
us who was white to play the part of Jane and those who were
black to take the part of the white customers. This suggestion
was met with excited laughter. Jane clapped her hands and
said 'It'll be good, it'll be good.' I asked her to show each member of the group exactly how to behave so as to mirror her own
experience. Robert was to take her part. She showed him how
she had walked in and explained to the others how they must
react to the entrance. I took the part of the waiter.

We began to build the scene to the point at which Robert was
to leave. After he had hurried out Jane asked a series of questions which served to focus the drama further. 'Why did you
have to be the one who kept staring at him?', 'What was you
thinking when you walked in?', 'Why did you run out the way
you did?' and 'Why didn't you immediately try and serve him?'
Those of us to whom these questions were addressed tried to
answer them from within the roles we had adopted in the drama.

By this time I was beginning to wonder what the value of the
work was for the various members of the group. Clearly, Jane

stood to benefit the most, for it was her experience we were
using as the basis of the improvisation. By being given the
opportunity to observe the re-enactment of this scene and ask
questions, the pressing urgency of which in actuality had
caused her to hurry out of the Wimpy Bar in confusion and
embarrassment, she was able to recollect in some degree of
tranquillity an experience which had obviously troubled her.
But what of the other pupils?

The device of adopting the role of someone whose skin is a
different colour from one's own might have proved effective if
I had prepared more fully for it. As it was, I question whether
Nina, Clara, Veronica and Marcus really 'felt' themselves to be
white. Their perception of the scene was probably such that
they reversed the situation rather than their own roles: what
was being enacted, as far as they were concerned, was a situation in which a white person walked into a restaurant full of
black people (a somewhat different predicament from that
experienced by Jane).

The work obviously meant something quite different to each
member of the group. Towards the end of the course the diversity of response resulted in the disaffection of certain pupils,
who perceived that the educational value of this particular drama
method was more strongly felt by the 'protagonist' (in this lesson, Jane). Marcus, in a later session, said that in future he
would like to work from a situation that was purely 'make-
believe'. This comment received much support. Perhaps what
he and his supporters were asking for was a return to a type
of drama which, although lacking some of the intensity of this
method, did at least distribute the insights more evenly
throughout the group. The use of one person's experience as
a focus demanded great patience and control from the other
pupils.

A brief discussion ensued during which we talked about the
value of the work. I shall quote this discussion in full, for it
contained some important insights which the pupils gained into
the particular mode of enquiry employed throughout the lesson:

TEACHER: Do you think you have learnt anything?
JANE: Yes.
MARCUS: Well, we haven't learnt. Sir, I don't think we have
    really learnt. We have just sort of experienced.
THEO: Learnt other peoples' experiences.
TEACHER: When you say not actually learnt, Marcus, what do
    you mean?
MARCUS: Everybody knows about racialism and all that. We are
    just trying to get inside everybody's mind - what they thought
    - that's all we have tried to do really.
TEACHER: Would anyone disagree with that?
JANE: No. But we know that not all white people are prejudiced.
TEACHER: How did people respond to what we have just been
    doing? It was quite different from the sort of work we have

been doing, wasn't it?

MARCUS: It was good.

JANE: It was real.

TEACHER: Do you think we could continue exploring that next week?

JANE: Yes.

OTHERS: Yes.

MARCUS: Depends what subject it's on really.

TEACHER: What do you mean by that Marcus?

MARCUS: Well, depends what subject it's on. It's got to be true to life you see. If it's fantasy it won't really work.

TEACHER: Why do you think it was different from the sort of drama we have been doing?

MARCUS: That was more kind of like - that was more imagination than this. This is more for exploring issues - getting your experiences together.

CLARA: This is something that everybody experiences some time.

JANE: I think we tend to act better at it because it is something that everybody feels strongly about.

TEACHER: What do you think is the point of doing something like this?

MARCUS: To show how you would react in certain situations. It doesn't make you understand. It just makes you think about it, because there is no real yes or no.

TEACHER: When you say 'it doesn't help you understand', what do you mean?

MARCUS: Well, it doesn't help you say 'racism is bad' or 'racism is good', but it makes you think about it so you could have your own view.

TEACHER: It doesn't help you make up your mind about anything.

MARCUS: It might help you make up your mind about your own view, but it wouldn't be - well, like in Maths, you get a question and you answer it and you just go straight through with it. In English if you get a question there is no proper answer. It's just how you answer it.

TEACHER: Does anyone disagree with that?

OTHERS: No.

TEACHER: Do you think it would be interesting for another lesson or so to go on exploring the racial issue?

ALL: Yes.

We may disagree with Marcus's use of the words 'learn', 'understand', and 'experience'. He seemed, for example, not to equate the process of 'Getting your experiences together' (which he nevertheless saw as being extremely valuable) with 'understanding' or 'learning'. This limited view of education as something which has very little to do with one's own experience may be a sad reflection on his schooling. To understand, as far as Marcus was concerned, is not only to have answers, but to have the right answers; to learn is to attain to a state of certainty. Thus, the sort of work we had been engaged in 'doesn't make you understand....because there is no real yes or no'.

Perhaps in any thoughtful lesson the pupils and teacher are learning as much about what it means to learn as they are about the particular issue which they have set out to explore. Certainly, the distinction which Marcus made between an inquiry which works within clearly defined guidelines and one which has to discover its own methods and procedures is vital, and may have been the most important insight he culled from the lesson.

The work I have just documented was only the first of a course of four lessons in which the pupils attempted to explore directly their own experiences of racial prejudice. Anyone thinking seriously of working along the lines suggested in this brief study might well consider what seem to me the more interesting questions to have emerged from the course as a whole:

1 Would this 'direct' approach work with a larger group of pupils?
2 Would its use be practical and ethical with a group of younger pupils?
3 Could it be used effectively by a group with a different ethnic composition?

These are questions for which, as Marcus put it, 'there is no real yes or no'. For the sort of issues which may or may not be introduced safely into the classroom depends ultimately upon the quality of the relationship between teacher and taught.

It is for precisely this reason that discussion of classroom practice must begin at the micro-level. Generalizations seem increasingly vapid when viewed in the context of specific lessons. I hope that the previous case studies of classroom drama will, if nothing else, prompt more teachers to think seriously about the problems and effects of using drama as a way of exploring potentially troubled areas of human experience.

NOTES

1 See Case Study 5.
2 Joel Badaines, Psychodrama: Concepts, Principles and Issues, 'Journal of the Association of Dramatherapists', vol. 1, no. 2, Autumn 1977, pp. 4-9.
3 Martin H. Davies, The Origins and Practice of Psychodrama, 'Journal of the Association of Dramatherapists', vol. 2, no. 1, October 1978, pp. 1-7.
4 J.L. Moreno, Drama as Therapy, in John Hodgson (ed.), 'The Uses of Drama', London, Methuen, 1972, pp. 130-42.
5 Margherita Anne Macdonald (with comments by

J.L. Moreno), Psychodrama Explores a Private World, 'Psychodrama Monographs', no. 24, New York, Beacon House, 1947.
6 Geoffrey Summerfield (ed.), 'Voices: an anthology of poetry and pictures', The Third Book, Harmondsworth, Penguin, 1968, p. 119. This poem was also included in the materials produced by the project in support of experimental teachers.

21 CASE STUDY 10: STRATEGY A. AN EXPERIMENTAL SCHOOL REVISITED

Patricia J. Sikes and David J.S. Sheard

A flimsy unimaginative structure of glass and prefabricated concrete, the school stands on the fringes of a grey, sprawling, mining village in south Yorkshire. The community it serves has grown up over the last sixty years and contains minorities of East European and Scottish immigrants with very few black families.

Inside, the school is neat and well cared for. Its regime is liberal rather than progressive: there is no uniform and no corporal punishment. There is a great deal of mixed-ability teaching, and relationships between staff and students appear to be relaxed, informal and friendly. While the staff is as mixed in age, outlook and temperament as at any school, the prevailing ethos is of reasonableness and rationality.

In the decade since the comprehensive school was established, perhaps the most significant change has been in the actual catchment area of the school, which now draws pupils solely from the immediate neighbourhood. Consequently, few pupils come from professional backgrounds and around half of the present pupils come from families who have associations with the pit. The implications of the loss of a more distinctly middle-class element are perhaps reflected in the present concern of the headmaster and staff about underachievement among the more able pupils. Although employment opportunities lack variety within the area, relatively few pupils stay on into the sixth form and academic ability seems to have relatively low status in the community.

One of the fundamental aims of the school is to provide its pupils with as broad an education as is possible. In an attempt to achieve this end, from the start of the fourth year the traditionally compulsory core subjects of maths and English have been joined by social and moral studies (with RE as an alternative to moral studies), plus a science subject of the pupil's choice.

Despite changes in staff, a new head of the Humanities Department and a new headmaster, the humanities course has continued with no major alteration through six years. Although characterized by continuous assessment at both O level and CSE, a more or less integrated approach to the humanities disciplines and mixed-ability teaching, its work is probably no longer seen as innovative by the pupils. The theme of 'Race', which is tackled by all fourth-year pupils for five hours of humanities work each week for half a term, is well established

234

and is generally accepted by the members of the department
as an important and significant topic.

Through the department's involvement with the Humanities
Curriculum Project, a tradition of dealing with controversial
issues (through discussion work in which the teacher submits
to the criterion of neutrality) has been built up. The HCP
technique is seen by the department to be a sensible way to
enable pupils to explore controversial issues, and it is the
basis of the moral studies course followed by the majority of
the pupils in the upper school for two hours each week. Oral
work is assessed by the teacher, the marks given contributing
to the pupils' overall examination grades.

Having used the HCP experimental materials on race relations
for some years, the Humanities Department joined the SSRC/
Gulbenkian Project, 'The Problems and Effects of Teaching
about Race Relations', in 1974 with some confidence. It would
be true to say that experimental innovation had become something of a tradition in the department, and at this time its members were perceived by the rest of the staff as a relatively
isolated group of young, radical intellectuals, who kept to their
own separate areas of the staff room and who were too busy to
socialize with their colleagues. This view has since been modified
as the members of the original team have left, their replacements
stepping into relatively well defined jobs and adopting more or
less conventional roles.

The teacher whose lessons are the subject of this case study
was, by 1978, a senior member of the department and the only
one of the original group left. He was said to be 'an intellectual',
but, in his sixth year at the school, less of an outsider. He is
a committed exponent of neutral chairmanship, and is convinced
of the need to teach adolescents about controversial issues and
to make available for their use difficult source materials. The
fact that he is seldom satisfied with the work produced by his
pupils does not seem to discourage him.

Perhaps the reason why he is such an advocate of the 'neutral
chairman' as a teaching strategy is that he does hold strong
opinions about the majority of the issues that are taught within
moral and social studies. Experience as much as training has
led him towards procedural neutrality in the classroom, without
which his views would be immediately communicated to the pupils
who might then adopt or reject them uncritically, depending on
their feelings towards him. Accepting the criterion of neutrality
encourages pupils, through discussion, to move as rationally
and objectively as possible towards an intelligently reasoned
viewpoint. On the whole, apart from being thought of as a teacher who sets difficult work, pupils respond well to him and
his attempts to create a relaxed and friendly atmosphere with
them are generally successful.

The seventeen pupils with whom we are concerned came to
the theme of Race at the start of their third term of discussion-
based moral studies. They had consequently had time to learn

to work as a group and with their teacher. They were accustomed to the presence of a tape-recorder, which the teacher sometimes uses as a means to monitor his own and the group's progress, and even though the teacher did not have time to listen to all of the consequent recordings himself, this did provide a means of observing the lessons without intruding, which in this context would have been unacceptably disturbing to the group's routine.

Work on Race began with an initial exploratory discussion, using photographs as stimulus, from which the teacher attempted to identify issues of interest to the group. These constituted the agenda, though in practice this was used mostly to fall back on in an emergency and on a number of occasions when pupils showed unwillingness to accept responsibility for the topic to be discussed.

Sessions tended to follow a pattern; the teacher had found it more productive to arrive after his rather boisterous group and then to accept a period of casual conversation. He would then focus attention on to the chosen issue, with copies of an item from the resource bank. Further items would be introduced where the teacher considered them relevant or supportive to discussion. Each pupil kept a diary of discussion work, which was written up towards the end of the one-hour period.

In ethnic composition, the group reflected that of the school and the wider local community: it was exclusively white. One girl had East European parents, one boy was a recent immigrant from Scotland. However, they all thought of themselves as British, and identified with the culture of the community.

Basically, group members got on well together and, though spirited, avoided major disagreements. The teacher suggests that the boys in the group support each other in discussion because a number of them belong to the same rugby team, the team spirit carrying over into other common activities. There are, as in most groups, a few pupils who never or rarely contribute, as well as a few characters whose personalities have a major influence upon interaction within the group and ultimately on the level of discussion.

Bryan is the most disruptive member of the group. Tapes of the lessons are punctuated with incidents when Bryan is fooling around (which he does very loudly, involving other boys), is being chastized, or is sent out of the room. Every class possesses its clown, and Bryan enthusiastically assumes this role. As is often true of such pupils, he is not stupid and, when he is taking a sensible part in discussion, he can raise and support some valid arguments. For instance, he raised on one occasion the question of how the repatriation of immigrants would affect Britain's trading relationship with their countries. However, the borderline between the useful contribution and the disruptive tends to be blurred, and Bryan is more likely to ask questions that challenge the teacher's willingness to take him seriously and have a deleterious effect on the behaviour of the rest of the group, such as: 'Why are the children of black and white parents striped like zebras?' Most of the time he just creates disturbances, and when he is absent group behaviour as a whole undergoes a transformation, with discussion following a more conventional pattern.

One of the more able pupils in the group is Victor. He seems to find the discussion convention easy to work in and his contributions show that he takes care to present succinctly and neatly the point he wishes to make. He is able to 'keep up' with the discussion and does not make his carefully worded point after the pertinent issue has passed, as is the case with some. On a number of occasions it is clear that pupils who are not very quick or forceful have thought out what it is they wish to say in connection with a certain point but have been unable to break into the discussion; when eventually they are successful, their point is no longer relevant.

As a robust and articulate pupil who cares more than most about academic rewards, Victor's role is important. He is able to set discussion on a serious and thoughtful path if he takes an early and positive initiative. If he allows David (large and genially aggressive) or John (quick-witted, articulate and flippant) to take the lead, the session tends to be lively rather than reflective, and participation by less confident pupils may be inhibited. Because Victor's status among his peers owes little to his intellectual qualities, he will sometimes remind the group that he can be as aggressive as anyone. He has a low opinion of most other group members (on occasion he makes this very clear) and this creates tensions which can interrupt the flow of discussion.

The success, or otherwise, of a particular session can sometimes be explained quite easily in terms of how leading members of the group are behaving towards one another. At other times it is not so easy for the teacher to understand the influences that are at work in the group. One session foundered halfway through the period. For no apparent reason, interest evaporated and the teacher could find no way to restart discussion. He did not realize that, while he had been out of the room finding a particular item of resource material, Victor had inspected the 'mark' book and decided that he had not been fairly treated. Victor's silent withdrawal of co-operation, supported on this occasion by other group members, was not explained until the end of the lesson.

The difficulties that the teacher or an observer has in understanding the important interactions within the group are multiplied when he attempts to evaluate the effects that discussion may be having on individuals. This may be particularly the case when discussion deals with an area that has led to many well publicized expressions of strong feeling. While race relations may have no immediate relevance for the pupils in this group, media coverage ensures that they are aware of, and have knowledge of, some of the major issues. Their opinions may be quite deeply held but show at first little evidence of careful consideration. Consequently, a discussion will often contain a series of dogmatic statements of personal belief. There can be no simple generalization about what happens to these beliefs in the course of discussion, in the light of printed or other evidence presented to the group, or in the face of questioning by teacher or peers. Stubborn resistance to an alternative point of view may be effectively concealed behind silence. On the other hand, one of the more open-minded and tolerant members of the group keeps her thoughts exclusively for her written work. It is easier to identify points at which pupils retreat behind the assertion that opinions are facts, than to point to signs that viewpoints are being modified and attitudes becoming more tolerant. Frequently it is difficult to identify the direction in which the discussion is going, and the pattern is seldom as systematic as a teacher might hope for. Similarly, pupils often seem to become entangled in words. It is frustrating for the listener, who can generally guess the point which the pupil is seeking to express; that it is frustrating for the pupil is obvious because he will often give up, unable to make himself clear because he lacks the language. As far as evaluation is concerned, lack of formal precision in language is a problem.

The group is 'working class', and on the whole reflective language does not come easily to its members. There is a tendency to mock anyone, including the teacher, who uses 'long' words. The teacher believes that problems with language are a root cause of many pupils' failure to make the progress that would normally be consistent with their intellectual ability. He hopes that this type of discussion work, associated as it is with some difficult reading, may improve the pupils' facility with language.

In the extract that follows (which is from a discussion about the film, 'The Eye of the Storm', in which a teacher attempts to give her class practical experience of prejudice by grouping them according to eye colour and then treating one group favourably at the expense of the others), it becomes clear that John knows and understands what this teacher was trying to do. However, he isn't completely confident about using the word 'prejudice', and initially gives a simplistic answer to the teacher's question which is not correct and which implies that he has not understood the point that the film was trying to make. Nevertheless, when pressed by the teacher to explain himself he is able to give a more accurate answer by using a word which he knows but which is not in his everyday vocabulary. Had the teacher not pushed for a fuller explanation, he would not really have been sure whether John had not understood, or simply did not have the vocabulary to express his understanding.

TEACHER: Do you understand what the lady was trying to teach the kids?

JOHN: To hate brown-eyed people.
VICTOR: No.
ROBERT: Goes opposite way, to hate blue-eyed people.
BRYAN: Yeh that's it. (sings) 'Paperback writer'.

(muttering)

TEACHER: John, was that a serious comment?
JOHN: What?
TEACHER: That she was trying to teach them to hate brown-
eyed people.
JOHN: Yeh but, but, you know, only as an example to be
prej...prejudiced against.

(muttering)

TEACHER: To be what?
JOHN: To be, you know, prejudiced against 'em.
TEACHER: Why, what was the point of, I mean, I asked you
at the end of the last lesson to write about why they become
prejudiced so easily, but what was the point of making, of
creating the prejudice in the first place?

(inaudible)

ROBERT: So you don't like being prejudiced against.
VICTOR: So that they won't be prejudiced against blacks.

Only Victor seems happy with the word, and he has had time to
phrase his statement. Other speakers have difficulty, which
suggests they do not grasp the idea behind the lesson in the
film.
    Next, the group moves through a series of concrete state-
ments about what happens in the film, claiming it is typical of
the way it works. The teacher is unsure whether to take them
as serious contributions, though the pupils seem happy to work
in this way towards some understanding. In the following
sequence, dealing with repatriation, he judges Bryan's inter-
vention to be deliberately ridiculous, though Victor in a passage later than that quoted takes it more seriously as an example of how repatriation might be effected, pointing out the
impracticalities. The teacher was unsure of dealing with what
may or may not have been an attempt to set up an amusing diversion.

TEACHER: So you're saying in fact that the idea of sending
them back isn't a very popular one, isn't that popular.
VICTOR: We can't send them back, can you?
TEACHER: Well?
ROB: Yes you can.
VICTOR: How? How?

ROB: 'Course you can.
VICTOR: How? Go on then.
ROB: I don't know how you're going to send them back.
LUCILLE: Well, you're saying that they should be sent back.
BRYAN: Put 'em in a submarine, it holds about what? eh? a
     hundred people. You'd need more than one submarine.
TEACHER: Well look, it's a serious part of a political party's
     programme, right? The National Front, isn't it? So I think
     you have to take the idea seriously, and the part of their
     programme is that Britain should be a country of white
     people.

The teacher's annoyance is to some extent suppressed because
he is reluctant to antagonize the boys concerned, feeling this
would have a damaging effect on the group for the rest of the
session. Had he remained silent, the diversion into fantasy
might have taken on less significance, but the teacher felt
there was a risk of the submarine idea taking hold at the
expense of the real issue. On reflection, Bryan might have stimulated a useful exchange about the practicalities of repatriation, since Rob is clearly at a loss for an example to offer.

In both of the above extracts the teacher is trying to achieve
a balance between the need to establish acceptable standards
in this particular learning situation, and the need to be supportive and encouraging to the members of his group. They
clearly do not find discussion easy, and the teacher tries hard
not to make them feel inadequate, though he is not always successful in concealing his frustration at their inability to match
his criteria of a 'good' discussion.

One element of the resulting compromise is his tendency to
accept without question the 'race relations' vocabulary of the
pupils. He argues that the issues discussed in the classroom are
likely to already have been talked about at home and among
friends. Pupils will, therefore, already have what is to them an
appropriate vocabulary. Clearly, the purpose of introducing
such issues into the curriculum is to promote a greater understanding than would develop in the normal course of events, and
this end may best be served by encouraging pupils to feel
secure in their ability to express themselves, rather than by
invalidating their existing vocabulary. In fact, through his
experiences with similar groups this teacher has come to believe
that pupils attach little significance to the implications of words;
and, listening to the group's discussions, it would seem that
language has little to do with attitudes, with terms such as
'blackie' and 'wog' being used purely descriptively, rather than
derogatively. While it is sometimes difficult to know in what
spirit the following statements were made, it is likely that they
are not all hostile towards blacks, and that terms such as
'darkie' are used solely to indicate people who are not white.

BOY: Them black people, Pakki-wogs.

VICTOR: A lot of white people would say, 'Oh, why should they go back?' and they'll go on t'blackies side.

LUCILLE: Sir, are there any darkies in Northern Ireland?

TEACHER: David, why did you pick that picture?
DAVID: Cus there's a, er, er, blackie, looks like he's foreman and all that.

David's hesitation does seem to indicate that he is rather uncertain, in the context of the school environment, how to describe a black man. He falls back on language with which he is familiar and which does not, in his understanding, carry the derogatory overtones bestowed upon it by liberal, middle-class opinion.
   Evidence that tends to confirm the hypothesis that language usually associated with prejudice is used both in that context and in non-hostile ways is contained in this contribution of Lucille's, which imagines the conversation between a prejudiced person and a non-prejudiced person who has been through the 'Eye of the Storm' lesson.

LUCILLE: 'Cus they can say to their mates who don't, who ain't been in the exercise, say, 'Oh look at that wog walking up t'street', could say, 'Well, 'ow would you feel if you were a wog?'

It is as well to remember that the use of acceptable language does not automatically preclude unacceptable attitudes. Nevertheless, it might be less easy to tolerate the kind of language illustrated above in a multi-racial group, particularly if used in conjunction with the kind of misconceptions about the lifestyle of coloured immigrants before coming to Britain which are common. On one occasion a boy expressed confusion at the fact that some Asians were able to set up prosperous businesses in English towns. As he pointed towards an Oxfam poster on the wall he explained that they would come from backgrounds of acute poverty, so how would they raise the money for a business? In the following extract it seems that Lucille's notion, that immigrants may not have the skills of civilized life, has been extended to blacks in general.

TEACHER: So, it's, it's, you'd say it's not really true that they live in worse housing than whites?

(shuffling)

LUCILLE: Well, probably some darkies have trouble because they, they don't know 'ow to do 'ousework.

(shuffling)

VICTOR: Eh?

LUCILLE: Come straight over from living in t'mud 'ut, they're not going to clean t'ouse properly.

VICTOR: Who says they live in mud huts?

LUCILLE: Well, they might do in them ghettos in America, wherever it is.

But while there was enough interest in the question, 'What sort of houses do immigrants come from?' for it to be placed on the group's agenda at the start of work on Race, other, more immediate, issues took priority, and it was never investigated in the depth at which a more formal, teacher-centred, course would probably have aimed.

The pupils tended to use personal stories to illustrate points they were making. Although recognizing that the subject under discussion can easily get lost under the weight of anecdote, and that pupils, lacking in discretion, may reveal embarrassing personal information, the teacher does not normally veto such contributions. He felt that they could be put to valuable use. In this extract, from a discussion about police attitudes, Jane, normally a non-contributor, spontaneously tells of an incident in which she was involved. The teacher presses her to elaborate on her experiences. She is reticent after having given the basic facts, and the teacher does run the risk of discouraging her. The point is that she joined in because she had relevant information which was interesting to the group, and it was important that she be encouraged to elaborate on her contribution. In fact, she later remarked that this had been the 'best discussion' she had been in.

JANE: Mr (name)? When me and me mates were walking from (name) we were with some coloured people, these lasses. The cops stopped us, but they never asked us where we were going, just where they were going.

TEACHER: Really? And you were part of the same group?

JANE: Yeh. (inaudible)

TEACHER: And they just picked on the black kids?

JANE: Yeh.

BOY 1: Are them black kids from (name)?

JANE: Yeh.

BOY 1: Cops might 'a' known them.

JANE: No.

BOY 2: Yeh, they might 'a' known them, they don't know you.

BOY 1: Do you know if them black kids had been in trouble before?

JANE: No, I don't think so.

(muttering)

TEACHER: Do, do you think they felt, 'Oh these black kids probably don't like us so we'll show them that they're not gonna get away with that?' 'Cus that's what Dave and Robert suggest.

JANE: No.

TEACHER: Do, do you think your friends could reasonably be thought to look more like troublemakers than you?

JANE: No.

TEACHER: So what did you think at the time?

JANE: Nothing.

TEACHER: Why?

JANE: Bastards.

(laughter)

TEACHER: Had, had you talked about it after it happened?

(shuffling)

JANE: No, they just asked them where they were going and they said they were going to (youth club) but they never said owt to us.

(shuffling)

JANE: They looked a bit suspicious at me but didn't say owt.

(noise - Bryan)

TEACHER: Sorry, what were you saying?

JANE: When we come away from (inaudible)...picked on.

TEACHER: What, the black girls?

JANE: Yeh.

BOY 2: Ah, they're bound to, aren't they?

JANE: Shut your face.

TEACHER: So did you get the feeling that they disliked white cops anyway?

JANE: No.

TEACHER: What, before they got picked up by the cops?

JANE: No.

TEACHER: But because they got picked up?

JANE: Yeh.

TEACHER: Any more than anyone else would?

JANE: Yeh.

TEACHER: If they got picked up by the police? Do you think the colour made any difference?

JANE: No, no, don't know.

BOY 3: How would they feel if a black copper came and stopped them?

TEACHER: Well, what would you think if a black copper stopped you?

This extract also illustrates what commonly happens when a girl makes a point. The boys in the group tend to join together in refuting the credibility of what she has said, regardless of the fact that they, previously, have made a similar point. In that particular instance the boys had been quite adamant that the police often picked on innocent people. As soon as Jane spoke about what would seem to be an unprovoked incident of police harassment, the boys, rather than supporting her, imply that there were grounds for the action of the police. In the context of other, similar, exchanges it seems that the boys' questions were a way of reasserting male dominance in the group. They tend to respond to the girls in a challenging and aggressive way. The teacher expresses concern that they may be exaggerating their lack of sensitivity on occasion because they fear the ridicule of peers. Thus, there may well be a greater disparity between what the boys say and what they really feel than seems likely in the case of the girls, but, even so, interpreting the contributions made by the girls is not a simple matter. Generally, they are reticent in discussion. When they do join in, they seem to be more willing to deal with affective areas and more able to empathize. However, in this group they are very much in the minority (five to twelve), tend to be absent more frequently, and take little part in these discussions. The exception is Lucille, who, being dramatically overweight, has already lost the approval of the boys without doing or saying anything. Lucille evidently rejects the more passive aspects of the female role in that she regularly joins in discussion, but nevertheless her contributions often show her in the role of conciliator, while the boys maintain a more aggressive stance. This occasionally causes her to contradict herself by expressing conflicting opinions in order to avoid conflict with the boys.

At the start of one session, when the boys were involved in making raucous, racist comments, Lucille said:

LUCILLE: Get an island or summat as far away from anybody and just stick 'em on there.

As discussion progressed a more tolerant atmosphere began to prevail, and, in keeping with the general mood:

LUCILLE: Some of t'doctors who come over to England are a lot better than white doctors 'cus they've got more qualifications.

(shuffling, mumbling)

TEACHER: Well, you've, from starting off with the idea that, that what would happen if we sent them home, you're now saying that we can't afford to do without them.
LUCILLE: No, not really.

BOY: No, not now.

Finally, the discussion turned to the possible sources of prejudice, and Lucille found herself in a trap that she herself had
laid at the beginning. The boys waste no time in attacking her,
and her response is to abrogate responsibility for what she had
previously said by claiming lack of interest in the whole subject.

LUCILLE: Both my parents, well one of my parents, my step-
father, is colour-prejudiced. That don't make me colour-
prejudiced.
JOHN: You were at the start of this lesson.
BOY: Yeh.
LUCILLE: I'm not, just that...
DAVE: You was.
TEACHER: You actually are the person that suggested that we
should stop blacks reproducing.
ROB: You said we should put 'em on an island.
LUCILLE: Yeh, that's what they're all saying, why don't you
tek'em all away. Well don't you just...

(all talking together)

GARY: Well if you weren't colour-prejudiced you'd be against
that, wouldn't you?
LUCILLE: I'm not bothered.

This is not the only occasion that a pupil seems to hold apparently contradictory opinions at one and the same time. The
teacher feels that such opinions are expressed as a means of
moving towards understanding, and that the willingness of
pupils to put forward alternative and sometimes contradictory
views may be a necessary preliminary to the growth of understanding and tolerance.
   Lucille's father is Polish, and on one occasion she found herself grouped with 'immigrants'. This brought the group into
a more immediate encounter with the problems of prejudice,
and Lucille was disturbed and upset by 'being discriminated'.
Even she had previously failed to show any real empathy
towards coloured immigrants, despite her preference for sensitivity and tolerance.

GARY: You've got a Polish name.
LUCILLE: My father's Polish.
JOHN: Well, go back to Poland.

(mumbling)

GARY: You're saying, ship all the black babies out what were
born in here, so you have to be shipped out.
JOHN: If it's colour of t'skin...

LUCILLE: I wouldn't mind going to Poland, it'd be a nice holiday for me.
JOHN: Ah, it wouldn't be holiday, it'd be permanent.
LUCILLE: Stay there.
ROB: Skin seems to be the main feature.
TEACHER: What, what you said is that, that this country is our country, right? And that therefore, whoever we are, whatever we do, we have the right to live here, but, it's it's not your dad's country is it?
BOY 1: No.
BOY 2: No.
TEACHER: That's what you meant.
JOHN: How can it be his country when he's Polish? Work that out.
ROB: I didn't say it was his country.
BOY 3: I'm not talking.
TEACHER: Has he got more right to live here than a person from India whose skin's dark?
BOY 1: No.
JOHN: No, that's what I said.
GARY: If you're gonna ship blacks out you got to ship all other immigrants out as well.
BOY 2: You've got no right to be over here.
TEACHER: Why?
LUCILLE: If you're getting on about my, you know, about me being half-Polish, what about them invaders that come years and years ago? They were all foreign.
DAVE: Yeh. (mumbling)
LUCILLE: What about people with white hair? Sticking them into...
BOY 3: (mumbles)
LUCILLE: People with blonde hair, sticking them into one country and people with dark hair, sticking them into another. People with different coloured hair, sticking them into another.

(talk about hair colour, LOUD. Teacher tries to intervene)

TEACHER: What you're saying then is, 'Right', once you're saying things like, once you start selecting who the country's for, where do you stop?
LUCILLE: That's just it.
VICTOR: When there's nobody left.

(mumbling)

JOHN: National Front aren't racialists, are they? They're just, they're just all about colour, aren't they?
BOY 1: Which colour?
JOHN: Yeh, you work it out, they're just trying to keep blacks out.

TEACHER: Yes, but they would say that we're were all of the
   same race.
JOHN: How are we? How does (foreign surname) sound English?
   Eh?
LUCILLE: I'm gonna stop coming to this discussion, I'm being
   discriminated.

LATER

TEACHER: Well don't, don't get upset.
LUCILLE: I am, I am upset. I don't know what's made me.
JOHN: What's she upset about?
LUCILLE: I shouldn't really be in this village, then. Me
   mother's Scots and me father's Polish. God!

Despite Lucille's anguish at the way the discussion has focused
on her Polish connections in order to test out some of the
implications of racism, there is evidence here that John at
least has grown a good deal more confident in his ability to
use the language of race relations than was the case in the
early discussion of 'The Eye of the Storm'. Even so, this
extract shows a number of the problematic characteristics observed in the group's discussion work. These can be summarized
as follows:

(1) lack of conceptual language;
(2) conflict based on sex divisions;
(3) a tendency to rely on anecdote and personal experience,
which reveals an insecurity in dealing with generalizations and
second-hand evidence;
(4) a tendency to hold a variety of apparently contradictory
viewpoints about race relations at the same time;
(5) the use of 'prejudiced' language in both a hostile and non-
hostile way;
(6) assumptions about the 'primitive' origins of immigrants;
(7) a difficulty in empathizing with people from different backgrounds to their own.

As suggested earlier, it is a lot more difficult to identify the
effects of such teaching over a six-week span than it is to
establish the problems. In Gary's contribution in the last
extract, for example, it is difficult to distinguish between his
apparent desire to turn the argument against Lucille and a possibly genuine desire to illustrate the problems of a repatriation
policy. John may really wonder what Lucille is upset about,
though he has been quite aggressive towards her, if to him the
outcome of the discussion has been a clearer insight into what
the National Front seems actually to want to do. There is a problem if, to reach this understanding, he has needed to think
aloud around the hypothetical case of repatriating Lucille!
   Not all teachers are prepared to engage in this kind of

speculative analysis: many will lack the sympathy for the rather inelegant process of class discussion that seems to be its necessary starting-point. It is easy to arrive at the view that the teacher should be 'teaching' more. A more formal lesson or lecture may on the surface be less easy to fault. Nevertheless, it ought to be more possible to make judgments about pupil attitudes from the evidence of discussion than from a lesson in which pupil responses and contributions are more tightly controlled.

The extracts that follow may be evidence of a modest improvement in attitude in some of the pupils. Not all readers will agree with this interpretation. To some it may still appear to be sloppy thinking, lack of clear structure, and ill-informed opinion that stand out. The extracts are taken, in sequence, from the group's eighth session (out of ten) on Race.

This particular discussion, on the issue: 'Do immigrants try hard enough to fit in with our way of life?', focuses on some Asian religious customs and is of interest because of the more specific hostility that tends to be directed towards Asians.

To begin with, the teacher has introduced a newspaper cutting about the problems of getting Sikh motorcyclists to wear crash helmets.

ROB: This were in 1973.
TEACHER: Yeh, well it's out of date now. Do you know what the situation is now?
PUPIL: They don't wear 'em.
BRYAN: T'is chap keeps comin' in t'paper, dun't he? 'Cus he dun't wear one, he just wears a turban (inaudible) in his helmet and puts a wig on top, dun't he?
TEACHER: Well, do we know what the legal position is now? Is it, it is compulsory to wear crash helmets, isn't it?
LUCILLE: Yeh, but them people aren't s'posed to wear 'em.
TEACHER: Sikhs?
LUCILLE: They don't have to wear 'em...I don't think that's fair. I don't think they should ride bikes if they don't wear their helmet 'cus if someone kills them they'll feel awful about it.

(mumbling)

GARY: Their own fault, innit?
LUCILLE: Everyone could wrap a towel round their 'ead and go on a bike, couldn't they? er, that way...
ROB: Who'd be daft enough to?

(laughs)
(silence)

LUCILLE: Not everyone's planning to fall off a bike, are they?
BOY: Should wear helmets.

(silence)

TEACHER: Well we've got a situation where everybody has to, whether they like it or not, except this particular group of people.

LUCILLE: 'Tin't fair, though.

ROB: They've come to this country, they should do what we say.

LUCILLE: They should, they should go by our laws, not their religion. Come to this country to get our money, so go by our laws.

(shuffling)

TEACHER: Any other comments? 'Cus what you're saying so far, well, most people who've talked, that they, it's a bit unfair, and that they should accept the fact that everyone has to wear a crash helmet and...

GARY: Yeh, but...if they don't wear a crash helmet everyone else would turn round and say they don't have to wear one.

(shuffling)

ROB: Our laws say, not what they want to do.

GARY: Should make it awkward for them if they make it awkward for us.

JOHN: They, they're supposed to wear them in case they get slapped on the head by a sword, by a Mongol warrior or summat.

BOY: Yeh.

JOHN: But that's not likely to happen in Bradford.

(laughter)
(silence)

TEACHER: Well I think it'd be fair to say it's now such a long tradition, well it's 1666 - three hundred years? Three-hundred year tradition.

BOY: Yeh.

JOHN: Yeh, but what's that got to do wi' it?

GARY: It used to be tradition for women not to show their ankles, innit?

(Gary's intention is to show that it is time Sikhs changed their ways. But his example might have helped the group to think about the problem in a more open way had things not been disrupted by Bryan. After he is sent out, the group eventually returns to the turban issue.)

VICTOR: If they don't want to look the same, why don't they just go back?

(inaudible, boys talking together)

VICTOR: That's why people tek notice of them, 'cus they look different, goin' round with a turban on.

GARY: Yeh, that's proof that they don't want to be like us, innit? They don't want to be like British people.

LUCILLE: They want our British money though, don't they?

GARY: Don't want to fit in.

LUCILLE: We'd look right idiots if we all wore them. Mind you, I s'pose it wouldn't be noticed if we all wore them.

ROB: Yeh, but that's taken in England, we don't wear 'em.

LUCILLE: We're British. Why did they come over here in t'first place? 'Cus I bet they bring none of them over 'ere as slaves and that lot.

(shuffling)

ROB: Come over because they get money for nowt.

(mumbling)

TEACHER: I think, I think...

LUCILLE: Most of 'em we civilized, so we made that a civilized country or summat.

TEACHER: Are you saying this isn't civilized behaviour?

LUCILLE: No (nervous laugh) I wasn't.

TEACHER: It's not?

LUCILLE: No, a bit daft.

ROB: It's a bit like...turban is a bit daft.

LUCILLE: Eh?

ROB: Well...

(inaudible, muttering etc.)

GIRL: Bars, private bars.

VICTOR: And temples.

LUCILLE: Seen that one in (   )? Sikh's temple.

GARY: Yeh, when I went to see me mam in hospital she said she walked in one day and, into the day room, and there was this woman in t'corner, who were like this. (makes praying motions)

LUCILLE: Eh? Do it again.

TEACHER: Well what did she think?

GARY: Dunno. Well she just said she walked out feeling a bit silly.

(Up to this point the group seems to have been building up a strongly ethnocentric consensus. The contributors seem satisfied that there is no more to be said about turbans. The teacher now uses Gary's remarks to justify introducing a newspaper cutting dealing with a request from Muslim leaders that employers accommodate Islamic prayer requirements. This is talked about in much the same way.)

BEV: It's stupid.
ROB: Why should their employers say got to provide for...
LUCILLE: They're not getting cheap labour or owt, why should they 'ave all t'good facilities? They, you've, you've got to pay them as much as you pay white people, else there'd be a great big stink up about it, wouldn't there?

(shuffling)

DAVE: While they're doing this praying will they get paid?
ROB: It says give 'em a day off.
LUCILLE: What about all t'Catholics what go to church every morning? Do they get paid?

(silence)

TEACHER: Does it look, then, in fact as if prayer is going to disrupt the...
VARIOUS: Yeh.
ROB: What about this festival...they 'ave to 'ave the day off. And I don't think that's fair. Why should they 'ave the day off?
LUCILLE: Brother said that when he were in Libya they used to get off ut t' tractors at certain times when they were working, you know, and all get this square mat out and start praying.
ROB: That's in their own country though, innit? It's all right there.
LUCILLE: Yeh, but he said it were stupid.
ROB: Come over here...
LUCILLE: ...said at certain times they all did it, you know, like clockwork animals, and...crazy!
VICTOR: There should be some kind of, you know, oath or summat, that before you come over here you've got to obey. Laws, 'cus if they come they should be prepared to accept everything.
TEACHER: You're saying they should become Christian?
VICTOR: I'm not saying that. I'm saying, you know, they should obey everything, you know, laws.
LUCILLE: They should keep their, should keep their religion to themselves.
ANDREW: Private. They can pray at home.
LUCILLE: Yeh, why can't they keep their...
ANDREW: 'stead of out on t'streets.
LUCILLE: To night-time instead of day-time?
ROB: Not while they're working, not asking for days off and all this.
VICTOR: They're making it public, aren't they? They stick out.

JOHN: Yeh, but they'll still be wanting them days off and they'll be wanting days off for Christmas and all.
ROB: Yeh, want our holidays, wi' Easter and Whit an' all that crap.

(shuffling)

JOHN: Bet they all 'ave Easter eggs.

(giggles)

JOHN: That's two lots of holidays they've 'ad.
VICTOR: Want the best of both worlds, don't they? Their own and ours.
JOHN: The English people don't get their days, what they get off.
TEACHER: Well what would you think then if we said, OK, there's lots of Muslims in the country, let's have the festival of Eid'?
BOY: Yeh.
TEACHER: As a holiday.
LUCILLE: Oh aye. Be on t'holiday all t'time.
ROB: Eid? We don't know what it's on about.
JOHN: You'd like days off school, wouldn't you?

(giggles - shuffling)

JOHN: They 'ave a holiday for owt they do, even May Day.

(shuffling)

TEACHER: There's nobody whose spoken who thinks it fair enough if somebody has a particular religion which involves them in praying regularly, having fasts and things like that, nobody thinks it's reasonable.
LUCILLE: Dunno.
JOHN: Not if it's gonna interfere with what they're s'posed to do...interfere with us, and I think it does.

(muttering)

JOHN: Say in Bradford, if all of them 'ad it off on a Friday half o' work force would 'a gone, wouldn't it, in a place like that?
ROB: That'd mean that half the English people wouldn't be able to get to work 'cus busses'd be stopped.

(shuffling)

TEACHER: I think if you're, if you think they shouldn't have, have their own religious holidays, then what you're saying,

and that they, they should just follow our sequence of
holidays, which are religious, Christian, then you're saying that they ought to become Christian.
ROB: They don't have to become Christians.
VICTOR: Why don't they encourage more factories owned by
Sikhs and that? Then they could do what they want in their
own factories.
JOHN: Yeh, but they're trying to get the best of both worlds,
aren't they?

(The group has taken an exaggerated and distorted view of
this particular problem, but rather than draw attention to that
the teacher has attempted in his last comment what he feels is
a more dramatic challenge to the views expressed. It does not
have much of an impact, and he follows Victor's lead with an
article about the movement for separate education for Muslim
girls. This tends to support Victor's suggestion, but some
group members now suggest ways in which Muslim requirements
could be satisfied within co-educational schools.)

TEACHER: Look, what you're suggesting, then, is that they
should meet us half-way. What, what do girls wear doing PE
in here?
BEV: Skirts and shorts or...
TEACHER: And so you think it'd be OK, if you had a Muslim
girl here, if she wore a tracksuit?
BEV: Yeh, wear a leotard or anything.
TEACHER: I think it's not got to show the body's shape.
GARY: Baggy tracksuit doesn't.
ROB: Yeh, but then it gets in the way, dunnit?
JOHN: Big deal, so does all them robes an' all that lot.
TEACHER: You seem to be accepting that the, that it's an
important thing for them.
JOHN: No.
LUCILLE: What happens to them when they go to hospital
to 'ave a baby?
ROB: Well they're married then, aren't the'?
LUCILLE: Yeh, I know, but a man doctor delivers t'baby.
ROB: It's all right when they're married.

(Comparing what Rob, Lucille and Gary are now saying with
their contributions at the start of the session, they seem to
have acquired some awareness that cultural differences cannot
simply be dismissed. John is more resistant, and half a minute
later explains his position more clearly.)

JOHN: Religion's the...cause of all t'wars, all t'trouble an'
all that.
GARY: Yeh, like wit' t'Jews.
JOHN: Who kill t'Jews? Hitler. They ought to write it off,
religion.

TEACHER: Well, what you're saying then is that, that disliking
somebody else's religion can cause a lot of bloodshed and, er,
misery.
JOHN: A lot of problems, dunnit?
LUCILLE: You can't marry into certain religions because your
religion won't let you and their religion won't let them.
JOHN: They ought to be like me, non-religious. I don't believe
in God.
GARY: Nor do I.
TEACHER: But do you believe that other people ought to have
the right to believe what they do believe?
JOHN: Yeh, if they believe in it.
TEACHER: Sorry?
JOHN: If they believe in it.
TEACHER: Is there any people, people who're religious are
wrong?
GARY: Wouldn't it be funny if there were no such thing as
God? All these churches and t'Pope and everything.

(These anti-religious sentiments are extended to the Northern
Irish and to Jehovah's Witnesses. To draw pupils back to the
more specific issue, the teacher invites the group to return to
the suggestion that factory routine should be adjusted for
Muslim workers. This time he intervenes more in order to
counteract the misapprehensions that have emerged. And what
follows has more to do with the practicalities of production
than with holidays.)

TEACHER: Right? But, but I think, in fact, they can just say
the prayers to themselves - like, like one or two members of
staff say Grace to themselves.
BEV: It were on telly the other day, there is somebody, break
off in work...this electrician.
BOY: No, plumber.
GARY: And if they're doin' like to themselves they're not going
to concentrate. Like, miss something out. Put it in a packet
and send it. Bloke opens it, see this lamp, right? Oh they're
no good, throws 'em away and he wants his money back,
don't he? Well they've wasted all them bulbs.
JOHN: Yeh, wouldn't buy that brand again.
ROB: Wasted the packaging and all that.
JOHN: And then they won't buy that type of bulb again,
maybe.

(mumbling)

LUCILLE: And when you're packing with about three bulbs in
each hand. You couldn't do that when they were thinking you
know, could they?
They'd be picking up one card, crazy.
TEACHER: Would you say that 'Ah, it's likely you'll make a

mistake: therefore we won't have it', or would you wait
until a mistake has been made and then sack them for it?
PHILIP: They should make 'em say them prayers when it's our
holidays. Change their dates.
TEACHER: They have to pray five times a day.
PHILIP: Five times a day?
LUCILLE: Can't do it all in't morning?
GARY: Fifty-minute tea break. Do it all then.
LUCILLE: Well them people what work on motor brakes, it's all
one big tea break for them, so...
ROB: Yeh, what about tea breaks?
VICTOR: Want to get a job on't council. Be all right then.

(There seems to be a more serious tone to this exchange than
there was when the particular problem was discussed earlier
in the lesson. Some group members are thinking through the
implications of making concessions rather than dismissing them
out of hand. A little later, even John seems to have shifted
his ground a little.)

JOHN: You 'ave to go round it.
BOY: You 'ave to.
GIRL: Yeh.
GARY: There's no way they're gonna give it up, is there?
TEACHER: I think someone said that they should not come if
they're not prepared to.
JOHN: Yeh but it's too late now, innit? They've come 'ere.
GARY: They're all in, they've bred now.
LUCILLE: They come in, they shouldn't have kids. They
shouldn't have kids when they come to this country, and
then, you know, when all their kids die out, the kids that
they've already had, they shouldn't be allowed to have any
more. 'Cus they, they've always got a hold on, say, 'Well
look I'm British, I was born in this country.'
TEACHER: The National Front say that as well.
GARY: Really, if they're born here, they don't know the Indian
religion. It's just what their parents have told them and
everything.
LUCILLE: Yeh, but a lot of them go back to their own countries,
to, you know, see their relations and recap on what they've
learnt.

LATER

JOHN: It might sort itself out after a bit. 'Cus all t'kids what
go to school like this, all be like us, get our ways and that.
Idle.

For the discussion to end in this way is far from conclusive, and
Lucille's final comments were evidently disconcerting for the
teacher. Nevertheless, of the dozen or so pupils who spoke in

the lesson, some at least seem to have progressed from being lightheartedly dismissive to a more reasoning, less obviously intolerant, approach to the issue. John's final comment is typically flippant, but suggests a form of optimism that is not clearly evident at the start of the lesson.

Not all the lessons of the series had been even as encouraging as the one documented here, but the teacher felt that, in general, progress had been made in the direction of understanding and tolerance, while being aware that movements in attitudes were uneven, in some cases might be negative, and overall were no more than slight. For a half-term sequence of lessons, he felt that it would be unrealistic to expect more than to turn racial issues into a subject for serious discussion by pupils; and to move some way beyond the kind of conversations the pupils might have outside the classroom.

22 PUPIL REACTION

Lawrence Stenhouse and Robert D. Wild

We have a lot of taped material in which pupils are discussing alone, with a teacher or with an interviewer the work they have been doing on race relations. The problem is, how to present it to the reader. To list the judgments made and the issues raised seems not to capture the context that allows the reader to pick up ambiguities and make his own judgments. There is, we think, no satisfactory way of reducing these data.

In this chapter, therefore, we present transcriptions of five such discussions selected on two main principles. First, we think they cover a number of interesting issues and points. Second, they raise questions about the kind of feedback any teachers undertaking work in the area of race relations can get and how they should organize it.

Our own view is that the use of outsiders - students, college of education staff or youth workers, for example - to gather evaluative material on one's teaching is not nearly so productive for the development of teaching as is breaking through to honest evaluative discussion with the pupils. However, the use of an outsider may help in the breakdown of barriers to open and honest mutual appraisals by teachers and pupils. The work of the Ford Teaching Project may have something to offer as a point of comparison with the project reported here.

What we have written in the last three paragraphs should make it clear to the reader that the transcript material to follow is intended to provide a comparative base both for the assessment of one's own situation and for the assessment of one's capability to gather evidence about one's own teaching. In the end, the second of these is probably the more important, because it is the key to the first.

The material presented in this chapter is not offered as in any sense typical - whatever that could mean in this context - though in a sense it is commonplace. It documents some ordinary realities, but, being selective, it provides no basis for judging evaluatively the work of the teachers involved; much less is it claimed as representative of the range of situations within the project. We are dealing here with particularities of a kind that can be cumulated in one's own teaching experience to form a basis of judgment, but which cannot be reported at the level of detail and intimacy which provides such a basis within the context of a national research project.

TRANSCRIPT 1:
Two students from Strategy A discussing (with a tape recorder) their experience of learning about race relations. Both students are white.

BOY 1: This is a commentary on race discussion no. 1. This discussion was about a random group of materials from the pack and was intended to raise issues for later inquiry.

BOY 2: We were listening to the tape on the discussion about the race relations and, er, we deduced some questions. First, we started off with a picture of the two roadsweepers who are both coloured, and the question that we thought the discussion was based round was 'Do you think that immigrants get the lesser jobs, e.g., roadsweeper which was on the picture?'

BOY 1: Well, people were saying (pause) in the group that they don't get lesser jobs and it's just the job that they got, you know, lots of white people do the job; do that road-sweeper's job.

BOY 2: Yeh. Then it went on to say, um, 'In education do the coloured people have as much chance as white people?'

BOY 1: Well, if they study hard I think they do, but it's different. You don't see many black teachers around, so the black people are really out of their, er, social background. If there were a few more black teachers it might even things up a bit.

BOY 2: Yeh. I think white people should get on with black people really, you know, I mean it's a good idea, but I think black and white people should get on already without having to put them in separate communities.

BOY 2: Er, the next question was 'Do coloured people strike more than white people?'

BOY 1: The answer to that is, if they obey their union and the union calls them to strike.

BOY 2: They've got to strike.

BOY 1: Well, then they'll strike, but I don't think you can say they're more militant than anybody else. This is what was said in the group discussion, that the black people don't strike, strike as much as white people, not less and not more.

BOY 2: Yes. As the discussion carried on we began to change the subject and began to look at the picture on the demonstration and, er, there were quite a few suggestions made about the demonstration, and then we started to base it around this visual evidence and we came to the question that 'Do British citizens, coloured people, have the right to stay here?'

BOY 1: Well, in the group it was said that they do have the right because they're born in Britain and they're just as much British as anybody else.

BOY 2: Yeh. I think the majority of the group agreed with this.

BOY 1: There were a few people saw the opinion of the Enoch

Powell supporters trying to kick the coloureds out whether they're British or not, but it was a very small minority of the group.

BOY 2: Yeh. In the demonstration there was one question that came up that 'Do you think that certain people want two either separate communities or do they just want the one either white or black?' 'Do they want to separate or do they just want the one?' I think Enoch Powell's followers just want the one really; you know, they'd like to kick them all out.

BOY 1: People living separately.

BOY 2: Separate quarters.

BOY 1: People in the group thought this about Enoch Powell, but most people in the group wanted it to be one group, one mixed group.

BOY 2: Yeh. They didn't think any prejudice was needed at all.

BOY 1: No.

BOY 2: No. um. What else?

BOY 1: Well, this brought on the question that prejudice sometimes didn't occur until you're late in years. There was a picture of, I think it was a young white boy and a young black boy playing with each other.

BOY 2: In a pram.

BOY 1: In a flat, no, in a pram, and this gave rise to the question 'Did, er, people influence their children in the, in prejudice?' Well, in the group we thought that it did quite a lot, it depended on what your mother or father told you and influenced on to you, you know...

BOY 2: When you were young.

BOY 1: Yeh, when you were at home.

BOY 2: Yeh, I think when you become the age of about 14 or 15 I think you, yeh, I think you begin to take your own opinions about...

BOY 1: Take things your own way.

BOY 2: Prejudice, yes. It's just when you're young that your parents seem to have (pause) these two boys who were playing in the pram seemed to be quite happy, didn't they? Playing with each other. I think they're young, too young an age to realize what prejudice was about. And the group discussed this, and there were certain opinions that this wasn't right, and we came to the conclusion that it is the parents' influence that does affect the children, and we started to change the subject and came to the picture about the biscuit factory. It was interesting here because we had two different thoughts. One person noticed that on one side they were all coloured people and on the other side they were all white people and this boy thought it was prejudice.

BOY 1: Er, it was found in one side there was coloured, there was one coloured person or more than one coloured people. But this boy still thought that the management had split them up or it could have been that they wanted to be on one, you know, the coloured on one side and the whites on the other.

BOY 2: Yeh. I mean they want to stick with their own, their own race or...

BOY 1: Yeh.

BOY 2: Their own colour, I suppose it could be. Er, there, then one brought up the question that he thinks that this picture shows that we've equal ability in the job. I think that's pretty true, seeing that they are both in the same place doing the same job. I think this comes back to the first question we were talking about, 'Do coloured people get the lesser jobs?' And I think this shows positive evidence that it's not true.

BOY 1: Yes, 'cos they were both doing the same jobs, weren't they?

BOY 2: Yeh.

BOY 1: You know, the only difference was the, we don't know, but we think the management might have been white. You can't really tell, can you?

BOY 2: No, you can't. (pause) After this there was a thoughtful silence and one boy, which was very interesting, brought us back to the demonstration and, er, he wanted to know what the National Front was, and we all tried to explain but we couldn't, we don't really know what it is, and one boy's views were that the National Front mean that there's a boundary of people round the outside of England who are trying to stop the immigrants coming in, not in the physical sense, but they're just trying to stop immigrant people coming in, and we'd like some information on this if possible. Er, I think then we began to look at the Black Power in America, and, er, we were looking at a picture about the men doing the sign.

BOY 1: Yeh, well, the sign was in the Olympics. Those two American coloured people running in this race and one got the gold and one got the silver, and they was up on the, er, rostrum for the American national anthem, and when the anthem started playing they were, well, they just ignored it, they turned their back on the flag, started swinging their medals around and raised their left hand in salute.

BOY 2: Yes. Then one boy brought up a very interesting... which I thought was the main point of the discussion, which was 'Was the black sign the sign of superiority or equality?'

BOY 1: Equality.

BOY 2: As we discussed the question there were two different views, one was that, um...

BOY 1: Um, that it was a sign of they were the same, they were not, they weren't bigger or more powerful, they were just the same, equality. The other sign was that they'd won gold and silver and they were really better than the whites so they were showing that they were superior. They being superior, they ignored the national anthem so they were eventually disqualified. This didn't prove much, but everybody saw it as it was being televised live.

BOY 2: Yeh. I think they were trying to put their feelings across.

BOY 1: In a big way. 'Cos the telly...

BOY 2: Yeh, because the telly...

BOY 1: Yeh, they knew all the world, they'd be on the telly and they'd be able...

BOY 2: Yeh, and it would be remembered.

BOY 1: Yeh.

BOY 2: That early round for the Black Power sign to win, I think they really won it for America because I think America's got a biggest, a bigger problem than we have in England of Black Power and black leadership. The majority of the people seem to think it was superiority in the group, didn't they? And there were a few who thought it was equality, but we've all got our own opinions. As the discussion progressed we came on to the question, um...

BOY 1: If we have no racial prejudice against coloureds would they object towards us? Well we hadn't got much information about this, but we thought, as the complete group, this was one of the occasions where we thought completely alike, that if we stopped saying 'coloured's go back' and things like that, they would, er, drop their racial prejudices and try and become part of society.

BOY 2: Yeh. Some of the group seemed to think that they wouldn't forget it so easily. You know, they wouldn't forget that we'd treated them this way so easily, and others seemed to think that they'd forget it straight away. We'd all settle down, but there were two different views on this.

BOY 1: Yeh. One thought was that as they wouldn't take to it so easily where, you know, they might get back at people.

BOY 2: Yeh.

BOY 1: Once we'd stopped it, they'd start it.

BOY 2: Yeh, but they (pause)... 'Can new coloured immigrants expect help from their assigned communities?' This question was raised by a very interesting and, er, confusing picture, where there was just a single man standing outside what seemed to be the door of his house with his name tag on it.

BOY 1: And, er, people brought up the views that he was, he expected help from people and, er, he was, he was being, er, he was shy about the cameras, he didn't like being filmed and that he was in a white community. No one had any real evidence but they were going on their own kind of fears, if you like; but he looked, well, timid, afraid and in need of company. Just because he had his name tag on him showed, we think, that he wanted help from other people.

BOY 2: Yeh, and, then we tried to get away from the subject but, rightly so, the chairman brought us back to that picture because it seemed to be again one of the main aspects of the discussion, and we began to talk about it and began to, er, deduct questions from it, such as 'Do most coloured immigrants expect help from white people?'

BOY 1: Yeh, that was, that was...

BOY 2: One of the more refined members of the group then brought out another picture and, er, it was a very confusing picture, and it began to give us a lead which we thought was very good. Somebody who didn't say anything in the group at all usually...

BOY 1: This was, er, he thought the woman who had a baby in her arms, that she was angry. But many other people thought that she was saying that she was equal. And another view was that coloured people could raise and bring up their children in exactly the same way as a white person; in a white community.

BOY 2: Having analysed the tape, we then moved on to a general question, which was whether certain members of the group were contributing more to discussion than others and we decided that, um, certain members were talking more than the others.

BOY 1: Yeh, and, er, people were talking, er, talking more on one-person pictures than they were on a group, for a group picture.

BOY 2: Yeh, I think that some of these mild boys, when one certain person made his opinion and he was one against seven, by the end of the discussion he was with the seven, which I think is wrong. I think he should be able to keep his, er, opinion whatever happened. Don't you agree?

BOY 1: Yes.

BOY 2: And what the last question was 'How successful was discussion as a means of explaining or naming the problems?'

BOY 1: With...this was only our second week with the race pack. It proved very helpful and I should think that the rest of the pack will prove even more so. (pause) The demonstration, you always see a demonstration on TV, they go in for the race relations rule, about...then you have the Race Relations Board...

TRANSCRIPT 2:
A short extract from a discussion between students from Strategy A and a teacher. Both students are white: the school is multi-racial.

TEACHER: Can I ask all of you, have you gained anything, do you think, or learned anything, from your study of race relations during this last couple of months?

BOY: Umm, well, from this discussion I've found that, for myself I've learned that, er, the race relations is a greater thing than what people say about it, but I haven't benefited from it whatsoever and I don't think that I could, er, help towards race relations, not unless it was done on a greater scale. It helped me, maybe, for myself, but I wouldn't, I wouldn't like to carry on with this because, er, I've found

that someone said something or other and it has embarrassed
me in a certain way, er, sometimes.

TEACHER: Can you think of any special times this has happened?

BOY: Umm, well, that someone said to me the other day in
school, er, somebody had said something to the other boys
and he said to me, 'What's this that you've been saying about
that you wouldn't like to see coloured, er, white, coloured
boys going out with white girls?' and I said, 'Well,' I said,
'This is true, I wouldn't like to see it, but I can't do anything about it and', I said, 'as far as I'm concerned it's none
of your business anyway.' That's just one incident what
happened.

TEACHER: Someone in the group or someone outside it?

BOY: Someone in the group said it to someone outside.

TEACHER: I see, and they tackled you about it afterwards and
it embarrassed you?

BOY: No, that made me feel I didn't particularly want to carry
on with it then. As far as I'm concerned it's nobody else's
business what I think.

TEACHER: But didn't you explain this to the person? Didn't
you say that we were trying to get over these - was this a
coloured lad that...?

BOY: Yeh, a coloured lad and a half-caste I think, in the
fourth year.

TEACHER: Didn't you say to him, 'Well, this is what we're on
about...'?

BOY: How it's about race relations and that? But he couldn't
really understand; he, as far as he was concerned it was just
that he didn't like coloured boys going out with white girls
and that's all he had in his mind.

TEACHER: I see. Have you had any embarrassing, embarrassment from the pieces, or have you found it interesting?

GIRL: No, I think I found it interesting, you know, because
before you didn't know what your friends felt about it. Now,
you're given the chance to talk freely and if you, if you give
an open mind to it, you know, you don't take offence. Of
course, there is the odd exception but, you know, it's helped
to clear the air, if you talk about it rather than just keep it
bottled up.

TRANSCRIPT 3:
An extract from a discussion between students and a teacher
from a Strategy A school. (Boy 1, black; Boy 2, white; Girl 1,
white; Boy 3, not known; Girl 2, white; Boy 4, black)

BOY 1: See, I live in a council home with that Indian kid, well
we haven't got any Indian kids now...and sometimes we all
fight this woman there. She called me 'ugly this' and 'ugly
that' behind yer back and went around for weeks like that,

until one of us apologized to each other.

BOY 2: I was just the same...

BOY 1: If we start arguing or she's been told us to do something he said 'No, why should I, what about them lot sitting down, I mean, why don't they do it theirself' and they start...this woman keeps saying 'these blooming foreigners, bloody foreigners coming'. When she used to say that, I usually used to laugh about that and then she'd...to say it was watching this thing on the telly and begin to argue and she said 'these blooming foreigners, why don't you go back to your own country' and we was there arguing, arguing...

INTERVIEWER: Oh, look, two minutes ago you said there was no problem.

BOY 1: Oh, there's no problem!

INTERVIEWER: Look, are you telling me that, honestly, when this woman said 'these bloody foreigners you want to go back to your own country'...

BOY 1: No, but you see...

INTERVIEWER: You don't feel annoyed?

BOY 1: But it's the way she said it then, see?

INTERVIEWER: Yes, but...

BOY 1: I'm not annoyed, I'll actually talk about it; this woman talked about it.

INTERVIEWER: Don't you feel annoyed that this woman said it? She said you argued with her because of it.

BOY 1: Yes, I did argue with her, I was trying to make her see my point.

INTERVIEWER: Yes, well, there's a kind of problem - you're not seeing it as a kind of gigantic problem, but there's a kind of problem, isn't there? You wanted her to see your point of view, you don't want her to feel like that.

BOY 1: No, but it's just the way she said it though. She was behaving badly, she got me mad. I mean, it's the same when we was talking about the £1.50 (bus fares) to go to school, I mean, come to school, and this girl was saying 'It's coming out of our bloody tax' and we were saying 'It's to save you being off the dole', so I was talking about (name). My mum being working in this country for donkey's years now...

INTERVIEWER: Yes, OK. Well, look, you've said that it was boring when you were doing it, but if you'd talked about a real issue like this would you have found it so boring? You know, this is something which is real to you, you've made the point, I think. I believe that if it's something to do with us, that we care about, you're going to want to talk about it, aren't you?

GIRL 1: Yes.

INTERVIEWER: If you'd talked about something like this - what I'm trying to find out is why you found it boring? It seems to me you found it boring because you felt it had nothing to do with you, am I right?

GIRL 1: Yeh, but if we start discussing it, right, whole-

heartedly sort of thing, weren't we just gonna pick little
points out of people that, who, I mean, we're just gonna
start saying things that we shouldn't say, which we might
not think, say, that white girls might not think that the
coloured girls aren't gonna think offensive then you're
losing your friends, aren't you, that you've already made?
BOY 3: But I'm thinking – that you talk about it with your
friends.
GIRL 1: But I could say...
BOY 3: You get more boring now when you talk about your
friends – if you talked to somebody else without your
friends...
INTERVIEWER: Yes.
BOY 3: You'd rather have not talked much about it; you
usually talk, say, about the Queen or something like that,
you know start playing about and calling each other names.
It don't seem to bother us.
INTERVIEWER: How do you feel, (name)?
GIRL 2: No, I don't know, I probably hate coloured people
at school.
INTERVIEWER: Oh, I don't – I'm not suggesting that there is
a problem...
BOY 4: I think we do, but, because last year's fourth year we
were saying how, that the English is happy with white blacks.
INTERVIEWER: The English?
BOY 4: The English is happy with white blacks, there's more
blacks in this school than the English people, but I think it's
only because more black people live around this area, they
come to this school, you can't do nothing about it.
INTERVIEWER: So you think there is a problem, yes?
BOY 4: But really, it's just, I think if you go, I think you'd
find the same...
INTERVIEWER: Yes?
BOY 4: Never any fights between black and white.
INTERVIEWER: Never?
BOY 4: Never any fights.
INTERVIEWER: No.
BOY 4: Isn't that bad.
INTERVIEWER: Now you've got me puzzled, because you're
saying on the one hand it's boring because it was nothing to
do with us. On the other hand you're saying – if it's some-
thing we care about which affects us, like baby bashing,
which you feel sympathetic about, you would be interested;
then you were telling me about this incident at the school –
and I'm saying, if you'd talked like that, would you have
been interested? And then you go back and say 'I thought we
didn't want to offend people in the group.'
GIRL 1: Yes, but we could talk all what we wanted to about
that woman, because she wasn't in the room.
INTERVIEWER: Yes, well, this is what...
GIRL 1: It's just that there's a group of us and we can talk

about say, ourselves and somebody we know outside the group, but it's when you're talking about other people in the group.

INTERVIEWER: OK, well, if you'd talked about things like this, which maybe affected you, but didn't involve another person in the group, couldn't this have brought you together as a group, West Indian, Asian and English, to see that there are people who do react against people?

GIRL 1: Yes.

INTERVIEWER: But, you know, there are regional things as well. We tend as people, I think, to be a bit afraid of what we don't understand, so you withdraw, and you say 'well, it's boring, we can't talk about this'. This seems to have been what happened, isn't it?

GIRL 1: Exactly, yes.

CHORUS: Yes.

TRANSCRIPT 4:
A student discussion (Strategy B)

GIRL 1: ...talks, there's no one to back them up and the pieces of evidence that (name) gives us aren't really good enough to argue about 'cos we're all on the same side. Also, I think that she should let us go out more and do other things as well as just sitting and talking.

GIRL 2: Yeh, 'cos the evidence she gives us is really long, isn't it?

GIRL 1: Yeh.

GIRL 2: And it's, it's boring and it, she don't even sometimes give us a little picture or anything...

GIRL 3: I think if the groups were made up, er, of people that were more against each other, then you could have better discussions, but in our group there's usually only about two people that're against the rest and so they get, they don't, can't say anything.

GIRL 4: When you've said something, she asks you 'ave you got a reason for saying it, and most people 'aven't got a reason. They just say it for something to say.

GIRL 5: Oh, yes. Since we've been 'ere, we've been accused of not talking and that, but when anybody talks nobody seems to...

GIRL 6: Follow it up.

GIRL 5: Follow it up because everybody agrees with it, because when the teachers tell you their opinion someone could be against it and then they could 'ave an argument about it...

GIRL 3: Mmm, start the lesson off, couldn't they?

GIRL 1: Yeh.

GIRL 2: Yeh.

GIRL 7: Instead of just saying, er...

GIRL 2: I mean, 'cos they've got their own opinions. Why

shouldn't they say 'em?

GIRL 7: Yeh, and most people wouldn't just agree with them for the sake of it. In fact, I think they'd argue against it, you know, a lot of the things.

GIRL 1: Mmm.

GIRL 7: Just because they *are* the teacher.

GIRL 2: I think that taping's really a waste of time in the lessons, 'cos you're waiting to start the lesson and she's taping and she can't work the machine so it takes hours...so, no, 'cos and then, then, you know, you've gone off the subject and by the time you're waiting for the tape recorder to record, you know, you're really going off the subject and it's really a waste of time and everything.

GIRL 1: Umm, going back to about teachers putting their views in, usually, at the end of the lesson, once the tape has gone off, the teacher says, umm, what she wanted, kind of edges us on and tells us, you know, what she, we should 'ave got out of the discussion.

GIRL 3: More people talk then.

GIRL 1: Then everybody starts talking and says 'oh, yeh', you know, they really start talking a lot, so I think it is better once the teacher gives her opinion.

GIRL 2: Mm. Yeh. And the evidence she gives us is miles too long. It takes hours to read...

GIRL 1: Mmm.

GIRL 2: And some of it you can't understand.

GIRL 1: Yeh, usually the evidence 'asn't got, it just states facts, you know, like when they say, she says 'what 'ave you got to say about this piece?'

GIRL 2: It's already said about it, 'asn't it?

GIRL 1: It's already been said about it in the actual piece itself. There's nothing to say.

GIRL 2: And, like when we was doing, in, in the city, the thing went on too long, we can't just do it for a little while and then go on to a new subject, start again, but everything drags on, don't it?

GIRL 3: Yeh.

GIRL 2: You know, you have to do it for one term and all this. I don't see why you 'ave to.

GIRL 4: Instead of just getting pieces of evidence and 'aving to read 'em and then talk about 'em, we should 'ave things like films, and...

GIRL 2: TV.

GIRL 4: And TV, and things like that...

GIRL 2: And going round and visit the places.

GIRL 4: Yes, and going trips and that.

GIRL 5: And actually seein' the conditions people live in and things like that.

GIRL 2: Instead of just readin' about 'em.

GIRL 6: Yeh, we'd like to see these things for ourselves, because we can't really believe some of the things they say.

GIRL 5: And, like, you could, um, instead of just reading about a boy going to an, an all-white school or a white boy going to a school where there's loads of blacks, you could, you know, go and see schools where your populations are different and all that.

GIRL 2: Mmm. And see how the, the kids feel then. Because it's much more interesting than just reading it, and talking about it.

GIRL 7: Mmm.

GIRL 2: And then we could come back and discuss it.

GIRL 7: Mmm.

GIRL 2: Couldn't you?

GIRL 7: Yeh.

TRANSCRIPT 5:
Three Asian girl students talking with a teacher (Strategy B)

TEACHER: OK. It's about, do you remember this time last year we split you up into groups?

GIRL 1: Yes.

TEACHER: And we were doing some work, you were with me, weren't you, and there were some people with (name) and (name). Do you remember what we were talking about?

GIRL 1: The world being broad and history and things like that. You know, you asked what Asian people were and things like that and what we thought, then we told you that ...we told you all the countries.

TEACHER: About the people?

GIRL 1: How the houses look alike and how they've come to England.

TEACHER: Did you enjoy doing that?

GIRL 1: Yeh.

TEACHER: Had you done it before in the school at all?

GIRL 1: In Pakistan?

TEACHER: No, in this school, had you ever found out about...?

GIRL 1: No.

TEACHER: ...your own country in this school? Not at all? What about the other people in the group?

GIRL 2: Oh, I don't know.

TEACHER: Did we just do things about your country, where you lived? How did this start off? Can you remember that?

GIRL 1: Yes, I told them that I'd come from Pakistan and India and you said which part and I said Bihar and you said I was to look it up and I told you...

TEACHER: What about before that, before we got to where you came from, did we do anything else?

GIRL 1: I can't...

TEACHER: You can't remember? That's all right. I just wondered. Part of the idea is to see how much you can remember from so far back. What do you think the idea was? Why do

you think we were doing that?
GIRL 2: We started from immigration and...
TEACHER: Oh, yes, we started from that.
GIRL 2: Yeh, and there was Jamaican boys on the group and
they showed the English, and we were discussing the
immigrants.
TEACHER: About immigration, yes. Do you think it was impor-
tant, most of this?
GIRL 1: Yes, I think so.
TEACHER: Why?
GIRL 1: Because we, we had to know each other.
TEACHER: And do you think it helped doing that, what we did
in those lessons?
GIRL 2: I think so.
TEACHER: You think so. Did it have any direct, can you think
of, say, West Indian children or white children who changed
the way that they've been treating you after we'd done the
lesson? Or lessons?
GIRL 1: I don't think I noticed.
TEACHER: You didn't notice.
GIRL 1: No.
TEACHER: Any change at all? How do they treat you, anyway?
GIRL 1: Sometimes they seem to hate us and sometimes they just
behave just like we're people.
TEACHER: What about you (name)? Because you can join in on
this. What about you? How do you find that the West Indians
and the English children treat you?
GIRL 3: Well, they don't really get along with you, not much.
Sometimes, er, when they're in a good mood they sort of
talk to you, but then when they're first years, then they
just ignore you and just swear and that and'll just push you
about. Especially the West Indians, not English much but some
do it to kids like that. They call me names like 'Paki' and like
that which I'm not because I don't like, I don't like children
calling me names, er, there was little kids, kids outside on
the street they said to me 'Paki', I said, 'Do you mind, I'm
not Paki, I'm an Indian'. Now I make it into a joke when I'm
talked to in this way, but I don't mind, I'm used to it by
now. They don't, they're not, they don't do this sort of thing
nowadays, not much, but they do suddenly.
TEACHER: They used to do it a lot?
GIRL 3: Yeh.
TEACHER: Why do you think they don't do it so much now?
GIRL 3: Well, I, maybe I'm growing a bit now, maybe I'm getting
bigger, somehow.
TEACHER: Because you're getting bigger?
GIRL 3: Yeh.
TEACHER: Do you think that, then, maybe in school we should
do something about it? Why do you think that they do call
you names or shout after you?
GIRL 3: Well, that's why I haven't, even the Indian children

they say to the coloured, and the English children start say-
ing, everyone starts saying to each other. It isn't that these
people say it to us, the English and the coloured, they say
it to each other, everyone. I mean they start calling everyone names. I don't know.
TEACHER: Do you just think...?
GIRL 3: I think it's with living miles away.
TEACHER: Yes.
GIRL 3: ...going on.
GIRL 1: The Jews were pestered.
TEACHER: Do you think it might be because they can't under-
stand you?
GIRL 2: No. They do understand we've got, not it's, er...
(name) and that lot, (name), they sort of, when they
will grow up like they start speaking Indian and these kids
come up to them and say, start copying them, they go
'bbbhhh bbbhhh'. They can't understand you see, but I
don't know, they used to, they start speaking in their own
language.
TEACHER: Have you got any English friends?
GIRL 2: Yeh.
TEACHER: They come home? Do you take them home?
GIRL 2: Yeh, sometimes.
TEACHER: But what about most of your friends, are most of
your friends Indian or...?
GIRL 2: Pakistanis.
TEACHER: Pakistanis. Why's that?
GIRL 2: Because their customs and our customs are the same.
GIRL 1: We can understand each other, you know, we can
speak our language, and...we can do everything with them.
When the English come round it's different, we can only
speak English rather than mix with us, you know.
TEACHER: Do you think that's the biggest problem, that they
don't speak your language?
GIRL 2: Oh, I don't think so because, you know, er...
TEACHER: Well, try and put it into words.
GIRL 2: Because they don't want it.
TEACHER: They don't want?
GIRL 2: Yeh, to learn our language or mix in our culture.
GIRL 3: Because our culture is higher than yours and why
we...
TEACHER: Who says that their culture is higher than yours?
GIRL 2: Some people think...
TEACHER: The English children?
GIRL 2: Yes.
TEACHER: Or the West Indian children say that?
GIRL 3: No, it's the English.
GIRL 2: The English.
TEACHER: The English, not the West Indian children?
GIRL 1: They do , you know, sometimes.
GIRL 3: You know, sometimes, but especially, say, the English

ones, you know.

TEACHER: Can you tell me what you mean by 'culture'?

GIRL 3: Like, um, you know, we don't wear short skirts and tights the way they do. You know, if we wear...they make fun of us which no one can bear that, that someone is making jokes at them.

TEACHER: Umm.

GIRL 3: And they make joke of the dinner that we eat...

TEACHER: Of their food?

GIRL 3: Yeh.

TEACHER: Do you think that's partly because they don't understand what you eat?

GIRL 3: Yeh.

GIRL 2: No, I don't.

GIRL 3: You know, they don't eat...they don't eat...

GIRL 1: Somehow it doesn't matter about the food.

GIRL 3: You don't eat chilli, do you?

TEACHER: Do you? Well, yes. Do...?

GIRL 3: It's Indians because they're not very free, you see.

TEACHER: Who aren't?

GIRL 3: Indians. The boys are, but girls are not and, like, English people, they like going out in the world, but we just stay in, I mean, the coloured children, they go out and English people, they don't sort of mix with, up with this sort of thing.

TEACHER: So you think one of the things might be that (name)'s said that they don't understand your culture, this is one of the reasons why you sort of, you don't have friends?

GIRL 3: No, it isn't. I've got plenty of English friends and I make friends quick.

TEACHER: Yes, but do you find it a problem that you can't go out, or you don't go out in the evenings?

GIRL 3: No, it's all right.

TEACHER: What about your English friends, do they ask you to go out with them in the evenings?

GIRL 2: Well, they do sometimes.

TEACHER: And that's a...

GIRL 2: We just say no, can't.

TEACHER: And what's their reaction to that?

GIRL 1: They condemn...

GIRL 2: No, they just say, 'Oh'.

TEACHER: Do you ever explain to them that you don't go out in the evening?

GIRL 3: Yeh, they get all excited.

GIRL 2: They say 'you don't deserve us as friends', and then they just go out.

GIRL 1: We've explained it to them on lots of times.

TEACHER: And what do they react to that?

GIRL 3: They say, 'Oh, I wouldn't like to be that'.

GIRL 2: 'I wouldn't like to be shut in'.

TEACHER: So it's sort of sympathy rather than anything else?

(silence)

TEACHER: And do you find this difficult?

(silence)

TEACHER: Would you like to be as free as they are to go
out?
GIRL 1: No, I wouldn't.
TEACHER: You don't mind?
GIRL 3: It, it isn't, no, we are free, well, it's only our
parents, they think, er, we go out and...
GIRL 2: It's from the beginning when, when, er, they didn't
used to let their girls go, daughters go out, and they're
doing it still up here, but some children like (name), she
can go out and my dad, some people would think is old
fashioned and they never let their children go out. But I
don't mind. But we can go out on the weekends, say, to
parties or that or things. But going out with boys, I
think, then we can't do that. It's just, it's about how we
grow up.
GIRL 3: I just go out with...
GIRL 1: People just don't understand.
GIRL 2: But we can go out with our friends.

23 A RESEARCHER'S SPECULATIONS

Lawrence Stenhouse

It is the role of the researcher to speculate rather than to instruct. In this spirit the hypotheses set out in the report on the measurement programme are gathered in this chapter, together with further thoughts on the case studies. Experience and experiment are the means by which the reader can test these.

HYPOTHESIS 1: In non-examination or CSE groups, teachers are liable to encounter a hardening of unfavourable attitudes towards school among adolescent pupils.

HYPOTHESIS 2: Adolescents in such groups show some trend towards higher self-esteem and presumably confidence.

HYPOTHESIS 3: Adolescents in such groups show a tendency towards a less authoritarian view of society and a less ready acceptance of authoritarian parental control.

HYPOTHESIS 4: Direct teaching about race relations in the age range 14-16 will tend to have positive rather than negative effects upon inter-racial tolerance as compared with not teaching about race relations.

HYPOTHESIS 5: In the case of attitudes towards Asians, there is a particularly marked negative trend of attitudes in groups aged 14-16 not taught about race relations.

HYPOTHESIS 6: This negative trend tends to be moderated rather than accentuated by teaching about race relations.

HYPOTHESIS 7: Strategy A and Strategy B are both moderately effective in combating inter-ethnic prejudice, and the data give no basis for prescriptive discrimination between them.

HYPOTHESIS 8: Schools will be wise to adopt whichever strategy accords with the context of teaching and the skill of the teachers involved.

HYPOTHESIS 9: Teaching about race relations through improvised drama does not lead to overall deterioration in inter-ethnic attitudes.

HYPOTHESIS 10: Schools would be unwise in general to rely solely on drama as a medium of teaching about

273

race relations if their objective is to maximize improvements in attitude.

HYPOTHESIS 11: Both before and after teaching, black pupils have markedly lower scores for racism and for negative attitudes to other races than do white pupils.

HYPOTHESIS 12: There is some evidence that for black pupils teaching about race relations may increase general racism, anti-Asian and anti-white scores, though these remain (where comparable) lower than those of white pupils. (In our sample this does not show in the anti-Asian scores in Strategy B or in the general racism or anti-Asian scores of Strategy C.)

HYPOTHESIS 13: Both before and after teaching, Asian pupils have significantly lower scores for racism and for negative attitudes towards other races than do white pupils.

HYPOTHESIS 14: Unlike black pupils, Asian pupils appear not to increase racism and prejudice scores between pre-test and post-test.

HYPOTHESIS 15: Experience of the discussion of controversial issues in the light of evidence and under a neutral chairman can lead to a position of 'open-mindedness' which transfers to new issues not previously tackled. (The characteristics of this 'open-mindedness' are not at present described, merely suggested (indicated) by trends in scores.)

HYPOTHESIS 16: Experiences in other styles of teaching may also transfer.

HYPOTHESIS 17: Transfer of open-mindedness will tend to produce a situation in which low racism scores on pre-test will harden somewhat, but remain low, on post-test ('idealism/realism shift').

HYPOTHESIS 18: One element in racism seems likely to be a perception of people of different races as competitors for scarce resources.

HYPOTHESIS 19: One element in racism seems likely to be an unwillingness of white people to accept the appropriateness of black people being placed in superior authority relationships to white subordinates.

HYPOTHESIS 20: The effects of teaching about race relations to adolescents in schools are not likely to be persistent in the long term without reinforcement.

HYPOTHESIS 21: The influence of school and social context is not likely to reinforce inter-racial tolerance in the absence of actions or policies actively designed to do so.

HYPOTHESIS 22: Teaching about race relations through the strategies studied in this project can, and by and large will, lead to more students moving in the desired direction (less racism) than in the undesired direction (more racism) on a measure of racism.

HYPOTHESIS 23: When teaching about race relations meets the educational criterion of appeal to the judgment of those who are taught, as opposed to adopting the stance of brainwashing, a fairly substantial minority of those taught will, during teaching, shift attitude in the undesired direction.

HYPOTHESIS 24: The experience of the teacher in the classroom in the face of racism as expressed by some of the pupils is likely to be sufficiently taxing to make it necessary to define explicitly the support and interest of figures of authority in her/his school and school system and to make provision for mutual support to be offered within a group of teachers sharing the problem.

HYPOTHESIS 25: Teaching about any subject or topic in association with which an attitude or outlook is valued by the teacher (i.e., there are affective as well as cognitive aims) can tend to lead to more students moving in the desired direction with regard to attitude than in the undesired direction (a general form of Hypothesis 22).

HYPOTHESIS 26: When such teaching meets the educational criterion of appeal to the judgment of those taught, a fairly substantial minority of those taught will, during teaching, shift attitude in the undesired direction.

These twenty-six hypotheses seem to me to hang together as a coherent theory, at least in the sense that there are no contradictions among them in the light of logic or common-sense experience. On the other hand, they constitute weak theory in the sense that they are not so well articulated that to disprove one is to call the whole theory into question. There is no obvious crucial experiment, though there is an obvious line of advance in the area of Hypotheses 15, 16 and 17 and again in the area of Hypotheses 22, 23, 25 and 26.

Our analysis of results by school in Chapter 9 might seem to suggest that schools where results were deleterious either knew that things were going badly or entered the project with motives complicated by local or internal political considerations. Such a generalization is almost certainly illusory: schools with good results were also often pessimistic about their teaching and led into the project by mixed motives. There is too much hindsight about this part of the report, but discussion of it by a school staff might nevertheless convert it to foresight.

The case studies are more difficult to summarize, though, in the hands of experienced teachers, easier to use. They also pose problems of understanding. In the first place, transcripts of classroom dialogue, wrenched from their context and deprived of intonation, timing and gesture, give a false impression. And second, these are records of transactions in what we might call, after Ball (1981), Band 2 and Band 3 classrooms. The distribution of readership for publications of this sort in our society suggests that few readers who are not teachers or Asian or black will have experience of such classrooms. They have existed for the 110 years of compulsory schooling, as we well know from log books. But the reader whose own experience of schooling was of blazered endeavour is likely enough to be shocked by the evidence that all schoolchildren are not – and were never – as he or she remembers them.

In my personal view, some of the transcripts used here show the need for an effective alternative pedagogy in a comprehensive and compulsory secondary education. We have been working with unusually able and competent teachers, and even they badly need such a pedagogy and a regime of schooling consistent with it. At the final conference some of them voiced their unhappiness at the masking of classroom difficulties by a rhetoric of complacency. Equally wide of the mark is the blackboard jungle view of the classroom situation. It is simply that in Band 2 and Band 3, pupil-teacher relations bear some resemblance to management-worker relations in British industry. And Band 2 pupils well know that the school is sponsoring the pupils in Band 1. Any teaching endeavour is played on this stage.

The teaching interaction takes account of this without expressing it, since it is tacitly assumed by teachers and pupils. Good teachers cope by tacking about, by humour or tolerance, by riding out some storms. Robert Wild talks of study of the classroom as 'a sociology of occasions'. Teaching and its effects are lodged in small behaviours – 'interactions' – that take place in the classroom; a kind of game held together by shared meanings and rules, but open to development through negotiation. As Sheard and Sikes have it, 'The success, or otherwise, of a particular session can sometimes be explained quite easily in terms of how leading members of the group are behaving towards one another.'

The meanings that enter this complex situation as the content of instruction are not easy to establish. The meaning achieved is socially constructed in the classroom. Pedagogy has not only to communicate an interpretative structure, but also to construct it as it goes along. This is particularly relevant when considering teaching about race relations, and is an important insight to bring to accounts of classrooms.

The experience of students is difficult to admit into the classroom. On the one hand, it threatens the teacher's position:

students often have experience the teacher lacks, and this is particularly true of race relations in a multi-racial school. On the other hand, the student who offers his own experience or views in the group becomes vulnerable to other members and perhaps - as one of the interviews shows - to students outside the group. In part, of course, this is one reason for using evidence - materials which open the experiences and views of others to discussion without putting those who discuss them at too much risk.

But evidence can readily be used not for discussion but as instructional material, and then attention to comprehension or style often serves to protect participants from facing content. Boredom lies that way, but boredom is for many students a familiar and relatively acceptable aspect of schooling - risk-free, at any rate! Wild sees it as possibly an attractive bolt-hole.

Boredom can be combated at one level by the teacher taking the role of entertainer or of ringmaster in the instructional circus. But the instructional leadership role is problematic when we are concerned with material infused with attitudes and out-side the teacher's trained expertise. These conditions generally apply in the area of race relations.

One relief for boredom that may be powerful as an influence on attitudes is conflict and tension. In one study Wild describes a group at loggerheads with one another, a high proportion of its members disliking one another, and suggests that this experi-ence of conflict may be projected on the topic of race relations, which serves as a medium in which the tension is expressed.

To use the case studies, however, it is not necessary to inter-pret at this level. More direct issues arise: the problem of the devil's advocate role; the problem of sensitivities within the group; the role of information about other cultures, and so forth.

With such issues, which speak rather directly to the experi-ence of the reader, he is not likely to need more commentary than has been offered in the case study chapters themselves.

24 A TEACHER'S REFLECTIONS

Alison Berry and Robert D. Wild

The teacher, who was to take a leading role in the project's
dissemination, is invited by the interviewer to recall the conference held in summer 1974 at which teachers from the three
strategies came together. This was the final event in the project's programme of activity.

INTERVIEWER: If you think back to the last conference, how
  you felt?
TEACHER: Yes, I think, to begin with, I didn't realize to what
  extent it was going to suddenly stop. Until that last session
  in the senior common room, I think we had this unrealistic
  expectation of everything being revealed at the follow-up
  conference. We, certainly in our place, and I think the
  (school name) people too, imagined that you would be able
  to analyse our tapes. I don't know whether they sent the
  tapes in, but we sort of imagined immediate feedback.
INTERVIEWER: From the tapes?
TEACHER: From our tapes, from our individual experience,
  from the team, so to speak.
INTERVIEWER: Because a lot of schools hadn't sent the tapes
  in.
TEACHER: Well, I didn't realize this, I thought they were all
  sending them in.
INTERVIEWER: Yes.
TEACHER: I think it was an unrealistic expectation, but still,
  as you were coming along, you see, 'Ah well, they will have
  listened to my tape by now that I made on such and such a
  date, and perhaps they can tell me why, what happened, or
  why it broke down, or how I should have handled this.' You
  know, you tended to think at a very individual level and want
  some kind of immediate insight into what had happened to
  you, and I think it wasn't until this last winding-up session
  that I suddenly realized that we were going to go back into
  our schools and it was all going to finish. And when the
  onus seemed to be put on us as well; when it was said to us,
  'Well, it's up to the teachers now', I'd been used to the idea
  of getting guidance from Norwich, so to speak, guidance from
  the team that the team was structuring it; and now we were
  going back and the onus was on us. It was just quite impossible for us to cope. We didn't have the kind of structure
  that would enable us to, I felt personally, the initiative, the
  ability to start doing things on our own and taking respon-

sibility for our own diffusion - if you like, of our experiences. And also, I had this acute feeling of, in the first conference, I'd met some people like (name), (name) and (name) and other people, and then, seeing them again at the second conference, you had the feeling of working together and working with them, and some of these people I'd seen at the HCP training scheme as well, and you had this great feeling of being in a team and working with them and it was coming to an end: we were splitting up; we weren't going to work together any more. All this thing that you'd felt happening had suddenly stopped. I think this is where you had the acute feeling of being let down. Then another element in it was that after each lesson I would sit down and write my account and I felt I was working towards getting some kind of understanding in what I was doing and I really enjoyed feeling, or imagining, that I was carrying out some kind of research role, or at least trying to look at what I was doing in school. I felt a feeling of support because I was taking part in a programme, because the team had structured it and because we felt we were working with you in some sort of way - it was like being a student again, in a sense, and I'm the sort of person who needs some kind of direction, I think, or guidance, and I felt I was getting it and this greatly enhanced what I was doing in the school. I felt very strongly this is what I would like all the time, this is how teachers should teach, with back-up from outside teachers in the school.

INTERVIEWER: Do you not feel that you can, within the school situation, develop this kind of relationship back-up from within your own colleagues?

TEACHER: I think to some extent we have, but in our particular school there are organizational problems of getting us to work together. For instance, when we talked about the problems of mixed-ability or we talked about the possibility of integration, we became much more questioning about what we were doing in the classroom, but at the same time those sort of sessions have fundamental differences, particularly integration, between the more subject-centred teachers and the ones who wanted integration, which had proved to be very divisive, partly I think because of the way in which the meetings were handled by the person responsible for curriculum development.

INTERVIEWER: Is that (name)?

TEACHER: No, (name).

INTERVIEWER: Sorry.

TEACHER: And in fact we'd been driven further apart as a result of these; there's still an exchange of ideas, but I somehow feel that people from outside, from research institutes and the Department of Education, have got a different kind of knowledge, a different kind of expertise and background, and that you need both. I'm not the sort of, I don't know whether it's because...

INTERVIEWER: You don't feel that it's just the idea of an outsider coming in and initiating something?

TEACHER: No. That it's somebody with a different kind of background and expertise who knows about – has perhaps a broader view of education, more knowledge about – trends of education and philosophies of education, I suppose, than the ordinary teacher has, and that this is necessary. I don't have the kind of attitude a lot of teachers have that busybodies intrude in the school – 'these people in colleges of education who don't know anything about what it's really like in school, it's about time they came back and did some teaching', that sort of attitude, which is common in our school. I think (name) to some extent is highly suspicious, and I know (name) much more so, from what I've heard. You know, sort of 'outsiders coming in and measuring things', and then 'measurement in itself is a threat and undesirable and against the interests of the children and that we shouldn't be using our children as guinea pigs', I mean that sort of attitude came across from (name) quite a lot of the time, you know, 'that these people at East Anglia are using our children and exposing them to stressful situations – perhaps bringing out conflicts which are best left uncovered – just for their own purposes of writing papers or doing something'. Well, I never felt like that, and that's probably partly my background; you know, I did two years of research work, unsuccessfully, and my husband's main activity in life is doing research, so I've had a different sort of attitude towards what research was for and what it could do. And I was keen to co-operate and interested in what the outcome would be, which I think is why I always wrote up the report and always taped, simply because I knew the necessity of accumulating the data and of being consistent and of not having gaps, and I understood why the control groups had to be different because I had some experience, however limited, of the need for a proper sample and of a proper amount of data.

INTERVIEWER: How far do you think this feeling of loss was felt by other members at the conference, and secondly, how far did other members at the conference feel as you did about research?

TEACHER: Well the feeling of loss, I stirred it – I don't know whether it was me, but there was a group of disgruntled elements in one corner of the room. I'm sure the people from (name) school felt it, and I think (name) felt it and one or two others because we were agitated. You know, I'd dig him in the ribs and say 'Isn't this terrible?' and 'What are we going to do now?' and 'Don't you feel let down?' and 'Why can't they tell us anything?' and 'When will the report come out?' and 'We've got a right to know what our findings are', and this sort of thing. So I think that was quite, for the people who felt involved and interested, I think it was a very common

thing. There seemed to be other people who were glad it was over and didn't want to know any more - you know, people who perhaps felt it was wrong to teach about race relations. There's a man from the north, from a (place) school; a girl...
INTERVIEWER: Oh, (name)?
TEACHER: Yes.
INTERVIEWER: And (name)?
TEACHER: Yes, well I was aware of (name) being what I considered to be obstructive, you know, it's a point of view very different from mine.
INTERVIEWER: Yes.
TEACHER: I don't know how people like that felt, but certainly in the group I'd associated with, I'd got to know vaguely the bloke from (name) school in the cross-strategy discussion group and there was a terrific amount of enthusiasm. We started off at the beginning of the conference quite hostile to the other strategies, I mean I had this feeling...
INTERVIEWER: This was general, was it?
TEACHER: Well, I don't know how general it was. Certainly I felt that HCP was the best way of doing it; it was the strategy that had the greatest amount of respect for the kids because it made them autonomous, it respected them, it didn't impose the teacher's views, it didn't rely on the character of the teacher thing, you know, you weren't God Almighty decreeing what you should think, and this was giving to me a much more humane - that's not the right word - but a way of handling children, that you were respecting their individuality; their need to realize their own ideas and measure them up against other people's, and you were freeing them of this kind of dependence on the teacher. So that was why I felt HCP was the superior approach, and I tended to be very disparaging towards some of the Strategy B things. Now (name) and (name) felt this even more acutely than I did, and I think got into some kind of strong verbal disagreement with other people in the particular wing that we were staying in - if you said something disparaging about HCP teachers ('aggressive women', I think was said) and this persisted. Then when we heard the local radio programme - we thought it was dreadful; we had a row, well it was a heated argument with, what was his name?
INTERVIEWER: (name).
TEACHER: Yes, there was (name) and (name) and I and (name) and a couple of other people, we were very rude, very crude, I think, in what we had to say; we said isn't this disgusting in a crude way, artificial working-class stereotype and middle-class stereotype that came across in these programmes and we thought that they were dreadful; an insult to the children to offer them this sort of thing. We had a really quite violent argument because (name) and (name) got friendly with the other two. I think they influenced them

quite a lot, and it came to a head in that meeting we had in
the other block, when some of us were turning to Lawrence
Stenhouse and saying: 'Come on, tell the rest what HCP
does and how HCP's better' and he didn't, and (name) and
(name) in particular reacted quite strongly to this.... And
I was waiting for the cross-strategy discussion, thinking,
'Right, we're really going to get them now' - and then,
of course, the cross-strategy discussions were so different,
so pleasant, and so enjoyable, and I had that bloke from
(name) school in my group...

INTERVIEWER: (name)?

TEACHER: Yes, and because of the influence (name) had on
the bloke from (name) school he was well disposed towards
HCP and wanted to know more about it and wanted to ask
questions about it, and at the same time I'd seen the exhibi-
tion as well and seen what the teachers from (name)
school had done and seen some of the materials the Strategy
B people had produced and been impressed by the amount
of stuff that they had actually prepared and the work that
they'd done, and the hostility had sort of been diffused quite
a lot and I found that cross-strategy discussion very worthwhile. I still feel that HCP is the best way of doing it, but
I could see what the other strategies had to offer and that
there were other ways of approaching teaching about race
relations. I've forgotten where I started now: what did you
ask?

INTERVIEWER: I started off asking how other people felt at the
end of the conference; how in general this feeling of loss
was also how you felt other teachers felt about being in the
role of the researcher?

TEACHER: No, I don't know about that one.

INTERVIEWER: When you returned back to the school after the
conference how did you feel then?

TEACHER: I think I continued to feel let down. Now I took part
in several things, I went and talked to this - I can't remember
whether it was an NUT sub-committee or what it was - but I
went and spoke at this and so did (name). Then we had an
HCP Association meeting where somebody from a Strategy B
school came in. But we seemed to get opposition from the new
inspector, or at least not opposition just a sort of coolness,
and he kept putting up objections. (Name) was saying things
like 'We must have a technician to keep the HCP packs up to
date'; 'We must look for materials'; you know, 'We can remedy
the problems that we saw in the race materials'; 'We must do
this, we must do that'; 'We need the services of a librarian';
'The Teachers' Centre must be prepared to disseminate
materials'; and he kept saying 'Well, that's not possible';
'Well, you can't have a technician'; and 'There isn't the
money' and so on. And he kept throwing it back to the

teachers and saying 'The teachers have got to do it'; 'You'll have to get together'. And we were saying 'When?'; 'We don't have the time'; 'We can't do this in addition to all the other teacher duties' and that tended to make you feel demoralized and sort of 'What's the use?'

This teacher became prominent in NARTAR, the National Association for Race Relations Teaching and Action Research, and took an active part in the earlier phase of the dissemination.

25 AFTERMATH

Jean Rudduck

The last chapter started with one teacher reflecting on the
final conference organized by the project team at Easter 1974,
and recollecting her sudden sense of the project being over.
Feelings of aggression towards the 'other' strategies faded, to
some extent, as all the teachers present faced the common
problem of ending. Feelings of irritation with the project team
for not bringing it all together in one final, satisfying set of
conclusions generated a mood of almost desperate independence:

> It's time we stopped hiding our light under a bushel and
> instead of waiting for somebody at the top to say to us: 'We
> believe you have been doing so and so; would you like to
> talk about it?' we should start going to teachers' centres
> and local education authorities and say: 'I've got the exper-
> tise' - and we have got a certain amount of expertise - 'Are
> you going to use me?' It's time we started to advertise what
> we've got ourselves.
>
> (A teacher at the conference)

The build-up to the final plenary session at which this statement
was made were meetings organized as 'commissions' - option
groups, each charged with the exploration of a particular topic;
for example, the political implications of teaching about race
relations, teaching about race relations in non-multi-racial
schools, and the need for materials to support teaching about
race relations:

> Through all the groups ran the sense of urgency - the need
> to do something - and at the same time there was growing
> awareness of the impotency that might face the teacher on
> returning to his own situation.
>
> (extract from the conference report)

It was clear that two concerns were emerging: a concern to make
accessible, outside the present group, the wealth of ideas and
experiences that the project had evoked; and a concern to keep
open the opportunity to continue the work in one's own school
and classroom. The project team may have disappointed many
of the teachers who took part through its insistence on teacher
independence and responsibility, but through its existence it
had legitimized the attempt to teach about race relations, even
in difficult settings. The ad hoc initiatives in dissemination

which the teacher quoted above had advocated would probably
not have served the long-term needs of dissemination; they
would certainly not have served the continuing needs of
individual teachers, or small school-based teacher ter.ns who
were trying to teach about race relations, for these teachers
needed the support of an organized reference group.

The narrative of what happened next is in one sense a story
about power v. potential. The project team, reincarnated in
a dissemination project, provided background support; teachers
who had been involved in the original project took responsibility
for the action, and tried, this time, to build authority in their
own group rather than rely on the borrowed authority of the
central team. In terms of teacher potential, the story is an
encouraging one; in terms of teacher power, the end is pre-
dictable to anyone who understands the structure of our
education system.

THE PROPOSAL FOR A FOLLOW-UP PROGRAMME

The first initiative after the ending of the original project was
taken by the central team. In January 1975 they had drafted
a proposal to the SSRC for funds to support the dissemination
of the projects and to study the progress.(1) While concentrating ostensibly on the task of making the ideas and experiences
of the project more widely accessible - the dissemination task -
the proposal went some way towards meeting the teachers'
other concern, in that it presupposed the existence of a network of teachers and a framework for co-ordinating their
actions.

The proposal warned against the dangers of easy generalization of the research experience yielded by the original projects.
Instead, it argued for an interpretation of research experiences
which were too diverse and too context-dependent to allow
generalization across settings. It argued for action planned in
the light of an analysis of the reported experiences, and of
the circumstances and structure of the situation in which
teaching was to take place.

The original project was characterized by the requirement
that participating teachers adopt a research attitude to their
own teaching. The logical next step was to suggest that teachers
new to the work were unlikely to benefit from or understand
what the project had to offer unless they were prepared to
adopt a similar attitude to their teaching about race relations.
The aspiration in the new project was, therefore, to make
accessible research attitudes and procedures as well as
research findings.

A boldly optimistic claim in the proposal was that, after one
year, the programme of dissemination would be self-supporting.
The basis for this prognostication was the likelihood that the
trial teaching materials from the original project would be

published (a publisher had already expressed what the team thought was firm interest in the enterprise). Royalties from the sales of the teaching materials would be placed in a trust fund and used to support a continuing programme of dissemination. The conferences, which were to be the main vehicle for dissemination, were to be self-supporting through fees, and the money available in the trust fund was to be used mainly to defray the expenses of teachers who would meet as a committee to organize and supervise the programme of dissemination.

The most urgent need, then, was for materials. In the summer of 1975 there was to be a conference of teachers who had taken part in the original projects and their task would be to prepare materials for handing to the publisher during the autumn of 1975. At the same time, the central team proposed that they should prepare case study material, which would demonstrate the diversity of project experiences and which would therefore be a useful resource at the dissemination conferences that the teachers were to run.

The next step was to be a course, organized during the Christmas vacation, at which a volunteer group of teachers who had taken part in the original project would be inducted as 'teacher disseminators'. The central team was to take responsibility for planning and staffing this conference, which would culminate in a formal handing-over of control from the project team to the teacher team. The project team also offered to notify LEAs of the programme of opportunities which the dissemination programme would open up.

It was proposed that dissemination conferences would need to be residential and about five days long if participants were to be inducted into research procedures, helped to interpret the range of experiences yielded by the original project and encouraged to consider the potential usefulness, in their own setting, of the teaching strategies and teaching materials used in the original projects.

What was proposed was appealing in terms of principle, logical in terms of the work that had gone before, but extremely ambitious. The scheme rested on the following propositions:

(1) that practising teachers could take responsibility for planning, staffing and effectively managing a series of national, residential conferences;
(2) that practising teachers could pass on to conference members an expertise in and respect for basic techniques in the monitoring of classroom performance;
(3) that practising teachers could encourage conference members to interpret case study material and measurement data in ways that would help them to plan a strategy for teaching about race relations which would be appropriate to the particular circumstances of their own schools.

DISSEMINATION IN ACTION

In January 1976, fourteen teachers from the original projects
(and five interested outsiders) enrolled for a residential
conference which was held in Norwich. A major outcome of
the conference was the formation of a national association, the
National Association for Race Relations Teaching and Action
Research (NARTAR). A committee was elected and at its first
meeting, towards the end of the conference, a draft constitution was drawn up:

(1) The committee shall plan dissemination and if necessary
appoint other associates to undertake planning.
(2) It shall collect and transmit information.
(3) It shall administer the funds available for it, and have the
power to seek funds if necessary.
(4) It shall maintain a register of, and communicate with,
associates.
(5) It shall maintain the corporate identity of the people involved with the experimental project on the Problems and Effects
of Teaching about Race Relations.(2)
(6) It shall liaise with other bodies working in the area of race
relations.

The constitution required that the committee meet at least once
a term and that an Annual General Meeting be held in January of
each year.(3) The subscription was set at 50 pence per year. It
was a demanding contract that the teachers had entered into.
Had the project director not had a serious heart attack in the
early days of the conference, the framework might have been
different:

> You see, basically, NARTAR came (into being) simply because
> the problem was how to get some group in whom money (i.e.
> royalties) could be invested, and the discussion was whether,
> for example, to make it a limited company....We went through
> all this with the SSRC and they weren't happy about the
> limited company solution, and we weren't awfully happy about
> it being CARE....Probably my absence from the conference
> robbed me of a voice in the definition of the task at that
> time....I can't tell exactly how things went, but my notion
> was that the association of teachers was simply to get a con-
> stitution which allowed them to handle money.
>   (Lawrence Stenhouse, interview, June 1976)

Stenhouse remained sceptical of the prudence of trying to establish a national association, rather than a formal working group,
especially with strong organizations already in the field such
as NAME - the National Association for Multi-racial Education.
However, the move was an understandable one in the circumstances. The first NARTAR secretary recalls her feelings at

the time:

> I think early on we felt particularly confused and we felt
> this crisis of identity very greatly when Lawrence was
> ill....It was very difficult to get a clear idea of what the
> project was about, how CARE saw us, of what our role
> should be....We felt we really did have to develop a sense
> of our own identity so that we knew what we were doing
> and why we were doing it....I think it's all very well to
> say 'OK, we'll make NARTAR into an association because
> of the problem of royalties and what have you', but once
> you make an association and you elect a committee, you've
> created something that wasn't there before, something
> that will become very conscious of itself and begin to
> function.
>
> (Interview, May 1976)

The first major dissemination event had actually taken place
in October 1975 – three months before NARTAR was set up.
A headmaster in the Midlands was organizing a short ATO/DES
course on multi-racial education and he invited the project
director to speak. His task was to 'get some names' so that
local teachers 'who knew the names would be attracted to the
conference'. Lawrence Stenhouse advised him that the intended
policy in dissemination was for teachers who had taken part
in the original projects to present the research. The head took
this well: 'Teachers will no doubt have a much more immediate
appeal to other teachers...so all I said to him (Stenhouse) was,
would he make sure that suitable teachers were available'.
The head acknowledged some anxiety – understandably so, for
there was a lot at stake for him: 'I wondered what they would
be like' (none of the other eighteen speakers were classroom
teachers), but after the event he was satisfied:

> Given that it's their first attempt – obviously they're going
> to have to be more selective, and with more experience of
> presenting it they probably will put the case more force-
> fully....If I were doing it again, I would put them in again.

And he did – a year later.
    The joint lecture was reasonably well received by the fifty
teachers present, even though most of them were junior school
teachers and the speakers were from secondary schools. The
two teacher-disseminators were, however, anxious about a
number of things. First, they acknowledged, as two Strategy
A teachers, an impulse to talk more extensively about their
own approach, and felt that they hadn't been fair to the other
two strategies. Second, they were worried about coverage, and
wondered whether they were right to try to include in their
talk an overview of the original projects, the research design
and tentative findings, personal accounts of classroom experi-

ences, and some reminders of general issues that teachers
contemplating starting work on race relations might give attention to. The two teachers concerned had put a lot of work into
their preparation, alone as well as together. They tape-recorded
the session and afterwards listened to the tape analytically to
try to improve their performance. They were given release from
school for the day; their expenses were paid, and they shared
a small fee. But what mattered most was that they were encouraged by the experience.

The next major event was a slot at the annual NAME conference in April 1976. Four teachers (two from Strategy A; one,
Strategy B and one, Strategy C) handled two three-and-a-half-
hour sessions for two different groups of teachers. This was
the first time that the teacher-disseminators had appeared
under NARTAR colours, and the first time that they had faced
a situation where what they had to offer was an option on the
programme. They were not disappointed: about twenty-five
people chose to attend each session. Their presence at the
conference had been negotiated internally - a member of the
NARTAR committee was an established member of NAME. There
was no attempt here to enlist the project director rather than
the teachers, for it was not uncommon for teachers to lead
sessions at the NAME conferences. The problems were of a
different order. The last conference was a one-off event; the
programme was fixed; there was no choice; the audience was
captive; the visiting lecturers and the conference organizers
were in the high-status positions. Here it was different. The
conference was an annual affair; the members were regulars
and they knew the ropes; the NARTAR team were outsiders.
The conference chairman, for example, was able to joke with
individual members of the 200-strong audience: 'Get back into
your box, Phil', and the audience would respond with knowing
laughter. It was like walking into a club that you don't belong
to and where the protocol hasn't been explained: 'I'm a bit
over-awed at the number of people here actually. It is very
much an "Oh, hello again!" sort of approach.' Observation of
an early plenary did not reassure the NARTAR team: 'I am a
bit terrified now, actually having seen the way they sort of
shot the Secretary of State, or whoever he was, down in
flames....' The NARTAR team was also worried because they
were white, because all the teachers in the original projects
were white, because one of the team was teaching in a non-
multi-racial school - and because a large number of the conference members were black. 'I obviously don't think people
should be entirely concerned with multi-racial schools, but I
think they (conference members) are.'

Experiences in the session were occasionally disturbing,
particularly when Strategy A was under scrutiny, but the
NARTAR teacher responsible for the session maintained his
cool in the face of sustained and long-winded attacks - leaving
it to other members of the group to take up the defence. He

was fortunately a fairly experienced conference-goer: 'I am always waiting for these people to show up. It doesn't really surprise me.' But it was valuable for the members of the team to have sympathetic colleagues around.

Some of the participants from the NAME conference who had opted for the NARTAR sessions were later interviewed by a member of the project's central team. (Shortly after this he accepted a post in Australia, and the data were not processed until 1979; had they been available earlier they might have provided useful feedback to the teacher-disseminators.) The ten participants were selected to represent the range of people present and included a remedial teacher, two secondary teachers, a primary headteacher, three lecturers, two advisers and a curriculum development officer. Reactions to the NARTAR team were generally supportive:

> From my point of view it was much better, because to listen to them, they were the ones who had a practical experience and so obviously to me they were the ones who could talk about it more. They weren't talking about what was reported to them; they were talking about what they'd actually seen and done...and this to me was one of their strengths.
>
> (Curriculum development officer)

> Great. Marvellous. Far better than people like me, or people doing research. It's terribly important that practical teachers are actually doing it.
>
> (College lecturer)

> The teachers talked about real experiences which were clear in their own minds.
>
> (Headteacher)

Good will was elicited by a perceived combination of commitment and slight uncertainty:

> They were clearly teachers and they weren't lecturers. They didn't have the easy sort of feeling of being relaxed in front of a large group of people....I think I wanted to make these people feel that they weren't in a difficult situation, that we were just people who were going to listen.
>
> (Headteacher)

Moreover, the NARTAR team didn't look all that different from the participants:

> Without wanting to give labels, the work was being done by two fairly middle-aged, acceptable teachers in that they weren't - they didn't look like, er, er - what's the word? They didn't look like left-wing radicals. They looked more like the normal teacher's conception of what

a teacher was....

(Headteacher)

The irony of this set of responses is that the teacher-disseminators were being valued more for their ability to talk
about their own practice in ways with which participants could
identify rather than for the challenge of the research-based
approach to classroom teaching which their practice exemplified.

The next event was a NARTAR presentation at the annual
DES course on multi-cultural education, a ten-day event. Four
NARTAR teachers took part (a fifth underwent an appendicitis
operation immediately before the course started). The team
handled one fifteen-hour unit (ten sessions) and two four-and-
a-half-hour units (three sessions) for two different groups of
participants. This conference was disturbing for the NARTAR
teachers, but it was not destructive of their morale or their
reputation. The first setback was the invitation. There were
to be two other team inputs at the course, one consisting of
well-known members of the NFER/Schools Council project on
multi-cultural education; the other consisting of well-known
members of NAME. Lawrence Stenhouse was invited to lead
the NARTAR sessions - and he refused, appealing to the
project's principle of dissemination as an explanation of his
refusal. HMI, not unnaturally, were concerned, having more
confidence in the project director whom they knew than in
teachers whom they did not know to sustain a major element of
the course. The NARTAR secretary recalled that the HMI in
charge 'told me quite clearly that if we couldn't change our
position he would find more conventional people to fill our spot
in the conference'. Some NARTAR committee members were
irritated and wanted to stand firm for the principle, but others
felt that if they lost the slot they might lose ground in the
overall dissemination campaign. A compromise was reached.
Lawrence Stenhouse was to accompany the NARTAR team and
to introduce them and then to take a back seat. He also tried
to help the team to see the conference organizer's point of
view:

> a new teacher organization in the area of race relations, not
> yet weighed up and evaluated, and still to prove itself....
> It's very difficult for people outside to see what we're doing
> because they can't see the teachers as part of the team.

The NARTAR team subsequently felt somewhat paranoid about
the conference:

> I was aware again at the first planning meeting that the
> course organizer was regarding me as somebody who should
> be made to feel quite clear about their place, I think.
> Actually he was very nice to me, but I still got this feeling.

A series of events made this a memorable course in practice as well as in preparation. First, the NARTAR team was informed before their first session that they had under-recruited in relation to the NFER and NAME teams: some teachers had been asked to transfer, and had agreed (but this meant that they attended as second-choice participants) and others had been asked and had refused. Second, the first NARTAR session blew up. The Strategy A/Strategy B suspicions, which had for some while been latent, suddenly flared up. A Strategy B teacher, departing from the agreed style, handled the first session in far from neutral chairmanship style, directly challenging and arousing the group members and accusing them of coming along merely to seek answers. Tempers unleashed themselves; some people stood up; some swore.(4) The team leader, a Strategy A teacher, was nonplussed. The HMI in charge of the conference appeared at the next NARTAR session – but this one, a Strategy A focus, was restrained, almost consciously so. The Strategy B teacher who had roused the group was due to leave after the first day anyway, and the rift healed. The final end-of-course review revealed the extent to which the NARTAR teachers were prepared to acknowledge a new closeness:

> The other thing that has come out of our experience is the way we've worked together.
>
> (A teacher)

> When you said this morning in response to that woman's comments about neutral chairmanship, and you said: 'What you've got to realize is it's a particular strategy, and a particular role' – now, if you remember that argument we had in Tom's room at Norwich (the January 1976 course, where the Strategy A/Strategy B sessions were particularly rent with divisions), it was over that very thing. And (now) your attitude, your stance, is different – amazingly. Maybe not your attitude, but your way of stating it is different, has shifted incredibly. I don't think that would have happened if we hadn't spent time working together.

This conference was also disturbing in that it called into question just what it was that the teacher-disseminators represented. At the preliminary planning meetings the issue had been raised but never resolved – perhaps the course was too close for the issue to be honestly faced. Now, in the final post-course review, it was raised and faced. The NARTAR teachers acknowledged that they were not all still involved in teaching about race relations in their own classrooms, and that this was a source of embarrassment.

> What we're training people in is a memory.

There is also the business about getting too glib about our interpretations of what we seem to half-remember from two years ago.

The outcome of the discussion was to look to 'further development' as a means of avoiding 'getting caught down memory lane'. An opportunity came at the first conference run exclusively by NARTAR (January 1977 - four days long) to attract new members and to embark on a period of further development of classroom work while maintaining the spirit of research-based teaching. The AGM, which was held during the conference, went ahead, even though it was not quorate; and a few new members were recruited, two of whom agreed to serve on the NARTAR committee where there had been some resignations.

So, NARTAR's first year was over. It had made a good beginning, but prospects were not encouraging. First, the financial climate was worsening, and money to support teachers attending out-of-county residential conferences was in short supply. One of the committee members, a deputy head, failed to gain financial support to attend the January 1977 conference, and he was reluctant to pay his own expenses. He made available the letter which he had received from his LEA:

> The Authority have had to reduce the financial provision for in-service education during the past year, and I am afraid that owing to the present economic situation it is not possible to meet all demands that are made, and we are obliged, therefore, regretfully, to decline grant aid to a number of colleagues wishing to attend courses....I must stress that this refusal in no way implies that the course would not be of value to you, nor that we are unappreciative of your keenness to attend.

The NARTAR committee member added a comment of his own:

> I feel that if other authorities are going to take the same stand we may find that our dissemination programme may possibly grind to a halt and certainly people will find it very difficult, with staff cuts and so on, even to get time off.

To communicate effectively its complex message about classroom research in the context of teaching about race relations, NARTAR needed the time afforded by a five-day residential conference. Instead, it was having to compress what it had to say into short spaces of one-and-a-half hours, three-and-a-half hours - rarely longer - and to work in settings over which it had no control and which may not have attracted the kind of audiences that NARTAR would have wished for. Moreover, there was some evidence that race relations was not yet a topic that had strong in-service appeal for teachers, although

LEA officers were concerned to promote opportunities for
their teachers to think about the issues. A teachers' centre
leader comments:

> I think the biggest problem is to get it into people's con-
> sciousness in the first place. If I advertised in my centre
> that this was going to happen, the very title would put
> off ninety per cent of the people, would stop them coming,
> because as far as they are concerned it's nothing to do
> with them – they are science teachers or maths teachers....
> And this is the big problem – trying to get it into people's
> consciousness.

Hence NARTAR's reliance on gigs in other people's shows –
NAME, ATSS, BERA.

Second, there was the problem of materials. It is a common
experience in curriculum development work that teaching
materials are perceived as an easy solution to classroom problems. Certainly, participants at short courses are inclined to
feel they have not had their money's worth if there is nothing
to take away – and materials may be more reassuring than just
a set of ideas that participants have to carry in their minds
and translate, later, into action. The teacher disseminators
were aware of this. They were worried about 'the way in which
dissemination implies a concentration on product' and noticed that
'people want to come in and grab the stuff and put it under their
arm'. They felt, therefore, somewhat ambivalent towards teaching
materials, but would have preferred to have them available, and
to re-educate their audience, than not to have them available
at the risk of losing the audience. And they were not
available.

In summer 1975 a group of project teachers had spent five
days preparing the trial teaching materials for publication – but
the publisher, who had originally seemed keen to take them,
turned them down. The climate was not one in which publishers
were prepared to take risks with investment, especially in the
sensitive area of race relations. Another publisher was found –
it all took time, of course – and a contract was offered to
NARTAR on condition that the materials were printed as bound
booklets and not as loose-leaf resource materials, as the teachers
had intended. In January 1978 a decision was made to abandon
NARTAR's constitution and committee meetings in order to concentrate on the preparation of the teaching materials; and committee members were translated, as was Bottom the Weaver, and
became editors. As drafts were submitted to the new publisher
it became evident that what was wanted was a fairly directive
commentary and a set of questions to accompany the 'evidence'
of photographs, journal articles, interviews, songs, poems,
etc., that the teachers had collected. With some distaste, the
editing team agreed to the compromise, but in summer 1979 the
publisher decided not to proceed with publication. However,

a collection of teacher education materials - brief extracts
from transcripts of interviews and classroom discussions which
illustrated common problems and occurrences and showing how
teachers and pupils responded - was put together by a NARTAR
associate on a short-term contract. She worked from the larger
case studies that had been prepared by the central team; these
materials were published and are available at CARE (Sikes,
1979). During this time, the costs supporting the work on the
teaching and teacher-education materials were met by grants
from the Gulbenkian Foundation.

Third, the committee members, who all had full-time jobs,
were over-stretched and had little time left from conference
planning, committee meetings and, later, editing meetings to
attend satisfactorily to unexpected domestic or professional
demands. The experience of managing to cope with the planning
for a major national conference during the school term is cap-
tured in this not untypical statement by the secretary of
NARTAR:

> I've now had two telephone conversations with the HMI,
> one Friday morning and one yesterday - that was Saturday.
> The first telephone conversation I was summoned from my
> classroom, and I'd like to describe the teaching situation
> or school situation which I had to leave in order to go and
> take that phone call....It was the last day before our half-
> term holiday and the school had decided to have a spon-
> sored walk to raise money. All the kids were expected to
> go on the walk. If they didn't, they were given something
> worse to do. A lot of them were keen, but they'd all
> turned up dressed as though they were going on holiday...
> in sort of festive mood, wearing odd clothes and very
> cheerful. So the teaching situation was lively to begin with.
> It also happened to be the Friday on which most of the
> fifth-years were going to leave, and by the time I got to
> the phone I'd already confiscated two raw eggs that hadn't
> been thrown - and the front stairs of A block had already
> had one or two eggs plastered over it as they'd been hurled
> from one fifth-former to another. So it was a bit hectic....
> I wasn't at my most reflective, to put it mildly!

Later, the same teacher filled out the picture:

> During the term I tried not to think about the conference
> at all under the pressure of more urgent but often more
> trivial problems - for example, a visit by 10 students to
> observe me teaching a class I can't control very well,
> attempts to get our sixth-form executive committee to func-
> tion, collecting resources for our Mode C Geography
> course, the school trip, preparing for a sixth-form con-
> ference, a school fair, a school evening, extra lessons for
> my two S-level pupils - and so on! By not thinking about

the conference I managed not to panic.

There was little opportunity for the NARTAR committee members to concentrate on building up the membership of NARTAR and establishing it as a credible organization. And yet there was an undeniable need for NARTAR to show itself as 'vigorous and confident...to earn its spurs' (reported comment of an LEA adviser). Sadly, little active support was available from the associates who had been involved in the original projects (despite their enthusiasm in 1974). Many had joined NARTAR when it was established, probably on a tide of good intent that was raised by the euphoria of the moment, but thereafter their direct contact with NARTAR was slender; and, despite five Newsletters in one-and-a-half years, for them NARTAR must have had an insubstantial reality. None of the founder members attended the first AGM held during the 1977 conference, and the 1978 AGM, which was planned as a seminar rather than as part of a residential conference, was cancelled for lack of support. New people joined, but the total membership never exceeded sixty-four. Gradually, NARTAR was attenuated to the few who were in the front line of action, the committee members. These were the staunch and reliable supporters, but even here there was some natural wastage - resignations relating to a new job, a new husband, increasing pressures in the old job.

Looking back, NARTAR in fact achieved a great deal, despite a difficult climate and despite numerous setbacks, not all of which were within their control. It contributed to a number of courses, both nationally and locally (not all of them have been mentioned in this chapter), and the contributions were efficiently and professionally managed; NARTAR produced a collection of teacher education materials, it produced three books of teaching materials in draft form; its teacher members contributed chapters to this book and wrote articles and chapters for other publiciations. NARTAR demonstrated that teachers can, with some training and some time for reflection, and with the reassurance of mutual understanding and mutual support, make a convincing contribution to the dissemination of ideas.

The principles that the dissemination programme worked to are best summed up in a short quotation which served as preface to the proposal:

> The real dissemination task is to increase the literacy of
> the consumer. But in education we seem to have preferred
> to dilute information in an attempt to 'meet the needs' of
> the consumer rather than to raise his skills, so that he may
> 'meet the requirements' of the situation.

The worthwhileness of the attempt is surely not in doubt, but it was an unrealistic aspiration in the circumstances and climate of the late 1970s. It may be that the teacher-as-researcher movement of which NARTAR was one part will gain momentum in the 1980s and establish circumstances and a climate in which such a dissemination task might succeed.

NOTES

1 A series of nine case records of different dissemination conferences was prepared by Jean Rudduck, who undertook to study the progress of dissemination. Page references are to these records, which are available at CARE.
2 The constitution makes reference to only one of the two original projects; the tendency of the Gulbenkian-funded drama project to be under-represented, and therefore to get overlooked, was a continuing problem.
3 The first chairman of the committee was in fact one of the interested outsiders – a university man with strong commitments to teaching about race relations. He resigned after a year, but remained in supportive contact.
4 The adviser who seemed most inflamed later invited the two Strategy B teachers to act as staff at a conference for sixth-formers on multi-racial education that he was directing.

APPENDIX

Gajendra K. Verma

THE BAGLEY-VERMA OPINION QUESTIONNAIRE

This questionnaire, used by Verma and Bagley (1973) in
studies of attitude change in British schools, has its origin
in the Wilson-Patterson (1968) Conservatism Scale. This scale
was originally developed in New Zealand, where its reliability
and behavioural validity have been clearly established. It has
subsequently been developed in a British setting, and has
also been used cross-culturally where its factorial validity has
been demonstrated (Bagley, Wilson and Boshier, 1970).

Wilson (1973) has shown that a strong general factor under-
lies the scale; that is, individuals who are conservative about
sexual matters also tend to be conservative about morality in
general, to defend the conventional position of religion, and
to express punitive and racialist attitudes. Higher-order rota-
tion of factors, however, produces two clearly distinct factors:
a religious-moralistic one and a racialist-punitive one. These
two factors are largely unrelated to one another (Bagley,
Boshier and Nias, 1973).

The Bagley-Verma development of the scale, carried out
after consultation with Wilson, expanded the racialist items in
the scale, at the same time retaining twenty-five 'core' general
factor items, so that General Conservatism (C scale) could still
be estimated. Item and factor analyses of the revised scale
(Bagley and Verma, 1972) indicated a high degree of internal
reliability for the Racialism (R) scale. The racial items tended
to be inversely correlated with the religious ones, however.
This is similar to Nias's finding (1973) with adolescents, which
indicates that they may be more committed to the 'intrinsic'
meaning of religious variables.

One of the merits of the Wilson-Patterson C scale is that it
avoids the problems of misunderstanding and response set and
yea-saying that beset many earlier scales in this area. Similar
item analyses to those carried out by Wilson (1973) indicate
that these advantages are maintained in the R scale.

Further modifications of the Bagley-Verma Racialism (R)
scale were made in the light of the changing political and social
climate of British race relations. A number of other scales
have been developed as well as the General Racism (GR) scales;
these are an Anti-West Indian (AWI) scale, and Anti-Asian
(AA) scale, an Anti-White (AW) scale, and a Black Power Ideo-
logy (BPI) scale.

The pilot version of this R scale contained eighty-one items, a substantial number of these being 'buffer' items. The items presented are short (e.g., 'West Indians'), and the subject is asked to respond to the question, 'Which of the following do you favour, approve of or believe in?' The three response categories are 'Yes', '?' or 'No'. Scoring takes account of the direction of response. Thus, 'Yes' in response to the item 'West Indians' is given a score of 0, '?' a score of 1 and 'No' a score of 2, while the scoring of the response to the item 'sending Asians home' is in the opposite direction. A high score on any of the scales indicates a marked prevalence of racialist attitudes.

Table A1   Correlations between Bagley-Verma Opinion Questionnaire and other scales (pre-test data)

L.S. Questionnaire	General racism	Anti-Asian	Anti-black	Anti-white
Attitude towards the British	0.01	0.10	0.02	0.23
Acceptance of people of other races	-0.29	-0.19	-0.29	-0.26
Competition for scarce resources	-0.45	-0.44	-0.45	-0.10
Subordination/superordination	-0.55	-0.47	-0.53	-0.07
Optimism/pressimism	-0.15	-0.13	-0.14	-0.26
Political policy	-0.46	-0.37	-0.46	-0.28
Perception of race-oriented theme	-0.24	-0.26	-0.18	0.01
General self-esteem	0.04	0.00	0.00	0.11

The pilot work of the new scales was carried out on 220 subjects in multi-racial areas of London and the Midlands, and the results of this study are reported elsewhere (Bagley and Verma, 1975). Data were subjected to various statistical analyses which reduced the number of items to fifty-five in the final scale, including twenty-seven 'buffer' items. The data were analysed in terms of four sub-scales: General Racism (GR), Anti-Asian (AA), Anti-White (AW) and Anti-West Indian (AWI). The correlations obtained from the pre-test data of the present study suggest that the Anti-white variable should be differentiated from the other two groups. The part-whole correlations on the scale show this difference. The score for General racism correlated +0.89 with the Anti-Asian score, +0.90 with the Anti-black score but 0.04 with the Anti-white score. These differences can also be seen in the correlations between the Bagley-Verma scale and other tests in the battery. The figures are given in Table A1. The correlations between the Bagley-Verma and the L.S. Questionnaire show a consistent negative relation-

ship - as one would expect. The fact that the Anti-white scale
also has negative, low correlations may suggest that there is
some element of generalized tolerance in the low anti-white
scores. However, since the vast majority of subjects were
white, this cannot be seen as judgments of an outgroup. This
section of the data has to be interpreted with caution.

The face validity of the scale has been discussed in Bagley,
Verma, Mallick and Young (1979).

This questionnaire asks for your opinions. There are no
right or wrong answers.

Which of the following do you favour, believe in or
approve of?

If you favour, believe in or approve of the thing, ring
YES, thus: (YES)

If you disfavour, do not believe in or disapprove of the
thing, ring NO, thus: (NO)

If you are not sure how you feel, ring ?, thus: (?)

Now begin:

Which of the following do you favour or approve of?

1	The United Nations	YES	?	NO
2	Hippies	YES	?	NO
3	Highly civilized Asians	YES	?	NO
4	British justice	YES	?	NO
5	West Indians	YES	?	NO
6	Bible truth	YES	?	NO
7	Black immigration	YES	?	NO
8	White superiority	YES	?	NO
9	Military drill	YES	?	NO
10	All-night parties	YES	?	NO
11	Asian inferiority	YES	?	NO
12	Patriotism	YES	?	NO
13	Pep pills	YES	?	NO
14	The death penalty	YES	?	NO
15	British morality	YES	?	NO
16	The Irish	YES	?	NO
17	Conscience	YES	?	NO
18	Black Power	YES	?	NO
19	Minority rights	YES	?	NO
20	Black superiority	YES	?	NO
21	Englishmen	YES	?	NO
22	Asian neighbours	YES	?	NO
23	The Race Relations Act	YES	?	NO
24	Asian businessmen	YES	?	NO
25	Gypsies	YES	?	NO
26	The British Empire	YES	?	NO
27	Black doctors	YES	?	NO
28	Co-education	YES	?	NO
29	Strict rules	YES	?	NO
30	Sex before marriage	YES	?	NO

31	Black People's Brotherhood	YES	?	NO
32	Modern art	YES	?	NO
33	White inferiority	YES	?	NO
34	Employing the handicapped	YES	?	NO
35	Abortion	YES	?	NO
36	Equality of races	YES	?	NO
37	Women doctors	YES	?	NO
38	Cypriots	YES	?	NO
39	Mixed-race marriages	YES	?	NO
40	Asian superiority	YES	?	NO
41	Royalty	YES	?	NO
42	Enoch Powell	YES	?	NO
43	Cinema-going	YES	?	NO
44	Employing West Indians	YES	?	NO
45	Space travel	YES	?	NO
46	Asian nurses	YES	?	NO
47	School uniforms	YES	?	NO
48	Having a black boyfriend or girlfriend	YES	?	NO
49	Mixed schools	YES	?	NO
50	Pakistanis	YES	?	NO
51	'Pop' music	YES	?	NO
52	Sending Asians home	YES	?	NO
53	Jamaican bus conductors	YES	?	NO
54	Mini-skirts	YES	?	NO
55	Divorce	YES	?	NO

THE L.S. QUESTIONNAIRE

This questionnaire is a new instrument, compiled by Lawrence Stenhouse for this research. Its main aim is to assess inter-racial attitudes through opinions expressed. Each item of the test presents two opposing points of view, A and B, between which pupils have to choose. There is a particular difficulty in the reliability of alternative-choice tests. There was an attempt to meet this by avoiding as far as possible parallel phrasing of alternatives.

This questionnaire is still in its developmental stage, and the psychometric characteristics have not been fully explored. It is hoped that future researchers will undertake further work to determine the validity of the sub-scales. In the interim, the results of this questionnaire have to be interpreted with caution. The face validity of the L.S. Questionnaire was ascertained by a group of thirty judges who were asked to classify the areas in terms of individual items which the author had distinguished on purely logical grounds at the construction stage. As a result of this scrutiny twelve variables finally emerged, which have been analysed separately. Five items on the trial questionnaire which showed considerable disagreement between the judges were discarded.

After having considered several possible scoring schemes, we decided to use the simplest one, which involved assigning +2 or +1 to each response. Since one of the statements in each pair is worded in a positive, the other in a negative way, any positively valued response contributes +2, and a negatively valued response contributes +1.

In order to ascertain the test-retest reliability of the questionnaire, a different sample drawn from two schools was tested twice, with two weeks between testing. The obtained value of the test-retest was 0.786 of combined sub-scales. We regarded this value as a satisfactory measure of internal consistency of the questionnaire.

Analysis of the questionnaire was undertaken in terms of twelve variables derived from responses. Six items were analysed separately. These were questions 1, 2, 4, 21, 22 and 28. Six sub-scales were analysed from the remaining items. These were:

(1) attitudes towards the British (B) - four items;
(2) acceptance of people of other races (A) - five items;
(3) competition for apparently scarce resources (C_m) - five items;
(4) interracial subordination and superordination (S) - three items;
(5) optimism versus concern or pessimism (C_n) - two items;
(6) problems of political policy (P) - two items.

Data from the pre-testing
As mentioned earlier, the L.S. Questionnaire is a new instrument, and further testing of the reliability and validity needs to be undertaken. The pre-test results were used to gain some perspective on the questionnaire as a measure of racial tolerance and an internally consistent test.

	Q1	Q2	Q4	Q21	Q22	Q28	B	A	C_m	S	C_n
Q1	–										
Q2	0.82										
Q4	0.90	0.80									
Q21	0.70	0.66	0.72								
Q22	0.80	0.76	0.82	0.75							
Q28	0.87	0.79	0.86	0.72	0.78						
B	0.12	0.01	0.13	0.07	0.01	0.08					
A	0.46	0.44	0.45	0.33	0.44	0.40	0.28				
C_m	0.04	0.17	0.00	0.01	0.00	0.08	0.05	0.31			
S	0.34	0.42	0.38	0.40	0.42	0.36	0.01	0.49	0.34		
C_n	0.41	0.44	0.40	0.51	0.46	0.44	0.09	0.28	0.02	0.23	
P	0.51	0.61	0.49	0.50	0.50	0.55	0.02	0.41	0.36	0.43	0.39

Figure A1: Inter-correlations between six questions and six sub-scales on the L.S. Questionnaire (pre-test data)

Figure A1 presents the inter-item and scale correlations for
the questionnaire. The six questions analysed separately intercorrelate highly. The sub-scales identified by analysis positively
intercorrelate at levels 0.3 to 0.5. The obvious exceptions are
the scales B and C_m: 'attitudes towards the British' and 'competition for apparently scarce resources'. It would seem that
the basis on which attitudes are expressed towards one's own
country is not necessarily related to the basis for attitudes
towards other ethnic groups. Certainly the limited information
for this table suggests that both positive or negative views of
the British (and of possible social competition) may co-exist
with racial tolerance. Levels of general racism from the Bagley-
Verma Opinion Questionnaire show a consistent, inverse relationship with the questions and scales of the L.S. Questionnaire (see p. 298 above). These results suggest a measure of
validity for the L.S. Questionnaire.

THE L.S. DISCUSSION QUESTIONNAIRE

Britain is a multi-racial society. People from many different
races live here together. When you hear them talking, they
are sometimes discussing what they think this society is like
or how best they should live in it. They often disagree.

On the next pages are printed some of the things people
say when they are disagreeing about this. For example:
A It is interesting to learn more about different ways of
life, cultures and languages.
B It's just a waste of time to learn about other people's
cultures and ways of life: everyone should just learn
about his own.

Imagine yourself sitting in the room where two people are
talking and saying these things. Each one is saying what he
believes to be right. Of the two, which do you think is more
right? Which do you agree with?
If you agree more with A and think it is more right, then
ring the letter like this: Ⓐ
If you agree more with B and think it is more right, then
ring the letter like this: Ⓑ
We hope you find it interesting thinking about these
things.
Now turn over and begin.

1 A People who come to this country from overseas have
a duty to try to become British in their way of
life.
  B People who come to this country from overseas are
perfectly entitled to live in their own way if they
choose.
2 A People from Asia, Africa and the West Indies make
a good contribution to life in this country.
  B People from Asia, Africa and the West Indies are
more of a problem than a help to this country.

3 A   It is wrong for people to come here from overseas and take jobs from British people.

   B   If people did not come here from overseas, Britain would be short of people to do jobs which are important for this country.

4 A   People of different races should feel quite free to marry one another.

   B   It is much better that we all marry people of our own race.

5 A   There is no reason why a white man should not accept a black man as a supervisor or boss.

   B   It is better in this country that white people should be supervisors or bosses.

6 A   There is very little prejudice against immigrants in Britain today.

   B   Britain has a big problem of racial prejudice.

7 A   Many immigrants work too hard, and this does not help the British worker getting better wages and conditions.

   B   British workers and those from overseas work well together on the whole and the immigrants have helped the British worker to go for better wages and conditions.

8 A   Immigrants expect too much of Britain.

   B   Britain could well do more to help immigrants.

9 A   There is a real need for more black and Asian policemen in Britain.

   B   On the whole, it is wrong to employ people as policemen unless they are British.

10 A   For an Asian or West Indian, the best way to establish yourself in this country is to make money and get yourself a really good house and car.

   B   It's not a good idea for an Asian or West Indian living in this country to buy too expensive a house or car: it just offends people.

11 A   The way things are in this country makes for racial prejudice.

   B   The British system is good: it is just some British people who are guilty of racial prejudice.

12 A   The British have made a lot of money out of Africa, India and the West Indies and they have a duty to people from these lands.

   B   The British did a lot to help Africa, India and the West Indies and people from these countries should be grateful for this.

13 A   When Asian, African or West Indian immigrants move into a neighbourhood, it tends to get slummy and broken down.

   B   Most Asian, African or West Indian immigrants can only afford cheap houses when they first arrive here, but they really work to make them nicer.

14 A   People who are very different from oneself are attractive.

  B   People are rather frightening when they are very different from oneself.

15 A   The British are often a bit boring and don't enjoy themselves much.

  B   The British are cheery and interesting and have a good way of life.

16 A   The British government spends too much money on helping countries overseas and not enough on the needs of this country.

  B   The British government should do everything it can to help countries that are not so well-off, even if it does mean a few sacrifices.

17 A   British troops ought to fight just as well if they were led by a black officer.

  B   You couldn't really expect British troops to fight as well if they were led by a black officer.

18 A   British people are rather cold and reserved and this makes them not very friendly.

  B   British people are friendly and are good at making people feel at home.

19 A   If you behave quite normally to people of a different race they are likely to think you are prejudiced or to act funnily towards you.

  B   You generally find you can get on well with almost everybody just by acting normally and being yourself.

20 A   Housewives from overseas have really quite a lot to teach British housewives.

  B   People from overseas are not usually as good at housekeeping as British people are.

21 A   It is pleasant to hear different languages being spoken as you pass along the street.

  B   It is dangerous to have many groups in a country all speaking different languages.

22 A   Asians often keep themselves to themselves because they are great family people and have their own customs.

  B   Asians often feel superior, and for this reason they don't mix with other people.

23 A   We probably don't do enough for children from overseas in our schools.

  B   Our efforts to help children from overseas in our schools could easily make things worse for British children.

24 A   The job opportunities here for black or Asian people are really very reasonable.

  B   It's very difficult to get the job you deserve in this country if you are black or Asian.

25 A   Now at last black people can be proud of themselves

and their traditions.

B The traditions that black people have brought to this country are not very valuable.

26 A It is difficult to understand people from a different background from yourself, and this tends to make people shy.

B Because there is so much to talk about, it is really quite easy to get on with people from a background different from your own.

27 A British people tend to be prejudiced because they got used to having an empire and bossing people about.

B British people are unusually free from prejudice against people from overseas because they have always travelled all over the world and met people from other countries.

28 A It is nice that people from overseas wear items of national or religious dress that are characteristic and colourful like turbans or saris.

B It is not practical to go on wearing your national or religious dress when you live in Britain and sooner people give it up the better.

29 A People often feel put off by the fact that they meet others who talk differently, dress differently or eat different food.

B Generally when people meet others who talk differently, dress differently or eat different food, they find them interesting and enjoyable.

30 A British people are very fair-minded and generally deal very justly and openly with strangers.

B British people are mean in a way and tease strangers and play jokes on them.

31 A On the whole the prospects of racial peace in this country are good.

B It is very likely that Britain will experience the problems and conflicts about race which have taken place in America.

32 A Immigrants who come into this country take up houses which should really go to Britishers.

B It's silly to draw distinctions between Britishers and immigrants when it comes to housing: anyone who is trying to work hard and bring up a family deserves a house.

Bibliography

BAGLEY, C., BOSHIER, R. and NIAS, D. (1974), The orthogonality of religious and racialist - punitive factors in conservatism in three cultures. 'Journal of Social Psychology', vol. 92.

BAGLEY, C. and VERMA, Gajendra (1972), Some effects of teaching designed to promote understanding of racial issues in adolescence. 'Journal of Moral Education', 1(3), 231-8.

BAGLEY, C. and VERMA, G. (1975), Interethnic attitudes and behaviour in British multi-racial schools. In 'Race and Education across Cultures', ed. G. Verma and C. Bagley, London, Heinemann.

BAGLEY, C., VERMA, G., MALLICK, K. and YOUNG, L. (1979), 'Personality, Self-Esteem and Prejudice', Farnborough, Saxon House.

BAGLEY, C., WILSON, G. and BOSHIER, R. (1970), The Conservatism Scales: a factor structure comparison of English, Dutch and New Zealand samples. 'Journal of Social Psychology', 81, 267-8.

BALL, Stephen J. (1981), 'Beachside Comprehensive: A Case Study of Secondary Schooling', Cambridge University Press.

BLOOM, Benjamin, ENGLEHART, D., FURST, E.J., HILL, H. and KRATHWOL, D.R., (1956), 'Taxonomy of educational objectives: the classification of educational goals. Handbook I: Cognitive domain', London, Longmans, Green & Co.

BRACHT, G.H. and GLASS, Gene V. (1968), The external validity of comparative experiments in education and the social sciences. 'American Educational Research Journal', 5, 437-74.

CAMPBELL, Donald T. and STANLEY, Julian C. (1963), Experimental and quasi-experimental designs for research on teaching, pp. 171-246 in 'Handbook of Research on Teaching', ed. N.L. Gage, Chicago, Rand McNally.

CANTOR, G.N. (1956), A note on a methodological error commonly committed in medical and psychological research. 'American Journal of Mental Deficiency', 61, 17-18.

CICOUREL, Aaron V. (1973), 'Cognitive Sociology', Harmondsworth, Penguin.

CORNFIELD, J. and TUKEY, J.W. (1956), Average values of mean squares in factorials. 'Annals of Mathematical Statistics', 27, 907-49.

CRONBACH, Lee J. (1975), Beyond the two disciplines of scientific psychology. 'The American Psychologist',

30(2), 116-27.

DAHLLÖF, Urban (1971), 'Ability Grouping, Content Validity and Curriculum Process Analysis', New York, Teachers College Press.

DEPARTMENT OF EDUCATION AND SCIENCE (1971), 'Education of Immigrants' (Education Survey), London, Her Majesty's Stationery Office.

DHONDY, Farrukh (1973), Overtly political focus. 'Times Educational Supplement'. 2 November.

FERGUSON, George A. (1976), 'Statistical Analysis in Psychology and Education', Tokyo, McGraw-Hill, Kogakusha.

GLASS, Gene and STANLEY, Julian C. (1970), 'Statistical Methods in Education and Psychology', Englewood Cliffs, NJ, Prentice-Hall.

GOFFMAN, Erving (1972), 'Interaction Ritual', London, Allen Lane the Penguin Press.

HALPIN, Andrew W. (1966), 'Theory and Research in Administration', New York, Macmillan.

HUMANITIES CURRICULUM PROJECT (1970), 'The Humanities Project: an Introduction', London, Heinemann Educational.

HUMBLE, Stephen and SIMONS, Helen (1978), 'From Council to Classroom: an evaluation of the diffusion of the Humanities Curriculum Project', Schools Council Research Studies, London, Macmillan Education.

JACOB, Philip E. (1957), 'Changing Values in College: an exploratory study of the impact of general education in social sciences on the values of American students', New Haven, Conn., Edward W. Hazen Foundation.

KRATHWOHL, D.R., BLOOM, B.S. and MASIA, B.B. (1964), 'Taxonomy of Educational Objectives. Handbook II: Affective Domain', London, Longmans.

LAWSON, John and SILVER, Harold (1973), 'A Social History of Education in England', London, Methuen.

LINDQUIST, E.F. (1953), 'Design and Analysis of Experiments in Psychology and Education', Boston, Houghton Mifflin.

LORD, F.M. (1960), Large-sample covariance analysis when the control variable is fallible. 'Journal of the American Statistical Association', 55, 307-21.

MILLER, H.J. (1967), A study of the effectiveness of a variety of teaching techniques for reducing colour prejudice in a male student sample (aged 15-21). Unpublished MA thesis, University of London.

MILLER, H.J. (1969), The effectiveness of teaching techniques for reducing colour prejudice. 'Liberal Education', 16, 25-31.

NIAS, D. (1973), Conservatism in children. In 'The Psychology of Conservatism', ed. G. Wilson, London, Academic Press.

NISBET, John D. and ENTWISTLE, Noel J. (1970), 'Educational Research Methods', London, University of London Press.

PARKINSON, J.P. and MACDONALD, Barry (1972), Teaching race neutrally. 'Race', 13(3), 299-313.

ROGERS, E.M. and SHOEMAKER, F.F. (1971), 'Communication of Innovations: a Cross-Cultural Approach', 2nd edn., New York, Free Press.
RUDDUCK, Jean (1976), 'Dissemination of Innovation: the Humanities Curriculum Project', Schools Council Working Paper 56, London, Evans/Methuen Educational.
RYLE, Gilbert (1960), 'Dilemmas', Cambridge University Press.
SCHUTZ, Alfred (1964), The stranger: an essay in social psychology, pp. 91-105 in 'Studies in Social Theory: Collected Papers II', The Hague, Martinus Nijhoff.
SIKES, Patricia J. (ed.) (1979), 'Teaching about Race Relations', Norwich, NARTAR, C.A.R.E., University of East Anglia.
SNOOK, I.A. (1972), 'Indoctrination and Education', London, Routledge & Kegan Paul.
SNOW, Richard E. (1974), Representative and quasi-representative designs for research on teaching. 'Review of Educational Research', 44(3), 265-91.
STENHOUSE, Lawrence (1967), 'Culture and Education', London, Nelson.
STENHOUSE, Lawrence (1975), Problems of research in teaching about race relations, pp. 305-21 in 'Race and Education Across Cultures', ed. Gajendra K. Verma and Christopher Bagley, London, Heinemann Educational.
VERMA, Gajendra K. (ed.) (1980), 'The Impact of Innovation', vol. 1 of the revised edition of the publications of the Humanities Curriculum Project Evaluation Unit. CARE Occasional Publication no. 9. Norwich, Centre for Applied Research in Education, University of East Anglia.
VERMA, Gajendra K. and BAGLEY, Christopher (1973), Changing racial attitudes in adolescents: an experimental English study. 'International Journal of Psychology', 8(1), 55-8.
VERMA, Gajendra K. and MACDONALD, Barry (1971), Teaching race in schools: some effects on the attitudinal and sociometric patterns of adolescents. 'Race', 13(2), 187-202.
WALKER, Decker F. and SCHAFFARZICK, Jon (1974), Comparing curricula. 'Review of Educational Research', 44(1), 83-111.
WEBB, Sidney and WEBB, Beatrice (1897), 'Industrial Democracy', London, Longmans, Green.
WILSON, G. (1973), 'The Psychology of Conservatism', London, Academic Press.
WILSON, G. and PATTERSON, J. (1968), A new measure of conservatism. 'British Journal of Social and Clinical Psychology', 22, 9-39.
WINDLE, C. (1954), Test-retest effect on personality questionnaires. 'Educational and Psychological Measurement', 14, 617-33.